Teaching
Seventeenth- and
Eighteenth-Century
French Women Writers

**Modern Language Association of America
Options for Teaching**

For a complete listing of titles,
see the last pages of this book.

Teaching Seventeenth- and Eighteenth-Century French Women Writers

Edited by
Faith E. Beasley

The Modern Language Association of America
New York   2011

© 2011 by The Modern Language Association of America
All rights reserved.
Printed in the United States of America

MLA and the MODERN LANGUAGE ASSOCIATION are trademarks
owned by the Modern Language Association of America. For information
about obtaining permission to reprint material from MLA book publications,
send your request by mail (see address below), e-mail (permissions@mla.org),
or fax (646 458-0030).

Library of Congress Cataloging-in-Publication Data

Teaching seventeenth- and eighteenth-century French women writers /
edited by Faith E. Beasley.
    p. cm. — (Options for teaching series ; 33)
    Includes bibliographical references and index.
    ISBN 978-1-60329-095-1 (hardcover : alk. paper)—
    ISBN 978-1-60329-096-8 (pbk. : alk. paper)
    1. French literature—Women authors—Study and teaching. 2. French
literature—17th century—Study and teaching. 3. French literature—18th
century—Study and teaching.   I. Beasley, Faith Evelyn.   II. Title: Teaching
17th- and 18th-century French women writers.
    PQ149.T34 2011
    840.9'928709032—dc23   2011021197

Options for Teaching 33
ISSN 1079-2562

Cover illustration of the paperback edition: *Portrait of Madame de la Sablière*,
by Pierre Mignard (1612–95). Oil on canvas. Chateau Bussy-le-Grand,
Bussy-le-Grand, France.

Printed on recycled paper

Published by The Modern Language Association of America
26 Broadway, New York, NY 10004-1789
www.mla.org

For Joan DeJean and Nancy K. Miller, who first showed me that teaching women writers is not only an option but a necessity

Contents

Part II: Teaching Specific Texts

Part III: Teaching Specific Courses

Acknowledgments

Over the course of the nine years that I have been working on this volume, I have been helped, inspired, and sustained by a number of colleagues. Joseph Gibaldi first approached me about developing this project and was a key interlocutor whose vision helped shape this Options volume. I am grateful that Sonia Kane agreed to oversee the volume's production upon Joe's retirement from the MLA. The expert advice of the many anonymous readers and of the Publications Committee improved the volume. I wish to thank Margit Longbrake for her editorial expertise and especially for her aid in designing the cover. Sara Pastel deserves not only thanks but a medal for her meticulous attention to every detail of the editing process and especially for her good humor. She is a pleasure to work with and the best editor anyone could hope to have. Finally, I would like to thank the contributors for their wisdom and especially for their patience.

Faith E. Beasley

Introduction: Reviving the Conversation

Asked to conjure up a few images from European history, twenty-first-century American college students would most likely list Versailles, the Enlightenment, and the French Revolution as elements of a foggy past that remain touchstones of Western civilization. They may not be able to insert such places, intellectual movements, and events into any kind of chronological frame, but thanks to films such as *Dangerous Liaisons*, *Ridicule*, *Vatel*, and Sofia Coppola's *Marie-Antoinette*, as well as the numerous books that continue to explore this period, seventeenth- and eighteenth-century France retains a place in the imaginary of our students. Moreover, if students are asked to list a few works that they believe they should read or at least say they have read, France's canonized authors of the same period, such as René Descartes, Molière, Jean Racine, Voltaire, Denis Diderot, and Jean-Jacques Rousseau, would most likely figure prominently on the list, as many of them do in courses devoted to the history of Western civilization, philosophy, and literature. Rarely, however, would a woman's text be included in this canonical pantheon. Rarer still would a dialogue between male and female interlocutors be suggested or occur in most pedagogical environments.

1

Yet ancien régime France has been celebrated as the period of conversation. Descartes's foundational philosophy; Racine's plays; the epistolary portraits of Marie de Rabutin-Chantal, marquise de Sévigné; Voltaire's cultural critiques; and Françoise de Graffigny's social satires were composed by their authors not in isolation but rather in constant dialogue with their contemporaries, other texts, and their culture. Since the 1970s some of the most innovative scholarship in French early modern studies has focused on recovering the dynamics of this culture of conversation. A large component of this work has been influenced by the resurrection of the strong tradition of women writers and female cultural participation that had been relegated to oblivion since the nineteenth century. Early work was devoted to unearthing specific women writers and their texts from dusty archives. Scholars offered what were then considered to be exceptional and daring courses on women writers to transmit the knowledge their work was uncovering. The next step in legitimizing the female literary tradition consisted of reinserting these writers into their literary contexts. Thus Marguerite de Navarre began to be included in Renaissance courses. *La Princesse de Clèves*, by Marie-Madeleine Pioche de la Vergne, comtesse de Lafayette, began to appear on the syllabi of great works courses. Some of these early modern French women writers have now reached almost canonical status and are regularly taught, although they are often still marginalized and taught out of a sense of obligation to include a woman on the syllabus. Few students, for example, would list Madeleine de Scudéry among the great authors of France's literary canon, even though her contemporaries predicted she would merit such a position.

A crucial step toward recognizing the importance and the contributions of women to history and culture thus remains to be taken: the conversations of the past need to be acknowledged and taught. While great progress has been made in making women writers known and their texts available (The Other Voice in Early Modern Europe series and the MLA's Texts and Translations series have been especially effective), most professors, when devising a syllabus for this period most associated with France's literary canon and national identity, create a foundation of men's voices to which they add a sprinkling of women's. Outside French departments these women's voices are almost uniformly silenced even as the texts of their male contemporaries figure prominently in courses on such topics as Western political thought, history of philosophy, religion, medicine, and Western civilization. But Descartes, Voltaire, and Rousseau, among others considered as the cornerstones of Western knowledge, lived and worked in dialogue with their female contemporaries. This volume is designed to offer new pedagogical practices and perspectives that reflect the enormous amount of research on women that has appeared in the past thirty years. The guiding principles for the volume as a whole are incorporation and integration. Women did not write alongside their illustrious male contemporaries; women and men in the early modern period in France worked together, in dialogue, to create their cultural and literary landscape. The contributions illustrate how to create the necessary dialogue among women writers, their male colleagues, and the cultural and literary context that nourished and inspired them all. Rather than focusing on courses that separate women writers from their cultural and literary contexts or that include them as an aside, this volume offers ways to incorporate women writers into general courses on literature, history, women's history, the history of science, philosophy, women's and gender studies, and European civilization across the curriculum, to show how these writers affected the historical, literary, and philosophical developments in later periods. Reconstructing the conversations between women and men of the ancien régime changes our view of the period as a whole, offers new interpretations of the canonical men's texts so celebrated in Western culture, and changes the very questions we ask as scholars and teachers. The ultimate goal of this volume is to have, for example, students and teachers alike cite Françoise de Graffigny along with Voltaire and Charles de Secondat, baron de Montesquieu, as representative of the Enlightenment thinkers who added to the conversation on cultural relativism. The contributors show how no course on the early modern period can be complete or even relevant without serious consideration given to the works of women writers.

In addition to the goals of incorporation and integration, *Teaching Seventeenth- and Eighteenth-Century French Women Writers* aims to create a conversation between early modern culture and twenty-first-century students. The intellectual climate of the early modern period offers much to stimulate the minds of today's students. Students are often surprised to learn that the questions raised by seventeenth- and eighteenth-century women writers are not only relevant but also often unanswered today: What is the relationship between the individual and society? How should individual rights be weighed against those of the society at large? What effect does access to education have on an individual's life? Are gender differences biologically or socially determined? What role should women and men play in child rearing? What are women's and men's supposedly natural functions in society? What are the standards by which literature and history are judged? What is taste? What effect does contact with different civilizations have on one's perceptions of oneself and of the world? Seventeenth- and eighteenth-century French writers grappled with questions that often still occupy the front pages of newspapers and stimulate discussion on *Facebook*. Their works can be used to add a level of complexity to discussions on contemporary feminist theory. Scudéry, Marie-Josèphe de Monbart, and Olympe de Gouges, for example, raised the issue of nature versus culture and women's supposedly natural place in the order of the universe long before today's sociologists and pundits (see, in this volume, Beckstrand and Marcellesi, as well as Tucker).

When first exposed to women's texts of these canonical periods for French culture, students often remark, If these women were indeed such an influential force, why haven't students ever heard of them before? Why are these texts only now being included in general histories and anthologies? Such questions can provide some of the most enduring teachable moments in our classrooms and allow for reflection on the question of how knowledge is constructed and circulated over time. The idea of what is natural for women and for men relied on the authority of Aristotle for centuries. Women's texts of the early modern period confront this authority; studying them in their historical context allows students to comprehend that patriarchy was constructed for a reason and has had and continues to exert wide-ranging consequences. History as a discipline can provide a particularly illuminating example of the influence of patriarchy on the construction of knowledge. Examining women's memoirs as historical documents, for example, raises the question of what value is assigned to various genres and disciplines. Women were not historians in the traditional sense until the twentieth century and thus could not shape the discourse or vision of the past as directly as their male counterparts. Women did seek, however, to inscribe their experience onto the historical record, and studying their works forces students to question how the past is constructed, by whom, and for what purposes. Women's texts of this period inspire students and teachers to reflect on the masculine discourse that has led us to consider and categorize women's works in ways that have often relegated them to inferior positions in the hierarchy of knowledge (see D. Goodman's conclusion in *Becoming*). Letters and memoirs, often women's preferred genres for expression, thus are nonliterary and too personal to be so-called real history. Our syllabi have reflected such masculine values. The pedagogical practices suggested by the contributors to this volume are reactions to the status quo and will no doubt spark as many conversations about the present as they do about the past.

Conversations in Early Modern France

This volume in the Options for Teaching series spans the period from the beginning of the seventeenth century to the French Revolution. What may at first glance appear to be a very long period is a logical choice for France. Seventeenth- and eighteenth-century France offers a sustained and relatively cohesive female literary tradition. As the essays devoted to the seventeenth and eighteenth centuries in *A History of Women's Writing in France* underscore (Stephens), women composed in every genre, from theater to poetry to fiction to political satire. They were largely responsible for the development of the modern novel and experimented with its forms throughout the period. Women's memoirs and letters illuminate the entire era. The salons, or *ruelles*, that fostered female literary production and philosophical, literary, and political discussions among men and women evolved during these years but remained an important social force. France led the way for a female literary tradition in Europe, and this rich and innovative literary culture provided examples and inspiration to shape other countries' cultures as well as France's. Participants in these salons inscribed the ideas they developed through such conversations in novels, political tracts, theater, poetry, fairy tales, travel narratives, and philosophy.

Since this volume aims not to introduce seventeenth- and eighteenth-century women writers but rather to offer ways to incorporate them into courses, I do not retrace here the history of early modern French women writers, a history that has already been more than adequately documented elsewhere (see in particular Stephens; DeJean, *Tender Geographies*; and D. Goodman, *Becoming*, "Letter Writing," *Marie-Antoinette, Republic*). Instead I focus in what follows on the dialogue that can be created among this female literary tradition, its context, and issues of pedagogical interest.

The beginning of the seventeenth century in France was marked by religious wars, struggles for political power, and the emergence of an institution that would come to dominate literary culture for the next two centuries, the salon. As many of the authors in this volume underscore, women were active participants in the public sphere throughout the period. First Marie de Médicis's and then Anne of Austria's reigns as regents until the mid-seventeenth century illustrate women's influence on the political stage (see Zanger in this volume). The civil war known as the Fronde involved a number of aristocratic women, including Louis XIV's cousin Anne-Marie-Louise d'Orléans, duchesse de Montpensier, who was famously, or infamously, known for ordering the cannons fired on her cousin's troops from the top of the Bastille. The figure of the *amazone* reflected these intrepid women and found its way into men's and women's writing alike (see Watt; DeJean, *Tender Geographies*; Beasley, *Revising*). Louis XIV's rise to power limited such seditious political activities but did not quell women's participation in the political realm. Their activities took other, primarily literary forms by the end of the seventeenth century, which were further developed in the eighteenth century. Women like Montpensier; Marie-Catherine Le Jumel de Barneville, comtesse d'Aulnoy; and later de Gouges realized that the pen was as influential a political weapon as the sword, and perhaps more influential (see Verdier, Beckstrand, and Goldwyn in this volume). Today's students are fascinated to discover these female political figures and their writings and are often amazed to see that women's and men's texts of the period raise many of the same issues concerning gender and politics that students recognize from their own culture.

In many ways, the development of the salon, addressed by contributors throughout this volume, allowed women to enter the public sphere in unprecedented ways. The use of the term "public sphere" might appear questionable to those who are unfamiliar with the construction of ancien régime society. Seventeenth- and eighteenth-century French society cannot be neatly divided into public and private spheres that correspond to Jürgen Habermas's formulations derived from nineteenth-century society. Salons, beginning with that of Catherine de Vivonne, marquise de Rambouillet in the 1620s, were social spaces dominated by women. These gatherings were usually convened in the private space of a woman's home, but the salon's influence radiated far beyond the walls of this domain (Lougee; Beasley, *Salons*; D. Goodman, *Becoming, Republic*; Russo, *Cour, Exploring, Style*). Philosophers, writers, politicians, and intellectuals of both genders and from across society gathered in these salons, which became a hallmark of French culture through the Revolution. They provided a space to develop the art of conversation that by the eighteenth century was seen by Germaine de Staël and others as a unique characteristic of French society. Salon conversations addressed all the major preoccupations of both centuries, from education to marriage, politics, science, literary taste and criticism, friendship, philosophy, race, individual rights, and cultural relativism. Indeed every facet of culture during this period bears at least a trace of salon influence. Students gain a new appreciation for and understanding of the maxims of François, duc de La Rochefoucauld, when they learn how the maxims grew out of a female-dominated salon context that encouraged literary production and critique by women. La Rochefoucauld's text is not a stand-alone example of the genre but a written reflection of a salon art that was practiced orally as well as in written form by both male and female participants. The availability of the maxims of Madeleine de Souvré, marquise de Sablé, allows students to re-create this context (see Steinberger and Harrison in this volume). As many of the essays in this volume show, reading ancien régime culture through the lens of the salons changes the way we interpret not just women's texts of the period but also the entire literary and social culture (see in particular Cherbuliez, Goldsmith, Gethner, and Beasley in this volume).

Through the middle of the seventeenth century, the shadow of the age-old *querelle des femmes* was still being cast on women's ability to par-ticipate actively in the political and cultural arenas. Did women have the capacity to understand complex philosophical thought? Were they geneti-cally weaker than the male sex, and did this difference justify their exclu-sion from education? Was it morally wrong for women to read and write? Writers such as Marie de Gournay, Scudéry, and Elisabeth of Bohemia addressed such questions early in the period and entered into conversa-tions with interlocutors such as Descartes (see Hogg in this volume). By mid-century, the answers to such questions appeared clear, as women be-came more and more active in the literary and social fabric of the period. The questions, however, did not disappear entirely, as Molière's satirical comedies *Les Précieuses ridicules* and *Les Femmes savantes* most famously illustrate. The backlash against women writers and intellectual figures that developed in the mid-1670s, championed by Nicolas Boileau and Molière, shows to an exceptional degree the position women had obtained in the intellectual realm. Had they wielded no power there would have been little reason to oppose them. Allied primarily with the avant-garde forces of the "moderns," women writers were dramatically altering the intellec-tual values of the period and offering their own models to replace those of the "ancients" (see DeJean, *Ancients*; Stedman and Cherbuliez in this volume). Charles Perrault and Bernard Le Bovier de Fontenelle, two espe-cially vocal moderns, were allied with d'Aulnoy, Marguerite de La Sablière, Catherine Bernard, and other women who defied any attempt to contain their intellect. D'Aulnoy was a polarizing figure who used her novels, fairy tales, and travel narratives to interrogate the representation of women as well as the political fabric of Louis XIV's France (see Verdier in this vol-ume). La Sablière, considered the most scholarly woman of her age, drew together an eclectic group in her salon, which included leading male intel-lectuals such as Perrault and Fontenelle and women writers like Lafayette and Sévigné. La Sablière was especially drawn to astronomy and worked

hard to advance scientific knowledge as well as to break down the psychological and societal barriers that prevented women from scientific inquiry.
She added travelers such as François Bernier, who had spent twelve years at
the Mughal court in India, to this mix (see Beasley in this volume). Such
progressive gatherings ran counter to the ambience at Louis XIV's court,
which by the 1680s was becoming increasingly conservative. Questions of
religious freedom were central in La Sablière's salon, among others, and
could be seen as particularly seditious in a climate that ultimately sanctioned the revocation of the Edict of Nantes, which since the sixteenth
century had guaranteed Protestants the freedom to practice their religious
beliefs in France. Huguenot women such as Bernard and La Sablière grappled with these issues in their work, while other such as Anne-Marguerite
Du Noyer wrote memoirs to document the fate of French Huguenots
and to plead for religious tolerance (see Goldwyn in this volume). This
period at the end of the seventeenth century represents a culmination of
the efforts of female intellectuals and writers not only to carve out a space
for their intellectual contributions but also to be accepted by their male
peers as valuable interlocutors on the major issues of the day. As many of
the essays in this volume show, this period at the dawn of the Enlightenment, often characterized as "le grand renfermement de la femme" ("the
great suppression of women"), is more complex and dynamic than it has
been previously portrayed (see Cherbuliez and Stedman in this volume).
Although Anne-Thérèse de Marguenat de Courcelles, marquise de Lambert, at the beginning of the eighteenth century could justifiably lament
the fact that fewer women were living up to their intellectual capacities
than in previous decades and that many of her contemporaries were more
accepting of the roles traditionally ascribed to the female sex, women at
the end of the seventeenth century had nonetheless proved that the female
intellectual was a force to be reckoned with and would remain an integral
part of French thought.

Women such as Lambert; Claudine-Alexandrine Guérin, marquise de
Tencin; Graffigny; and de Gouges continued the tradition of the female
salon intellectual criticized by Molière. And while one can trace the resur-
gence of a sentiment that a woman's place was more properly outside the
realm of public debate and that education should be primarily a male domain, women's advances in the seventeenth century and their literary and
philosophical contributions had made it impossible to silence the voices of
their successors. As in the seventeenth century, women in the eighteenth
century used their pens and their voices to comment on every major issue,

culminating in and indeed helping to create the tumultuous events of the Revolution (see Hesse; D. Goodman, *Republic*). Isabelle de Charrière and Tencin used their novels to interrogate the institution of marriage, much as Lafayette and Scudéry before them had done (see Trouille and van Dijk in this volume). Women were also inspired to add their voices to new areas of debate, such as colonialism and cultural relativism. Graffigny's Peruvian woman gripped eighteenth-century society as much as the celebrated Persian of Montesquieu (see Goldsmith and Stone in this volume). A friend of Voltaire, Graffigny drew on her experience as a female intellectual to highlight issues of particular relevance to women, questioning, for example, the value of a convent education and advocating women's choice in marriage. Graffigny also takes up notions of class, racial prejudice, and individual rights, prefiguring the work of de Gouges (see Beckstrand in this volume). Other women were drawn to political commentary, often, like their male contemporaries, couching it in fiction. Inspired by the colonization of Tahiti, Monbart's *Lettres taïtiennes* reveals how France was formulating its relationship to other civilizations and complicates the concept of orientalism that is frequently too neatly and unproblematically associated with such works (see Marcellesi in this volume).

In the wake of the Revolution, France witnessed a dramatic shift in the status of women and an accompanying change in the position of the woman writer. Salons and their strong ties to literary and philosophical developments were replaced by gatherings devoted almost entirely to sociability. The result was the creation in the nineteenth century of a pedagogical canon designed to disseminate what it meant to be French, a process that had disastrous consequences for a collective understanding of the female literary tradition (see Beasley, *Salons*; DeJean, "Classical Reeducation"). Seventeenth-century French literature was chosen as a cornerstone for the foundation of French collective identity. Pierre Corneille, Racine, and Boileau were crowned the kings of this canon, and theater was designated as the most representative genre of the period and the only one worthy of being taught. In this process, not only were women writers denigrated and relegated to the sidelines, but their works were systematically erased from literary history. Moreover their influence on literary culture suffered a similar fate: canon formation extended its influence and changed the way the entire period was viewed. The seventeenth-century salon was transformed from a place of literary critique, innovation, and interrogation to a foyer of politeness whose only goal was to refine behavior and promote sociability. Much of the scholarly work since the 1990s has focused on ridding our understanding of the seventeenth and eighteenth centuries of this nineteenth-century overlay. Resurrecting the strong female literary tradition that existed in France before the nineteenth century, a tradition unsurpassed by that of any other country, serves to reveal the gendered construction of France's collective identity as created and propagated by the late nineteenth century and perpetuated by succeeding generations.

Conversations across This Volume

This volume is loosely organized to facilitate interactions among the various contributions. The essays included in the first part, "Cultural and Literary Contexts," illuminate the specific context of this period and raise the questions that preoccupied ancien régime France. They provide much of the background necessary to teach women writers of the period and are designed to help colleagues identify places in their courses across the curriculum that could be enriched, enhanced, or even altered dramatically when women's participation is taken into account. Holly Tucker's examination of women in medical contexts can be used to add another dimension to the history of science. Faith E. Beasley's contribution on the salon serves as a foundation for all the texts in this volume. In part 2, "Teaching Specific Texts," contributors focus on central writers and genres of the period. In many instances, well-known figures are reexamined in the light of the philosophical, cultural, and literary trends discussed in part 1. Some contributions focus on texts that are not well known, such as Volker Schröder's discussion of Antoinette Deshoulières's poetry and Thomas M. Carr's exploration of convent writing. Suzan van Dijk pairs Graffigny's well-known text with those of her contemporaries Marie-Jeanne Riccoboni and Charrière. The essays in part 3, "Teaching Specific Courses," emphasize the construction of actual course syllabi. Contributors offer concrete course descriptions that include many of the writers and issues evoked in the first two parts.

Teaching Seventeenth- and Eighteenth-Century French Women Writers attempts to reestablish the conversations of the past as well as generate new conversations about the past, its authors, and how we teach them. Since the focus is on dialogue, there are few essays devoted solely to one woman writer or to one text. Rather, each essay reflects the period's art of conversation; contributors place women's texts in dialogue with those of their male colleagues or with a particular historical characteristic or issue of the period. In addition, many of the same authors and texts are treated by numerous contributors, creating a conversation among the various essays. It is hoped that these internal conversations will lead to even further pedagogical innovation. One can imagine, for example, a colleague creating his or her own dialogue among John D. Lyons's consideration of Sévigné as a philosopher, Richard E. Goodkin's treatment of the relationship between Lafayette and Descartes, Juliette Cherbuliez's examination of Fontenelle in the light of women's texts, and Francis Mathieu's analysis of Blaise Pascal and Lafayette. In a similar vein, Harriet Stone's suggestive use of art to explore Lafayette and Graffigny can be profitably paired with Abby Zanger's discussion of print culture and with Mary Ellen Birkett and Ann Leone's work on women's efforts to visually change the world around them. Gabrielle Verdier's discussion of the publication history of d'Aulnoy's texts can be used to teach valuable lessons in literary history and its ideological underpinnings. Many of the essays, such as Harriet Stone's, Katharine Ann Jensen's, and Donna Kuizenga's, explicitly pair writers across the two centuries in question and, in the case of Kuizenga, across cultures. Women's conversations with the literary establishment and their generic innovations during the period are evoked in many essays, including those by Elizabeth C. Goldsmith, Roxanne Decker Lalande, Schröder, Kathleen Wine, Perry Gethner, Kuizenga, and Allison Stedman. Many of the essays address women's reactions to the roles society prescribes for them. Thus Jensen's analysis of motherhood could be read in the light of Mary Trouille's exploration of marriage and Carr's enlightening discussion of the convent. Louise K. Horowitz, Verdier, and Henriette Goldwyn examine women's reaction as authors to historical events. Nicholas Paige's essay on the importance of language and the difficulty of translation provides an essential corollary to every essay in the volume. Through a careful analysis of some of the key words of the period, Paige argues that these texts need to be approached as products of their culture, and readers need to be careful not to fall into the trap of anachronism. David Harrison develops this point by exploring the very different connotations politeness and sociability had in the early modern period. In a similar vein, Goodkin takes two key terms in Lafayette's seminal *La Princesse de Clèves* and explores how they resonate with the period, specifically with Descartes, thus re-creating a conversation between these two forces of the seventeenth century. Cherbuliez reminds us that, just as we must be careful to interpret the language of these texts in their own cultural and historical contexts, so too must we be attentive to the way premodern readers and writers categorized knowledge, for such models for understanding and organizing the world were much "fuzzier," in Cherbuliez's words, than today's methodologies and ways of thinking. Horowitz's analysis of Lafayette's relation to history provides an example of this meticulous contextualization and further enriches the conversation about this novel that has not stopped since its publication. Chloé Hogg and Claire Goldstein, as well as Zanger, explore the relation between women writers and the history of the book, investigating how this history affected the dissemination of texts and ideas. One can teach the Revolution in a new light by using Caroline Weber's and Lisa Beckstrand's essays individually, but also by putting them in dialogue with each other or adding other voices, including Laure Marcellesi's illuminating discussion of Monbart's, Diderot's, and Rousseau's very different approaches to colonialism and female sexuality. Katherine Montwieler and Deborah Steinberger, like many of the other contributors, shows how these women's voices have a lot to say to present-day students.

All the essays in this volume attest to the fact that seventeenth- and eighteenth-century French women writers, their texts, and the issues that inspired and surrounded their production can be profitably integrated into courses ranging from the traditional survey to those that developed using the most cutting-edge research in a variety of fields. The essays show that the essential conversation created when women's voices are added to those of their male contemporaries in their literary and historical contexts changes the way we conceive of the period that constitutes one of the building blocks of French national identity and Western civilization. Ideally, *Teaching Seventeenth- and Eighteenth-Century French Women Writers* will prompt such interrogation, rejuvenate the teaching and experience of one of the most exciting and well-known period of Western civilization, and inspire many future conversations.

Note

Unless otherwise noted, French-language quotations from *La Princesse de Clèves* in this volume are taken from the Flammarion edition, edited by Jean Mesnard, and English-language quotations are taken from the Terence Cave translation published by Oxford. Instructors comparing the English with the French text will be surprised by a significant difference common to all English translations of the novel. Mesnard's edition reads:

> [La princesse] eut soin d'y faire porter de grands tableaux que M. de Clèves avait fait copier sur des originaux qu'avait fait faire Mme de Valentinois pour sa belle maison d'Anet. (205)

> She . . . [took] care to give instructions that a set of large paintings should go with her: these were copies she had had made from originals that Mme de Valentinois had commissioned for her fine house at Anet.

All previous French editions read "elle eut soin d'y faire porter de grands tableaux qu'elle avait fait copier," a line English translations generally translate as "these were copies she had had made" (125). Mesnard provides no explanation for his decision to alter the French text. The most recent Gallimard edition by Dorian Astor follows Mesnard and also denies the princess agency in this key scene. Since these are the editions most frequently ordered for classroom use, I have opted to use the Flammarion edition, but I believe it is important that teachers be aware of this change and of the resulting difference between the French and English texts.

Part I

Cultural and Literary Contexts

Nicholas Paige

The Complexities of
the French Classical Lexicon

The statistic is familiar but still bracing: Jean Racine, by any account one of the greatest poets in the French language, used fewer than three thousand different words to compose his eleven tragedies. This lexical sobriety was not Racine's alone: seventeenth-century efforts to excise words that appeared erudite, technical, or outdated have been well documented (Brunot, vol. 3, pt. 1, and vol. 4, pt. 1; François 1: 231–82), and many of the women writers of the period whom students are likely to encounter use a similarly reduced vocabulary. A small lexicon is a boon in the French literature classroom—one can imagine the perils of presenting John Milton to students with five or six semesters of English—but it also brings challenges. Writers of the period place much pressure on a seemingly innocuous group of words—*générosité*, *galanterie*, and *honnêteté*, for example—whose import may be occulted by their apparent counterparts in modern French (and English). Worse still, these words may not strike readers as particularly "poetic" or "literary": linguistically speaking, Honoré de Balzac or Aimé Césaire or Marguerite Yourcenar probably puts more stress on the beginner's skills, but the struggling student may very well take such difficulties as a mark of the work's aesthetic prestige.

The treacherous simplicity of the classical lexicon, however, is also an excellent way into the literature of the period, for the key words of the time can hardly be said to possess stable meanings that can simply be footnoted for the neophyte. On the contrary, writers of the period, and especially women writers, returned again and again to a limited number of terms that provided the means of mapping a contested and evolving cultural terrain. At stake was nothing less than a reconceptualization of the way people thought about feelings, selfhood, and human relationships of all kinds. And this reconceptualization was a process: the words that matter in the literature of the period did not have meanings etched in stone and certified by the Académie Française but jostled for prominence; a term popular one generation could be nearly extinct ten or twenty years later.

One of the most crucial literary-cultural revolutions of the time involved ways of talking about love. The amorous vocabulary of the Middle Ages and the Renaissance, as elaborated in chivalric romance and Petrarchan poetry, largely revolved around the idea of *service*: a male lover served as perfectly as possible his chosen lady in the hope of obtaining her favors. This metaphor, clearly homologous with the political obeisance owed by a vassal to his sovereign, gradually lost its currency in the course of the seventeenth century: still central to Honoré d'Urfé's hugely successful *L'Astrée* (1607–27), service was no longer a master trope by the time Madeleine de Scudéry was writing in the 1640s and 1650s. At least in part, the incompatibility between service and Scudéry's writing needs to be understood in the context of the period's salon culture, which gave women an active role (DeJean, *Tender Geographies*; Timmermans). It no longer made sense for the literature of passion to revolve around the discourse of the man in love.

Instead, a novel such as Scudéry's *Clélie, histoire romaine* (1652–60) privileged terms that referred to the reciprocal recognition of excellence between man and woman. This vocabulary can appear strange to students, since it is based neither on the uniqueness of the person loved nor on the desire of the person who loves, but they will have little trouble assembling a list of terms used when characters are turned on to others. Many of these—*honneur, valeur, vertu, générosité*—have caste connotations that can be uncovered by students. Period dictionaries such as Antoine Furetière's *Dictionnaire universel* are very useful, as is the precise etymological information in Alain Rey's *Dictionnaire historique de la langue française*. There students will discover that *générosité*, for instance, was virtually a synonym for *noblesse* and comes from the Latin word *genus*, or "race": a *généreuse* action demonstrates a character's resemblance to his or her noble ancestors. Above all, it will become clear quickly that the distinct meaning of each term is less important than the general overlap between terms that are nearly interchangeable: their main function is to repeat again and again the social distinction of the people to whom they apply. From this insight, students can try to ascertain whether some terms apply more to men than to women; or, if reading Scudéry in conjunction with Pierre Corneille, the playwright to whom she is substantially indebted for her heroic ethos, they can debate about the extent to which she innovates. They can also be urged to think about what it means for such prized characteristics to be recognized not only by the person in love but also by society as a whole: it is not that Scudéry's Clélie and Aronce are bound by some idiosyncratic fit between two unique individuals but rather that their union symbolizes the triumph of aristocratic values over threatening elements such as impostors or ill-bred foreigners.

Such attention to vocabulary need not, then, turn the professor into a walking glossary. Instead, the reading process can become an active exploration of a strange planet where students discover that this most basic of human emotions, love, has a history. As I have alluded, Scudéry's amorous lexicon comes partially from Cornelian heroism. Her most famous contribution to the evolving language of love, however, is her "Carte de Tendre" ("map of tenderness"), which appeared in the first volume of *Clélie*. In it she provides an allegorical map of sentiment with no fewer than three different towns labeled "Tenderness." One could not hope for a better illustration that, for Scudéry's contemporaries, words did not have discrete and clear meanings about which everyone agreed. On the contrary, Scudéry's splitting of hairs, in her map and in the explanatory conversations that accompany it, shows the efforts required to think up a new vocabulary of love, centered on the word *inclination*. While two towns named Tenderness can be reached by traveling overland through villages with names representing either the old service tradition of courtship (Soumission, Obéissance, Amitié Constante [Submission, Obedience, Constant Friendship]) or a newer one emphasizing personal traits (Sincérité, Probité, Respect [Sincerity, Probity, Respect]), a third, the mysterious and central Tenderness-on-Inclination, can only be arrived at by navigating the river Inclination. *Inclination*, which would remain a mainstay of romantic discourse well into the nineteenth century, implied a new way of falling in love, one that had little to do with the mastery of behavioral codes or the recognition of excellent breeding. Love, in Scudéry, is starting to be seen as a natural process that one feels in the heart; the heroine Clélie can make such an authoritative exposition of the subject because she speaks from experience alone: "c'est parce que mon cœur m'a appris à en bien parler, et qu'il n'est pas difficile de dire ce que l'on sent" 'it's because my heart has taught me how to talk about these matters and because it's not hard to say what one feels' ([Morlet-Chantalat] 1: 177; my trans.). By putting this heretofore unknown town on the map, Scudéry can be said to found a qualitatively new view of the emotions that will make possible the Enlightenment cult of *sensibilité* (DeJean, *Ancients* 78–123).

Scudéry's map and its accompanying conversations can thus be used to introduce students to a range of slightly later texts that put overflowing, unstoppable passion front and center. For the generation of writers that followed Scudéry, a prime motor of romantic narrative lies in the desperate attempt to control feelings that no longer follow predictably from the moral and social excellence of the love object. The works of Marie-Madeleine Pioche de la Vergne, comtesse de Lafayette, are central here. Her *Zayde, histoire espagnole* (1669–70) is virtually devoid of the heroic vocabulary still prominent in *Clélie*; instead, her lovers are all swept away by various forms of jealousy. The reader's attention is not held by an orderly Cornelian standoff between passion and reason; rather, Lafayette develops a supple vocabulary for enabling us to peer inside the minds of characters and follow their twisted logic and dubious inferences. No one word suffices for such a task, and students can orient their reading by looking for the various terms Lafayette adds to Scudéry's *inclination* (which, in Lafayette's predecessor, is overwhelmingly positive)—*agitation, trouble, chagrin, inquiétude, caprice*, and *dérèglement* are some of the most frequent. Once again, delineating precise meanings is less important than understanding that this cluster of terms is one writer's response to a sea change in conceptions of the emotions. *La Princesse de Clèves* (1678) shares many of these terms and others still; some, holdovers from an earlier heroic vocabulary, Lafayette systematically subverts. Students might be asked to pay attention to the vocabulary of the will and decision making that figures prominently in Corneille's *Le Cid* (1637)—notably in Rodrigue's famous *stances*, where he grapples with demands of filial duty (act 1, sc. 7)—and to observe what happens to it in Lafayette's masterwork. For example, if *résolution* and *se résoudre* occur regularly in Lafayette, this is precisely because the princess, under the onslaught of passion, is powerless to keep the numerous resolutions she makes when alone and reasoning calmly.[1]

La Princesse de Clèves is a virtual laboratory for observing other classical key words and the decisive scrutiny Lafayette devotes to them. The novel's very first sentence is the perfect starting point: "La magnificence et la galanterie n'ont jamais paru en France avec tant d'éclat que dans les dernières années du règne de Henri second" 'Never has France seen such a display of courtly magnificence and manners as in the last years of the reign of Henri II' (69; 3).[2] A quick English translation will provide matter for at least a class's worth of work and crucial orientation for subsequent reading. Students may well settle on "magnificence" for *magnificence* (as Terence Cave does), but not before being alerted to its resonance with the legend engraved everywhere in Lafayette's time, *Ludovicus Magnus* ("Louis the Great"; see P. Burke) and to the way the word seamlessly links visible spectacle and social distinction. No one term can render *galanterie*, whose ambiguities can be approached through excerpts from Scudéry's conversation on the subject, "De l'air galant"; by a look, in facsimile or in the original, at the periodical *Le Mercure galant* (in which Lafayette's novel was vigorously promoted alongside the latest fashions); or through an illustration of the long-standing enthusiasm for commitment-free relationships, as first set forth in *L'Astrée*'s famous "Tables d'amour falsifiées par l'inconstant Hylas" (Urfé [Vaganay] 2: 194–97) and then summed up by Mme de Villedieu's "Articles d'une intrigue de galanterie" (1661).[3] Whatever their translation, students will, in the course of their reading, need to reconcile the clearly positive meaning the term possessed with the dangerous sexual charge Lafayette's novel imparts to it, a connotation that would become prominent in the eighteenth century. *Éclat*, or "brilliance," is equally important. Although readers will not be able to grasp the irony of its appearance here until reaching the end of the third part of the novel, when the king is killed by an *éclat*, or "splinter," of a sporting lance, the word, as well as this entire superlative register of visibility, can be contextualized through a glance at the period's abundant panegyric.[4] Finally, the aptness of Lafayette's verb choice — *paraître*, "to appear" — needs emphasis as well: whereas *générosité* in Scudéry (or Corneille) always provided an unambiguous and visible access to the character's inner worth, or *être* (see Starobinski), appearance is systematically devalued in Lafayette's work as misleading or downright mendacious. Students may find it challenging to find an English verb that will allow their translation to flow smoothly, and indeed they may not be able to agree at all on how to render this difficult sentence. They will, however, have grasped the importance of these four key words and stand ready to appreciate the critique to which Lafayette subjects them.

The words Lafayette opposes to the surrounding culture of appearance and permissiveness include the initially perplexing *repos*. Why, beginners may wonder, is the princess so concerned about getting her "rest" (Beasley, "Teaching" 127)? Elucidating Lafayette's use of this and related terms—*tranquillité*, *retraite*—could take several directions, depending on the aims of and the audience for the course. An advanced seminar on seventeenth-century literature might want to emphasize the appropriation here of a key component of the period's philosophical and moral thought. This tradition, at once secular and religious, runs clearly from Michel de Montaigne's "De la solitude" (1580) to "De la retraite" (c. 1686), by Charles de Marguetel de Saint-Denis, seigneur de Saint-Evremond, and Blaise Pascal's great fragments on *divertissement* (1669; a problematic term for those brought up to think of "entertainment" as an unalloyed good).[5] Or Alceste's repeated use of *sincère* in Molière's *Le Misanthrope* (1666), perhaps coupled with Scudéry's conversation "De l'ennui sans sujet" (1684), which describes a melancholic who is unable to enjoy the company of others, could be used to produce a lexical map of fault lines between the period's enforced sociability and resistant elements. A broader course on an omnibus subject such as solitude, selfhood, or the individual could guard against an overly conceptual focus—and anchor itself in the literary text—by paying attention to the precise terms used to oppose the individual to society. A semester-long exercise might involve the collaborative creation of a "dictionary of the self," in which key words (like *repos*) would be illustrated, analyzed, and historically located.

In a women's studies course covering the long eighteenth century, Lafayette's *repos* could also provide an entry into an alternative feminist tradition of critiques of prevailing social arrangements that often operate to the detriment of women. English and French works could be paired, and students could be encouraged to follow the evolving vocabulary that allows writers to configure relations between women and men, public and private. Aphra Behn's *The Fair Jilt* (1688) or Delarivier Manley's *Adventures of Rivella* (1714) could be read alongside its French precursor, Villedieu's *Mémoires de la vie de Henriette-Sylvie de Molière* (1672–74); Françoise de Graffigny's *Lettres d'une Péruvienne* (1747) and Charlotte Lennox's *The Female Quixote* (1752) instructively part ways over the proper role of women; the heroines of Isabelle de Charrière (*Lettres de Mistriss Henley* [1784]), Sophie Cottin (*Claire d'Albe* [1799]), and Fanny

Burney (*Cecilia* [1792]; *Camilla* [1796]) are similarly "smothered" (Spencer 163). The interest here would come not only from diachronic change—one thinks of the considerable slippage between classical *vertu* and its later Enlightenment avatars—but also from the extent to which the conflicts described are translatable, both culturally and lexically. The enduring popularity of Jane Austen's novels might furnish a particularly apposite end point for such an investigation: her innovative use of free indirect discourse aside, Austen is deeply indebted to the vocabulary of courtship that had been evolving for a century and a half.

Finally, any course that teaches French works exclusively in translation can use inevitable deformations (or downright inaccuracies) to underline the specificity of the original text (while avoiding the discouraging suggestion that the version under study is completely inadequate). The idiosyncrasies of the classical lexicon, which prevent the key words of the period from simply mapping onto the distinctions and emphases of current English usage, constitute one source of difficulty. Another problem for the instructor who would like students to trace the use of selected words stems from the lack of seventeenth-century taboos regarding repetition: works like *La Princesse de Clèves* or *Zayde* so insistently reuse key terms that translators, hoping to bring the works in line with modern stylistic habits, may reach for synonyms that dilute the author's prose. With careful prereading such gaps can be productively exploited. Two passages in which a single word has been rendered with different terms might be brought together; students could then speculate on the author's lexical linking of situations that to a modern reader are presented as distinct. *La Princesse de Clèves* has the advantage of having multiple translations that, for important scenes, might be read in tandem: Which seem more modern (or archaic) and why? Are there differences in rhythm or tone or register? Many other works—by Villedieu, Graffigny, Cottin, or Marie-Catherine Le Jumel de Barneville, comtesse d'Aulnoy—have early modern English translations (frequently available in microfilm or online) that can be used for in-class group work. At the very minimum, the exercise will raise awareness regarding both the massive changes in English usage and the European prominence of French fiction in the period. The interest of this sort of lexical excursion is not merely scholarly. Certainly, it is to be hoped that students will come away from their study with a rough idea of classical aristocratic values or of the decisive innovations that Enlightenment *sensibilité* brought to conceptions of what it means to be human. And attention to key words is indeed a way to focus discussion on the texts themselves, to turn the subject from ill-defined ideas to an author's actual expression, which is partially determined by the culture of the time. Yet a last, and crucial, benefit lies in the examination of the subjective lexicon that twenty-first-century students might otherwise assume to be natural: "needs," "goals," "choice," "fun," "fulfillment," "supportiveness," and so on are all words whose use reinforces historically bounded conceptions of the individual. How would we go about defining such notions for a hypothetical visitor from early modern France whose coordinates are *honnêteté* and *repos*? Such an experiment in estrangement may well have the happy effect of leaving students feeling less sure about their feelings than when they started.

Notes

1. Lafayette's extensive vocabulary of emotion can also be productively juxtaposed with the distinctly more rhetorical or euphemistic flourishes one finds in Guilleragues's *Lettres portugaises* (1669) or with Racine's tragedies.

2. All quotations from *La Princesse de Clèves* are from Jean Mesnard's edition and Terence Cave's English translation.

3. For a brief history of the term, see DeJean, *Tender Geographies* 135–40; for more extensive background, see Pelous; Denis, *Parnasse*; Viala, *France*.

4. The sixth and final *intermède* of Molière's *Les Amants magnifiques* (1670) provides a particularly fine example.

5. Background on the culture of retreat and withdrawal can be found in Stanton, "Ideal"; Beugnot.

Abby Zanger

Woman and Iconography: Early Modern Women and Their Images

Women have a deeper and more interesting relation to iconography than simply as objects of a visual gaze. While images can flesh out the ideas about women found in literary narratives, women's iconography might be about matters other than content, such as usage, production, and the vagaries of agency related to images in this period. And so-called depictions of women might be found in less obvious places; for example, in the ways women read images, in the manner women's ideas intersect with images, even in the ways women create images of themselves and others. All these facets of women not just *as depicted* but also *in relation to depiction* are available to us as scholars of early modern women and can enhance our readings of literature and other cultural texts. Indeed, I propose that, as we teach about early modern women in the context of the study of literature and culture, we teach about women and iconography, not simply the iconography of women. I propose we illuminate and complicate the relation between women and images on many levels in order to move beyond important work already done on the representation of women in iconography (see, e.g., Matthews-Grieco).

Posing the question of women and depiction underscores the fact that women in early modern France could be both objects and agents of iconography. In fact, women in history perform in a dialectical relation to these two positions. It is thus promising and enriching to encourage students to look at many dimensions of women's relation to iconography, not just their depiction or cultural output, but also their social, political, and economic activities. This mixing of multiple levels (and academic disciplines) involves eliminating an artificial separation of genres (within literature and among the arts) and of topics, texts, and disciplines. It means looking at areas that are potentially unconventional to the discipline in which one teaches. The result is that teaching about women and images can put into question not only our picture of men and women, our mental iconography, but also our notions of teaching.

The following overview of four specific teaching scenarios engages the problem of iconography and women. These cases can serve as jumping-off points or as models. In the first, woman as icon, the way that the icon of a woman is used to sell the earliest printed books in France is examined. In the second, women in iconography, representations of noble women demonstrate the complexity of capturing women's experience through images that are produced as part of the apparatus of power. In the third, woman as iconographer, the example of a female artist is used to enlarge the notion of woman as author. Finally, the fourth case, women reading images, considers one woman's reception of an image, suggesting a broadened notion of woman as reader. The four vignettes offered here are not neat packages. They are scenarios meant to complicate paradigmatic ideas about women in iconography and to encourage students and teachers to think beyond the depiction of women to consider how women touched, were touched by, and experienced images as consumers, models, and producers.

Woman as Icon: Hélisenne de Crenne

Hélisenne de Crenne is not a seventeenth-century figure but a sixteenth-century one. The name Hélisenne de Crenne does not even refer to a real person. It is a pseudonym for Marguerite Briet, who we believe is the author of Crenne's four texts. Briet's writing is relevant to teaching seventeenth- and eighteenth-century French women because Briet was the first female to author a sentimental novel in the French language. Briet/Crenne can thus serve as a point of departure for discussions of writers such as Marie-Madeleine Pioche de la Vergne, comtesse de Lafayette; Madeleine de Scudéry; and Françoise de Graffigny. Like the works of those later writers, Briet's first novel, *Les Angoysses douloureuses qui procèdent d'amours*

(1538; *The Torments of Love*), has entered the university curriculum as it has become available in inexpensive editions. The pedagogical interest of the novel is likely greatest for the story line of the first of its three interior books: the saga of a young woman, Hélisenne, who is married to an older man but falls in love with a young man she sees one morning outside her window. When her husband catches her in the deceit of illicit love, he tears up her precious writings, beats her black and blue, and, at the end of the first book, imprisons her in an isolated tower. To make matters worse, in book 1 the lover betrays Hélisenne's confidence, although he is rehabilitated in books 2 and 3, which recount his quest to find and free Hélisenne. This quest is accomplished at the end of book 3. The lovers flee, but Hélisenne dies, as does her lover, stricken by her death. This narrative is formulaic. Parts of the story may reflect the biography of Briet (c. 1510–after 1552), about whom we have only scant information. Court documents and a will indicate Briet separated from her husband and went to Paris to live and write. Between these two poles of text and historical woman is a larger story to tell and teach, about how Briet became an icon, Hélisenne de Crenne, for an emerging reading public. That story about how one woman writer became an icon in her own time could anchor any course on seventeenth- or eighteenth-century women writers.

It is not entirely Briet but also her printer-publisher, Denis Janot, who was responsible for Crenne's iconic status. It is important to teach students this fact, to remind them that books were produced as commodities and that the voices of women and the images they painted, even of themselves, were mediated by corporate influences. Businessmen like Janot took advantage of the attraction of readers to women-in-distress narratives (sentimental novels) in what was, in the early sixteenth century, a new media, the printed book. Indeed Janot was emerging as a prominent editor-printer (*libraire*) in 1530s Paris, a crucial period for the evolution of the Parisian book, still in its infancy at this time. Janot's list focused on newer genres and nonerudite books in the vernacular, including fiction like Briet's novel, polemical writings on such topics as the *querelle des femmes*, and translations into French of classical texts and of contemporary Spanish and Italian writings. These kinds of books appealed to emerging literates—the rising legal class and, of course, the growing population of female readers. Briet's first book, which was very popular with this audience, was republished several times and was also pirated by a publisher in Lyon. A talented and prolific writer, Briet would write three more works for Janot, a collection of invective letters (*Les Épistres familières et invectives de ma dame Helisenne, composées par icelle dame De Crenne* [1539]) connected to the themes of *Les Angoysses;* an allegorical text (*Le Songe de Madame Hélisenne composé par ladicte dame* [1541]); and a translation of the first four books of Vergil's *Aeneid* (*Les Quatre Premiers Livres des Eneydes du tres elegant poete Virgile, traduictz de latin en prose françoyse par ma dame Hélisenne* [1541]). The first three of Briet/Crenne's books are available in French editions, and *Les Angoysses* and *Les Épistres* are available in English translations.[1] They are didactic texts that have much to teach about early modern French women's voices.

For the topic of this essay, what is particularly interesting about these texts is the way the eponymous character of *Les Angoysses*—actually, a pseudonym—becomes the author-function of the ensuing books, whose title pages all bear the name Dame Hélisenne. She is both the topic of the books and their author, a point made visual and material in her books' title pages. Even the Vergil translation features her name prominently, a rarity in this period and a rarity in Janot's list, which contained many translations of classics. It is important to note that the title page was a relatively new invention in the early sixteenth century and that Janot was a pioneer in developing its visual format. As a pioneer, Janot used the author-function to draw readers to this new form. To further reinforce the feel of the brand, he reused the familiar iconography of the framing compartments commissioned for the title pages of *Les Angoysses* throughout Crenne's books as well as for books of other authors, now anchored by the popularity of Briet's work. A woman's novel thus became the prototype for Janot's style of book (see Mortimer for the images of the various title pages and the reuse of framing compartments).

The appeal of Briet/Crenne's writings, therefore, lies not just in her words but also in the way her books were fashioned and manipulated on the market. While Janot determined this fashioning, Briet may have had some interest in the emerging book form and market since she concludes her three-part narrative with an epilogue that explains how the book the reader is holding passed into print. These concluding pages follow the heroine's death, describing how Mercury, coming to gather the souls of the lovers, discovers a package wrapped in white silk next to Hélisenne's body (see Chang, "Clothing," on this episode). It is the manuscript of her adventures that she wrote while imprisoned and that she had finished upon reuniting with her lover. Mercury takes this package first to Jupiter's court, then, on the king's orders, to Paris, where it will be published. This remarkable epilogue is perhaps one of the first allegories about publication ever published. Its focus on the manuscript of a woman who must die for her work to be published can lead to class discussions about the fate of other fictional figures, such as the princesse de Clèves; of other female writers, such as Lafayette and Scudéry; or of their fictional counterparts, such as Graffigny's Zilia, from *Les Lettres d'une Péruvienne.*

We cannot know who wrote this epilogue. Was the corporate nature of publication an interest of Briet's? or of Janot's? Or did Briet and Janot write it together? What we can trace is the hand of Janot in the publication of Briet's works at a time when the material presentation of the French printed book was taking shape. One aspect of this evolution is the way Crenne becomes an icon. Another is the way the material presentation of her books is repeated. This repetition occurs not just in the title page but also in the approximately one hundred ten woodcut illustrations found in *Les Angoysses.* Some of these vignettes were recycled for Briet/Crenne's book, but many were created specifically for this text. These illustrations can be seen in Christine de Buzon's edition of *Les Angoysses* or found online in the editions posted on *Gallica,* the digital library of the Bibliothèque Nationale de France (BNF). Since it was rare in the early modern period for an author, let alone a female author, to have any input into aspects of the material presentation of a book, including illustration, Janot was probably responsible for those decisions. That Janot invested so much in the book underscores his belief that he would sell it. Readers of early French printed books loved illustrations, and by the 1530s readers wanted illustrations in their books, even nonluxury editions like the 1538 *Angoysses* and even if the pictures often did not correspond to the text. The popularity of illustrations would continue into the seventeenth century, when the durability of copperplate would lessen the expense of illustrations, even if it shifted them to the frontispiece or intercalated page, since copperplate, unlike woodcuts, could not be put directly into a typeset page. With woodcut, Janot was able to punctuate Briet's text, using small vignettes inserted right onto the text's page. These vignettes could illustrate the story, or they could, by their repetition, draw connections among parts of the book.

One example of interest is an image of a woman holding an open book. The image is used as decoration for a prefatory epistle from Dame Hélisenne to her readers, in which she warns her female readers not to act as she has and pleads to higher forces to steady her trembling hand in writing and in completing her work. Students can easily link the vignette of a woman holding her book to the themes of the epistle and the book in general. But what might they make of its inclusion in the opening of the second book of *Les Angoysses*, which is written in the male lover's voice? The woodcut could connect the preface to the second book with its female author, Hélisenne. She is not its reader but its producer, even when the narrative voice is that of her lover. The magpie, a sign of profligate orality, is situated behind the female figure. She turns away from it as she turns her back on gossip against her unfaithful lover in rehabilitating him in book 2. Note that the magpie's voice is blocked out by the book held (and produced?) by the woman. The image is also utilized a third time, in the midst of a debate between the lover and his traveling companion concerning the superiority of love over war. In this instance, it is hard to connect image to text. Is Janot simply repeating the image as filler? Or does it have another use? Since the image has appeared earlier in the text, students could be shown that it might function as a form of narrative punctuation, linking moments within the text. Here perhaps it reminds the reader that the book is indeed Hélisenne's treatise about the tension between folly and reason and that the words of her lover's companion are really her own. Janot thus not only used Crenne to sell Briet and reused images from Briet's books to sell other volumes on his list, but he also manipulated images within the book to reinforce the author-function of this valuable commodity, Crenne.

Teaching Briet/Crenne demonstrates how one female writer's relation to images extends beyond her role as simply agent (writer) or object (icon), casting new light on her writings. This scenario underscores the link between women, the marketplace for women writers, and the materiality of their printed books. It proposes a new and more multidimensional way to read between form and content, person and persona, using the topic of images to look beyond literary history to the cultural and economic role played by women as agents and icons.[2]

Women in Iconography: Anne of Austria and Marie-Thérèse of Austria

While early modern French women wrote memoirs, devised verbal or poetic portraits as part of salon society games, or hired artists to paint their portraits, not all representations of women were self-generated. It is important to discuss and contrast the multiple venues in which women were portrayed by themselves and others. One can undertake this task by considering an array of texts that describe and depict women verbally and visually, although the sheer mass of material might become a course unto itself. The figure of the queen can be an interesting case study for looking at the iconography of elite women. Marie-Antoinette, of course, offers a rich teaching case since she was both an active patron and an object of the artistic gaze (see Weber in this volume; D. Goodman, *Marie-Antoinette*). Likewise, the Medici queens have left a large iconography produced through their own patronage and through their enemies' (Crawford). Elizabeth I of England can also be referred to as a model. Important seventeenth-century royal figures are the Spanish Hapsburg princesses Anne of Austria and Marie-Thérèse of Austria, queens of Louis XIII and Louis XIV, respectively.

It is possible to link the iconography of these last two women, since many motifs are repeated in their portrayals. Accounts of both queens at the time of their marriages are found in diplomatic reports, pamphlet descriptions, engravings produced for popular consumption in objects such as almanacs, luxury publications, and a myriad of memoirs. There are also allegorical images connected to the queens' pregnancies and the births of the dauphin, or first male heir, including images by engravers such as Abraham Bosse. Many such texts and images are easily accessible on the BNF's *Gallica* database and on its *Banque d'images*, as well as in catalogs of Bosse and almanacs (Join-Lambert and Préaud; Cojannot–Le Blanc; Reed).

It is perhaps easiest to use the representations of Louis XIV's bride (for images see esp. Zanger, *Scenes*). A woman who was largely depicted as invisible at court, particularly after the birth of the dauphin, Marie-Thérèse was quickly eclipsed by Louis XIV's many mistresses. She did not leave any correspondence, nor is she known as a patron as was her mother-in-law, Anne of Austria, who commissioned the building of the highest monument in seventeenth-century Paris. Marie-Thérèse was simply known for being an overly pious woman. In part, her invisibility was a result of Anne of Austria's visibility: Marie-Thérèse was contained and isolated because her mother-in-law, as queen regent, was too visible in taking power. But Marie-Thérèse's portrayal in letters, memoirs, and engravings shows how the Bourbon monarchy relied on the image of a queen to portray the king as virile, ready to rule, and, perhaps most important, able to buttress the dynasty by reproducing it. Almanac images dating from the late 1650s serve this purpose in the way they position the royal family as compared with portraits of potential queens (Zanger, *Scenes*, ch. 1; Norberg, on teaching uses of these images; and Harth, *Ideology*, on interior portraits).

Analyzing these types of historical images in class allows students to see not only the triumphs and trials of these elite women but also their function as crucial foundations of state building even if they were not actively ruling (see Zanger, "Making"). It can also help students situate the writings of other noble women, such as Françoise Bertaut de Motteville and Anne-Marie-Louise d'Orléans, duchesse de Montpensier, who both wrote about the queens in their memoirs (Beasley, *Revising*; Cherbuliez; Zanger, "Marriage"). Scudéry also wrote about Marie-Thérèse in the preface to her novel *Célinte*, which was published the year after the marriage. Scudéry's discussion of the new royal couple's entry into Paris in August 1660 can be compared with journalistic pamphlets on the same topic available on *Gallica*, allowing comparisons of descriptions of queens by men and by women, across media and genres (see Zanger, *Scenes* and "What"). This multidimensional focus takes the emphasis off asking if the iconography depicts a woman (or women) accurately to ask larger questions about how women are depicted, by whom, and how the source and purpose of the depiction must be weighed in looking at the representation. The iconography may be politicized, but the pedagogical lesson in such an exercise can be about narrative construct and narrative and visual perspective. Indeed, when the duc de Nemours spies on the princesse de Clèves in Lafayette's novel, he is actually in part reenacting a Bourbon marriage ritual in which the king's first view of his bride is an act of clandestine viewing or voyeurism. This ritual is described in widely disseminated pamphlets, and it is interesting to explore the crossover between fiction and history in these texts, which depict noble women, real and imagined (Zanger, *Scenes*, ch. 3).

Woman as Iconographer: Claudine Stella

While large-scale oil paintings of this period tend to focus on elite portraiture or on history (ancient, contemporary, or biblical), early modern copperplate prints most often feature scenes of daily life, both public and private. They are thus an obvious place to look for early modern women and their history. Like the woodcut engravings that embellished books in the sixteenth century, copperplate technology provided even more economy and durability to the printing process. Copperplate prints decorated all sorts of books, as well as almanacs, broadsides, playing cards, games, and even ladies' fans, as we see in Bosse's engraving *La Galérie du palais* (Join-Lambert and Préaud 186–87). People at every level of society, from the buyer of luxury goods to the illiterate woman in a shop, encountered objects printed with images. Engravings and etchings were sold on the streets, in front of the churches and in boutiques near the law courts. They thus provide a rich field of evidence for studying women on many levels. Engravers such as Bosse offer insight into how women dressed, studied, married, and so forth (see BNF's online image bank; Join-Lambert and Préaud; Cojannot–Le Blanc). Bosse also reproduced versions of age-old proverbs about women, such as the one about women tricking and beating their husbands (Join-Lambert and Préaud 126–27). Another source for this latter genre is Jacques Lagniet, whose engravings concern proverbs and proverbial situations in which gender often figures. Natalie Zemon Davis's essay "Women on Top" is an excellent entry into this genre and gives examples of pertinent images.

While engravings are rich sources of depictions, several important aspects about the format must be explained to students. First, prints are a highly mediated form: engravers often worked from designs that they had not created or modeled designs after already extant images by other artists. Indeed an engraved or etched image often passed through many artistic interpretations. As mentioned earlier, it was usually the printer or publisher, not the artist, who decided how the image would be used in a book. Images were, furthermore, often commissioned by the printer or another commercial agent. Thus it is difficult, if not impossible, to impute intention to copperplate images, even if they are quite detailed. This multiple authoring agency, however, makes them good sources for discussing how ideas about women travel, as well as how market forces influence imagery, since copperplate images containing women were reproduced in large numbers (versus the select few oil paintings or enamels produced) and so respond to the demand of an emerging market economy of print. The images that have survived are images people in the early modern period wanted or producers wanted to produce in large numbers for various reasons, including political propaganda. If we have access to these images today, it is because someone cared about these pieces of paper enough to keep them for generations in their original form.

We do not have records of many female engravers, although the nature of the field as artisanal (rather than fine art) likely means that women in the families of engravers might have engaged in this work as they did in other family businesses, even if they would rarely have received credit for it. One woman who did make a name for herself was Claudine Bouzzonet Stella (1636–97), the niece of Jacques Stella (1596–1657), a well-known artist of Poussin's generation and circle. Jacques Stella was childless and took in his sister's four children, three girls and a boy, training them as artists. Perhaps the girls gravitated toward engraving (the boy chose to paint) because their father was a metalsmith and many in this profession turned to engraving. We have a record of Claudine Stella's work from Pierre-Jean Mariette's *Abécedario*. Stella had a relatively large output for a female artist, although the images she reproduced were typical of what women produced, that is, largely religious images. She also printed books; an inheritance from her uncle included his printing business as well as his rooms in the Louvre. Two books she published and illustrated using images left by her uncle can be interesting to teach in relation to different kinds of literary and cultural texts. The 1657 *Jeux et plaisirs* (*Games and Pastimes*) is a fascinating set of images of naked putti engaged in children's games (Stella and Stella). The fifty vignettes each illustrate a so-called child's game, with a six-line verse commentary below the image. The scenes are at once innocent and emblematic. These images could be contrasted to the fables of Jean de La Fontaine, the vignettes of Lagniet, or even Renaissance emblem books. Like these forms, many of Claudine Stella's images and vignettes carry a deeper meaning and a darker message about power. The critic Julia Dabbs has characterized the work as a hidden commentary on the Fronde, although she sees the commentary as that of Claudine's uncle Jacques and does not make the connection between women and the Fronde as Joan DeJean does in *Tender Geographies*.

Also useful in teaching is *Pastorales*, a volume of images Claudine Stella published one year later, again engraved from her uncle's sketches (Stella and Stella). While these images are idealized and sanitized, they do offer insight into village life and into contemporary ideas about such life at a time when pastoral settings were used by some of the most popular writers, including Honoré d'Urfé, Scudéry, and Pierre Corneille.[3] The volume's last three plates are of particular interest for the study of women and gender and could be used when teaching works like Paul Scarron's *Roman comique* or Antoine Furetière's *Roman bourgeois*, Molière's comedies such as *Georges Dandin* and even his pastoral ballets. One plate in *Pastorales* shows a gathering in a house with a notary, who is finishing the documents for a marriage. The interior shows several groupings of people and the food being prepared as well as the characters involved in the new alliance. The next plate shows the marriage procession. This image is well known for its reproduction of musical instruments, but it also reveals a great deal about the marriage rituals. The final scene of a domestic interior may take place a year or two after the marriage since it features a woman diapering a baby, a group of men sitting around a table drinking, and other domestic activities. Whether considered together or separately, all the plates tell stories and provide glimpses of everyday life and might offer a useful contrast to the visions of elite women in Racinian tragedy, for example. Since marriage is a perennial topic in women's (and men's) writings in this period, these engravings can provide a counterpart to many idealized narratives.

Note that these images are arranged and interpreted by Claudine Stella, but they were not invented by her. They are engraved from her uncle's drawings. We can only speculate on how she might have put her own spin on the arrangement, interpretation, and commercial import of these tableaux. Hers is nonetheless an authoring act, even if we cannot know the exact extent of her agency, just as we often cannot trace the agency of female and male artists and authors in the early modern period. This conversation is important to have with students as they read or look at female- (and many male-) authored work from this period. And, even if we do not know the extent of Claudine Stella's input into the images she engraved, we do know that she thought these images were important and commercial. She functioned in relation to them as Janot did to Briet's work. Hers is an authoring position that confounds simplistic notions of agency to ask, in the mode of Michel Foucault, What is an author of images? Stella, as an artist and a corporate force (a publisher), occupies a niche that forces us to deal with the complexities of female authorship in the early modern period.

Woman as Reader of Images: Elizabeth Chéron

As we read images of women, a logical question we might ask is, How did early modern women respond to images? Again, beyond knowing that women bought images, we do not have many instances in which we can trace how women read and interpreted visual imagery. Salon conversations offer some insight into women's ideas about culture. Access to such conversations is found in the letters of Marie de Rabutin-Chantal, marquise de Sévigné, and other correspondence and memoirs. From Lafayette's *La Princesse de Clèves* and Scudéry's *Le Grand Cyrus*, we know women had their portraits painted in miniature to share. The *Mercure Galant* also offers information about the *salonnières'* reception of culture, although it is largely (although not entirely) male authored. Claudine Stella provides a possible entry into this question not only because she interpreted images as she produced designs for engraving or the engravings themselves but also because, as heir to her uncle, parents, and siblings, she had an enormous collection of paintings, drawings, engravings, books, jewelry, and silver. We know she was aware of the monetary value of these objects, since she penciled in numbers on her hand-written five-page will (a document that also sheds light on her professional status and personal choices in maintaining a family legacy).

One interesting and provocative case of a woman's reception of a particular image concerns a poem written by the female painter Elizabeth Sophie Chéron (1648–1711). Personally presented to the Académie Royale de Peinture et de Sculpture by Charles LeBrun in 1672, Chéron is noteworthy as one of only seven women elected to that institution in the seventeenth century (Démoris and Delpierre, "Femmes" 112). She was elected for her skill as a portrait painter. Few of her paintings survive, however, and we gain insight into her ideas about women and images not from her capacity as academician but from a poem she wrote in 1669 or 1670 as part of a controversy over a fresco painted in the dome of the Val-de-Grâce Cathedral by Pierre Mignard ("Coupe"). The cathedral, the highest point in Paris in the seventeenth century, was a project undertaken by Anne of Austria in 1645 to commemorate the birth of her son, Louis XIV, after twenty-three years of a barren marriage (Mignot). Anne died in 1666 before her project was finished, but the fresco had been completed by 1665. A large, Italianate fresco of the apotheosis, it filled the church's enormous dome with over two hundred figures from the Bible and from history. (Mignot and various online sites devoted to this monument include images of the fresco.) The choice of painter and style caused controversy, particularly in the light of the focus of the painting academy under LeBrun on a contemporary French style. In 1668, Charles Perrault published the poem *La Peinture*, championing this style and its author, LeBrun. LeBrun made illustrations for the poem when it was published in pamphlet form. One year later, the actor-playwright Molière answered this encomium with his own poem praising Mignard, his style, and his fresco (while also paraphrasing recent art theory). Mignard, likewise, provided designs to illustrate Molière's pamphlet, which was titled, *La Gloire du Val-de-Grace*. Both these poems can be read in class and provide an opportunity to teach the legacy of the king's versus the queen's patronage (the king's founding of the painting academy and the queen's erecting of a monument to her own and to the dynasty's fertility). They also offer an introduction into the early stirrings of the *querelle des anciens et des modernes*, since Perrault's poem sketches out a preliminary version of the advocacy of contemporary French art over ancient models while Mignard's fresco may be seen as retrograde in its Italianate style.

Chéron's intervention in the debate is interesting in this context. A painter of portraits and religious images, as well as an engraver of some note and a poet, Chéron was a protégé of LeBrun. Her poem "La Coupe du Val-de-Grâce" depicts the dome, addressing Molière as it stages a trial of the fresco the playwright defended. The fresco's diverse viewers are the dome's witnesses. The poem comes to us not as a published pamphlet but as several manuscript copies and an eighteenth-century edited version as well as a recent edition drawn from two of three extant manuscripts. While looking at the manuscript reveals the lack of strict training in grammar afforded even the most talented women, the edited version provides fodder for a class discussion of how Chéron read the debate between male intellectuals and artists as well as how she saw the fresco and, by extension, its monument. Critics are quick to see her as a censor of the fresco and an ally of her patron LeBrun and his perspectival tradition (Poiron). But her poem can also be read as a celebration of the genre of the fresco, for in her text she seems to stress how it is necessary to adopt a flexible viewpoint to grasp the circular painting of the apotheosis, a moment in which all time is telescoped together. Because the image is on a ceiling, it requires constant displacement to take in the scene. Chéron makes this point by offering differing viewers' comments and by highlighting their need to shift positions in order to evaluate the painting. They do not have the luxury of the rationalizing gaze of the proscenium stage. One can link this shifting view to the reality of Anne of Austria's patronage and remind the students that Anne, figured in the fresco on her knees offering the monument to God, may be depicted at the center of the image, but she struggled to bring her project to fruition.

Chéron's poem celebrates the complexity of the viewing experience created by the fresco, which can be seen as offering a parallel to the complexity of female patronage positions (see Mignot on Anne of Austria's travails). Unlike the Italian scenic mechanism of French neoclassical art, the unidirectional gaze of absolutist political culture promoted in LeBrun's work and Perrault's poem, the fresco requires of viewers the kind of flexible, subaltern habitus we might attribute to women as artists and as cultural consumers of art (and even royal patrons). Chéron makes such a statement in her intervention into a large-scale debate among male poets and painters. To see, she tells her readers, a viewer needs to move about and look at all the angles. This advice might apply to any viewer, but it seems to apply particularly to women, regarding their relation to images of themselves and others, and to us, as scholars and teachers of early modern women and their images.

The above teaching scenarios move any discussion of women and their images beyond iconography as testimony to consider how women in early modern France produced, utilized, commented on, and generally experienced images. It is not necessary to adapt all these angles in teaching or research. The concepts behind each scenario, however, can inform the understanding of many other dimensions of early modern women. Rethinking women's relation to images should be a crucial facet of any course on the subject of women and gender in early modern France.

Notes

1. Modern French editions of Crenne's works include the editions of *Les Angoysses* by Beaulieu and by Buzon, Nash's edition of *Les Épistres*, and Beaulieu and Desrosiers-Bonin's edition of *Songe*. English translations include Neal and Rendall's translation of *Les Angoysses* (*The Torments of Love*) and Mustacchi and Archambault's translation of *Les Épistres* (*A Renaissance Woman: Hélisenne's Personal and Invective Letters*).

2. On women and publishing see Chang, *Into Print*; Broomhall; and Davis.

3. In particular, see Henein's online edition of d'Urfé's *L'Astrée* and Madeleine and Georges de Scudéry's *Artamène ou le Grand Cyrus*.

Holly Tucker

Books and Bodies: Early Modern Women in Medical Contexts

In the 1990s, a significant transition in early modern French studies began to take shape. Groundbreaking research by Joan DeJean, Erica Harth, Linda Timmermans, as well as many of the scholars included in this volume, demonstrated in new and thoughtful ways the important and historically neglected role of women and women's writing in the late seventeenth century. Building on the work of Carolyn Lougee's detailed study of salon life, our scholarship explored and continues to explore the complex dynamics between men, women, and knowledge during the reign of Louis XIV. Among these early studies, DeJean's work focused on genre and gender as a driving force in the rise of prose fiction. Demonstrating the ways in which women served as "principal architects" of the genre (*Tender Geographies* 8), DeJean was careful nonetheless to note that her use of the term "women's writing" referred not exclusively to women but rather to a "French female tradition" of writing to which male writers also contributed in varying degrees (16).

At the same time that scholars in French were beginning to rediscover and to think in new ways about women's writing broadly understood, the first glimpses of foundational theoretical texts in gender studies emerged as a developing field (see, e.g., Scott, "Gender"; Butler, *Gender Trouble*; Sedgwick; Rubin; Haraway). Turning the focus on disentangling naturalized intersections of sex and gender, gender studies as a field emphasizes the cultural and social constructions of femininity, masculinity, and sexualities. Moving away from an essentialized notion of identity to one of postmodern fluid identities, gender studies focuses on regulatory discourses and practices in the construction of social practices and roles. As Robyn Wiegman discusses, the tensions between women's studies and gender studies have had important implications on academic program building (and naming) and carry high stakes for feminist political struggle.

However careful our academic discussions on women are, our students often remain deeply attached to the notion of gender roles as part and parcel of corporeal difference, heteronormativity, and reproduction. My teaching experiences have convinced me of the need to unsettle notions regarding bodies, texts, and women before engaging in focused discussion of "women's writing" and what it meant in the late seventeenth century. The purpose here is not to work on the side of "gender studies" or "women's studies" as a type of mutually exclusive choice but rather to work in the productive gaps between the two to gain a deep appreciation of the cultural politics and feminist stakes of examining women's writings, both in regard to our studies of the early modern era and as part of self-reflective practices for our own moment.

This essay describes the ways in which both early modern and recent debates on medical representations of the female body can serve as a pedagogical framework for courses on seventeenth- and eighteenth-century women's writings. My aim here is to discuss how early medical texts and dissection illustrations can be used in the classroom to help trouble the notion of woman and by extension the notion of women writers. To what degree do modern uses of the term "women writers" represent or not core debates regarding the nature of woman as a category in the early modern era? How can an understanding of medical approaches to sexual difference in the seventeenth and eighteenth centuries help us understand the relation among gender, genre, and writing more generally? And, finally, what does a thoughtful study of sex, gender, and genre tell us not only about the early modern period but also about the preoccupations of our modern era?

These are broad and complicated questions whose answers are neither easy nor obvious. Instead of attempting to resolve the issues they bring up, I offer here an overview of major lines of thinking about the early modern female body as they might apply to courses on women's writing in the ancien régime, at both the undergraduate and graduate level. The resources and teaching approaches mentioned below can be used as the core of a semester-long course or can be shortened to a two- or three-week preliminary segment for the wide range of syllabi and teaching strategies discussed later in this volume. All texts referred to here are easily accessible either in print or online.

Sex, Gender, and Writing

The establishment of male academies in the seventeenth century (most notably, the Académie Française in 1634 and the Académie des Sciences in 1666) placed specific emphasis on the gendered nature of public and private spheres of knowledge and writing. As we know with increasing precision and nuance, the salon represented a privileged space where women, who were otherwise progressively becoming isolated from the public intellectual domain, could pursue a life of the mind—socially, collaboratively, and through the written word. In her *Cartesian Women: Versions and Subversions of Rational Discourse in the Old Regime,* Harth cautions, nonetheless, against understanding early modern knowledge making strictly in terms of gendered binaries:

> The sexual division of intellectual labor involved in these social spaces cannot be convincingly mapped onto public and private spheres. Victorian "separate spheres" are not relevant to seventeenth-century French aristocrats. (22)

Indeed, the fluid borders and contours of the public and private spheres are especially evident in the ebb and flow of scientific and medical knowledge—and it is here that we can appreciate the ever-shifting and highly tentative dynamics of gender in the last decades of the seventeenth century. We know that well-placed *salonnières* in particular rubbed shoulders with high-profile academicians such as Bernard Le Bovier de Fontenelle, Charles Perrault and his brother the doctor Claude Perrault, and others. Members of the celebrated *bureau d'esprit* ("ministry of wit") of Anne-Thérèse de Marguenat de Courcelles, marquise de Lambert, also had opportunities to interact closely with the president of the Académie des Sciences, l'abbé Jean-Paul Bignon, and its director, l'abbé Jean Gallois. Moreover, there is ample evidence that salon women read and discussed the official publication of the Académie des Sciences, *Le Journal des sçavans,* which presented and critiqued cutting-edge research in science and medicine. Mme de Lambert subscribed to the journal and owned an impressive collection of the most important medical texts of the time. The court surgeon Pierre Dionis's *L'Anatomie des hommes* ("The Anatomy of Men") was included among these texts, and Dionis held a place of honor among the medically minded female aristocracy for the private dissections that he performed at the request of Queen Marie-Thérèse (see Tucker 17, 43–53).

Anatomy and Physiology

The queen's interest in anatomical demonstration shows how difficult it is to establish firm gender boundaries around learned and lay communities when it comes to medicine in the ancien régime. To introduce students to the world of medicine as it pertains to women and women's writing, I first reach back into the sixteenth century and dip at times into antiquity. I begin with book 1 of Laurent Joubert's *Erreurs populaires* (*Popular Errors*), which provides a rich overview of the ways that "wives' tales" and the therapeutics recommended by university-trained physicians were not as distinct as medical writers would have liked them to be. For modern readers, Joubert's text poses as many questions as it answers — questions about tradition, authority, and legacies of knowledge making regarding general medical practice, humoralism, and (in later chapters) understandings of the female body. An excellent resource for course preparation is Nancy Siraisi's *Medieval and Early Renaissance Medicine: An Introduction to Knowledge and Practice,* which offers coherent overviews of medical education, medical practice, and humoral theory. Visual supplements to Joubert's text might include engravings by Abraham Bosse (such as "La Belle saignée," "Le Clystère," and "L'Accouchement" ["The Beautiful Bloodletted Woman," "The Enema," and "Childbirth"], all available at the Bibliothèque Nationale de France [BNF] Web site). Literary supplements might also include excerpts from Molière's *Le Médecin malgré lui* (*The Doctor in Spite of Himself*), which mocks humoral medical practices and shows how Joubert's concerns about tensions between medicine and society in the Renaissance continued well into the seventeenth century.

Following this overview, I turn to a presentation of dissection practices in their historical and visual contexts to show students what anatomists could know, did know, and could not know about the human body—

particularly about the female body. This visually engaging prelude paves the way for more detailed discussion of sex and gender dynamics and socially constructed identities as they pertain to women and, by extension, to women's writing later in the course. Several top medical libraries offer early anatomical illustrations and exhibition catalogs online. Notably, the National Library of Medicine's outstanding exhibition *Dream Anatomy* offers a clear and helpful overview of the history of early dissection and is accompanied by high-quality reproductions of dissection images. Similarly, the image bank of the Wellcome Library for the History and Understanding of Medicine provides a rich resource for anatomical, humoral, and surgical imagery from the Middle Ages into the modern era.

The frontispiece to Vesalius's *De humani corporis fabrica* (1543), available on the Wellcome Library's site, is a must for any course that uses the history of medicine to preface discussions of women's bodies, women's texts, and women as texts. I have students contrast this image with earlier, medieval illustrations of dissection scenes. Focusing especially on the works of the preeminent medieval anatomist Mondino de'Luzzi, we consider the role of the dissectionist (who, in the medieval representations, takes orders from an academician sitting up high), the audience (which is sparse and sedate), and the positioning of the cadaver in the composition (male and off-center). With this historical context in mind, students are usually quick to note the dramatic representational shifts in the Vesalius frontispiece. The anatomist himself performs the dissection, and there is substantial hubbub around the body, which is situated squarely and centrally in the composition. Interestingly, however, students often neglect to take note of the sex of the cadaver. Unlike the work of de'Luzzi, Jacopa Berengario da Carpi, and other anatomists of the Middle Ages and the early Renaissance in which male bodies figure most prominently, the cadaver here is a woman's. We discuss possible meanings of this shift and consider underlying messages of the anatomist's clear gesturing toward the uterus of his subject with one hand and the title *De humani corporis fabrica* ("On the Fabric of Humans") with the other. A skeleton mediates the anatomist's gesturing toward the title and creates a continuous vertical plane from life (womb) to death (skeleton) to knowledge of man (title). From here, we turn our focus to other representations of female bodies in, for example, the works of Charles Estienne, Adriaan van den Spiegel, and Jacques Guillemeau. Students soon see that female anatomical studies frequently (if not almost exclusively) demonstrate a fascination for the reproductive body and, particularly, the female body in pregnancy. A number of accessible texts on the history of dissection can be used as reading assignments or supplements to lecture notes (see Siraisi; French; Sawday). An interactive Web version of four anonymous, seventeenth-century flap anatomies is available from Duke University's History of Medicine Collections; this resource provides students with a hands-on experience of exploring early representations of the male and female bodies (*Four Seasons*).

The Anatomy of Gender

Having introduced students to humoral theory in its therapeutic contexts as well as to general understandings of dissectionist practices and iconography, I turn to more detailed discussion of how the female body was framed and understood within the humoral physiological paradigms that dominated Europe from antiquity to the mid- to late eighteenth century. Two texts in particular work well to introduce the concept: Galen's discussion of male and female anatomy (14.6–7) and excerpts from Hippocrates on menstruation and childbirth (qtd. in Mauriceau). Helpful visual resources can be found at the companion Web site for the exhibition *Anatomy of Gender: Arts of the Body in Early Modern Europe* on display at Northwestern University's Mary and Leigh Block Museum of Art in 2006.

Over the past two decades of early modern gender studies, there are few images that have figured as prominently—and as controversially—in both interdisciplinary scholarship and the classroom as Vesalius's illustrations of male and female anatomical isomorphism. Thomas Laqueur used these images and other examples from medical and cultural documents to christen what he called a pre-Enlightenment "one-sex model" of anatomy and physiology (*Making* 8). Women, argues Laqueur, were not considered as being anatomically different from men until the mid-eighteenth century. Dominant physiological paradigms, which were based on Galenic and Aristotelian writings, described female anatomy homologously, rather than in comparison with, male anatomy. In humoral frameworks, women were similar to men, with one fundamental exception: they lacked sufficient heat and dryness to allow their reproductive organs to remain outside their bodies. Instead, their organs remained tucked up inside their bodies. It is, asserts Laqueur, only in the eighteenth century that anatomies began to be represented in terms of binary difference. These claims echoed those of Londa Schiebinger, who similarly asserted through a careful study of early illustrations of female skeletons that presentation of anatomical differences of sex does not appear in medical contexts until the Enlightenment (*Mind*).

Both intriguing and visually provocative, the one-sex model has had tremendous traction in early modern scholarship. However, there is a truism in academic scholarship: the stronger a notion or theory takes hold, the more likely it is to be criticized and contradicted. In the past several years, researchers have presented numerous counterexamples to the one-sex model as paradigm and have asserted that representations of biological sexual differences can be found in medical texts long before the eighteenth century (e.g., Cadden; Stolberg; Schleiner). Their arguments have met with varied reaction and, in a debate published in *Isis* in 2003, have garnered a strongly worded response from Laqueur that "stray observations do not discredit worldviews" ("Sex" 300).

These recent controversies can provide a rich frame for classroom explorations of the early modern female body. My goal in bringing medical theory and practice into a course of this type is to demonstrate the ways in which our understandings of what we mean by "women" and therefore what we mean by "women's writing" are as much up for debate as they are framed by historical and cultural contexts. With this background in mind, I have students judge the merits of the one-sex model after they do a close reading of excerpts of Laqueur's *Making Sex* along with two articles that take direct aim at his conclusions: Michael Stolberg's "A Woman Down to Her Bones: The Anatomy of Sexual Difference in the Sixteenth and Early Seventeenth Centuries" and Winfried Schleiner's "Early Modern Controversies about the One-Sex Model." Given the direct and contentious register of these articles, students are generally very eager to read Laqueur's reponse to Stolberg—which is equally direct. After students judge the merits of the articles and weigh in on the nuances of anatomical differences in the early modern era, we spend a good amount of time talking about what is at stake in this academic debate. Why do we care, and care so deeply, about early modern anatomy? Why does it matter if the early modern era understood there to be clear differences between men and women or whether a one-sex model could be considered the dominant view? How does this debate shape the way we might proceed as we think through questions of "*women's* writing" of this same time period? And, finally, how does our own inquisitiveness about the history of women, their bodies, and their texts tell us about our cultural frameworks and preoccupations?

Enter Descartes

An overview of the medical contexts for early debates regarding women's bodies and woman as a more general category offers an opportunity to problematize as well temptations to create steadfast dichotomies between public and private, male and female in the early modern era. Following Harth, I move then to a discussion of the mind-body dynamic and the potential impact of Cartesian notions of mind-body duality on women's writing and scientific engagement. Students read René Descartes's *Discours sur la méthode* (*Discourse on the Method*) and *Traité de l'homme* (*Treatise on Man*), either in their entirety or as excerpts depending on time and emphasis. I also assign excerpts from François Poullain de la Barre's *De l'égalité des deux sexes* (*On the Equality of the Two Sexes;* the chapter titled "Que les femmes . . . sont autant capables que les homes de toutes sortes de connoissances" is especially effective) as well as Marguerite Buffet's assertions that differences between the sexes are important only for the survival of humanity and do not have an impact on the intellect (224, 215). Molière's *Les Femmes savantes* provides, of course, the quintessential literary example of the tensions inherent in Cartesian dualisms, its stakes for women, and the mockery that female intellectual pursuits could garner.

This foray into the medical and philosophical contexts of women's writing challenges notions that bodies and texts, as well as historical truths, can be seen as inherently stable or consistent across time and place. In this way, writings on the body—and especially women's reproductive bodies—offer important insights into the fluidity that existed between male and female and help add nuance to our understandings of perceived divisions between salon and academy as spheres of knowledge making. Other essays in this volume address how social and cultural tensions relate to questions of space, mind, and body and how conjugal and reproductive duty plays out in texts penned by women in this period. Along medical lines, several other readings could be added to a syllabus of this sort: writings by the midwife Louise Bourgeois (which include descriptions of her practice, beauty recipes, and a letter of instruction to her daughter as she follows in her mother's footsteps); excerpts from Mme de Fouquet's home remedy manual, *Les Remèdes charitables* ("Charitable Remedies"); and Marie de Meurdrac's alchemical instruction book for women to help heal family members, *La Chymie charitable et facile, en faveur des dames* ("Charitable and Easy Chemistry, in Favor of Women"). These texts are fascinating and show women's writing and women's work in action. As I hope to have shown here, however, medical texts and related philosophical texts can also be used to demonstrate the wide and contested range of understandings of the female body as well as the high stakes of sexual difference and textual difference. In all, such an inclusion of early modern medical and dissection manuals allows for an exploration of the theoretical tensions and practical implications central to gender studies and acknowledges in the richest ways possible the theoretically sophisticated legacy of scholarship on early modern French women's writing.

Mary Ellen Birkett and Ann Leone

Gardens of Change: The Landscapes of Early Modern Women Writers

The recent emphasis on culture in French studies has dissolved disciplinary boundaries, thereby creating options for teaching literary works using different lenses. Evoking one of these perspectives in a 2006 report on the changing profession, Ursula K. Heise observes that environmentally oriented literary studies "promises to become one of the most intellectually exciting and politically urgent ventures in current literary and cultural studies" (514). Indeed, as many students are discovering, the optic of landscape studies gives them a way to link their interest in the natural environment with its construction in architecture, landscape architecture, the sciences, engineering, art, and literature.

Teachers who wish to experiment with this approach need not be specialists in landscape studies. Historical and theoretical background sufficient for introducing the topic and directing student work can be gleaned from good histories of garden landscape (e.g., Berrall, chs. 8, 10; Gothein, chs. 12, 15; Rogers, chs. 4, 5, 7; Thacker, chs. 8, 9, 10, 12, 14). We ourselves have successfully linked landscape studies to works of French literature in courses that include a bridge course from language to literary studies, a first-year seminar, and courses in French and comparative literature. In 2003–04, we codirected Elizabeth Anderson's senior honors thesis that brought landscape studies to bear on the writings of Marie-Madeleine Pioche de la Vergne, comtesse de Lafayette (1634–93), and Marie de Rabutin-Chantal, marquise de Sévigné (1626–96). We draw on that collaborative learning experience in this essay, particularly for the original research on Mme de Sévigné.

Garden landscapes occupy a privileged place not only within landscape studies—as interfaces between natural and constructed environments—but also within cultural studies, as Anne Desprechins observes: "[L]e jardin apparaît aussi révélateur de l'esprit qui anime une époque que les œuvres de ses écrivains et de ses artistes" 'Gardens are as revealing of the mentality of an era as are the works of that era's writers and artists' (395).[1] Teachers of courses that span the seventeenth and eighteenth centuries in France can exploit gardens' emblematic status effectively. What do the *jardins à la française* ("French gardens") of Louis XIV (1638–1715) and the *jardins à l'anglaise* ("English gardens") favored by Jean-Jacques Rousseau (1712–78) reveal about the changing relationship of people to the natural world during this time period? How does the study of two women writers—Mme de Lafayette and Mme de Sévigné—and their gardens, both literary and real, inflect our view of this evolution? Is there material here for reflection on our place in the world of the twenty-first century?

Le Jardin à la Française

Before examining these questions, it is useful to ask another: What is a landscape? The *Oxford English Dictionary* says it is "a view or prospect of natural inland scenery, such as can be taken in at a glance from one point of view; a piece of country scenery." In *Discovering the Vernacular Landscape*, J. B. Jackson cites the definition of landscape as "a portion of the earth's surface that can be comprehended at a glance" (8). Sight thus defines a landscape; but it is also true that a landscape can be constructed that defines, directs, and limits our gaze, thereby controlling our understanding of space.

Louis XIV and his architect, André Le Nôtre (1613–1700), understood this perhaps better than anyone before them in their interpretation of the formal *jardin classique* ("classical garden") or *jardin à la française*. Simply put, this kind of garden is a landscape where human intelligence and effort shape nature into *la belle nature*, that is, nature that is a manifestation of the human power to control, dominate, and embellish it. The ultimate realization of this formal aesthetic is of course the vast garden complex at Versailles that from its beginning in 1663 took more than a half century to complete. Images of the gardens at Versailles show an all-pervasive geometry, a strong axial orientation, and the artifices of linear perspective transforming natural elements into a display of human dominion over an otherwise inhospitable natural world (see Baridon; Pincas and Rocher-Gilotte; Fryberger).

Louis XIV's guide to Versailles, *Manière de montrer les jardins de Versailles* (*The Way to Present the Gardens of Versailles*, composed between 1689 and 1705), underscores that this human control over nature is nothing less than royal "visual imperialism" (Apostolidès, *Prince* 34–35). For example, the king's first peremptory sentence orders:

> En sortant du chasteau par le vestibule de la Cour de marbre, on ira sur la terasse; il faut s'arrester sur le haut des degrez pour considérer la situation des parterres des pièces d'eau et les fontaines des Cabinets. (*Manière* 1)

> On leaving the château by the vestibule of the marble courtyard, go out on to the terrace: pause at the top of the steps to view the layout of the parterres, the pools and the fountains. (*Way* 19)

Louis XIV controls not only the spectacle of his power but also how that display is seen. All the pauses in *The Way to Present the Gardens of Versailles* constrain the visitor to view the gardens from set viewpoints, usually elevated, so that she or he perceives the gardens as static, unchanging tableaux composed of elements owing their existence to their powerful royal creator.

These design choices are collaborative elements in Louis XIV's politics of absolutism, as well, as William Howard Adams (*French Garden*, chs. 2, 3), Jean-Marie Apostolidès (*Roi-machine*, chs. 3–5), and F. Hamilton Hazlehurst (chs. 4, 17) underscore. All elements of Versailles—château, mythological decor, gardens—have as their point of origin and point of perspective the Sun King himself. The landscape of Versailles is thus a kind of three-dimensional metaphor and theater for Louis XIV's absolute power. Louis XIV defines for all time the *jardin à la française* as a political entity, an instrument of power—power of man over nature, power of man over humankind.

Mme de Lafayette, *La Princesse de Clèves*

One of the privileged seventeenth-century visitors to Versailles—privileged in that the king served as her guide to the gardens—was Mme de

Lafayette (Sévigné, *Correspondance* 1: 226–27; letter 157, 17 Apr. 1671; Sévigné, *Letters* 1: 157; letter 98). As students read Mme de Lafayette's famous novel of 1678, *La Princesse de Clèves*, they should think about the ways in which Mme de Lafayette's firsthand acquaintance with Versailles's aesthetic of power transmitted through vision appears in the representation of gardens in her novel. Despite the minimal visual presence of landscape in *La Princesse de Clèves*, three scenes important to the plot take place in a garden.

In the first of these scenes, in the formal garden at Coulommiers, the princess confesses to her husband that she loves another man (169–75; 93–99).[2] By bringing her husband into a garden that is primarily *her* space, the princess gains control over one man (her husband); but her authority over men is not absolute, for the duc de Nemours sees all, without being seen. The one who sees is the one who retains power.

In the second scene in the princess's garden at Coulommiers, the princess indulges in a semierotic reverie while toying with a cane belonging to the duc de Nemours, with whom she is still in love (208–09; 127–28). Once again, because the princess is in her garden and has set the scene in which she figures, she retains a certain control. Once again, Nemours sees without being seen. But in this instance, Nemours's "role as omniscient and unique observer of the whole interlude is taken from him" (Leone 41). One of the princess's servants catches him in his act of voyeurism, thereby calling into question the masculine prerogative to the power of vision.

In the third garden scene (222–23; 140–41), this precarious balance of power definitively shifts: the princess discovers the secret vantage point from which the duc de Nemours, unobserved, watched her comings and goings in her garden. It is this reversal of perspective that empowers the princess, finally, to accede to absolute authority when, in the garden "hors les faubourgs" 'outside the suburbs' (222; 141), the princess sees the duc de Nemours without his seeing her. When, unsuspecting that he has been observed, he wakes and leaves the garden, "Mme de Clèves va s'asseoir dans le même endroit d'où venait de sortir M. de Nemours" 'She went and sat in the spot which he had just quitted' (223; 141). As the princess takes Nemours's place, as she becomes the viewer instead of the viewed in a garden landscape, her power equals that of Louis XIV in his garden at Versailles. She achieves the self-determination that brings her to renounce the demands of the duke, of court life, and indeed of all of society.

The princess, however, is not Louis XIV, nor are her gardens Versailles. She uses the garden not to control the natural world or to dominate the lives of others so much as to foster the discovery and affirmation of her autonomous desires. In short, power associated with seventeenth-century gardens in *La Princesse de Clèves* is not an absolute male ruler's power politics but rather one woman's power of will over her emotions. Mme de Lafayette, while keeping the form of *le jardin classique*, alters its function: the formal gardens of *La Princesse de Clèves* are the site of a relocation of power from the realm of the political to the realm of the personal.

Mme de Sévigné, *Correspondance*

For Mme de Sévigné, Mme de Lafayette's friend, the discovery that the garden is a private space is but the point of departure. Students should consider the relation between function and form in Mme de Sévigné's garden, as well as think about the ways in which she positions herself in the landscape.

Les Rochers—the Breton property Mme de Sévigné inherited from her husband Henri de Sévigné when she was twenty-five years old—was the private space that Mme de Sévigné preferred to the public sphere of Paris and life at court (Sévigné, *Correspondance* 2: 931; letter 764, 17 May 1680; Sévigné, *Letters* 5: 28–32; letter 628). The experience of the garden for Sévigné is at heart an experience of solitude:

> Je vous avoue que c'est un de mes plaisirs que de me promener seule; je trouve quelques labyrinthes de pensées dont on a peine à sortir; mais on a du moins la liberté de penser à ce que l'on veut.
> (1: 310; letter 187, 29 July 1671)

> I own that I take great pleasure in walking by myself; we get, it is true, into a certain labyrinth of thought, from which it is sometimes difficult to extricate ourselves; but then we have the liberty of thinking on what pleases us most. (1: 234–35; letter 121)[3]

This concept of garden landscape—fundamentally opposed to the reigning theatrical and socially determined garden forms accepted by Mme de Lafayette—frees Mme de Sévigné to transform the estate at Les Rochers into a *parc* that favors not only movement but also personal participation. Mme de Sévigné never used professionals to design or execute the plans she made (Desprechins 399; see also Sévigné, *Correspondance* 3: 924; letter 1224, 30 July 1690; omitted from Sévigné, *Letters*). As she works, what matters to her is not formal control over the landscape but rather being part of it. She designs her garden herself, enlarges it herself, plants it herself, tends it herself, walks and meditates in it:

[C]e matin . . . je me suis mise dans la rosée jusqu'à mi-jambes pour prendre des alignements. Je fais des allées de retour tout autour de mon parc, qui seront d'une grande beauté.
(1: 371; letter 213, 28 Oct. [1671])

I do not know what you may have been doing this morning; but I have been half-way up my legs in dew, laying lines for some walks that I am making round my park, which will be very beautiful when finished.
(1: 296; letter 147)

Nothing about these vast, serpentine lanes or about measuring them out in wet, knee-high grass suggests the human domination of space, the rigid configuration of perspective and point of view, or the geometrical design of parterres characteristic of classical French gardens.

Because Mme de Sévigné's garden is not the static *jardin classique* appreciated primarily through vision but instead a representation of the passage of time, it fosters in its creator bittersweet feelings. Trees grow, plantings thrive, the garden changes layout and shape as new lands are added; these changes also mark the duration of the absence of her daughter, Françoise-Marguerite de Sévigné, comtesse de Grignan (1646–1705), who appears to have shared at least some measure of her mother's "passion" for Les Rochers (1: 380; letter 217, 15 Nov. 1671 [1: 305–07; letter 151] and 2: 116; letter 433, 2 Oct. 1675 [3: 35–39; letter 344]). Mme de Sévigné writes to her daughter with mingled delight and sadness:

Je viens de ces bois; vraiment ces allées sont d'une beauté à quoi je ne m'accoutume point. Il y en a six que vous ne connaissez point du tout, mais celles que vous connaissez sont fort embellies par la beauté du plant. (2: 186–87; letter 457, 15 Dec. 1675)

I come from my woods; the walks in them are beautiful, and I should never be tired of them. There are six new ones you have never seen, and those you have seen are very much improved. (3: 109; letter 368)

Indeed, Mme de Sévigné's maternal feelings are so abundant that they overflow to all trees, "ces petits enfants que j'ai plantés" 'these little children that I have planted' (3: 604; letter 1113, 29 May 1689 [omitted from *Letters*]).[4]

Mme de Sévigné's garden landscape—a landscape where humans seek intimacy and harmony with nature rather than power over it—marks a turning away from the form and function of *le jardin classique* and the values associated with it. For Mme de Sévigné, the garden is no longer the site for domination by a political self (as it was for Louis XIV) or for affirmation by a socially determined self (as it was for the princesse de Clèves). It is the place where beauty consists in one's private emotional response to, personal relationship with, and participation in a nature nourished by humans but free to follow its own development. Mme de Sévigné sums up this aesthetic that dissociates vision (and power) from the pleasures of the garden when she writes to her daughter, "Notre jardin est très beau; je crois que j'y coucherai" 'Our garden is so beautiful; I believe I'll spend the night there' (2: 575; letter 620, 15 Oct. 1677 [omitted from *Letters*]).

Le Jardin à l'Anglaise

The work of male English landscape architects and theorists in the early decades of the eighteenth century echoes the garden aesthetics that Mme de Sévigné—a French woman, writing personally and at times intimately about her life—developed at Les Rochers. John Vanbrugh (1664–1726), the designer of Blenheim, and Joseph Addison (1672–1719), the author of articles for the *Tatler* and the *Spectator*, also contested the rigid aesthetics of *le jardin à la française*.

Rousseau's immensely popular and influential epistolary novel *La Nouvelle Héloise*, published in 1761, evokes the new garden aesthetic that emerged from these writings and from their realizations—"le jardin à l'anglaise" (609)[5]—in his description of Julie's garden, "L'Elisée" (572; a letter composed as early as 1757 [*Œuvres* 4: 11]). Nothing about this "lieu retiré dont [Julie] fait sa promenade favorite" 'secluded spot which is her favorite place to walk' resembles the gardens of Versailles (470–71; 387). Plantings no longer embody politics: "des touffes obscures, impénétrables aux rayons du soleil" 'these groves so shaded' underscore the values of mystery and imagination rather than of control and vision (473; 388). The living force of nature has priority over static vision: fruit-bearing shrubs grow "çà et là, sans ordre et sans symétrie" 'here and there without order or symmetry' in exuberant defiance of Versailles's disfiguring geometry (473; 388); "des allées tortueuses et irrégulières bordées de ces bocages fleuris" 'torturous and irregular alleys bordered by these flowered woods' invite visitors to follow their own paths within this realm of protected abundance (473; 389); aromatic herbs, bird song, and the sound of flowing water, too, hold the visitor in thrall to leisurely delectation of all the senses (472–75; 388–91).

Woman's Place

It is no coincidence that L'Elisée is a woman's garden: "[I]l est vrai, dit-elle [Julie], que la nature a tout fait, mais sous ma direction, et il n'y a rien là que je n'aye ordonné" 'It is true, she said, that nature did it all, but under my direction, and there is nothing here that I have not designed' (472; 388). But Julie's design, unlike Louis XIV's, is destined not to dominate nature but rather, like Mme de Lafayette's, to represent emotional self-possession, and, like Mme de Sévigné's, to create harmony with the world around her, for "la main de jardinier ne se montre point" 'I see no human labor here' (472; 388). The garden becomes a metaphor for Julie's inner self, "an expression of the passionate side of her being that her social position as Mme de Wolmar does not permit her to avow" (Birkett 118).

This is nothing short of a revolution in taste and mentality. Students who have read *Discovering the Vernacular Landscape* will recognize this new kind of garden as coinciding with Jackson's contemporary definition of landscape as "a composition of man-made or man-modified spaces to serve as infrastructure or background for our collective existence" (8): in short, a landscape defined not only by vision but also by our sense of place in it. They will be sensitive to the fact that this transition from one aesthetic to another, far from being remote from twenty-first-century concerns, lies close to the heart of our relation to the natural environment today. As precious parts of our natural world disappear, gardens and landscapes have begun to regain the importance they had in the past, as ground—literally and figuratively—for debates about aesthetics, metaphysics, and the value of physical place for our well-being and our identity as individuals in that world. Students' consideration of Mme de Lafayette and Mme de Sévigné along the continuum from classical garden, exemplified by Louis XIV's Versailles, to picturesque garden, evoked by Rousseau, will have suggested to them that, no matter how rigid, how politically determined a culture's vision of human beings' place in the world may be, it is susceptible to new ways of seeing and that women can and have been significant agents of this change.

Notes

1. All unattributed translations are by Mary Ellen Birkett.

2. All references to *La Princesse de Clèves* are to Roger Duchêne's edition and Terence Cave's English translation.

3. See also 2: 69; letter, 4 Oct. 1679 (4: 202–04; letter 567) and 3: 4; letter 805, 8 Sept. 1680 (5: 156–60, letter 663).

4. See also 2: 111; letter 431, 29 Sept. 1675 (3: 32–35; letter 343).

5. All references to *La Nouvelle Héloïse* are to Bernard Gagnebin and Marcel Raymond's edition and Philip Stewart and Jean Vaché's English translation.

Claire Goldstein

Textual Production
and the Woman Writer

Not so long ago, faculty members interested in teaching a course on French women writers of the ancien régime faced an almost insurmountable obstacle in the scarcity and expense of modern editions of their works. This is no longer the case, since publishers large and small capitalize on the reassessment of the canon made possible by a generation of iconoclastic academic research. Such assessments, especially of emergent prose fiction genres, like Faith E. Beasley's *Revising Memory*, Joan DeJean's *Tender Geographies*, Margaret Anne Doody's *True Story of the Novel*, Chantal Morlet-Chantalat's *La* Clélie *de Mademoiselle de Scudéry*, and Alain Niderst's *Madeleine de Scudéry, Paul Pellisson et leur monde* have dramatically rewritten accepted narratives of Western literary history. With Louise Labé in the headlines, along with Marie-Madeleine Pioche de la Vergne, comtesse de Lafayette, and *La Princesse de Clèves* (one recalls the debate surrounding Nicolas Sarkozy's derogatory statements about the novel in 2009 [see, e.g., Girard]) — and novels, fairy tales, plays, and *nouvelles* by women coming out in affordable anthologies and pocket editions — the challenge has become which texts and authors to include in a single semester rather than how to find enough available material to teach.

So it came as a surprise, when planning a new class on early modern women writers, that I felt a sense of regret as I contemplated the range of prerevolutionary women's texts easily available from mainstream online French bookstores. Certainly advances in the field have been astonishing and positive. My students would not have to use interlibrary loan and photocopy to read Madeleine de Scudéry's novels or Mme de Villedieu's plays. They could find the two volumes of Perry Gethner's anthology of ancien régime women playwrights in the library and purchase single fairy tales in attractive and inexpensive editions such as those published by Mille et Une Nuits. Even Scudéry's *Clélie* is now teachable in Delphine Denis's affordable Folio Classique abridgement. For the first time, I could, like my modernist colleagues, simply fill out an order with the bookstore and wait for desk copies to arrive. Perhaps never before have ancien régime women writers had such an uncomplicated relation to the publishing industry.

But in fact, even before they were written out of the canon, when they were widely read and acknowledged as avatars of the literary scene, women writers in prerevolutionary France occupied an ambivalent position vis-à-vis the book trade. While it is wonderful to find bookstore shelves stocked with titles by women beyond *La Princesse de Clèves*, it is important to give our students a sense of the stakes and challenges of writing (as well as publishing and reading) as a woman in the seventeenth and eighteenth centuries. For this reason, I designed my advanced undergraduate course on early modern women writers with a secondary focus on the history of the book. The course's double focus allowed me, first of all, to expose my students simultaneously to two vibrant fields of literary research. Second, and even more important, I hoped to use the book history to add nuance to students' understanding of texts we read, to lead them to see these works not just in terms of (occasionally strange) plot, structure, and character development but as interventions in a rapidly changing cultural scene, filled with particular opportunities and risks for women writers. Giving students the opportunity to learn about and handle old books stimulates them to learn about the historical and social contexts in which early modern women wrote, read, and published. As students scrutinize title pages and *privilèges* (the "permission" to publish, included at the beginning of works of the era), they are curious to know more about the publishers and booksellers whose names and addresses they see. This scrunity offers an *entré* to readings about women in the book trade and the sometimes positive, sometimes critical (even hostile) reception of women authors by the reading public. The anonymity or complex staging of women authors (as mothers, for example) on title pages, frontispieces, and prefaces raises similar questions regarding the way the ancien régime construed authorship and authority and the various strategies women from different strata of society used to appropriate or subvert these entrenched male values.

Let me acknowledge from the outset that teaching the history of the book at a Research I institution with an old and well-stocked library, or in close proximity to venerable public collections, is not the same thing as attempting to do so at a small, new, or less-endowed institution. I designed and taught the course I am discussing here at Miami University, a medium-sized public, largely undergraduate institution in the rural Midwest. We have an old but relatively limited library, with a small collection of rare books and manuscripts that have been neither fully cataloged nor always properly conserved. I have discovered since coming to Oxford, Ohio, to teach, however, that each library and locale presents its own prospects, not only the predictable deficits. To make this essay as usable as possible, I try to present easy and portable (often Web-based) solutions in addition to ways I used resources particular to my institution. I concentrate less on the primary literary readings—the rest of this volume provides many rich possibilities for teaching these—than on the annex activities I used to contextualize women's writing in the prerevolutionary book market and to train students in primary research methods. I should also note that Miami University has a particularly long semester—fifteen or sixteen weeks—and that the course I am describing met three times weekly, which allowed me to plan two days of reading discussion and one of research enrichment each week. Rather than insist on the specifics of the course exactly as I taught it, I describe research activities and assignments that would be easy to adapt as homework or in-class activities.

Databases, some with digital facsimiles of early modern books, others with searchable text, provide a range of engaging classroom opportunities, even for beginning students of French. These resources allow our students to become armchair archivists and make possible a kind of primary research previously unimaginable at great removes from important research centers. Before unleashing my computer-literate, *Wikipedia*-addicted undergraduate readers into the computer lab, however, I wanted to give them some tactile experience of old books. It was capital that they understood from the start that books constitute objects in their own right, with myriad layers of meaning, and do not coincide totally with the texts they contain. Fortunately, the rare books room at my institution is not only open to undergraduate classes but under new direction that actively encourages students and faculty members to make use of the collection. I arranged to meet the students in special collections for the second class session. In advance of the visit, I asked them to write a paragraph or two in their reading journal in which they tried to capture the experience of (buying, holding, carrying, reading) their favorite book. This exercise gave me an early chance to detect any severe French or writing problems, established the routine of regular writing before class meetings, and, finally, put my students in the right frame of mind to discover the materiality of the text.

I wanted the experience to be as memorable as possible. The librarian and I met the students at the door to the special collections reading room. Although students are not required to sign in for class visits, I had them all sign the register and follow every step a researcher would normally take to enter the collection. As they consigned coats, bags, and pens, I described for them the steps a researcher would take to gain entrance into the Bibliothèque Nationale de France (BNF) or the British Library or the Newberry. Pencils and blank notebooks in hand, we were ready to go in. This mise-en-scène, although admittedly dramatic, makes a more indelible impression than my often repeated assertion that old books and primary research are irreplaceable. I also wanted to share with my students in the most tactile way what it is that scholars do. I had selected a variety of books, which the librarian had prepared on cradles scattered around the room. While I am always tempted to begin by showing students things, I divided them immediately into small groups to examine a book, guided by a questionnaire I had prepared. After a few words on the care needed to handle old paper and fragile bindings, students set out observing their assigned books: the size, shape, paper, binding, condition; the title, author, date, frontispiece, illustrations; notes in margins and on flyleaves; objects placed between pages. I asked each group to present their book to the class and to try to describe what kind of book it was, who might have used it, when, and for what purposes. With no prior knowledge of seventeenth- and eighteenth-century books, the students did a wonderful job of understanding the different potential uses of a folio versus a duodecimo. They observed some books had been well used, bearing signs of wear, inscriptions, marginalia, and splotches from ink and food, while others seemed to have passed their lives on protected shelves. They observed the relative quality of paper stocks, typefaces, and illustrations. They made some interesting guesses based on frontispieces (I deliberately included several with the typical male author portraits as well as allegorical images of female bodies and images of solicitous maternal pedagogy). They determined that some of the books contained incomplete publication information or seemed to be anonymous or printed and sold abroad rather than in the type of Paris bookshop advertised on most title pages.

After the class visit to the rare books room, we began filling in the blanks—the cultural context of both women and books and where they intersect—with secondary sources alongside our program of literary readings. Within the first few weeks of the semester, I assigned several chapters from Elizabeth Goldsmith and Dena Goodman's *Going Public* as well as shorter selections from Beasley's *Revising Memory*, Roger Chartier and Henri Jean Martin's *Histoire de l'édition française*, Robert Darnton's *Forbidden Bestsellers of Pre-revolutionary France*, and DeJean's *Tender Geographies* and "Lafayette's Ellipses" to introduce institutions and practices from the salon and collective writing to censorship, the book trade, and prerevolutionary concepts of authorship and authority. When I next teach the course I will also include readings from Beasley's *Salons, History and the Creation of Seventeenth-Century France*.

Since so much seventeenth-century women's writing experiments and innovates with genre (see Stedman in this volume), I felt it important to offer students the experience of reading texts they might not at first know what to do with. Scudéry's *Femmes illustres* gave us the opportunity to go to the library and learn how to use microfilm, which none of the students had seen—or even heard of—before. The new generation of microfilm readers mercifully allows users to scan pages as PDF files, which are clearer than the photocopies of old, to the point of permitting analysis and discussion of the woodcut images embedded in the text. (Teachers of courses in translation will be happy to find two nearly contemporaneous translations of the text on *Early English Books Online* [*EEBO*].) The attribution of the young author's text to her brother and the genre of the work—a portrait gallery of speeches by exemplary women—opened class discussion on the concerns of women authors and readers. To help students make sense of the values advocated by the *harangues*—what it means to be a heroic woman in word and in deed—I asked them to identify what they thought were key terms in the assigned selections (the introduction, Clélie's speech, Sappho's speech, and one additional speech per group of two students). We then consulted historical dictionaries to grasp the nuances and associations related to these words.

After introducing students to sources in the library's reference collection (our library has recently been able to purchase a facsimile of Antoine

Furetière's *Dictionnaire universel*), I guided them to the online *Oxford English Dictionary* and historical dictionaries on *American and French Research on the Treasury of the French Language* (*ARTFL*), a subscription-only database. I created a worksheet activity to help students discover some of *ARTFL*'s many other research capabilities. I had them explore the partial *French Women Writers* database (under "Collections of Texts") and gave them guided tasks to discover linked full-text databases (*EFTS*) and *Electronic Open Stacks* (*EOS*) (both under "ARTFL Collaborations"). Students can become easily overwhelmed by the number of unfamiliar choices, and it is important to give them very specific tasks (for example, find the *Artamène, ou le Grand Cyrus* hypertext and answer several factual questions about the introductory page) as well as more open-ended quests to locate and describe for the class what might be interesting leads. Finally I demonstrated how to do word-frequency searches ("the FRANTEXT DATABASE using PhiloLogic"). This tool allows researchers to locate all uses of a word or phrase within a specific historical period in the *ARTFL* database. A search can also be narrowed by author, title, and genre. For the purpose of our exercise, I chose a few of the key words students identified in Scudéry's *Femmes illustres* and searched for occurrences between 1600 and 1800 or 1600 and 1715.

We accessed the next literary text of the semester, selections from Scudéry's *Conversations*, on the BNF *Gallica* database, which offers free use of digitized facsimile texts, images, and sound recordings. Again, I created a worksheet to guide students through the BNF Web site (www .bnf.fr/). I asked directed questions, which had them navigate through a virtual exhibition and one of the pedagogical dossiers on the main BNF site. Then I instructed students to enter *Gallica* (http://gallica.bnf.fr/). It is useful to explain step by step how to select a document, view the bibliographical information ("notice complète"), view the document, and download it as a PDF ("télécharger"). Since I wanted to accustom my students to independent research in preparation for their final project, I also assigned each group of two or three students an author, subject, key word ("recherche simple") or title that might guide them to a text not included in the syllabus but relevant to our study of early modern women writers. Students wrote up their findings in their weekly journal entry and reported briefly in class. Although undergraduates typically blanch at the prospect of reading in seventeenth- and eighteenth-century typeface and orthography, using printout facsimiles for the first two readings allowed students a kind of experiential proximity to old books that helped them understand the difference between a book and a text and helped dramatize the stakes of women's access to and circulation in print.

Conversations predictably baffled students, who began by demanding a more recognizable plot structure. However, writing pastiches proved an effective way of guiding them toward a better understanding and appreciation of the rhetoric and values of Scudéry's text. Our contextualized readings of Scudéry's *Femmes illustres* and *Conversations* prepared students to read Denis's abridgement of *Clélie* with an eye to issues of gender and authority. My students seemed especially sensitive to textual stagings of the act of narration and the relative glory assigned in the text to literary and verbal versus military prowess. Students reported that their experience with old books made these themes seem much less abstract.

Students returned to *Gallica* to read from the *Mercure galant* as a way of providing context to fables written by Marie-Catherine Desjardins (Mme de Villedieu) and fairy tales by Marie-Catherine Le Jumel de Barneville, comtesse d'Aulnoy; Charlotte-Rose de Caumont La Force; and anonymous women writers. The *Mercure*'s inscription of communities of female readers and its particular mix of news (on politics, fashion, society, technology, curiosities, etc.), fiction, reader submissions and reactions, and assorted novelties such as enigmas and riddles offered students a sense of the preoccupations and reading, writing, and reception practices of worldly readers. Since Miami University's special collections have a focus on educational books, broadly defined, my class was also able to work with quite a few late-eighteenth-century collections of fairy tales written by women. We examined the presentation of women authors and women readers on title pages, prefaces, and frontispieces as well as which scenes were illustrated and how. I asked small groups of students to follow themes of their choice. Some of their concerns included representations of power, maternity, marriage, literacy, and education.

The semester's other literary readings included Villedieu's play *Le Favori*, which we read in conjunction with articles by Jeffrey N. Peters ("Kingship") and Chloé Hogg and the author's description of its *fête* performance; Lafayette's *Princesse de Montpensier*, with selected readings around the *Princesse de Clèves* controversy (see Beasley and Jensen's *Approaches*); the description of court life and etiquette in *De l'esprit des étiquettes de l'ancienne cour et des usages du monde de ce temps*, by Stéphanie-Félicité Du Crest, comtesse de Genlis; several novels and novellas in Raymond Trousson's anthology *Romans de femmes du XVIIIe siècle*; and Gabrielle-Emilie Du Châtelet's philosophical meditation *Le Discours sur le bonheur*.

For their final project, students worked individually or in small groups to present a document of their choice to a salon of their peers. Most groups chose to work with volumes from the special collections. Students presented several different collections of fairy tales; women's periodicals; "secret" histories attributed to important French women, including Marie-Antoinette and Mme Du Barry; and education manuals for and by women, including guides to rhetoric and letter writing, history, and comportment. One group analyzed images of women painted by Élisabeth Vigée Lebrun and Adélaïde Labille-Guiard. The quality of their work and their enthusiasm demonstrated to me that the students' experiences with old books—virtual and real—enriched their understanding of and interest in early modern women writers.

Faith E. Beasley

Salons and Innovation

Until relatively recently, the image that most readily came to mind when one evoked a woman during the ancien régime was not that of a woman writing but rather that of a woman socializing, surrounded by her friends in a *ruelle*, or salon. Abraham Bosse's influential engravings of seventeenth century salons are devoid of the instruments of textual production; they depict women eating, conversing, and gazing through telescopes but not writing or even reading. Eighteenth-century artistic renderings of female activities often portray an individual woman with a pen or a book in hand or an intimate group engrossed as one member reads aloud but do not portray salon participants actually writing. Until the late twentieth century, historians and literary historians alike maintained the distinction between salons and literary creation illustrated by this visual record. Salons and their conversations provided civilizing gentility that came to characterize ancien régime society but, according to the prevailing view, had little if any influence beyond the realm of sociability. Above all, the institution of the salon supposedly had no influence on or any serious connection to literary production, the history of ideas, and what in hindsight was deemed mainstream thought and literary expression of this foundational period of French history.

Research on ancien régime France since the 1970s, however, in particular the fruitful collaboration between literary and social historians outside the hexagon, has questioned the image of the salon as merely an institution of politeness. The work of scholars such as Dena Goodman, Joan DeJean, Domna Stanton, Elena Russo, and many of the contributors to this volume has resurrected the essential relation of the salons, textual production, literary practices, and the creation and diffusion of knowledge during the ancien régime. The move to rehabilitate the salon has encountered critics; there are those such as Antoine Lilti who contend that the influence salons, especially the women associated with them, exerted was primarily social as opposed to intellectual or philosophical. The stakes of this debate are high given that the specific periods associated with the salons are also those that produced what are arguably the literary and philosophical works most associated with France's intellectual capital. Re-creating the dialogue that existed in and was facilitated by the salons between relatively unknown, primarily female salon figures and writers and philosophers such as Molière, René Descartes, Voltaire, and Jean-Jacques Rousseau not only resurrects salon influence but also transforms the way we read and interpret classic texts and even French culture as a whole. While such an intellectual shift may appear threatening to some, to many others it is essential and long overdue.

In what follows I present ways to incorporate recent scholarship on the salons into classes on French history, literature, philosophy, the history of the book, French culture, and the history of feminist thought. In my courses I focus on giving students a sense of how the salons functioned during the ancien régime, how they were viewed by their contemporaries, and what lasting influences they had on literary culture. While I direct students to the wealth of recent scholarship available on the salons—in particular Erica Harth, DeJean, Elizabeth C. Goldsmith, Carla Hesse, Goodman, and Linda Timmermans—I find that using primary texts of the period illustrates more convincingly the ways the salons functioned, the influence they exerted, and their multifaceted nature. Using primary texts also allows me to underscore that distinctions between sociability and literary production are anachronistic and impede our understanding of how texts and knowledge were produced and circulated during the ancien régime. We explore this complex, "utterly French" 'purement français' institution and analyze the myths associated with it and how they came to exist (Picard 19; my trans.). Placing the salon in its cultural and literary context reveals it to be much more than a private club for conversation among elite women with nothing else to do; nor are salons of the ancien régime the equivalent of Oprah Winfrey's book clubs (an analogy made by one of my colleagues).

In this essay, I organize my discussion around some of the principal salon figures and issues raised particularly well by their salons. Incorporating all these important *salonnières* into a class gives the full range of the salons, but each figure could easily find her way into other courses. Throughout my discussion, I raise broader pedagogical possibilities associated with the salons, especially how they can be used to illuminate canon formation, the construction and reconstruction of history over time, the French educational system, and French collective memory. I emphasize the dialogue that one can and should create between what have traditionally been considered the margins, that is, the worldly culture of the salons, and the center, or France's rich literary and philosophical culture associated with the ancien régime. Given the vast scope of this enterprise, in this essay I suggest various approaches rather than describe in detail specific texts that could be used to create this dialogue.

Catherine de Vivonne, marquise de Rambouillet; Madeleine de Scudéry; Marie-Madeleine Pioche de la Vergne, comtesse de Lafayette; Marguerite de La Sablière; Anne-Thérèse de Marguenat de Courcelles, marquise de Lambert; and Germaine de Staël are the principal salon innovators and habitués who can most easily and profitably be used to reconstruct the salon milieu. The marquise de Rambouillet and her *chambre bleue* ("blue room") are a logical starting point for defining the phenomenon of the salon. The marquise is generally viewed as the founder of the salon movement in France in the 1620s, although others, such as Marie de Gournay, had salons beginning in the late sixteenth century. The marquise de Rambouillet was not recognized as a writer, but she surrounded herself with a group of intellectuals who included academicians and intellectuals like Jean Chapelain, poets and writers like Vincent Voiture and a young Scudéry, as well as worldly interlocutors and political figures. Students are often surprised to learn that such "serious" male intellectuals and writers as Chapelain and Pierre Corneille not only frequented salons but also coveted invitations. Of Italian descent, the marquise was especially desirous to refine French manners and language (Aronson, *Madame de Rambouillet*). Baldesar Castiglione's *The Book of the Courtier* can provide a good entry into a discussion of *politesse* and *galanterie* and how the French conceptions of these terms differ from those espoused by Italian court culture (see also Harrison in this volume). The history of the development of worldly court society, emphasizing women's intellectual roles, can also be developed under the umbrella of the *chambre bleue* using the work of Carolyn Lougee, Alain Viala (*France*; *Naissance*), Timmermans, and Harth (*Cartesian Women*; *Ideology*).

Posterity has tended to focus on an exaggerated conception of the effort to refine on the part of habitués of the *chambre bleue*, to the exclusion of its other purposes and activities. The notion of *préciosité* is derived above all from this association of the activities of the *chambre bleue* with extreme refinement, as satirized by Molière in *Les Précieuses ridicules* (Lathuillère). When one resurrects the *chambre bleue*'s cultural milieu, however, the charge of *préciosité* can be interpreted as a move to discount the salon's true power and influence. As Stanton has persuasively argued, the "fiction of preciosity" is actually a fear of female influence and a reaction against women's incursion into the cultural, especially literary, sphere ("Fiction"). From this discussion, an instructor can move to an analysis of what effect women's salon activity had on the cultural milieu as a whole. The reaction against women's participation illustrates how the age-old *querelle des femmes* continued, despite and indeed because of women's new roles in the cultural arena. Even Armand-Jean Du Plessis, cardinal and duc de Richelieu, recognizing the potential for uncontrollable influence deriving from worldly gatherings such as the *chambre bleue*, founded the Académie Française in part to counter this movement (see Beasley, *Salons*, ch. 1).

Richelieu recognized that the key to controlling French culture, political and literary, lay in securing control over its essential building block, language. The *chambre bleue* was associated with refining the French language during this crucial time of its and the state's development. Richelieu can be viewed as establishing the Académie Française to rival its worldly alternative and specifically to exclude female influence from the cultural realm. Several texts from the period point to a perceived rivalry between the salons and the Académie Française over the control of language. Of particular interest are the *discours de reception*, the acceptance speeches given by newly admitted academicians, in which authors make explicit the connection between language and politics that was developed and exploited by Louis XIV. Dominique Bouhours's *Entretiens d'Ariste et d'Eugène* can be used to illustrate the influence of the worldly salon public, especially its highly developed art of conversation. Composed in the form of a dialogue, *Entretiens* is an excellent illustration of the appropriation of language to exert cultural influence. Finally, a text that deserves to be better known today, Marguerite Buffet's *Nouvelles Observations sur la langue française*, explicitly reflects the links among salons, language, female literary production, and women's influence on the cultural sphere through their activities as critics and writers in the salons (Beasley, *Salons* 50–66). Buffet's observations on language are followed by a series of portraits of her female contemporaries in which she underscores their cultural achievements and influence. She emphasizes conversation as a serious form of criticism and as a creative medium (see Harth, *Cartesian Women*). Indeed, conversation in Buffet's text is equivalent to actual literary composition and is equally influential and deserving of recognition.

Bouhours's and Buffet's texts, as well as their contemporaries' descriptions of and references to the *chambre bleue* and to other salons throughout the period, all highlight the growing influence of the worldly public, developed and exerted by the salons, on literary production and critique. Analyzing Corneille's *Le Cid* and the quarrel that surrounded it is a compelling way to illustrate the emerging force (Merlin-Kajman) of the salon context, which affected the composition as well as the reception of this canonical play (Beasley, *Salons* 102–14). The texts documenting the quarrel are available in Armand Gasté's edition. The success of Corneille's play among the worldly public sparked the clash: Corneille provoked the professional jealousy and ire of his contemporary playwrights by composing the poem "Excuse à Ariste," in which he boldly advances that the pleasure the public derived from *Le Cid* compensates for any creative liberties he may have taken with his play, such as not respecting the *trois unités* ("three unities") to which classical theater was supposed to be wedded. It is to the worldly salon public's criteria of pleasure that Corneille adheres, instead of that of classical theater's traditional critics, the *doctes*, or learned scholars. Corneille was known for reading his plays aloud in salons and for seeking the counsel of nontraditional critics such as his sister. Practices like these, which would increasingly become the norm, provoked more-traditional playwrights and critics to try to control the worldly public's influence on the literary arena.

The quarrel surrounding *Le Cid* is especially interesting to students because much of the debate centers on the character Chimène, who dares to accept an offer of marriage from her father's murderer. Corneille's critics condemned Chimène and the play, considering Chimène an unacceptable character for the stage; she is *invraisemblable*—that is, she does not conform to moral dictates. Corneille retorted that the salon public, and women in particular, applauded Chimène. Critics judged this taste reprehensible; while *Le Cid* may please and instruct (the goal of French theater), it should not, because its lessons are morally corrupt. Richelieu considered this debate so important that he instructed his newly formed Académie Française to enter it. After rejecting numerous drafts, Richelieu finally managed to force the academy to compose a document that established the learned scholars of the academy as the principal critics of the literary world, to the exclusion of the worldly public. Richelieu's difficulty in instituting this policy reveals how enmeshed the *doctes* and the salon public really were.

The quarrel generated by *Le Cid* suggests that salon values (such as those represented in an exceptionally strong and independent-minded female protagonist) and salon practices associated with literary creation and critique were viewed as posing a threat to the cultural realm. As the century progressed, more and more satirical representations of salon culture emerged in an effort to control this influence. Read within this context, Molière's *Les Précieuses ridicules* and *Les Femmes savantes* acquire new meaning (Beasley, *Salons* 44–46, "Molière's Precious Women"). Since much of posterity's view of the salons is premised on Molière's satirical depictions, it is essential to read these dramas not as history but as literary texts in dialogue with their historical context. Molière's *salonnières* critique literature and attempt to refine language, both salon practices that rivaled those of the *doctes* and the Académie Française. The salons' innovation was seductive and exciting for some, threatening to others, but always a powerful influence (Viala, *Naissance*).

While Molière satirized Rambouillet's *chambre bleue* and other salons, his most virulent attacks were centered on Scudéry and her *samedis* ("Saturdays"). As the century progressed, the emphasis in the salons turned from literary critique to literary creation, as more and more salon habitués, especially women, put their values into practice to produce new literary genres. Scudéry and Lafayette are representative of this second wave of salons; their works and those associated with them are especially useful for depicting salon innovations in literary genres and content. Scudéry's harangue on Sappho from *Les Femmes illustres*, now available in English translation, provides a good entry into this discussion. In the fictional conversation between Sappho and her protégée, Erinne, the poet raises many of the issues regarding women's intellectual capabilities and concludes by urging Erinne to rely on her writing rather than her ephemeral beauty for her immortality. Scudéry and the contemporaries who surrounded her—such as Lafayette; Marie de Rabutin-Chantal, marquise de Sévigné; Madeleine de Souvré, marquise de Sablé; Anne-Marie-Louise d'Orléans, duchesse de Montpensier; and Mme de Villedieu (Marie-Catherine Desjardins)—were doing precisely that, developing the novel as well as other genres emanating from conversations in the salons. It is important to explain to students the impact Scudéry's heroic novels had on the period. They were not only romans à clef portrayals of her contemporaries but also experiments in prose writings, as Scudéry incorporated the art of literary portraiture and conversation, two salon activities, into the novel genre (DeJean, *Tender Geographies*). The length of these works makes them difficult to include in the classroom, but one can illustrate Scudéry's art by using *The Story of Sapho*, which Scudéry interpolated into *Le Grand Cyrus* and which, along with a volume of her letters and a few conversations, has been published as part of the series The Other Voice in Early Modern Europe. Montpensier's letters to Françoise Bertaut de Motteville composed during Louis XIV's marriage to the Spanish Infanta have also been published in that series and can be profitably paired with Scudéry's text to evoke how marriage and the status of women were discussed in the salons (*Against Marriage*). We may not have a transcript of what happened in a *samedi* or in the *chambre bleue*, but works such as these as well as Sévigné's letters, which were often read aloud in salons throughout the period, can give us an excellent sense of the institution.

Conversations in the salons led, in fact, to some of the period's most revered texts, such as *Maximes*, by François, duc de La Rochefoucauld, and Lafayette's *La Princesse de Clèves*, as well as her lesser-known *Zayde* (available in English translation in the Other Voice series). It is interesting to pair *La Princesse de Clèves* and its maxims with those of La Rochefoucauld as well as Mme de Sablé's, to discuss the ambiance of a seventeenth-century France at the beginning of absolute monarchy (see also Steinberger in this volume). The letters between salon participants regarding the composition of works, such as the maxims, illustrate how literature was imagined, produced, and critiqued during the period. These texts also reveal how the individual was subsumed into a social apparatus in which *paraître* ("appearance") was essential to survival. The complex salon society and the difference between the salon and the court become evident when such literary texts are read in the light of Norbert Elias's *The Court Society* or Louis Marin's *Le Portrait du roi*. The salon can be viewed as an alternative space in which one could escape or, equally seditious, question Louis XIV's all-encompassing agenda.

The generic innovations developed in the salons mirror the literary tastes and values first associated with Rambouillet's worldly public. Another literary quarrel, this one around the most celebrated novel of the period, again underscores the power of the salon public and its profound influence on literary culture. Even before the princesse de Clèves stepped onto the literary stage, her behavior inspired criticism and incomprehension (Goldsmith, "Quarrel"; Beasley, *Revising*). The debate that erupted over the novel, much like the one over *Le Cid*, can be analyzed as an attempt to curtail salon influence over literary innovation and as an effort to ensure that figures applauded by the salon public such as the princess and Chimène not become models for society (Beasley, *Salons* 114–34). Jean-Baptiste Trousset de Valincour's text and the response from Jean-Antoine, abbé de Charnes, are useful for elucidating the effect salon culture had on the development of the novel, since each author examines the novel's effect on society (a few excerpts from the quarrel in French and in English can be found in app. 1 of Beasley and Jensen [183–91]). Both authors use the epistolary and conversational forms developed in the salons to examine the criteria against which literature should be judged, the authority of various publics, authorial liberty and responsibility, and the use of history and the development of the novel as a genre, among other issues at the heart of literary practices of the period. Teaching the quarrel with the novel helps students gain insight into the *mentalités* ("mentalities") of the salon milieu. Issues that were debated in salons, such as women's education and the role of women in society and marriage, are interwoven into the novel and then heatedly contested during the debate.

The debate over *La Princesse de Clèves* illustrates how the arts of conversation and sociability perfected in salons led to innovations in literary criteria, genres, and forms for literary critique. Academicians, writers, historians, philosophers, scientists, Protestants and Catholics, aristocrats and members of the bourgeoisie, men and women joined the conversation. The eclecticism of salons and the expanse of their networks are epitomized by Mme de La Sablière's salon, which flourished in the 1670s and early 1680s. As with the *chambre bleue*, the *samedis*, and Lafayette's gatherings, it is possible to get a sense of this salon and its importance through the texts of the salon's habitués and their contacts. La Sablière is the quintessential learned woman of the period, as evidenced by Nicolas Boileau's vitriolic satire against her. Astronomy and Descartes were among the principal subjects of conversation in her salon, where we find many of the same figures who peopled Rambouillet's, Scudéry's, and Lafayette's as well as intellectuals like François Bernier and Bernard Le Bovier de Fontenelle, who lent a new tone to the conversation. Bernier was a disciple of Pierre Gassendi and dedicated his published scholarship on Gassendi to La Sablière. Bernier also spent twelve years at the Indian Mughal court and composed the memoirs of his travels while he was one of the principal habitués of La Sablière's salon (Beasley, "Versailles"). This knowledge of India spread through La Sablière's salon and influenced, among others, the fabulist Jean de La Fontaine, who lived with La Sablière during her salon period and produced the second volume of his India-inspired *Fables* in 1678, the same year that his friend and fellow salon habituée, Lafayette, published *La Princesse de Clèves*. Charles Perrault and Fontenelle, both assiduous moderns, were also prominent members of this milieu, and their works can be added to the conversation of La Sablière's salon (see Cherbuliez in this volume). Indeed, Fontenelle's marquise in the *Entretiens* is La Sablière's daughter. Perhaps inspired by La Sablière and her guests, Perrault inscribed women's literary authority into his *Parallèle* as a hallmark of the moderns. The web of relationships and conversations that developed around La Sablière can be used to construct a portrait of the period very different from the one centered on Louis XIV. Diversity and appreciation of difference, in particular religious beliefs and practices, are among its defining characteristics, at a time when Louis XIV was revoking the Edict of Nantes. Works such as Fontenelle's *Entretiens*, La Fontaine's *Fables*, and Perrault's modernist manifestos take on new meaning when read in the context that inspired their production.

Salons such as La Sablière's were also responsible for producing a new literary genre: the fairy tale, developed initially by women such as Marie-Catherine Le Jumel de Barneville, comtesse d'Aulnoy, and Marie-Jeanne Lhéritier de Villandon, who embedded the first fairy tales in their novels (see Stedman in this volume). These tales do not entirely resemble Perrault's later works (often cited as the beginnings of the fairy tale in France); rather they are clearly products of the salon milieu and can be used to convey its values and interests. D'Aulnoy's "La Chatte blanche," for example, turns the traditional tale upside down as her female feline heroine prizes her castle's library above all else and remains in control over her domain and eventually that of her husband and his father. Similarly, in Lhéritier's "Les Enchantements de l'éloquence" the salon values of learning, creativity, and oral expression take precedence over female beauty, in sharp contrast to the traditional values expressed in Perrault's version of the same tale. These works reflect how far salon influence had come by the end of the century, in particular how salon taste had shaped the composition of literary works, the values expressed through literature, and the composition and values of criticism in the literary world at large.

Straddling both centuries is the marquise de Lambert, who can be seen as reminiscing about the apogee of the salon tradition, which she considers pre-Molière, and as a harbinger of what the institution would become during the Enlightenment. In her *Réflexions sur le goût* ("Reflections on Taste"), Lambert, like many of her salon predecessors, specifically associates women with an innate capacity to judge literary quality (see Beasley, *Salons*). One can learn and benefit from this art, she suggests, through contact with women in the salons. In her later treatise on education, Lambert criticizes her society for censoring women who practice this art as well as those who pursue other intellectual activities. She identifies Molière as the culprit who heaped the shame on the *salonnières* that led to a devaluation of women's literary and academic pursuits. In Lambert's view, society as a whole has suffered a loss, for many women are reluctant to tread the intellectual path opened to them by female forebearers such as Rambouillet and Scudéry out of fear of ridicule. Instead of considering themselves equal to their male counterparts and capable of engaging in writing and conversation, they are content to be society's passive and silent ornaments. Lambert herself strove to keep the earlier salon activities and influence alive, but as the visionary and strong architects of that worldly culture passed from the scene at the end of the century, so did a conception of the salon as a place that fostered women's creativity and critique and that influenced culture as a whole.

The salon movement continued through the eighteenth century, but women's roles within the institution changed dramatically. As Lambert predicted, social mores relegated women increasingly to the margins, or at least the shadows, of public intellectual debate. Once critics and composers, women salon figures adopted the role of hostess, facilitating male discourse rather than altering or challenging this discourse by writing (Russo, *Style*; Beasley, *Salons*). This is not to say that female intellectuals no longer existed or that women did not continue to influence eighteenth-century philosophical and literary movements (see Hesse; D. Goodman, *Republic*; Russo, *Style*; Trouille, *Sexual Politics*; Beckstrand, *Deviant Women*). Figures such as Françoise de Graffigny tended to join the entourage of a Voltaire rather than heading their own salon. Many major salons of the period were controlled by male intellectuals and politely presided over by women such as Julie de Lespinasse, many of whom were content to animate the conversation and draw together the participants but not actively engage in writing (see Craveri for a portrait of the eighteenth-century "age of conversation"). As a result, while the salons clearly had an impact on the development of Enlightenment thought (see in particular D. Goodman, *Republic*; Russo, *Cour, Style*; and Hesse), the salons were increasingly dominated by men, and *salonnières* became better known for their social than for their literary skills. Tellingly, Graffigny's Peruvian heroine delights in her library at the end of *Lettres d'une Péruvienne*, but she does so alone.

One obvious exception to the literary and even intellectual effacement of the *salonnière* is Germaine de Staël at the end of the eighteenth century. In many respects, Staël can be viewed as renewing the seventeenth-century salon tradition of Scudéry or La Sablière, although her salons, such as the one at Coppet, were frequented more by men than by women. Staël not only had a profound effect on the intellectual realm through her influence on writers such as Benjamin Constant, but she also enriched this realm through her own compositions. Many of the same questions addressed by early *salonnières*—women's place in society, education, marriage—are center stage in Staël's *Corinne*, *De l'Allemagne*, and *De la littérature*. In "De l'esprit de conversation," Staël pays homage to her female predecessors as she points out how the art of conversation developed principally by women in the salons altered French culture and shaped the nation's collective sense of identity. She argues that if France is known for its conversation, it is because of the salons and their influence.

Studying the salons through the work of Staël can lead to a class discussion of the relationship between salons and French collective memory or identity. Exploring the place of salons in France's *patrimoine* ("patrimony") raises the question of how the history of the salons has been constructed over time. After having studied the salons, students often question why and how they became primarily associated with politeness and not with serious literature, much less with France's classical canon. Even after studying the intellectual nature of the salons in class, they still wonder if salons can really be serious cultural institutions if Pierre Nora's *Les Lieux de mémoire*, with its vast exploration of the building blocks of French national identity, does not include an essay on the salon. The instructor might then show students that this lack of recognition can be viewed as revelatory of France's construction of its cultural past and the place accorded to female influence and women's literary production (see Beasley, *Salons*). An analysis of the role of the French educational system from the late nineteenth century to the present in the creation of the *patrimoine* associated with the seventeenth and eighteenth centuries illuminates the forces at work in the shaping of collective memory (see Thiesse and Mathieu; DeJean, "Classical Reeducation"). Such work allows instructors to bring the salons into dialogue with present-day theoretical interests like memory, historiography, and national identity and in the process restore the salons to their place of prominence. Indeed, the study of the institution of the salon reveals to students how knowledge is constructed and produced, not just in the far-off world of the ancien régime but also in today's world.

Elizabeth C. Goldsmith

Letters and the Epistolary Novel

Teaching the Epistolary Novel

Numerous studies have explored early modern women's entrance into the literary sphere through epistolary writing. Since the early 1990s scholars have documented the progressively strong connection during the seventeenth and eighteenth centuries between women's style of oral and written expression and the art of the familiar letter (Beebee; Cook; Duchêne, *Écrire*; Goldsmith, *Writing*; Jensen, *Writing*; Plantié). The epistolary genre gradually came to identify the love letter as a genre at which women excelled. Praise of women as writers of love letters did not, however, encourage women to write and publish; on the contrary, it tended to confine women's perceived abilities as writers to this single genre, which was best published anonymously, if at all. The development of a certain type of epistolary novel, based on the fiction of "found" letters, was strongly motivated by the fascination of a reading public for the intimate letters of women.

But the connection between women writers and the epistolary genre extends well beyond the love letter. Letter writing offered women a way of entering and participating in dispersed intellectual communities; letters and the developing postal system opened the way for women to circulate their writings to readers at a distance and to a public that extended beyond their immediate entourage. Through their letter writing, early modern women participated in the development of modern diplomacy and inserted their voices into religious debates. The way women spoke and, by extension, the way they wrote were topics of great interest not only to ecclesiastics, fascinated with the "purity" of the female voice speaking to God, but also to authors of letter manuals and conduct books, attracted by the supposedly unselfconscious, natural voice that women brought to good conversation. Women authors of letters responded to these expectations by both encouraging and resisting them. They exploited developments in technology and cultural practices to create a new space for women's writing and used letters as a means of entry into the public sphere.

Like conduct books, letter manuals published in the seventeenth century gave progressively more space to women's voices in the models of written sociability that they promoted. Jacques Du Bosc published a collection of model letters for women in 1635, and other epistolary collections followed suit (Puget de la Serre; Richelet). Theorists of sociability and polite interaction recommended that letter writers learn to express themselves by frequenting female society and imitating women's way of speaking. The style of letters that was increasingly admired during the course of the seventeenth century is described in much the same way as women's speech: it avoids pedantry, it is not overpolished (*le style négligé*), it is natural.

The idea that the most admirable quality of women's writing was its freedom from literary pretention may have had an inhibiting effect on the publication and printing of women's letters. In the sixteenth and early seventeenth centuries, several women, such as Hélisenne de Crenne (Marguerite Briet) and Madeleine and Catherine Des Roches, orchestrated the publication of their letter collections, and various types of letters by women were included in letter manuals (Altman, "Letter Book"; see Zanger in this volume). During the seventeenth century, however, women's letters were increasingly considered separately, applauded for their conversational style and their capacity to express intense emotion.

Katharine Ann Jensen has coined the term "epistolary woman" to describe the model of feminine writing, based on the trope of seduction and abandonment, that came to be touted in letter manuals and produced in epistolary fiction, mostly written by men (*Writing*). The popular interest in women as writers of love letters, in the wake of the publication of *Lettres portugaises* in 1669, fueled discussions of the particular aptitude of women for a kind of negligent eloquence, unschooled, natural, and deriving from emotional experience. The experience of passion was promoted as the best school for women who would write, as Molière's character Horace had proclaimed in his praise of the love letter that he receives from the previously inarticulate Agnès in *L'École des femmes* (1664).

Women writers, not surprisingly, viewed the new attention to the female epistolary voice with some ambivalence. Madeleine de Scudéry, in her novel *Clélie* (1654), included a dialogue on letter writing that praised the new importance of women as practitioners, readers, and judges of good epistolary technique. Thirty years later she rewrote this dialogue for inclusion in one of her collections of "conversations," adding a debate about whether women should write love letters ("De la manière"). One speaker, a poet who is being prodded to try her hand at letter writing, insists that love letters are too dangerous for women, for such letters are inevitably circulated without the writer's consent, misinterpreted, and used to condemn the author on moral grounds, even as her writing is admired.

Scudéry's revision of this dialogue may have been inspired by the experience of the prolific novelist and playwright Marie-Catherine Desjardins de Villedieu (1640–83). The well-known author, who had recently died, had not been able to prevent the 1668 publication of her "gallant letters" addressed to her lover. Sold to the publisher Claude Barbin by the unfaithful Antoine de Villedieu, whose name she had taken (although they never married), Mme de Villedieu's *Lettres et billets galants* records the unhappy relationship and also illustrates the popular demand for women's love letters. The correspondence had been generated by a bargain struck between the two: he promised to visit her if she would write him letters. The resulting collection, recently translated (Love Notes), offers a fascinating example of the contradictions and risks of the new cultural currency that women's love letters enjoyed.

Epistolary fiction has frequently been produced in response to other letter novels. An interesting approach to teaching the historical gender-genre link between women and epistolary writing is to read a pair or cluster of epistolary novels that seem to take contrasting views of an issue. Many such novels favored the Ovidian image of the abandoned woman, but several written by women in the eighteenth century do not always conform to this popular model. *Lettres portugaises* inspired an array of sequels and continuations, which can be interesting to study for their variations on the theme of seduction and abandonment. Françoise de Graffigny's *Lettres d'une Péruvienne* (1747) was inspired by *Lettres persanes* (1721), by Charles de Secondat, baron de Montesquieu, and also by *Lettres portugaises*. Graffigny's heroine is both foreign traveler and abandoned woman, but she takes control of her fate and ultimately avoids the conventional enclosures to which her predecessors had been confined. Marie-Jeanne Riccoboni's novel *Lettres de Mistriss Fanni Butlerd* can also be read as a response to *Lettres portugaises* as well as to Samuel Richardson's epistolary novels *Pamela* and *Clarissa*. Riccoboni's letter novel is monophonic, like *Lettres portugaises*, but the seduction is reciprocal, and in the end the woman freely chooses to publish her correspondence and comment on its social implications. Isabelle de Charrière's short novel *Lettres de Mistress Henley* (1784) was written in response to Samuel de Constant's popular novel *Le Mari sentimental*, a pathetic tale of a country gentleman who marries a well-educated wife who drives him to suicide. Charrière's novel is a series of letters written by a young bride to a female friend, recounting her slow awakening to the dull and confining realities of married life in the English countryside.

Jean-Jacques Rousseau's *Julie, ou la Nouvelle Héloïse* inspired many imitators and responses. *Les Contre-confessions: Histoire de Madame de Montbrillant* (1756–62), by Louise Tardieu d'Esclavelles, marquise d'Épinay, can be read as a challenge to many of the premises and ideals set forth in Rousseau's work; Épinay's female voices stress the obstacles to intellectual and emotional development posed by domesticity, promote the value of extramarital contacts for the woman writer, and provide liberal commentary on the material conditions of family life. The letter novel *Adèle et Théodore* (1782), by Stéphanie-Félicité Du Crest, comtesse de Genlis, reiterates but also revises Rousseau's ideas on female education, and Genlis's novel *Les Petits Émigrés* (1798) explores the consequences of a Rousseauesque formation among revolutionary exiles scattered throughout Europe.

In a comparative or cross-cultural course, in addition to contrasting the novels of Richardson and Riccoboni, profitable pairings might include *Lettres portugaises* and Aphra Behn's *Love Letters between a Nobleman and His Sister*; Villedieu's *Mémoires de Henriette Sylvie de Molière* (written as six letters) and Delarivier Manley's *Adventures of Rivella*; and *Relation du voyage d'Espagne* (written in letter form), by Marie-Catherine Le Jumel de Barneville, comtesse d'Aulnoy, and the travel letters of Mary Wortley Montagu.

Teaching Letter Correspondences

Numerous letter correspondences by seventeenth- and eighteenth-century women have been published, and many are available in modern editions. These are sometimes difficult to teach, because of the often dense historical context that needs to be explained to students. Anthologies can provide the needed explanatory material (Goldsmith and Winn; Maison). In a course concentrating on a specific historical period, this context is less of an obstacle; otherwise, teaching a selection of letters relating to a single event or historical topic can be the best approach.

Marie de Rabutin-Chantal, marquise de Sévigné, enjoys the unique status of being recognized as a great writer solely on the basis of her private letter correspondence. Sévigné's letters are widely available in numerous published editions and in many languages. Her correspondence can profitably be used as a resource in history classes (or in the history of philosophy; see Lyons in this volume) as well as in courses addressing early modern women's writing. Her long letters range freely over many topics and offer some of the best examples we have of the conversational style of salon culture, the early modern discourse of intimacy, and the beginnings of journalism, which drew heavily on epistolary models. Some sections of her correspondence are readily excerpted and can be introduced to students as a serial commentary on a political event (such as the trial of Nicolas Fouquet or the Affair of the Poisons). Her letters to her daughter, which receive most of the critical commentary on Sévigné today, record her passionate attachment and also trace how the expression of that passion led to her discovery of her vocation as a writer. Sévigné's letters lend themselves to selected reading and have the advantage of being available in inexpensive and well-annotated editions, sometimes organized around themes or events.

Many letter correspondences by women who are known principally as historical figures, rather than as literary authors, were published in the nineteenth century, and some have been reedited more recently. The best selection of new paperback editions of early modern correspondences is in the Mercure de France series Le Temps retrouvé. Two noteworthy editions of women's letters in this series lend themselves to classroom use: *Lettres de la princesse Palatine, 1672–1722*, by Charlotte-Elisabeth de Bavière, duchesse d'Orléans, and *Correspondance de Madame de Maintenon et de la princesse des Ursins, 1709: Une Annèe tragique*. The duchesse d'Orléans, commonly referred to as la princesse Palatine, was the German-born wife of Philippe d'Orléans, brother of Louis XIV. Her letters to her sister and friends offer sharp and entertaining portraits of court life. They are astounding in their frank critiques of the French nobility and of the codes of sociability being cautiously cultivated around her. The 1709 correspondence between Françoise d'Aubigné, marquise de Maintenon, and Anne-Marie de la Trémoille Orsini, known as la princesse des Ursins, is an exchange between two powerful political figures who late in life reflect freely on their lives and the history in which they had each played such important roles.

In English, the series The Other Voice in Early Modern Europe includes several excellent pedagogical editions of letters by important political figures, notably a series of letters on marriage by Anne-Marie-Louise d'Orléans, duchesse de Montpensier, and the correspondence of René Descartes with Princess Elisabeth of Bohemia.

Another approach to teaching real letters, most likely in an upper-division or graduate class, is to consider correspondences together with other writings by the same author, to show the ways in which letters functioned to facilitate women's entry into the literary and public spheres. The letters of Anne-Marguerite Du Noyer offer a rich and lively commentary on social issues relating to women (marriage practices; social, economic, and legal status; family relations) as well as on topics of interest to the Huguenot community in exile. A French Protestant refugee living in Holland, Du Noyer edited a news journal and published a multivolume correspondence blending fiction and real letters under the title *Lettres historiques et galantes* (1707). The work enjoyed great success and multiple reprintings. Du Noyer drew on her letters from this collection to write her memoirs, which she published in 1711.

The letters of Marie-Jeanne Philipon Roland de La Platière, begun in her youth and continued until her death on the scaffold, in 1793, constitute, when read with her memoirs written in captivity, a fascinating autobiography drawing on a lifetime of energetic conversation and epistolary communication. Recent scholarship on her youthful correspondence with her friend Sophie Cannet suggests ways in which the memoirs grew out of the autobiographical project begun in the correspondence (Diaz; D. Goodman, "Letter Writing").

The Catholic reform movements of the sixteenth and seventeenth centuries encouraged new forms of self-expression among women in religion.

The devotional practice of self-examination through interior conversation was thought by some to be easier for women, because of their lack of schooling and formal education (Certeau; Loskoutoff; Timmermanns). As in the secular world of the salon, where women's speech was appreciated for its natural qualities, in the religious sphere the female voice in prayer and confession was appreciated for its simplicity, and some religious directors encouraged their protégées to write their private reflections in letter form and circulate them. Interest in the voice of the abject, abandoned woman (dating back to Ovid's *Heroides*) and fascination with a woman's particular way of expressing religious passion merged explosively in *Lettres portugaises*, ostensibly six letters written by a nun to a soldier. Meanwhile, real letter correspondences by women in religion circulated and were published. Jeanne de Chantal (1572–1641), Marie de l'Incarnation (1599–1672), and Jeanne-Marie Guyon (1648–1715) are three figures who played important roles in the religious revival and whose correspondences are available in modern editions (see Carr in this volume). Chantal, who with François de Sales founded the order of the Visitation, maintained a vast web of epistolary relations with religious and secular figures throughout her adult life. Marie de l'Incarnation, an Ursuline who was a founding member of the first settlement of nuns in French Canada, wrote lengthy epistolary accounts of life in Quebec and the colonies that were circulated in France and eventually published by her son Claude Martin, who interspersed her letter writing with text from her memoirs along with his own commentary. Guyon's letters and autobiography offer a vivid picture of the language of charismatic mysticism that built on new religious and aesthetic ideas about the superiority of untutored forms of self-expression and prayer (*Correspondance*, *Vie*). Guyon enjoyed a huge following and was close to powerful figures (including Fénelon and Maintenon), with whom she corresponded. For women in particular, Guyon's "short way" to God held a strong appeal, for it glorified the maternal bond as well as the value of a childlike "naturel" 'naturalness' (*"Moyen court"*).

Courses on women's writing that include letter correspondences can offer valuable opportunities for teaching students how to use archives, prepare an edition, or undertake a translation project. Letter correspondences by early modern women are still largely unpublished, and many university libraries hold at least a few autograph letters from this period. The material aspects of an early letter, from ink and handwriting to paper and sealing wax, are as fascinating to students as they were to many epistolary novelists. Recent scholarship on the practice of early modern letter writing has shown how rewarding it can be to study women's letters in the context of the history of material culture (D. Goodman, "Letter"; Harrison). Developments in transportation, architecture, furniture design, fashion, and portrait painting all reflected the new reality of the modern, letter-writing woman.

Perry Gethner

Women and the Theatrical Tradition

Although there were roughly a dozen women in France who published plays in the seventeenth century and over twice that number in the eighteenth and although the authors often succeeded in getting them performed, this branch of female creativity remained largely forgotten until the final decades of the twentieth century. There are many reasons to bring these works into the classroom, not least that many of them are thought-provoking and enjoyable to read. While the corpus is so heterogeneous that it might not be feasible to devote an entire course to these plays, even on the graduate level, there are many productive ways to introduce these early French women playwrights into general courses devoted to the seventeenth or eighteenth century.

One reason for the traditional absence of these works in the classroom was the lack of modern editions. Today that problem is rapidly being corrected. In addition to the two-volume collection *Femmes dramaturges en France* (Gethner), made up of twelve works by ten authors from the period 1650–1750, several other works have recently appeared in critical editions. Two volumes of the planned five-volume collection *Théâtre des femmes de l'Ancien Régime* have been published (Evain, Gethner, and Goldwyn). This collection is designed for use by university students in

France and covers a large number of works by some thirty authors from the sixteenth, seventeenth, and eighteenth centuries. Both collections use modernized spelling, in the hopes of reaching an audience of students as well as scholars.

Arguably the most effective pedagogical use of specific plays is to integrate them into the study of women's literature as a whole or into the general literary history of the period. In either case a play can be juxtaposed with works by other authors, in the same or a different genre, to demonstrate how the texts bring complementary or opposing perspectives to the treatment of similar issues.

An intriguing lesson to be learned from the study of these playwrights in the context of the expansion of female readership and authorship is the critical role played by women in the development of the salons. These informal gatherings, organized by women, who also made up a sizable percentage of the participants, helped integrate cultivated women into the cultural life of their time. The salons created a climate in which women felt empowered to write and to make their works public: they brought women into social contact with eminent men of letters; increased attendance by women at important cultural events, including theatrical performances; fostered the view that the greatest French writers of the seventeenth century were at least as valuable as models for aspiring writers as the celebrated figures from classical antiquity (which also meant that a knowledge of Latin, a subject typically left out of women's education, was no longer perceived as crucial); and gave rise to the belief that women possessed a naturalness of style that typically surpassed that of men. Women authors, whether or not they wrote to make a living, were convinced that they were capable of meeting the same literary standards as men and that they too had something of value to communicate to their audiences. Indeed, they felt worthy to compete with men in what was widely viewed as the preeminent branch of French literature, drama. Despite the difficulties of dealing with theatrical companies, a problem that got even worse in the eighteenth century, many women playwrights succeeded in getting their works staged, sometimes with considerable success. Moreover, contrary to what one might expect, most of them were not embarrassed to publish under their real names. The exceptions were mostly women from the nobility, for whom, as for their male counterparts, writing for profit was seen as incompatible with their rank.

Presenting the plays in the more general context of women's literature can also encourage a focus on issues of special interest to women authors, not least those connected with the *querelle des femmes* that raged for much of the late medieval and early modern periods. Hotly debated questions involved whether girls should be educated at all and, if so, what subjects they should be allowed to study. Significantly, the playwrights tend to take women's education for granted. The heroines of tragedies are models of eloquence, whose rhetorical skills rival or surpass those of the men. The female characters in comedies are well-read and capable of appreciating good poetry, music, and dance. In Françoise Pascal's *L'Amoureux extravagant*, for example, the young women are just as quick as the men to recognize the incompetence and pomposity of a male poet. The heroine of *Le Favori*, by Marie-Catherine Desjardins, Mme de Villedieu, makes her first entrance reading a book of poetry. In Catherine Durand's proverb comedies we find a girl who reads every book in her parents' library before deciding to rebel against her confinement in a remote rural area and several women who make accurate references to classical mythology. The young heroine of *La Mode*, by Marguerite-Jeanne Cordier, baronne de Staal-Delaunay, impatient with the overelaborate costumes and grooming demands required by court society, prefers to spend her time reading Roman history, to the dismay of her snobbish mother. With very rare exceptions, women are presented as having good minds and as being eager to cultivate them. Olympe de Gouges, in *Molière chez Ninon*, presents a salon in a positive light, showing the hostess (the much maligned Ninon de Lenclos) both as a noble human being and as a source of inspiration and encouragement to distinguished male authors.

Debates about the role of the women during the early modern period were not limited to the realm of education. Some writers dared to suggest that women could competently exercise real power in the areas of government and war. In drama, owing to the fondness for plots based on classical history and mythology, it was possible to create situations where women could assume roles denied to them in seventeenth- and eighteenth-century France. In Anne-Marie Du Boccage's tragedy *Les Amazones*, an all-female society is as competent as male (Greek) society in politics and war. There were, in fact, women warriors in real life during this period, including Alberte-Barbe de Saint-Balmon (also a playwright), but this phenomenon would not be mentioned on the stage until the Revolution. The outspoken champion of women's rights, de Gouges, featured real-life women warriors in her current-events play, *L'Entrée de Dumouriez à Bruxelles*.

A handful of tragedies present reigning queens, but their administrative competence gets overshadowed by two standard problems: first, the common people's distrust of female leadership and insistence on bringing in a male leader in time of war, and, second, the queen's inability to control her passion for a hero who does not return her love. The playwright may choose to emphasize the pathos in the character's predicament, like Catherine Bernard (*Laodamie reine d'Epire*), or her stoic fortitude, like Madeleine-Angélique de Gomez (*Marsidie reine des Cimbres*), but in every case the queen's career ends in political failure and death, either by suicide or assassination. Another option for female participation is to direct a conspiracy or counterrevolution from behind the scenes, exerting some of the real power but ensuring that male leaders get all the visibility and all the credit. Arrie, in Marie-Anne Barbier's *Arrie et Pétus*, exerts effective political leadership, although her attempt to overthrow the inept Roman emperor and reestablish a republican regime ends in failure. The title character of Barbier's *Cornélie mère des Gracques* likewise chooses to remain in the shadows, inspiring her son with her eloquence and idealism but entrusting him to carry out her agenda by himself. Perhaps the most daring example of female empowerment occurs in Pascal's *Endymion*, where the goddess Diane, the only deity worshipped, is seen as all-powerful and is able to subject the hero to a variety of physical and psychological tests before deeming him worthy of becoming her consort.

If female playwrights only occasionally accorded political power to women, they were far less reluctant to display the incompetence or tyranny of male authority figures, whether kings, fathers, or husbands. Ruthless, bloodthirsty, and unprincipled rulers, while far from unknown in tragedies and tragicomedies by male authors, occur in nearly all the plays in these genres written by women. Perhaps the most egregious of these tyrants is Cambyse in Villedieu's *Nitétis*, blamed for introducing the previously unknown practices of incest and divorce into Persia, as well as committing a variety of abuses such as blasphemy, religious desecrations, and wrongful executions. Competent and moral rulers are a rarity, though occasionally a tyrant may reform in the final scenes. Father figures fare little better, whether they are well-intentioned but self-centered and peevish, as in the dramas of Françoise de Graffigny, or brutal and so uncaring that they are prepared to put their children to death for flimsy reasons, as in Villedieu's *Manlius* and Antoinette Deshoulières's *Genséric*. Rude and abusive husbands, however common in real life, are generally kept off the stage. Probably because of censorship considerations, serious discussion of divorce was rare until the revolutionary period, notably in de Gouges's *La Nécessité du divorce* (where, curiously, the knowledge that it will be possible to terminate a troubled marriage helps the couple reconcile). Some notable exceptions occur in plays destined for private performance, such as the comedy proverbs of Durand and Françoise d'Aubigné, marquise de Maintenon. The latter, writing for students at her school, Saint Cyr, reminds them that once a husband decides to exert his legal authority to the fullest, the wife will ultimately be forced to submit. Durand takes a somewhat more optimistic view, allowing a scorned wife to reach an agreement with her husband, though hardly a moral one (each will henceforth live openly with a lover).

One issue that appears frequently in the works by women is genuine friendship between two women—something that many male writers deemed impossible. To be sure, most plays that feature two prominent female characters make them rivals in love, but female authors often allow these characters to respect and like each other. *Laodamie* shows two sisters whose mutual affection is so strong that each is prepared to sacrifice her love interest on the other's behalf. In *Manlius* and *Nitétis* the two virtuous women esteem each other and try to help each other, even though they do not become close. *La Mode* shows a firm friendship developing between two women who find that the other is the only person capable of understanding her true feelings and giving candid advice; at one point they even consider the possibility of trading a lover between them. Durand's ninth proverb comedy presents a young woman who displays not the least resentment when the man she hopes to marry decides instead to wed her best friend, whose reputation is acknowledged to be purer; instead, she calmly maintains amicable relations with both of them. In Louise-Geneviève Gillot de Sainctonge's *Griselde* and Françoise de Graffigny's *Cénie*, close bonds are formed between women of different ages that develop well before they discover that they are mother and daughter. Sisters-in-law can likewise be very affectionate, even sharing the same views on all subjects, as in the opening scene of Saint-Balmon's *Les Jumeaux martyrs*. In *Le Favori* it is possible for two women of radically different temperament and philosophy to genuinely enjoy each other's company, disagreeing but never quarreling.

As for the other main option for teaching this body of work, to pair a play by a woman writer with a canonical work by a male writer, the possibilities are almost unlimited. One technique is to read two texts on the same or similar subjects that were written at roughly the same time, especially if one of the authors knew the other's work. An obvious example is Villedieu's *Le Favori* and Molière's *Le Misanthrope*. Not only do the two plays feature many common themes, but they also were written within a year of each other, and it was Molière's troupe that gave the premiere of Villedieu's play. The question of whether Villedieu directly influenced Molière is undecidable and ultimately of little importance. *Le Favori* is more overtly political in that the king and his chief minister are among the principal characters and that the conventionally virtuous lovers chafe under the constraints of the new style of court life, whereas their comic counterparts in *Le Misanthrope* openly admit to reveling in a world of intrigue and artifice. One could also argue that Villedieu adopts a more sympathetic stance toward women in her play: the coquette Elvire and the prude Léonor genuinely like each other, despite their disagreement on every subject and the coquette's open and unashamed expression of her views. Indeed, Elvire, far from feeling publicly humiliated, even gets the last word.

An especially fruitful method of pairing is to select works by women that deliberately echo well-known works by men but contain a subversive intent. Typically, the female author is more supportive of women's abilities, needs, or rights, while questioning the superior competence and integrity attributed to male authority figures. The tragedies of Barbier have numerous situational parallels to and verbal reminiscences of works by Pierre Corneille and Jean Racine, but there is no slavish imitation involved. In *Arrie et Pétus*, for example, the presence of Agrippine and Narcisse calls to mind Racine's *Britannicus*, which also features those two characters. There are, however, crucial differences between the plays: Barbier's Agrippine is shown at the pinnacle of her power, rather than at the moment when she realizes she is about to lose it, as in Racine's play; Barbier's Claudius is far more inept and less sinister than Racine's Néron, both as a tyrant and as a rejected lover; the prophecy of eventual divine judgment on the villain is more credible in Barbier; Agrippine's worthy rival in *Arrie et Pétus* is more politically astute and heroic than in *Britannicus*; Barbier's virtuous male lead is shown as competent, courageous, and less naive than Racine's hapless Britannicus. *Arrie et Pétus* also contains explicit references to Corneille's *Cinna*, especially in the scene where the two conspirator-lovers discuss their plans and in the later scene where the emperor confronts the conspirator who has plotted to murder him. Whereas in Corneille Cinna is the principal organizer and Emilie is little more than a spectator, Barbier makes Arrie the organizer, who enlists the help of Pétus only when an unexpected emergency arises. When the plot is discovered, Pétus is more outspoken and has stronger convictions than Cinna, while Barbier's Claudius lacks the magnanimity of Corneille's Auguste. This overt intertextuality can only work if it is assumed that the original audience knew the earlier plays well and could grasp the radically different viewpoint suggested by the later author.

Pairing need not be restricted to thematic similarities. One could equally well compare two plays from the same dramatic subgenre. Among Christian martyr tragedies, for example, *Les Jumeaux martyrs* was presumably inspired by Corneille's *Polyeucte*, but the differences are at least as significant as the similarities. Instead of having an aggressively assertive and isolated hero, Saint-Balmon makes her protagonist a set of twins, Marc and Marcelin, and surrounds them with a loving and caring family (parents, wives, friends). The emphasis on community leads to the conversion of nearly all the characters by the end of the play and to the sense that living a committed Christian life is compatible with the preservation of personal relationships. In the genre of comedy-ballet, the plot of Anne de La Roche-Guilhen's *Rare-en-tout* contrasts with those of the hybrid plays of Molière in the disappearance of the father figure, the refusal of the title character to take love and marriage seriously, and the fuller integration into the main plot of characters who sing but never speak. Indeed, apart from the prologue and epilogue, La Roche-Guilhen seems to owe nothing to the examples of her illustrious predecessor, and the Molière plays with the closest plot parallels are nonmusical comedies, such as *Dom Juan* and *Le Misanthrope*. That Rare-en-tout, the main character, far from being a dangerous seducer, is an ineffectual and narcissistic fop, whose interest in women seems largely confined to their singing voices, suggests a questioning of both the traditional marriage plot and the physical and mental competence of court males.

Since comparative studies need not be limited to other dramatic works, one may also pair plays by women with works by men in a different genre that were or might possibly have been the source of the plots. For example, Sainctonge's *Griselde* borrowed its plot from Charles Perrault's first verse tale, "Grisélidis," but the play is more a response than an imitation. Sainctonge makes the husband more cruel, more tyrannical, and more of a misogynist than Perrault does, while the heroine is more assertive and less willing to view her sufferings as a trial imposed by God. The role of the daughter is far more developed: she is shown as a self-confident, level-headed, and even heroic figure. The confidants invented by the playwright function as surrogates for the audience, intervening in the action and challenging the outrageous views and actions of the main players. The improbable happy ending, relying on the stock device of switched infants, may have been intended to suggest the cynical view that only a miracle could make evil husbands and rulers change their ways.

In short, these remarkable plays address a variety of literary and social issues, indicate how women writers viewed their role within the world of letters, and express concerns and grievances shared by many women of the time. Covering a surprisingly wide number of dramatic forms and intended for a variety of theatrical venues, they shed new light on French literary history and on the development of feminist thought.

Katharine Ann Jensen

Daughters as Maternal Masterpieces: Teaching Mother-Daughter Relations in Lafayette and Vigée Lebrun

Focusing on mother-daughter relations is a rewarding way to teach several seventeenth- and eighteenth-century works by women, such as *La Princesse de Clèves*, by Marie-Madeleine Pioche de la Vergne, comtesse de Lafayette; *Selected Letters* of Marie de Rabutin-Chantal, marquise de Sévigné; Françoise de Graffigny's *Cenia*; Isabelle de Charrière's *Lettres écrites de Lausanne*; and passages from Élisabeth Vigée Lebrun's memoirs, *Souvenirs*. In this essay, I discuss Lafayette's novel and Vigée Lebrun's *Souvenirs*. I describe how to approach these works in the context of a course I have designed specifically to study mother-daughter relations in a range of works from various time periods and cultural traditions. This approach easily lends itself to integration into other courses and into a broader analysis of any one of the works mentioned above.

The course, which I teach in a women's and gender studies program at a large state university, emphasizes issues of identity: how does a woman become an individual self and how does her relationship with her mother or with her daughter influence that self? The course draws both graduate and undergraduate students from a variety of disciplines. At the beginning of the semester, we read our first three theoretical texts, selections from

Adrienne Rich, Jane Flax, and Nancy Chodorow. Briefly, these theories have argued that because of gender arrangements in modern United States society, mothers have identified more closely with their daughters, whom they see as versions of themselves, than with their sons. These theories posit a preoedipal symbiosis, whereby mother and infant supposedly feel merged with each other, as the source for later identity confusion between mother and daughter. While girls are brought up to maintain this deep emotional connection to their mother and others, boys are trained to give up their intense bond with their mother. Boys and men in our culture are expected to be emotionally distant as a way to claim autonomy and individuality. Women are also expected to be autonomous individuals—at school and in their careers, for example. Yet the intense connection fostered initially between mother and daughter can work against a girl's or woman's desire for autonomy. The tension between identification with each other and autonomy has often created conflict between mothers and daughters.

As a transition to our early modern French works, I emphasize to students that we will witness this same tension in mother-daughter relations long before the twentieth century. In both the past and present, however, there are reasons other than an extended preoedipal bond for identity confusion between mothers and daughters. Later in the semester we see how intersubjective theory contests the reality of mother-infant symbiosis and proposes the infant's capacity and need to recognize her mother as distinct from herself. Throughout the seventeenth and eighteenth centuries, meanwhile, when mothers in the privileged classes rarely tended their own infants, an ideology of reflectivity seems to have produced confusion between self and other for many mothers and daughters. Since this was also the period when the notion of the individual as distinct and autonomous from others, as unique and specific, gained great cultural importance, we see the historical roots for the modern problems that often beset mother-daughter relations and that psychoanalysis tries to theorize—often ahistorically.

To illustrate the ideology of mother-daughter reflectivity, we discuss excerpts from François de Grenaille's 1640 behavior manual, *L'Honnête Fille* (*The Virtuous Daughter*). I explain that this book, like many others on behavior, conversation, and letter writing, was enormously popular in early modern France, providing ideals according to which aristocrats—and bourgeoisie aspiring to act like aristocrats—could model themselves. *L'Honnête Fille* is a conservative work intended to preserve class and gender hierarchies. Grenaille enlists aristocratic mothers in the reproduction of these hierarchies by calling on them to form daughters in the mothers' own virtuous image. Mothers are to train daughters to be sexually pure, modest, pious, and submissive wives, like themselves. We read together excerpts such as the following:

> Or est-il que les mères ayant les mêmes humeurs et inclinations qu'on remarque dans les filles connaissent parfaitement leur naturel, en se connaissant elles-mêmes, elles s'efforcent de lever toutes les tâches d'une glace qui les doit représenter. (86; pt. 1)

> So it is that mothers, having the same moods (humors) and inclinations one notices in their daughters, know their daughters' nature perfectly, by knowing themselves; they strive to remove all the flaws from a mirror that must represent them.[1]

> L'honnête fille est l'image et le chef d'œuvre de l'honnête femme. (75; pt. 1)

> The virtuous daughter is the image and masterpiece of the virtuous woman.

I explain that mother-daughter mirroring was intended to reproduce a certain kind of feminine behavior that served patriarchy well. Although the feminine qualities of virtue, modesty, piety—and even sociability, which in some circumstances counteracted submissiveness—were granted social and moral value in seventeenth- and eighteenth-century France, they never made women as culturally powerful as men. Indeed, as the concept of the individual was elaborated, it defined men as autonomous individuals in opposition to women, who were deemed inferior and dependent objects. On the one hand, mother-daughter mirroring was supposed to prevent women from becoming individuals by reproducing female submissiveness to men. On the other hand, many women aspired to distinguish themselves as individuals despite the obstacles. Mother-daughter mirroring would have been one of these obstacles: because of the identity confusion endemic to mirroring, a mother's or daughter's attempt to differentiate herself from the other was often a highly vexed matter.

Thus the ideology of mother-daughter reflectivity conflicted with the ideology of individualism. Yet mother-daughter mirroring probably owed much of its enduring power to the fact that many mothers gained narcissistic satisfaction in creating daughters to fulfill maternal desires. While the goal of reflectivity was the transmission of proper behavior from mother to daughter, the mirroring structure would also have produced a psychological mindset. I call this mindset maternal narcissism: a mother's tendency to construe her daughter as an aspect of the maternal self—an alter ego—rather than as her own independent center of desire. We notice in Grenaille's work that daughters belong to their mothers as objects they create. We also notice that as maternal "masterpieces," fully formed, adolescent daughters stand as their mothers' crowning life's achievement.

Our discussion of Grenaille's excerpts prepares the ground for Lafayette's 1678 novel, *La Princesse de Clèves*. I give students the following reading questions before class:

> In what ways can Mme de Chartres be seen to make her daughter into her own masterpiece?
> What role does virtue play in the mother's creation of her daughter?
> Why is female virtue an exceptional quality for women at court, and why would female virtue be a way for Mme de Chartres to distinguish herself at court as an exceptional mother—and individual—through her daughter?

In the class period devoted to *La Princesse de Clèves*, we notice that the narrator describes Mme de Chartres as "extrêmement glorieuse" 'exceptionally proud and ambitious' where her daughter is concerned (77; 10).[2] The mother's pride and ambition seem linked to gaining public recognition at court for herself as an individual through her exceptional daughter and masterpiece. We can gauge the success of Mme de Chartres's project to create a uniquely virtuous daughter and alter ego through the princess's utter disinterest in love affairs. After her arranged marriage to the prince de Clèves, several attractive, powerful men pursue her; yet

> Madame de Chartres joignait à la sagesse de sa fille une conduite si exacte pour toutes les bienséances qu'elle achevait de la faire paraître une personne où l'on ne pouvait atteindre. (89)

> Mme de Chartres reinforced her daughter's own good behaviour with such an exact respect for all the proprieties that she finally succeeded in making her appear unassailable. (22)

Here I point out that Mme de Chartres has completed her masterpiece and created her ideal second self. She has succeeded in making her daughter renowned not simply for relative virtue—for conjugal fidelity despite possible illicit desire, the norm at court—but also for absolute virtue: erotic unattainability. This perfection implicitly elevates the mother's prestige as a uniquely effective creator-educator.

We see that Mme de Chartres's masterpiece becomes a failed work of art, and the mother-daughter mirror shatters when the princess falls in love with the duc de Nemours. At first, the princess does not recognize her erotic feelings for what they are, but her mother certainly does:

> Cette connaissance lui donna une douleur sensible; elle jugeait bien le péril où était cette jeune personne, d'être aimée d'un homme fait comme Monsieur de Nemours, pour qui elle avait de l'inclination. (100)

> The knowledge was acutely painful to her. She well understood how dangerous it was for her daughter to be loved by a man as handsome as M. de Nemours to whom she was also attracted. (32)

As I suggest to the class, we can interpret the mother's pain as symptomatic of maternal narcissism. Mme de Chartres is wounded not only on behalf of her daughter's eventual grief from Nemours's betrayal but also, especially for herself, for the loss of her perfectly virtuous, ideal alter ego.

The first sharp pain that Mme de Chartres feels soon becomes a fatal illness. Her total dependence on her daughter for the fulfillment of her ambitions to be acknowledged at court as an exceptional woman, or individual, makes her completely vulnerable. Even though the princess has not acted on her illicit desire for Nemours, the very existence of this passion is enough to cause her mother despair, for she has lost herself in losing her ideal. We can read her illness and death as emblematic of the destructive force of the mirror dynamic.

After Mme de Chartres's death, the question is whether her daughter can extricate herself from maternal narcissism and define a subjectivity of her own. By opposing the princess's relationship to her mother with her relationship to Nemours, Lafayette reveals that the primary avenues for a woman's self-definition are either the mother-daughter mirror or heterosexual desire. The students' task is to decide whether the princess defines a subjectivity of her own and support their interpretation with textual evidence. I consider either response valid as long as the students can support their view convincingly.[3]

Before reading passages from Vigée Lebrun's *Souvenirs*, I prepare the students by comparing this real-life mother and artist with Mme de Chartres, a fictional invention. They both attest to the ideological force of mother-daughter mirroring in contradiction to emerging individualism. But where Mme de Chartres channeled her ambition for public recognition of herself as an individual into creating her daughter as her work of art, Vigée Lebrun gained public recognition of herself as an individual through her career as a uniquely talented artist—in fact, as the renowned portraitist of Marie-Antoinette. Yet Vigée Lebrun shows herself to be as narcissistically invested in her daughter Julie, nicknamed Brunette, as was Mme de Chartres in the princess. And like Mme de Chartres, Vigée Lebrun construes her daughter's heterosexual desire as a wound to her maternal ego. Whereas the princess's desire for Nemours was, at least initially, beyond her control, Brunette actively chooses her heterosexual love object from the start. Moreover, she specifically chooses to love a man her mother deems unworthy, thereby openly and explicitly defying maternal desires. We want to see, then, how Vigée Lebrun responds to this defiance.

To prepare for discussion of the *Souvenirs*, I ask students to respond to these questions:

> In what ways does Vigée Lebrun seem to see her seventeen-year-old daughter as her masterpiece?
> How does the mother represent Brunette's desire for Nigris?
> How does Vigée Lebrun portray Brunette in order to show her own superiority?
> What do you think Brunette's desire for Nigris meant for her?

I highlight certain passages in discussion to reinforce or guide the students' interpretations. For example, Vigée Lebrun asserts that her daughter

> était charmante sous tous les rapports. . . . Elle avait une voix charmante et chantait l'italien à merveille: car à Naples et à Saint-Pétersbourg, je lui avais donné les meilleurs maîtres de musique . . . mais ce qui me charmait par-dessus tout, c'étaient ses heureuses dispositions pour la peinture, en sorte que je ne saurais dire à quel point j'étais heureuse et fière de tous les avantages qu'elle réunissait. (2: 49)

> was charming in all respects. She had a charming voice and sang Italian perfectly: for in Naples and Saint-Petersburg, I had provided her the best music teachers, but what charmed me above all was her fortunate predisposition for painting, such that I don't know how to say to what extent I was happy and proud of all her advantages.

We notice that the mother focuses on her own pleasure in her daughter's accomplishments rather than on Brunette's. Vigée Lebrun also implicates herself in Brunette's musical talent because she gave her daughter the best training possible. The daughter's unusual musical abilities thus reflect back on the mother as the product of her superior knowledge about how to cultivate those abilities. In this way, Vigée Lebrun views her daughter narcissistically, as an aspect of the maternal self. Similarly, Brunette's predisposition for painting implicitly belongs as much to the artist mother as to the daughter since this gift was maternally transmitted. The students can see, then, how Brunette functions as her mother's masterpiece—a perfect object that represents the mother.

Vigée Lebrun's pleasure in seeing her daughter as a talented painter like herself is dispelled, however, when Brunette falls in love with Gaétan Bernard Nigris, the secretary of family friends. According to Vigée Lebrun, Nigris is "sans talents, sans fortune, sans nom" 'without talent, without fortune, without a name' (2: 51). Although Vigée Lebrun may have worried about Nigris's qualifications as a husband worthy of her exceptional daughter, she nonetheless represents the marriage issue as a battle of wills waged with Brunette:

> En vain je m'efforçai de faire comprendre à ma fille combien sous tous les rapports, ce mariage était loin de pouvoir la rendre heureuse; sa tête était trop exaltée pour qu'elle voulût s'en rapporter à ma tendresse et à mon expérience. (2: 51)

> In vain did I strive to make my daughter understand how far this marriage was, in every respect, from being able to make her happy; she was too carried away to wish to rely on my tenderness and experience.

To make someone understand something is to assert one's will as dominant. And to refuse that effort is to signal that one has desires of one's own, independent from the other's.

Vigée Lebrun reads her daughter's refusal to yield to maternal desires not as the sign of autonomous filial desires but as a simple opposition of wills. Maternal narcissism blinds Vigée Lebrun to Brunette's desire as having any existence outside its relation to Vigée Lebrun herself. Moreover, she diminishes her daughter's opposition by attributing it to a kind of feverish state: "sa tête était trop exaltée" 'she was too carried away.' As a result, the mother's desire to impose her will on her daughter—to make her understand—is portrayed not as a wish for supremacy but as superior sanity, the proof of maternal "tenderness and experience."

Vigée Lebrun reduces her daughter's power as maternal opponent even further—and further to her own advantage—by attributing Brunette's potential independence to outside influences:

Sa vieille gouvernante, madame Charrot . . . s'était totalement emparée de son esprit, et l'aigrissait contre moi au point que tout mon amour de mère se trouvait impuissant pour combattre cette funeste influence. (2: 51–52)

Her old governess, madame Charrot . . . had taken total possession of her mind and embittered her against me to such an extent that all my mother's love was powerless to combat this deadly influence.

By representing her daughter as the passive victim of the evil governess, rather than as an agent choosing to ally herself with a surrogate mother, Vigée Lebrun is able to highlight her pathos as a loving but helpless and suffering mother. We can see, then, that Vigée Lebrun uses to her advantage Brunette's desire and opposition.

When Brunette falls ill, however, the loving mother gives in, writing from Saint Petersburg (one of the cities she inhabited after fleeing from the Revolution) to her husband back in Paris for his consent to the Nigris match. When the consent arrives, Brunette apparently takes it as her due. But her mother wants acknowledgment that she conceded her will to her daughter's: "la cruelle enfant ne me témoigna pas la plus légère satisfaction de ce que j'avais fait pour elle en lui sacrifiant et tous mes désirs et toutes mes répugnances" 'the cruel child did not show me the least satisfaction for what I had done for her in sacrificing all my desires and all my loathings' (2: 53). As evidence of the force of maternal narcissism and the power of mother-daughter reflectivity, Vigée Lebrun wants Brunette to recognize maternal desires but cannot acknowledge her daughter's autonomous wishes.

If Brunette had been raised to reflect and fulfill her mother's wishes, what might her desire for Nigris have meant to this daughter? Students see that desiring Nigris was probably a way for Brunette to claim something for herself, something that did not belong to her mother. It could have been a way for her to try to define herself as an individual. I ask them how they interpret the fact that Brunette left Nigris five years after their marriage. Many students think that she probably only imagined she loved Nigris as a way to get away from her mother. Once married, she realized she was stuck with him and eventually broke away. Others suggest that she purposely used Nigris to get back at Vigée Lebrun—to fight a battle of wills. There is no clear answer, and students enjoy speculating.

The relational dynamics that our early French texts put in relief—maternal narcissism, mother-daughter identity confusion, filial rebellion—

recur throughout the semester. Although in other texts, the intense identification between mother and daughter provides women emotional gratification unavailable from men, such identification is also often at painful odds with women's desire for individuality.

Notes

Portions of this essay are adapted from material that appeared in *Uneasy Possessions: The Mother-Daughther Dilemma in French Women's Writings, 1671–1928* (U of Delaware P, 2011) and are published with permission.

1. All translations from Grenaille and Vigée Lebrun are my own.

2. All quotations from *La Princesse de Clèves* are from Jean Mesnard's edition and Terence Cave's translation.

3. See Michèle Longino's "The Mother-Daughter Subtext" and my "Making Sense of the Ending" for diverging interpretations about whether the princess creates a subjectivity of her own after Mme de Chartres's death.

Allison Stedman

Jean Racine, Marie-Jeanne Lhéritier de Villandon, and Charles Perrault: A Revised Triumvirate

I pair Marie-Jeanne Lhéritier de Villandon's literary fairy tale "Les Enchantements de l'éloquence" ("The Enchantments of Eloquence"; 1695) with Jean Racine's classical tragedy *Andromaque* (1667) and Charles Perrault's classical fairy tale "Les Fées" ("The Fairies"; 1697) when I teach the seventeenth-century unit of a literature survey course covering texts from the Middle Ages to the French Revolution. While Racine's play and Perrault's fairy tale provide examples of classicism, a style of literary production popular at court, Lhéritier's fairy tale offers an introduction to what I refer to as "worldly" literary production, an aesthetic that emerged from the cultural context of the salon, informed the evolution of the novel as a literary genre, and was initiated and dominated by women writers. Read in chronological sequence, these three works expose not only the formal and stylistic differences of classical and worldly literary production but also the deep-seated ideological underpinnings of these differences.

I introduce Lhéritier's fairy tale with a brief *PowerPoint* presentation, which enables students to see a picture of Lhéritier, read facts about her biography, and even view pages from seventeenth-century journals describing her work. We discuss the visual elements of her engraved portrait by Étienne Desrochers (1697), elaborating on the signifiers that confirm

Lhéritier's social position as an educated, low-level aristocrat. We discuss the scope and chronology of her literary corpus. Students are surprised to learn that Lhéritier was received into several prestigious literary academies both in France and abroad, including the Palinot Society of Caen in 1692, the Academy des Jeux Floraux of Toulouse in 1696, and the Academy dei Ricovvrati of Padua in 1697 (Stedman). These accolades emphasize the historical importance of the fairy tale we are about to read and invite students to question why, with the exception of a privately maintained Web site ("Les Enchantements" [Rousseau]), it is currently unavailable in modern French. A brief list of Lhéritier's mentors, among them Madeleine de Scudéry, whose salon Lhéritier inherited in 1701, provides an opportunity to discuss the evolution of the Parisian salon network and the female-dominated novelistic tradition into which Lhéritier inscribes herself and her writing.

Since students have already read Racine's *Andromaque* in conjunction with the short chapter on "La Monarchie absolue" ("The Absolute Monarchy"; Mathiex 44–55), they are familiar with the major tenets of the classical literary aesthetic promoted by Louis XIV and enforced by the Académie Française: purity, symmetry, hierarchy, unity, and centralization on the level of form; the prioritization of appearance over essence, duty over passion, and order over disorder on the level of content. We apply this outside knowledge to Lhéritier's biography and lifestyle, hypothesizing the repercussions that Louis XIV's policies may have had on the salon network in the years before Lhéritier began writing. We discuss factors such as the establishment of the court at Versailles, the loss of patrons, the forced exile of friends, and the increasing authority of the Académie Française. As they begin reading, students keep in mind the following question: How might authors working in a society where every published work required a "privilege du roi" 'royal privilege' express disdain for Louis XIV and for the aesthetic system that bolstered his regime without becoming the victims of censorship?

Lhéritier's fairy tale is interpolated into a letter addressed to Anne Louise Christine de Lavalette, duchesse d'Épernon, an important fixture of late-seventeenth-century salon society whose portrait may also have appeared in *Divers Portraits*, by Anne-Marie-Louise d'Orléans, duchesse de Montpensier (1659). This letter provides a useful introduction to the worldly literary enterprise by revealing the ways that those who frequented late-seventeenth-century salons used literature to memorialize salon interaction and to inscribe models of worldly conversation and community in the form and the content of their works. In Lhéritier's model, the conversational framing letter interrupts the fairy tale at numerous intervals in the form of narra-tive digressions, emphasizing that the tale is not suspended in an ambigu-ous and therefore universal context. Rather, it is the subject of a projected epistolary dialogue between salon women, an arrangement that empha-sizes worldly society's prioritization of the particular over the universal (Beasley, *Revising* 20–31).

The presence of the framing letter also underlines the traditional lack of emphasis on generic purity in the literary production of the salon. Work-ing in pairs, students scan the letter's interventions to uncover moments where the narrator highlights the generic ambiguity of her interpolated tale, alternately referred to as a "Fable" 'fable'; "conte" 'tale'; "bagatelle" 'trifle'; "Histoire" 'history' or 'story'; and "Chronique" 'chronicle' (163, 164, 165, 185). We discuss the relationship between this ambiguity and the identity of the narrator, who refers to herself as both a "conteuse" 'storyteller' and a "Historienne" 'historian' (165, 185), even though she is ultimately closer to an epistolary novelist. I circulate a bound photocopy of the *Œuvres meslées*'s 1696 edition, now available online through *Gal-lica*, so that students can see the original context of their reading; both the fairy tale and its framing letter are inserted into a compilation of letters created by the same narrator and addressed to members of the author's real-life literary entourage. We discuss the generic variety that the letters contain: two short novels, two fairy tales, two treatises on the process of literary creation, a tribute to the late poet Antoinette Deshoulières, and an array of poetic forms, including odes, sonnets, and eclogues. We then compare the "haphazard" structure of the *Œuvres meslées* to the five-act symmetry of *Andromaque*. This exercise illustrates how differing ideologi-cal perspectives on variety, novelty, and creativity are reflected not only in narrative content but also in choices of genre and narrative form.

Perhaps most significant, the contrasting of Lhéritier's framing letter with Racine's second preface to *Andromaque* reveals the degree to which worldly and classical authors relied on fundamentally different genealogies to bolster the legitimacy of their literary enterprises. While Racine estab-lishes the origin of his tragedy with the ancient Greek poets Euripides, Homer, and Sophocles (40), Lhéritier's narrator derives her text from a group of anonymous, medieval French troubadours:

> [C'est] une de ces Fables gauloises, qui viennent apparemment en
> droite ligne des Conteurs ou Troubadours de Provence, si célèbres
> autrefois. (163–64)

> It is one of these Gallic fables passed down, apparently in direct line, from the Provencal storytellers or troubadours, so famous long ago.[1]

The genealogy of the fairy tale not only differs from *Andromaque*'s in terms of origin; it also revises the more recent French authors and subcultures responsible for facilitating the trajectory of the story from remote past to recent past to present. While Racine alludes to *La Franciade*, an epic by the sixteenth-century poet Pierre de Ronsard (40), Lhéritier's narrator credits an anonymous female intellectual and the oral culture of the seventeenth-century salon:

> Une Dame très instruite des antiquités Grecques et Romaines, et encore plus savante dans les Antiquités Gauloises, m'a fait ce Conte. (164–65)

> A woman very learned in Greco-Roman antiquity, and even more learned in Gallic antiquity, told me this story.

We discuss why Lhéritier's narrator might feel compelled to create an alternative genealogy for the story that follows. The explicit statement that the narrator's most recent source was well acquainted with "[les] antiquités Grecques et Romaines" eliminates the possibility that the classical genealogy is passed over out of ignorance. Rather, the choice appears related to the illustration of a particular proverb: "une maxime fort sensée quoique Gothique . . . que *Doux et courtois langage* / *Vaut mieux que riche héritage*" 'a very sensible maxim even though it dates from the high Middle Ages . . . that *Sweet and courtly language is worth more than a rich inheritance*' (165). Students analyze the value system implicit in this maxim, particularly with respect to its ranking of eloquence (an interior signifier acquired in private in the context of the fairy tale) over riches (an exterior signifier intended for public display). We relate this perspective to the classical tradition's emphasis on the incompatibility of private, individual impulses and desires and the public sphere, reviewing how tragedy befalls the characters of *Andromaque* largely because they are unable to sublimate their private desires (passion) to their public obligations (duty). This exercise helps students comprehend the degree to which the differences they have observed in worldly and classical literary plots ultimately reveal deep ideological divergences—particularly with respect to the value attributed to privacy, authenticity, and self-expression. While in the salon tradition individual merit is cultivated, internalized, and initially rewarded in private, in the classical tradition individuals must learn to efface the authentic, interior, private self—conforming their identities instead to the dictates of preestablished social roles to achieve public success.

In reading the fairy tale, we pay particular attention to its heroine, Blanche. We examine the positive effects that her affinity for novels has had on her personality, augmenting her natural beauty and kindness with knowledge, moderation, impeccable manners, good taste, and, most important, eloquence. As Blanche's father attests, novels are of particular benefit to innately eloquent readers like his daughter, since they model the practice of fine speech:

> On ne peut pas nier que les Romans bien faits n'apprennent le monde et la politesse du langage. Blanche a déjà assez de disposition à parler juste, et j'espère que la lecture de ces agréables ouvrages achèvera de lui en donner l'habitude. (183)

> No one can deny that well-written novels teach the worldly and polite use of language. Blanche is naturally predisposed to speak eloquently enough, and I hope that reading these agreeable works will put her into the habit of doing so.

As they continue reading, students consider the role that eloquence plays in the heroine's ability to orchestrate her own upward social mobility, transforming herself from a member of the "noblesse ruinée" 'impoverished nobility' into a wealthy, respected, and benevolent future queen (182).

In preparation for our second class on "Les Enchantements," students map the narrative structure of the three main encounters that drive the fairy tale's plot: Blanche's encounters with the prince, the fairy godmother Dulcicula, and the fairy Eloquentia. I distribute a table that lists these three encounters vertically down the left side, with three subject headings across the top: *Action* ("initiatory action"), *Suite* ("immediate repercussion"), and *Conséquence* ("ultimate conclusion"). Completing this chart with plot details and page numbers allows students to see the structural similarities that underlie the superficial differences of each event. All three are initiated by a singular dramatic action: the prince wounds Blanche during a hunting accident, Dulcicula applies a magic balm to Blanche's wound, and Blanche provides Eloquentia with a drink of water. Each is then followed by an in-depth conversation, during the course of which Blanche's interlocutor is impressed with her eloquence and decides to reward the heroine with a gift. The sum of the three gifts—a return to physical health (proffered by the prince, who sends his fairy godmother to heal Blanche), the most beautiful voice in the world (offered by Dulcicula), and the power of precious stones falling from Blanche's mouth each time she finishes a sentence (given by Eloquentia)—supplies the advantages necessary for the heroine to transform disparate, private encounters into publicly recognized social success. While in the classical tradition the public overwhelms the private to the point of obliteration, in the worldly tradition authenticity in private is essential to public triumph.

The chart also enables students to notice the pivotal importance of eloquent, polite discourse in driving the fairy tale's plot; worldly conversation consistently figures as the central, unifying factor among dramatic events, and its central role is amplified three times over. This theme provides a transition into a discussion of how worldly authors often subverted the classical aesthetic popular at court by manipulating the tropes of this aesthetic against itself. In groups of two or three, students find examples of how ideals such as symmetry, amplification, and centralization are reconstituted in the fairy tale and used to promote a worldly agenda. Inevitably, the three-by-three structure of the chart helps the group charged with the classical unities to appreciate the fairy tale's manipulation of the number three, thereby promoting a worldly vision of social success through both the sequence and structure of narrative events. Students also appreciate the fact that, in the worldly universe of the fairy tale, passion and duty are not in opposition but rather united in the mutually beneficial marriage of inclination that marks the tale's conclusion.

Often one of the most fruitful outcomes of this discussion is the analysis of Lhéritier's use of symmetry. We had begun our discussion of *Andromaque* the previous week by diagramming the symmetry of the cast of characters (44). During this exercise students had observed how the tragedy's lead roles (Oreste, Pyrrhus, Hermione, and Andromaque) are each symmetrically balanced with a subordinate confidant (Pylade, Phoenix, Cléone, and Céphise, respectively). Only Astyanax, the origin of the modern French monarchy according to Racine, is left to stand alone atop a metaphorical, classical pyramid (44, 51). Students are given the task of finding a similar pattern in the fairy tale, organizing primary and secondary characters into columns. The task is not as straightforward as it appears since, for classical symmetry to balance out, all the characters in the left column must have a similar relationship to the characters on the right. After working through various possibilities and occasionally drawing their interpretations on the board, students begin to conceptualize the fairy tale's symmetry in terms of family relations, whereby the younger generation of characters (Blanche, her stepsister Alix, and the prince) corresponds to *Andromaque*'s lead roles, while the older generation (Blanche's father, Alix's mother, and the prince's fairy godmother, Dulcicula) stands in for the tragedy's confidants. Only the fairy Eloquentia, the literary embodiment of worldly, polite conversation, is left to replace Astyanax atop the revised classical pyramid. The substitution of Louis XIV's "ancestor" with the salon ideal of eloquence offers insight into how worldly authors were able to subvert the classical tradition, and even the monarch's authority, without engaging in overt political criticism.

The seventeenth-century section of our survey concludes with a comparison of Lhéritier's salon fairy tale and Perrault's classical fairy tale "Les Fées," driving home the major differences between court and salon aesthetics by examining Perrault's diverse interpretation of a similar genre and subject matter. Even though "Les Enchantements" and "Les Fées" are derived from the same oral tale-type (AT480 [Aarne and Thompson 164–67]), the absence of a framing letter in Perrault's version foregrounds the classical penchant for generic purity; the tale appears as part of a collection of seven, all with similar structures and moral agendas. Even more revealing, however, is the marked contrast in the portrayal of the story's heroine. While Lhéritier's Blanche is an avid reader who impresses both the prince and the fairies with her eloquence, Perrault's nameless heroine, referred to simply as the "belle fille" 'pretty girl,' is the epitome of naïveté and ignorance (135). Rather than converse with the fairy she encounters in the forest, she simply responds, "Oui-da" 'yup' to the fairy's request for a drink of water (135). She is rewarded with the gift of a flower or a precious stone that falls from her mouth each time she speaks, not because she is eloquent but because she is obedient (136). The prince, whom she subsequently meets in the woods, decides to marry her not because she impresses him with her intelligence but because she is pretty, naive, and rich: "[C]onsidérant qu'un tel don valait mieux que tout ce qu'on pouvait donner en mariage à une autre, [il] l'emmena au Palais du Roi son père, où il l'épousa" 'Considering that such a gift was worth more than all the dowries he could hope to get from another, [he] took her to the Palace of the King his father, where he married her' (138). The triumph of Perrault's "belle fille," affirmed by the fairy tale's concluding "autre moralité" 'alternative moral,' is similarly a far cry from the medieval proverb of Lhéritier's tale. Rather than encouraging the cultivation of individual talents such as eloquence, the moral urges the individual to be patient and complacent and to conform to standards of behavior deemed appropriate for one's age, gender, and social class until the sovereign sees fit to offer a reward:

L'honnêteté coûte des soins,
Et veut un peu de complaisance,
Mais tôt ou tard elle a sa récompense,
Et souvent dans le temps qu'on y pense le moins. (138)

Social propriety requires care
And a certain degree of complacency,
But sooner or later it will be rewarded,
And often at the moment when one least expects.

A few decades ago, the decision to use Racine's *Andromaque* and Per-rault's "Les Fées" as a backdrop against which to foreground Lhéritier's "Les Enchantements" would have suggested what some have referred to as a feminist approach to "masculine history," defined by Maria-Milagros Rivera as "a tendency to look to a 'past' where women were not present and to try to insert them into that past." Thanks to the work of Faith E. Beasley, Joan DeJean, Elizabeth Goldsmith, Erica Harth, Carolyn Lougee, Ian Maclean, Aurora Wolfgang, and many others, we now know that by the 1690s women writers were outpublishing their male contemporaries by a ratio of 38 to 29, salon literary production dominated reading prac-tices and sales, and classical tragedies like Racine's were increasingly being relegated to the level of court spectacle (Wolfgang, Rev. 5–6; Hoffman 165–70). Positioning literary contributions like Lhéritier's at the center of a survey chapter on seventeenth-century French literature thus seems more a logical than a radical choice. While the reprinting of salon-inspired primary sources such as Lhéritier's has not kept pace with the reprinting of classically inspired texts, the benefit of giving students access to such materials ultimately outweighs the inconveniences, allowing students to experience the early modern literary landscape's diversity and complexity, even in the context of a literature survey.

Note

1. All translations are mine unless otherwise indicated.

Juliette Cherbuliez

Ways of Knowing: Fontenelle and Gender

Male writers have provided many of the most enduring insights I have had into the relation between women and writing in the premodern period. The proposition in this essay—that a volume on women's writing and women writers should include a reflection on male writers and male voices— proceeds directly from scholarship and teaching on women's writing, women's history, gender theory, and the history of Enlightenment epistemology. It builds on thirty years of feminist methodologies, whether uncovering women's voices (King and Rabil, "Editors' Introduction"), pairing women and men alongside each other (Miller, *French Dressing*), or incorporating the wave of masculinity studies that is changing early modern French studies (Connell; Butler, *Undoing*; Bray; Seifert and Reeser, *French Masculinities*; Seifert).

In this essay, I discuss how teaching Bernard Le Bouvier de Fontenelle's 1686 *Les Entretiens sur la pluralité des mondes habités* (*Conversations on the Plurality of Worlds*) underscores the complex status of women in literature, in literary culture, and in society. To teach the diversity of views on relationships between men and women, through this text and others like it especially, is also to examine a world before certain academic divisions and distinctions came to apply absolutely: divisions between science and literature, distinctions between experiential knowledge and theorized ideas. It prompts students to make connections between gender and knowledge and between social institutions and learning conventions. It also reveals some common pitfalls of instructors' historiographical choices, which are not always obvious to the literary scholar or student.

Teaching male writers, or traditionally male-oriented subjects, is fruitful for understanding the stakes of gender in late-seventeenth-century France. My choice of period is not incidental; the period 1680–1715 is historically what might be called a bridge period, a threshold separating the classicism of Louis XIV's court from the epistemological revolution of the Enlightenment. Constrained by the demands of periodization, this literature is seen either as degraded, fossilized, even decadent—the remains of the court society's day—or as embryonic, germinating the seeds of Enlightenment thought. Consequently, when literary scholars speak of Louis XIV's waning years, we invoke the severe piety of Françoise d'Aubigné, marquise de Maintenon, or the moral disarray of fairy tale writers such as Henriette-Julie de Castelnau, comtesse de Murat, or Marie-Catherine Le Jumel de Barneville, comtesse d'Aulnoy. Or we examine the influence of their contemporaries, whether Pierre Bayle, Fénelon, or Robert Challe, on eighteenth-century thought. It is not a surprise, then, that textbooks consider this bridge period ambivalently as at once "twilight" and "dawn" (Hepp 405), as either the beginning or the end, but never constituting anything in itself.

That the literary culture of these decades has been framed in a deterministic manner has limited our interest in teaching the products of them. At the undergraduate level in particular, we have little time to delve into historical intricacies, and it might seem redundant or belabored to read books that reiterate what already took place or embryonically exemplify those innovations to come. When it comes to teaching gender and women, however, we should consider making an exception of texts from such bridge periods. Resisting the impulse to see them as leading to or from a moment of greater significance, we might instead see them as accounting for or even producing a specific effect of such a transitional moment. Literary texts from this era compel us to disrupt a historically continuous picture of the premodern period by presenting a moment of possibility, however fleeting or interrupted, for women and their relation to social change, knowledge, and hierarchy.

Getting beyond Binaries

I have taught *Les Entretiens* in undergraduate courses on science, the idea of nature and the natural, libertine (or free-thinking) literature of the seventeenth and eighteenth centuries, as well as in courses on the literature of early modern philosophy. It would be an important addition to courses on women and science, on education, or on spaces of sociability; I have taught it alongside both *La Princesse de Clèves* (1678), by Marie-Madeleine Pioche de la Vergne, comtesse de Lafayette, and Françoise de Graffigny's *Lettres d'une Péruvienne* (1747).

The structure, language, and themes of *Les Entretiens* lend the text to such diverse presentations. Through a series of five evening conversations, Fontenelle portrays an excitable natural philosopher and a radiant member of the aristocratic leisure class who flirt their way through a discussion of Cartesian cosmology together. Topics of their conversations include Nicolaus Copernicus, travel to the moon, René Descartes's notion of the physics of the vortex, and the possibility that each star is a sun with its own planetary system. The unnamed philosopher entertains his hostess with witty observations on the nature of scientific inquiry: "Toute la philosophie, lui dis-je, n'est fondée que sur deux choses, sur ce qu'on a l'esprit curieux et les yeux mauvais" 'All philosophy is based on two things only: curiosity and poor eyesight' (*Entretiens* 62; *Conversations* 11). In contrast, the Marquise's contributions are seemingly nonscientific, humanizing attempts to understand the cosmos. In response to the Philosopher's description of planetary rotation, the Marquise personifies celestial bodies:

> Toutes ces planètes, dit la Marquise, sont faites comme nous, qui rejetons toujours sur les autres ce qui est en nous-mêmes. La Terre dit: *Ce n'est pas moi qui tourne, c'est le Soleil. La Lune dit: Ce n'est pas moi qui tremble, c'est la Terre.* (85)

> All those planets are like us, blaming the others for what we ourselves do. The Earth says: "It's not I who turn, it's the Sun." The Moon says: "It's not I who sway, it's the Earth." (26)

Thus metaphorical language and natural philosophy combine, under the stars in the Marquise's country estate, to illuminate the possibility of other inhabited worlds in the universe. At first glance, then, Fontenelle's text seems obvious on questions of gender and obscure, or at least outdated and irrelevant, on science, knowledge, and philosophy. In this regard, *Les Entretiens* appears easy to categorize and yet difficult to theorize.

Similarly, it is hard even to describe its author in today's disciplinary terms. Fontenelle (1657–1757) was at once historian of mathematics, opera librettist, and dramaturge, as well as permanent secretary to France's Académie des Sciences. Not so much a philosopher as a kind of broker among different social spheres and institutions, Fontenelle created works and occupied positions that we would see today as interdisciplinary or hybrid. To call them such, however, presents us with two problems, one epistemological and the second methodological. In the first instance, the categorization validates our modern, differentiated disciplines over premodern categories of knowledge whose boundaries were far fuzzier. Second, it forecloses those instances of knowledge making beyond the progressivist version of history that tells us how we got to our disciplinary distinctions, by treating them as exceptions, dead ends, or simple instances of insignificance. The same might be said for the culture of gender during the 1680s and 1690s and for Fontenelle's engagement with science through the question of gender. Indeed, literature in particular is rich fodder for an approach to history that sees disciplines as less divided, gender positions as less ossified, and historical time as rather more "wrinkled," to borrow from Michel Serres's vocabulary (129). Fontenelle's writings take up the question of what it might have meant to be a woman, to think like a woman, or to write for a woman during a period of immense change and possibility and so allow us to entertain the possibility of a more complex relation between gender and knowledge making.

Such is the case with *Les Entretiens*, published first in 1686 and translated into English in 1688 (Gelbart's introduction to the 1990 translation provides a fine historical overview). Yet *Les Entretiens* traditionally is taught through the numerous binaries that define its central concerns. Whether taught in literature or culture classes or alluded to in courses on the history of science, the work is generally introduced as a scientific text that was made almost instantly obsolete, since it promoted Cartesian cosmology less than a year before Isaac Newton's *Principia* (1687) appeared. As the standard history goes, despite this obsolescence *Les Entretiens* was by far Fontenelle's most successful written endeavor, with at least thirty editions in his lifetime, translations into ten different languages, and a reputation for having inspired the popularization of science. This historical narrative identifies in the text's conversational form a model for how science can be taught to the nonlearned.

Because the text is structured as a pedagogical conversation—in the great tradition of the philosophical duologue—it is particularly susceptible to facile binary divisions. My first task is to point out these oppositions by asking students to pay attention to form. Very quickly the reader seizes on the distinction between the Philosopher and the Marquise as emblematic of the binary categories that structure the text. The Philosopher is also initially a seducer and so draws readily from the period's standard seduction imagery; thus he first broaches the subject of astronomy by commenting on the beauty of the stars, which prompts a digression into the relative beauty of blonde and brunette women (Gelbart xiv–xv). This flirtation seems to suggest traditional gender norms: the female voice speaks for women, and the male voice speaks for men. Their roles also echo the kinds of unreconstructed stereotypes we persist in imposing on male-female relationships: educated versus uneducated, strong-minded versus feeble-minded, scientific versus imaginative, predator versus prey, learned and rigorous versus curious yet impetuous, elite versus anonymous masses. Even the setting suggests a very old division of labor: the sedentary, cloistered female who welcomes the adventurous philosopher to her château. Thus the Marquise declares a particular affinity to a study of the stars: "Heureusement encore nous sommes à la campagne, et nous y menons quasi une vie pastorale: tout cela convient à l'astronomie" 'Happily, . . . we're in the country, and here we lead a fairly pastoral life, quite conducive to astronomy' (*Entretiens* 66; *Conversations* 13), and the Philosopher may delight in having "softened" Ptolemaic science for her, since, "Si je vous le donnais tel qu'il a été conçu par Ptolémée son auteur, . . . il vous jetterait dans une épouvante horrible" 'If I gave it to you as it was conceived by Ptolemy . . . it would throw you into a horrible fright' (68; 14).

Generating this series of binaries allows us initially to consider the assumptions we make about the period, about the relation between men and women, and about their respective roles in a wide range of social, cultural, and intellectual debates. In this regard, *Les Entretiens* is an ideal text for a course on European thought; it provides the context for student-led presentations on the *querelle des anciens et des modernes*, the debate between Cartesianism and Newtonianism, as well as the era's questions about women and science. Further, it inspires students to consider the many spaces of sociability that defined early modern France: academies, salons, the court, the city. The salons, a perennial favorite topic for students, allow us to return to the text and examine our assumptions about the symbolics of the gendered relationship between the Marquise and the Philosopher. While I do work to interrogate the stability of the gender binary, I think it is important to acknowledge how such categories structure *Les Entretiens*—as they do many texts from this period—along with the many cultural phenomena that are its context.

Social Roles and Gendered Knowledge

After acknowledging the dichotomies guiding our assumptions about the premodern period and our general reading of the text, we turn to a closer examination of *Les Entretiens*. With some cultural and historical background, the idea that the Philosopher conquers the *mondaine* or *salonnière* is shown to be inaccurate. I use elements from Christophe Martin's excellent introduction to the French edition of the text to clarify the economic and social role of the salons and women's gatekeeper role in them. Women, we discover, represent two distinct sources of contribution to scientific inquiry in this text. The first is socioeconomic. Women in the early modern period presided over the mixed-gender social and educational events that, along with the academies, were major institutions in the circulation and innovation of knowledge. Philosophers like Fontenelle needed these salons for publicity and patronage. Here Fontenelle uses woman as a stand-in not for the popularization of science but for social power and privilege. Looking at the text from this angle, we complicate our analyses of the text's dichotomous structure.

Women's second contribution to scientific inquiry emerges through a close rereading of the text, focusing on the Marquise's role in the conversation. We note the discourse of seduction that the Philosopher initially uses to entice the Marquise, and I point out his worldly vocabulary (florid metaphors, liberal uses of allegories, explanations that are rather more social than technical), which has been categorized as "neoprecious" (Martin 60n1). In this way, we uncover a discourse—seemingly about conquest and seduction—that also reveals the Philosopher's need for the Marquise's approval and sanction of his ideas. We unearth the ways in which the Marquise increasingly masters the conversation and comes into her own way of being knowledgeable, that is, "savante" 'a scholar' (Fontenelle, *Entretiens* 157; *Conversations* 73). Especially in classes where we have also read Lafayette's *La Princesse de Clèves*, we revisit Fontenelle's assertion:

> Je ne demande aux dames pour tout ce système de philosophie, que la même application qu'il faut donner à *La Princesse de Clèves*, si on veut en suivre bien l'intrigue, et en connaître toute la beauté . . . [J]e suis sûr qu'à une seconde lecture tout au plus, il ne leur en sera rien échappé. (51–52)

> I ask only of the ladies, for this whole system of Philosophy, the same amount of concentration that must be given to *The Princesse de Clèves* in order to follow the plot closely and understand all of its beauty . . . one cannot read [it] more than twice at the very most without grasping [it] very accurately. (4–5)

Here, feminine-coded modes of knowledge also indicate sophisticated reading habits; Fontenelle elsewhere lauded *La Princesse de Clèves* and spoke of reading it repeatedly ("Lettre" 22). Thus we try to establish a multifaceted notion of science in its etymological sense of knowledge. One success of teaching this text has been to broaden students' understanding of how we limit our perception of other periods, cultures, and knowledge systems by imposing our own epistemological divisions on them.

Other Voices in the Classroom

One of the best ways to show students how different (and not immature, prefeminist, or unmodern) the mentality of the late seventeenth century was—and how many possibilities there are in an early modern text—is to create a dialogue of disciplines in the classroom. To this end, I invited a colleague of mine in the history department to join the conversation. This historian happens to have written on the history of science and on *Les Entretiens* in particular. That I have a colleague in the history department who specializes in this period, with a particular interest in the history of science, is fortuitous. I could have invited a philosopher, women's studies scholar, sociologist, or anthropologist, with equally productive results, since it is the productive tensions between interpretive approaches that is important. In contrast to my approach, which situated the text in our tradition of reading women as subjected to male-dominated institutions, my colleague offered as background the history of scientific thought as historical context along with received ideas about what we call the Newtonian scientific revolution, thus showing what the text implies about sound scientific inquiry. As my colleague has said in print, historical readings of this text, especially ones that see it as a mere popularization of science, rely "without scrutiny [on] a set of assumptions about the nature of scientific inquiry, texts, institutions and actors that are deeply anachronistic for the late seventeenth century" (Shank 89).

This kind of in-class encounter demonstrates that we deliberately choose an approach to texts and that in doing so we rely on inherited methodologies and received ways of thinking. During this discussion we observed the difference between positioning this text in the history of scientific thought and in discourses of seduction. When a historian talks about the ways in which we limit the relevance of *Les Entretiens* when we see it as a hybrid of science and literature, instead of understanding the text according to categories that were relevant at the time, students are better able to read the text through its own distinctions. Furthermore, for students of literature, the idea that a book featuring an intimate garden party where moonmen and Cartesian vortices are subjects of flirtatious banter might also intervene in the history of science is a powerful one.

There were some other fortuitous aspects of this public intersection of literature and science. The most obvious is that the historian of science is male and I, the literary scholar, am female, a binary opposition that mirrors Fontenelle's gendered Philosopher and Marquise. Gender in the classroom, like gender in the text, appears to correspond to certain kinds of authority, certain domains of interest and knowledge. It was particularly useful, then, for students to hear the historian's take on the text's philosophy of gender. For my colleague, "it was a philosophy that . . . offered a gender alternative to the excessively patriarchal and masculine philosophical cultures that both preceded and succeeded it" (Shank 88). In this reading, the idea of pleasure plays a theorized and fundamental role in the science Fontenelle is espousing: it is not a tool for educating the ignorant. Delight and pleasure are not superficial or feminized; rather they are the conditions for scientific inquiry, and the dialogic structure of the story emphasizes these conditions. Thus "Fontenelle articulates the complicated, intersubjective, and essentially mixed-sex method by which natural knowledge should be produced" (106). Students contrast this reading with a literary approach meditating on the textual complexities of these relationships, in which philosophy emerges from a failed seduction. The Philosopher initially relies on the perverse truism that knowledge can be power—over other people. His philosophizing is an excuse to seduce the Marquise, yet she is far more interested in cosmology than intimacy and so continually rebuffs his advances in favor of more astronomy lessons. Far from exhibiting an essential epistemological "difference" in the service of philosophy (Delon 67), the Marquise controls both the narrative and her education, in the service of herself.

Following either the historian or the literary scholar, we see how gender remains entrenched in the story. Indeed, the shift occurs in what we mean by science, writ large: science in the early modern period as a synonym for knowledge included also how to know, where to know, and who gets to know. It was only by jostling the categories we associate with gender that we could see how closely notions of gender relate to the social, epistemological, and methodological questions of science. This process opened up more fields of inquiry: What can literature do that other kinds of writing cannot do? What is science? What is authority? Who is the authority in the classroom? Which kinds of knowledge are socially constructed?

There are multiple consequences of this dialogue. On the most super-ficial pedagogical level, it shows students—and faculty members—how our disciplines shape our ways of thinking. Students in my class tend to interpret through the lens of their respective majors, labeling certain as-sertions as being from a history or political science perspective. A more important consequence of this dialogue is the insight it gives us into the ways in which these discipline-specific outlooks do not work for the pre-modern period. Our disciplinary dialogue shows us not only where histo-rians and literary scholars differ but also where these divisions simply miss the point of premodern literature. It reminds our students to think in a predisciplinary manner.

Predisciplinarity: Pleasure and Knowledge

I am making a case for what I would call an early modern predisciplinary position on women and, in this example, science. If we really want to un-derstand the historical reality of women and to study early modern litera-ture and other sites of knowledge production, we should attempt to rep-licate the period's models of knowing within our own modes of inquiry. Gender roles in the early modern period corresponded in many ways to what we consider traditional gender roles, but at the same time they af-forded opportunities and possibilities that no longer exist. Fontenelle's text is by no means alone in providing access to this holistic view of gen-der and knowledge making. Indeed, the works of Margaret Cavendish and Aphra Behn would complement a course that included Fontenelle's text—not coincidentally, Behn offered the first English translation of *Les Entretiens* in 1688. The idea, then, is not simply to get past gender but to look at it squarely to see what else was tied to gender, to get past, or rather before, disciplinary divisions that have occluded some of those possibilities.

In courses exploring the role of women in premodern France, the questions elucidated by texts such as Fontenelle's can challenge us to re-tain the complexity and contradictions characteristic of this period. *Les Entreteins* positions gender, its pleasures, and women's self-determination at the center of debates on knowledge and sociability. In this respect, it might provide an important counterpoint to much later novels. Nearly one hundred years after *Les Entreteins* was published, one of the Enlight-enment's most famous fictional women is unable to have both pleasure and knowledge. Pierre Choderlos de Laclos's 1782 *Liaisons dangereuses* (*Dangerous Liaisons*) portrays a radically knowledgeable woman in Mme de Merteuil, who declares her refusal of sexual pleasure to gain access to knowledge: "Ma tête seule fermentait; je ne désirais pas de jouir, je voulais savoir" 'I did not want the delights of love; I only wanted to know' (265; 164). While we continue to debate whether Laclos's novel is profeminist or deeply misognynstic, we might agree that texts such as *Les Entretiens* demonstrate a much more ample place in society for women's knowledge and their delight in knowing. We would do well to examine the conditions under which mixed-gender inquiry might draw such pleasure and innovation.

Caroline Weber

Memoirs and the Myths of History: The Case of Marie-Antoinette

In her anthology *Marie-Antoinette: Writings on the Body of a Queen*, the historian Dena Goodman examines how, in the age of tremendous political upheaval that was the late eighteenth century, representations of Marie-Antoinette became key sites of conflict and contestation. Although, as its title suggests, Goodman's volume focuses exclusively on the ways in which Marie-Antoinette's body became a vexed political and cultural signifier for the people of France, such an analysis can easily—and appropriately—be extended to include Marie-Antoinette's biography as well, especially when brought to bear on the large corpus of memoirs by eighteenth-century women that inscribe her life into their narrative.

In the turbulent century that followed the Revolution, the controversial life and death of Louis XVI's bride assumed new meanings as the French government assumed new forms. Particularly during the Bourbon restoration (1815–30), when several of the best-known memoirs of her contemporaries were published, discussions of Marie-Antoinette's conduct and character proliferated with much the same urgency as they had while she was alive. During the restoration and throughout the nineteenth century, moreover, the legends attached to her name were invariably shaped (as they were during her lifetime) by contemporary biases and pressures.

Memoirs relating the story of the infamous queen make for rich pedagogical material, because they allow students to consider firsthand how
historical truth tends to mutate as a function of a given political context.
Teaching students to recognize this correlation is a chief intellectual goal
of my advanced undergraduate seminar Myths of Marie-Antoinette. The
course's title is meant to sensitize participants from the outset to the ficti-
tious and constructed nature of her legend, and the memoirs written by
people who knew her well stand as a prime case in point.

Because so many of the memoirs that purport to tell Marie-Antoinette's
story were written by women, this corpus of texts has the added advantage
of showcasing women as the agents — not merely the voiceless objects — of
history. Teaching as I do at a women's college, I try to strike a judicious
balance between fielding my students' sometimes hair-trigger harangues
about the objectification of women and encouraging them to look at ways
in which women have, at times, colluded with men in the construction of
given ideological systems. Eighteenth-century women's writing on Marie-
Antoinette complicates any facile claims about the queen as a victim of contemporary, exclusively male rhetorical manipulations — be they idealizing
(like Edmund Burke's), denigrating (like Jules Michelet's), or both (like
Edmond and Jules de Goncourt's). Admittedly, the female authors who
include anecdotes about Marie-Antoinette in their memoirs tend to present her in a positive light: the glaring misogyny to which the Goncourts
sometimes give voice is nowhere in evidence in the writings of some of the
best-known of the female memoirs published in the Revolution's wake:
Mme Campan; Marie Du Deffand; Élisabeth Vigée Lebrun; Henriette-
Louise de Waldner de Freudstein, baronne d'Oberkirch; Henriette-Lucy
Pillon, marquise de La Tour Du Pin; Marie de Donnissan, marquise de La
Rochejacquelein; Rosalie Lamorlière; or Mme Royale. But, as I urge my
students to remember, even a favorable presentation of the slaughtered
Bourbon consort — whether composed under Napoléon, who was hostile
to the royalist cause, or the restored monarchs Louis XVIII and Charles X,
who strongly encouraged displays of monarchist loyalty — has far-reaching
implications. Just as surely as their male counterparts, women writing
about Marie-Antoinette engage in political myth making. In the age of
Hillary Clinton, Condoleezza Rice, and Ann Coulter, this lesson seems
worth imparting to students at single-sex and coed institutions alike.

Although neither critic addresses the case of Marie-Antoinette, Roland Barthes and Paul de Man have convincingly identified the pretense
of unvarnished truth as a prime identifying marker of all ideology. For this

reason, in my seminar on Marie-Antoinette, I have learned that teaching short extracts from Barthes's *Mythologies* and de Man's *Aesthetic Ideology* prepares the students to look more thoughtfully at texts that might at first strike them as neutral, even banal, statements of biographical fact. For instance, Barthes's essay on the Citroën as an embodiment of a set of particular French cultural ideals opens their eyes to the semiotic richness of an ostensibly utilitarian object like an automobile. And while de Man's writing is somewhat less accessible than Barthes's, it still works well as a pedagogical tool. By devoting ample class time to a few important passages in, for example, *The Resistance to Theory*, I have found that de Man's meditation on the inherent facticity of truth claims makes eminent sense to students and conditions them to examine their primary texts with a more critical eye. By receiving this theoretical preparation before they turn to the memoirs, students are less likely to fixate on uncovering the real story of Marie-Antoinette and more prone to explore the ways in which culture and politics shape all stories—especially those of prominent public women.

But it is the memoirs themselves that provide the most abundant fodder for investigations of this kind. To maximize their pedagogical effectiveness, I prefer to assign excerpts from these works in a host of comparative exercises. Students never fail to notice that the memoirists emphasize, again and again, many of the same characteristics of the queen. These include her physical beauty, her sexual purity, her devotion to motherhood, and her generosity toward the unfortunate. As supplemental readings from the feminist historians Lynn Hunt and Chantal Thomas quickly reveal, the pamphleteers of the Revolution depicted Marie-Antoinette in exactly the opposite way: as a hideous monster, a shameless harlot, a "bad mother" (Hunt 89–123), and a greedy spendthrift who stole bread from her subjects' mouths and money from their coffers. When compared with the examples cited by Hunt and Thomas (whose book is especially helpful for the revolutionary tracts it reprints in translation in an appendix), the passages that, for instance, Vigée Lebrun, Campan, and Lamorlière devote to establishing their royal heroine's physical and moral beauty assume a new meaning—as deliberately conceived antidotes to the propaganda campaign that the Revolution's supporters waged against her to such devastating effect.

Indeed, to impress on my students how powerful that propaganda campaign turned out to be, I follow this assignment by distributing excerpts from the proceedings of Marie-Antoinette's October 1793 trial, where prosecutors, condemning her as an adulterous and incestuous sexual pervert and a hideous "sangsue des Français" 'bloodsucker of the French,' by turns repeated and embroidered on the charges that the revolutionary media had been leveling against her since the liberalization of the press in July 1789 (Castelot 65). Although none of the memoirists wrote about the trial per se, suggestive counterpoints to the prosecution's virulent rhetoric appear in the writings of Marie-Antoinette's daughter, Mme Royale, with whom she was incarcerated in the Temple from August 1792 to August 1793, and of Lamorlière, who acted as Marie-Antoinette's ladies' maid in the Conciergerie from the time of her transferal there in August 1793 until her execution three months later. Both writing during the Bourbon restoration (to which Mme Royale had close ties, given not only her own royal birth but also her marriage to her cousin, the duc d'Angoulême, son of the future Charles X), these women offer detailed and emphatically moving accounts of Marie-Antoinette's travails in the period leading up to her fateful summons before the revolutionary tribunal. Both women insist on the state of extreme material deprivation to which her captors reduced her (e.g., forcing her to unstitch by hand the fleurs-de-lis embroidered on the wall hangings of her prison cell), the psychological cruelty she endured from the Revolution's more militant avatars (many of whom visited her in jail merely to taunt her, and some of whom took it upon themselves to take her young son away from her so that he might be "reeducated" as an enemy of the throne), and the saintlike calmness and dignity with which she allegedly bore up under her travails. When compared with the brutally pejorative character assessment that was put forth at her trial, these pathos-ridden, quasi-hagiographic narratives emerge as highly charged correctives to the revolutionary myth of "the wicked queen" (Thomas).

Another fruitful, compare-and-contrast assignment involves selections from the memoirs of two noblemen who, during the ancien régime, each briefly enjoyed pride of place in Marie-Antoinette's inner circle: Armand-Louis Gontaut, duc de Lauzun, and Pierre de Besenval. In their memoirs, both tried to capitalize on their erstwhile friendship with the famously prudish sovereign by implying that she had been (or had wanted to be) their mistress. Against the self-congratulatory, kiss-and-tell narratives of these two men, I find it useful to juxtapose the detailed refutations of their claims made by Mme Campan, Marie-Antoinette's longtime *femme de chambre*. To be sure, no definitive proof exists to establish whether Campan, who insists that her mistress had no sexual involvement with either gentleman, is telling the truth. But the comparison between her text and the two noblemen's reveals how all three presented her sexual conduct as a key component of her story. Assigning the introduction from Goodman's *Marie-Antoinette* as an added resource, I ask students to write short response papers to this trio of memoir excerpts, examining how and why Marie-Antoinette's sexual body assumes such importance for those writing about her. What might the queen's sexual morality (or lack thereof) have to do with her political stature and with the soundness of the body politic over which she and her husband once ruled? Does her erotic misconduct, as reported by Lauzun and Besenval, retroactively justify her demise, or even explain that of the ancien régime? Conversely, does the unfailing decorum that Campan attributes to the queen enhance Marie-Antoinette's posthumous glory? If so, how does this presentation stand to benefit her surviving Bourbon relatives—like her brother-in-law Louis XVIII, who had regained the throne by the time Campan published her memoirs?

Posing these questions necessarily requires at least a brief consideration of each memoirist's biography and of the circumstances under which his or her reminiscences were published. Unfortunately, no published source that I know of covers these issues in exhaustive detail. Emmanuel Bourassin, however, has provided a very useful and reasonably comprehensive overview of the best-known (male and female) memoirists who wrote about Marie-Antoinette in the preface to his edition of *Souvenirs du comte d'Hézècques*, written by a former page of Louis XVI. Since this preface is a mere fifty pages long, I include it in the packet of readings for Myths of Marie-Antoinette and urge my students to refer to it for further information about the people whose testimonies constitute the bulk of the class's material. As Bourassin relates, during the period immediately following the Revolution, Mme Campan became a suspicious figure in royalist circles for transferring her loyalties to Napoléon Bonaparte and receiving conspicuous signs of his favor. After the restoration brought Napoléon's royal enemies back to power, Campan was thus desperate to remind her contemporaries (and the Bourbon government) of the many services she had performed for Marie-Antoinette. In this light, Campan's protestations about the queen's sexual innocence register as so many protestations of her own political innocence, while at the same time echoing other contemporary paeans to the sublimity and virtue of the Bourbon dynasty as a whole. The personal and the political here coalesce, since Campan's memoir reveals as much about its author as about its purported subject and as much about current political concerns as about past ones.

Students reach a similar understanding when comparing Campan's version of Marie-Antoinette and Louis XVI's failed 1791 escape from France—the so-called flight to Varennes—with relatively neutral, scholarly accounts of the same episode (e.g., Schama; Tackett). As this comparison readily reveals, Campan invents for herself in the drama of Varennes a prominent role that she by no means played. In fact, as Jean Chalon, the editor of the 1988 paperback edition of her memoirs, points out in his preface, by 1791 Marie-Antoinette had come to suspect Campan of harboring revolutionary sympathies and took great pains to exclude her from the escape plot—a fact that Simon Schama's and Timothy Tackett's narratives soundly confirm. Marie-Antoinette's suspicions may, moreover, have given rise to the rumors that Mme Campan was the palace insider who betrayed the royals' flight to revolutionary officials and thus brought about their ultimate capture at Varennes. By 1816, one year after the Bourbons' return to power, these rumors were still so persistent that Campan had to beg another former member of the queen's retinue, Louise Élisabeth de Croÿ d'Havre, duchesse de Tourzel, to make an official statement on her behalf, describing her as a loyal servant of the throne. In his preface to the memoirs, Chalon reprints this letter in full and explains Campan's reasons for soliciting it. Reading this letter and the Varennes accounts by Schama and Tackett in connection with Campan's paragraphs about the royals' escape, students again confront the mythical dimension of Marie-Antoinette's alleged life story. The ostensible truth of the consort's doings is embedded in a tangled web of personal interest, political intrigue, and patent narrative distortion.

As this last observation suggests, Campan is a skilled and savvy teller of tales—and so, it turns out, are most other eighteenth-century memoirists claiming to know the queen and her life story, each in a distinctive fashion. From Du Deffand's worldly, laconic wit in relating Marie-Antoinette's earliest days at court to Mme Royale's dignified understatement in narrating her mother's tragic time in prison and from Vigée Lebrun's effusive admiration for her patroness's warmth and kindness to La Tour Du Pin's knowing, lightly barbed reminiscences of the queen's preoccupation with her looks, each writer has a tone, a style, and a set of preoccupations all his or her own. These differences allow for an illuminating creative assignment, which is to have students adopt one memoirist's voice to narrate an episode contained in another's text. How might Vigée Lebrun have written about the difficulties Marie-Antoinette faced in prison? How would Mme Royale have explained her mother's purported vanity? How might Mme Du Deffand have construed the sexual boasting of Besenval and Lauzun—for which Mme Campan so righteously condemned them? This project deepens students' awareness not only of the stylistic and thematic diversity of the texts studied but also of the striking shifts that occur when a given biographical tidbit is retold from another perspective. I have found that students enjoy this exercise enormously, because it allows them to work in a creative vein. Practically without exception, the papers they give me for this assignment are the most entertaining and thoughtfully crafted essays I receive all term.

With all this training in the mythical underpinnings of Marie-Antoinette's story, students are primed by the end of the semester to consider more current variations on the same problematic. In years past, I have paired selections from Antonia Fraser's unabashedly royalist biography, *Marie Antoinette: The Journey*, with Simone Bertière's highly critical, even condemnatory *Marie-Antoinette, l'insoumise*. Like their eighteenth-century counterparts, these women frame their subject in wildly divergent ways, which I ask students to examine in class by doing a comparative close reading of a short passage from each work. A third female storyteller has recently entered the ranks of Marie-Antoinette's mythologizers: in May 2006, Sofia Coppola unveiled her film *Marie-Antoinette* at Cannes. And as Coppola has acknowledged in interviews, this portrait of the queen as a young party girl takes the most extravagant liberties with its subject. Transforming Marie-Antoinette's rigid, tradition-laden Versailles into a giddy world of drug use, Converse sneakers, and 1980s pop music, Coppola presents a version of the queen almost unrecognizable from all previous iterations—a version that some critics have suggested reflects Coppola's carefree and fun-loving life as a Hollywood princess more than any deep understanding of the French queen's complex existence. (Tellingly, the filmmaker avoided reading historians when writing her screenplay, on the grounds that, as she told the *New York Times*, "I didn't want to get bogged down with history.") Yet Coppola's is a vision of the queen that I suspect students will take great pleasure in dissecting, not simply because it seems custom-made for the MTV generation, but because it reiterates what their memoirs have already taught them. Today, as at the close of the early modern era, representations of Marie-Antoinette reveal at least as much about the creators as they do about the infinitely protean queen.

Mary Trouille

Giving Voice to Women's Experience: Marital Discord and Wife Abuse in Eighteenth-Century French Literature and Society

In a 1984 article, Ruth Nadelhaft observed that "domestic violence has not yet been identified, let alone studied, systematically in literature" (244). Although the issue has received considerable attention among literary critics since the mid-1970s, relatively little work has been published to date concerning domestic violence in eighteenth-century France and descriptions of it in the literature of the period, and seldom has this subject been explored in the classroom. Eighteenth-century France is particularly relevant to discussions of this issue, for during this period, French society experienced profound changes in family and legal structures, an increased separation between public and private spheres, and the emergence of a feminist consciousness.

As a specialist in eighteenth-century French literature and women's studies, I regularly teach courses on gender issues and women writers of early modern France. Among these is Marriage and Domestic Violence in Eighteenth-Century French Literature and Society, drawn from the research for my book *Wife-Abuse in Eighteenth-Century France*. In this course, we read letters and autobiographical works by eighteenth-century French women, fictional and fictionalized accounts of marriages gone awry, writings on marriage by theologians and moralists, and documents from court cases, as well as background material on the social history of the period. The central focus is to explore the interconnections between life and literature by comparing incidents of abuse described by victims in court testimony, letters, and autobiographical writings with fictional or fictionalized incidents depicted in the literature of the period.

The sixteen-week course is divided into three main parts: an examination of the views on spousal abuse expressed in eighteenth-century French laws, religious doctrines, moral treatises, and popular culture (proverbs, farces, and street theater) and how these views compare with actual behaviors; a study of six court cases from the period involving various kinds of spousal abuse; and a selection of eighteenth-century French fictional works depicting wife abuse.

Central Questions and Issues

Among the questions we address in the course are, What limits and punishments were prescribed for spousal abuse in eighteenth-century French laws, religious doctrines, and moral treatises? To what extent was such abuse tolerated by the police, magistrates, and the public, and what justifications were given and accepted for such behavior? To what extent were these attitudes and behaviors influenced by the social class of the perpetrators and victims (e.g., was physical abuse more common and more widely tolerated among the poor and working classes)? How did narratives of domestic violence differ in tone and substance depending on the form adopted (letters, memoirs, court testimonies, newspaper articles, fictional or fictionalized accounts, etc.) and the gender and social class of narrator and audience? What motives—reformist, reactionary, sensationalist, vindicatory—prompted people to write and publish these accounts? How did these attitudes, practices, and laws evolve over the course of the century, and how were they affected by changes in social, political, and ideological structures? For example, did the legalization of divorce in 1792 following the French Revolution lead to a decline in spousal abuse? Finally, to what extent did the twin ideals of companionate marriage and domesticity advocated by Jean-Jacques Rousseau and others beginning in the 1760s affect people's expectations of marriage and the norms of marital behavior?

To draw comparisons among texts of different decades and genres and to trace the evolution of social structures and attitudes, I find it helpful to use the same set of questions for each of the primary texts. We begin each class by discussing how the form of expression (genre and voice) affects the tone, substance, and effectiveness of the message. For example, what are the advantages and disadvantages of expressing one's views in a work of fiction as opposed to a work of nonfiction or of adopting first-person as opposed to third-person narrative? We then discuss the tensions in the marriage, how the couple's social origins and financial assets affected their relationship, and the character traits and circumstances that may have predisposed the couple to problems. If spousal abuse was involved, we discuss what form(s) it took, what provoked it, and whether anyone intervened. Finally, if the couple had children, we discuss whether they played an important role in the story's outcome. As readers some two centuries later, are we surprised by the children's importance—or lack thereof? Do the children tend to play a more important role in the fictional works than in the court cases? What does this difference suggest concerning the social or sentimental function of literature? The remainder of the class discussion is devoted to an analysis of point of view, tone, and rhetoric in the text and the motives that may have prompted its publication. We conclude by examining what the couple's story reveals about the problems underlying the institution of marriage in eighteenth-century France, as well as the changes we see in attitudes concerning marital conflict and spousal abuse when we compare texts from different decades.

Background Readings

To serve as a framework for discussion of the primary texts, four kinds of background materials are assigned: writings on marriage and spousal abuse by eighteenth- and nineteenth-century theologians, legal scholars, social critics, and reformers; recent studies by social historians on the attitudes, practices, and laws in early modern France regarding marriage, spousal abuse, separation, and divorce; pertinent studies of the primary texts by contemporary literary critics; and recent studies on the law as literature. The first group of works include Mme de Cailli's *Griefs et plaintes des femmes malmariées* (1789; "Grievances and Laments of Unhappily Married Women"), Simon-Nicolas-Henri Linguet's satirical *Lettre du marquis de C* ** au comte de F* ** contre le divorce* (1790; "Letter against Divorce from the Marquis de C*** to Count F***"), and Antoine Blanchard's 1713 confessional guides "Péchés des maris à l'égard de leurs femmes" ("Sins of Husbands toward Their Wives") and "Péchés de l'épouse à l'égard de son mary" ("Sins of the Wife toward Her Husband"). To trace the evolution in the laws regarding separation and spousal abuse, we also read pertinent articles from Joseph-Nicolas Guyot's 1785 index of case law *Répertoire universel et raisonné de jurisprudence* and from two editions of Guy Du Rousseaud de La Combe's compendium of civil law *Recueil de jurisprudence civile*, published in 1736 and 1769.

Among the historical studies we read are Nadine Bérenguier's "Victorious Victims: Women and Publicity in *Mémoires Judiciaires*"; selected chapters from Suzanne Desan's *The Family on Trial in Revolutionary France* and several chapters of my *Wife-Abuse in Eighteenth-Century France* examining French laws, attitudes, and practices concerning spousal abuse during the period and the separation cases included in the course. To broaden the scope of our inquiry, we also read excerpts from the essay "Wife-Torture in England," published in 1878 by the pioneering British reformer Frances Power Cobbe; Benoite Groult's preface to the French translation of Erin Pizzey's groundbreaking *Scream Quietly or the Neighbors Will Hear* (1975) about wife abuse in the United Kingdom; and Bruno Frappat's 1975 article published in *Le Monde* in response to Pizzey's book. Finally, to acquaint students with current scholarship on the law as literature, I have them read Paul Gewirtz's essay "Narrative and Rhetoric in the Law."

The Norms of Spousal Abuse in Eighteenth-Century France: Social and Legal Contexts

Unlike its Protestant neighbors, Catholic France of the ancien régime did not permit divorce. Until passage of the divorce law of 1792, French marriages could be ended only by means of separation or annulment. Unhappiness and incompatibility were not valid grounds for a separation; only abusive behavior could be invoked. However, the laws concerning spousal abuse traditionally were heavily weighted in favor of the husband. In eighteenth-century France, as in most other European countries of the period, wife beating in moderate form was permitted—even expected. Because the husband was legally responsible for his wife's misdeeds, it was considered reasonable that he should have the right to control her behavior and to discipline her when necessary, just as he would his children and servants, for whom he was also responsible in the eyes of the church and the courts. The limitations lay in the severity and in the motivation, which was to ensure obedience and good behavior. If a husband went beyond these limits, his wife could sue for a separation. Yet for judges to grant a separation on the grounds of physical abuse, the abusive behavior generally had to be frequent, excessive, and life threatening.

The right to "moderate correction" was only one facet of a husband's authority over his wife, referred to in French law as *la puissance maritale*. The various French legal codes—royal, ecclesiastical, and customary—all recognized this principle, which gave a husband wide-ranging legal powers over his wife. These included control over her property, the need for his consent before she entered into contracts or testified in court, and his right to control her domicile. Under eighteenth-century French law, a married woman could not leave her husband's home to take up residence elsewhere without his permission; if she did so, he could obtain a court order to have her forcibly returned. His control over his wife's domicile also gave him the right to evict her or to lock her in. As Roderick Phillips explains, *puissance maritale* was simply a variation of *puissance paternelle*, the principle of a father's authority over his children. Both forms of authority were derived from the laws of ancient Rome, where a husband had a wide range of powers over his wife, including the right to kill her if she committed adultery. By early modern times, this right had been considerably attenuated in most Western countries, although some legal codes still permitted a husband to kill his wife with impunity if he found her in flagrante delicto. This right was enshrined in French law until it was repealed in 1907, after a public campaign against it (Phillips 110). Yet as Desan points out, even before the Revolution, there was much variation in attitudes and customs in different parts of the country: "women . . . in many cases exercised more power over property and decision-making than the letter of the law allowed, and family patterns differed immensely from region to region" (2).

Over the course of the eighteenth century, French legal standards evolved concerning what was considered a husband's acceptable behavior toward his wife. The evolution is especially clear when one compares the article on separation in the 1736 and 1769 editions of Du Rousseaud de La Combe's compendium of civil law, *Recueil de jurisprudence civile*. In the fourth edition, published in 1769, Du Rousseaud de La Combe writes:

> Il faut, suivant le Droit Canonique, que les sévices et mauvais traitements pour opérer la separation de corps aient été capables de faire craindre pour la vie de la femme, et qu'ils aient mis sa vie en danger; mais suivant nos mœurs, cela n'est pas requis, il suffit que les faits soient graves, qu'ils rendent la vie insupportable et infiniment triste et disgracieuse, et qu'ils soient d'une nature à pouvoir être admis.

According to canon law, to serve as grounds for separation, the ill treatment suffered by the wife must be serious enough to endanger her life. But in current legal practice, the ill treatment need not be life threatening; it is enough that the incidents be serious, that they make life unbearable, and that they be of a type admissible as evidence.[1]

He then adds the following caveat: "Il faut encore avoir égard aux personnes: car ce qui ne serait pas un moyen de separation entre gens du commun en peut server entre personnes d'une condition plus relevée" 'One must also take into account the couple's rank; for what would not be a means of separation among couples of undistinguished rank may serve as a means of separation among persons of higher rank.' The original 1736 edition, by contrast, makes no such class distinctions, nor does it distinguish between the provisions of canon law and civil law. In the thirty years between the two editions, the provisions for separations on the grounds of ill treatment clearly had become more flexible, especially for couples of distinguished rank. Yet there continued to be considerable subjectivity in the interpretation of these standards of behavior among judges, lawyers, and the police, as well as among the general public. Even after passage of stricter battery laws in 1791 and the liberal divorce law of 1792, the courts often retained the older legal standards and traditional attitudes toward women. Although the divorce law made no distinction between justifiable and unjustifiable marital violence, requiring only proof of violence per se, many courts persisted in judging the husband's violence in terms of his wife's alleged misconduct. The fact that women from all social classes filed battery charges against their husbands and that battery is very often mentioned in separation suits (and later in divorce suits with equal frequency) suggests that wife battering—that is, forms of correction exceeding the limits of what was considered acceptable—was widespread in eighteenth-century French society.

Notions of violence and abuse are, of course, culturally determined and specific to a particular time and place; they evolve over time and are shaped by changes in personal circumstances, as well as by developments in the society at large. In eighteenth-century France, as now, spousal abuse took a wide variety of forms, the most common of which included mental cruelty, verbal abuse, public humiliation, confinement, deprivation of food and shelter, and many kinds of physical mistreatment. Then, as now, there was a broad range of levels of violence—from a single slap to persistent assaults causing serious injury and sometimes death.

Court Cases

To see how incidents of spousal abuse were presented in the French tribunals of the period, we first examine four marital separation cases included in a popular anthology of causes célèbres drawn from eighteenth-century French judicial memoirs and published from 1773 to 1789 by Nicolas-Toussaint Des Essarts, a lawyer turned writer, editor, and cultural critic. Judicial memoirs—in which lawyers published their legal arguments for a particular client—had both a theoretical justification and a practical use. In theory, they were addressed exclusively to the presiding judges. In practice, however, lawyers circulated these texts widely in the hope of swaying public opinion in their client's favor. The most important or unusual cases were then published in collections of causes célèbres such as Des Essarts's. By the choice of cases, the selection and sequencing of excerpts from the lawyers' briefs, and the way the editors framed the accounts with narrative and commentary, these collections shaped judicial practice and public opinion on important legal issues of the day.

Like most separation cases in Des Essarts's *Causes célèbres*, the four we read all involve various kinds of spousal abuse. The first case dates back to 1771 in Reims and concerns a wife's successful defense against her husband's suit to overturn a separation granted in 1757, fourteen years earlier, after he had knowingly infected her with syphilis ("Mal vénérien").[2] Rejecting the traditionalist view that a wife's duty was to stay with her husband for better or for worse, Mme Blé's lawyer, Linguet, successfully argued that transmission of venereal disease to a spouse constituted life-threatening physical abuse. It was the first time a French court granted a marital separation on these grounds. The decision reflects advances in the medical understanding of the disease, its insidious nature, and its effects on children infected in the womb and presents interesting parallels to current laws that criminalize the transmission of HIV.

The second case we examine is the separation suit brought in 1775 by the marquise de Mézières against her second husband, Collet, her former financial adviser ("Cause").[3] She had filed for a separation within a year of her marriage, but, after much legal wrangling and blaming of the victim, the suit was rejected. Ordered to return to her husband, the marquise found herself a prisoner in her own home, mistreated daily and surrounded by servants loyal to Collet, who was living openly with another woman and rapidly dissipating his wife's substantial fortune through gambling and extravagant spending. After nearly six years of persecution, the marquise finally succeeded in obtaining a separation in 1775 on the grounds of financial mismanagement and physical abuse. The case is intriguing for several reasons. First, it shows that even the wealthiest and most privileged women were by no means immune to domestic violence. Second, the marquise — for reasons perhaps not fully understood even by her and glossed over by her lawyer, Jacques-Vincent Delacroix — had married a much younger man, far below her in both rank and fortune. Had she been in love with him, but ashamed to admit it in court? Her lawyer claimed that Collet had taken advantage of the depression and disorientation brought on by menopause to force the marquise to marry him and to sign over a large portion of her fortune to him. Third, despite the strong evidence presented of her husband's violence, unscrupulous behavior, and gross mismanagement of her wealth, the lower court had rejected her petition. This defeat confirmed her worst fears, as her lawyer, later explained in her appeal:

> Ce n'était qu'avec repugnance qu'elle s'avançait vers les tribunaux. Elle sentait combien son âge éleverait de soupcons injustes et offensants. "Je produirais, se disait-elle, des preuves de mes malheurs plus claires que le jour. Pourquoi, répondra-t-on, a-t-elle, à son âge, épousé ce jeune homme? Il la ruine; il la rend malheureuse; cela est dans l'ordre." (115)

> It was only with great reluctance and trepidation that she approached the courts. She sensed how much her age would raise unjust and offensive suspicions in the judges' minds: "Why, they will ask, had she, at her age, married this young man? He's causing her financial ruin, but she's merely getting what she deserves."

Finally, the case is compelling because of the misogynic stereotypes it reveals in eighteenth-century views of menopause as an illness that makes women weak and vulnerable to melancholy and to the unscrupulous behavior of others.

The third case is a separation suit brought by Jeanne Fouragnon, the wife of a prominent merchant in Toulouse, who accused her husband and her adult stepson of physical abuse. The husband, Pierre Rouches, accused his wife of theft and hinted at various improprieties, including adultery ("Demande" [Rouches]).[4] Rouches was represented by Guillaume Jean Desazars de Montgaillard, his wife by Jean Raymond Bastoulh. At the time of their marriage in 1772, Rouches, a widower with five children, was in his late forties. His bride, an innkeeper's daughter, was only twenty and brought little or no dowry to the marriage. The husband's lawyer presented his client as an embodiment of the bourgeois values of frugality, simplicity, and hard work. By contrast, he described Mme Rouches as a symbol of the corrosive influence of aristocratic tastes and values on the merchant class. He claimed that her immoderate taste for luxury, fashion, ostentation, and independence—tastes reflecting aspirations inappropriate for her rank—were the real reasons behind her separation suit and not the mistreatment she claimed to have suffered. In March 1782, the court granted Mme Rouches a four-year separation and modest alimony. This decision, based on evidence earlier courts might well have considered inconclusive, was in keeping with the trend toward increasingly liberal interpretations of the laws governing separations in the decade leading up to the 1789 Revolution.

The fourth case is a separation suit brought by Mme Aubailly de La Berge against her husband, a retired commander of a provincial military regiment, whom she had married in early 1785 ("Demande" [Aubailly de La Berge]).[5] She claimed that he had dissipated her fortune to support a series of mistresses and accused him of a wide variety of abuses that increased in frequency and gravity during the two years she lived with him, ranging from verbal insults to attempted murder. After fifteen months of legal proceedings, she finally was granted a permanent separation, recovery of her property, and custody of their young son. The case is noteworthy because of her lawyer's successful challenge to traditionally accepted norms of male behavior concerning adultery, spousal abuse, and control of a wife's property. Under eighteenth-century French civil law, adultery was largely a female offense, in contrast to canon law, which viewed it as a sin for both sexes. In the civil courts, which increasingly had jurisdiction over marital disputes, a husband's adultery was grounds for separation only when accompanied by aggravating circumstances (such as bringing his mistress into the home or dissipating his wife's fortune to pay for his debauchery). French laws concerning spousal abuse and property rights traditionally favored the husband as well. The court's judgment in this case therefore suggests a significant shift in practice.

What makes these cases interesting from a historical and pedagogical perspective is how they reflect conflicting views of marriage and the role of women in society. The main voices in the texts—the husband's lawyer, the wife's lawyer, and the editor Des Essarts—serve implicitly as spokesmen for competing interpretations of the laws concerning separation and spousal abuse. The accounts of domestic violence in these cases, the rulings made by the presiding judges, and the commentaries added by the editor all provide valuable insight into the attitudes, practices, and laws of the period. Particularly interesting is the way the women's lawyers drew on legal precedents and reinterpreted the law to challenge the norms of male behavior, such as the double standard and tolerance of wife abuse. By challenging traditional inequalities between spouses, progressive lawyers of the period helped prepare the way for the liberal divorce law of 1792 and the other radical reforms of family law adopted in the 1790s.

Our sampling of court cases concludes with two cases defended by the well-known lawyer Nicolas-François Bellart in 1803 and 1805, following the partial repeal of the divorce law in March 1803. In the first case, Bellart successfully defended Mme de l'Orme in her divorce suit against her husband. In the second case, he represented Pierre Mandonnet in a failed appeal to overturn the separation his wife had been granted earlier that year. In his judicial memoirs for both these clients—despite the sharp differences between their cases—Bellart applauded the stricter divorce law put into place in 1803 under Napoléon ("Mémoire," "Réflexions"). In his view, irreparable damage had been done to marriage as an institution during the decade in which the no-fault divorce law was in force. Bellart maintained that the 1792 law and the "agitations de la Révolution" had led to the revolt of women against their husbands, the undermining of marital authority, the disorder of families, and, more generally, the moral decline of French society ("Réflexions" 504). Bellart's traditionalist pronouncements are representative of the prevailing views on marriage and divorce among Napoléon's conservative Catholic supporters, who played a key role in the drafting of the more restrictive laws on divorce and separation.

An Approximation of the Truth

Like the other separation cases included in the course, Bellart's memoirs for de l'Orme and Mandonnet offer a behind-the-scenes look at the private lives of couples. As Cornelia Hughes Dayton remarks in her study of women's experiences in the courtrooms of colonial Connecticut:

> [C]ourt records provide an extraordinary window into behaviors [and] self-fashionings . . . that would otherwise go unrecorded. In a period when few adults left letters or diaries, women and men speak through court records more openly than through almost any other set of documents. (4)

But Dayton also underlines the challenges of deciphering court cases from centuries past:

> [A]s historians we can capture only a small fraction of the information that came before the bench. . . . The gestures of the various participants, the gasps and sighs and catcalls of the audience, and in general the dramaturgy of the courtrooms — these are almost always lost to us. Much of what the judges said from the bench went unrecorded. . . . Thus our interpretations of what happened in court are inevitably dependent on records full of omissions and silences and on testimonies refracted through faulty memories and calculation. (5–6)

The "truth" of what really happened in any separation or divorce case remains elusive because the versions of events presented by husband and wife are necessarily biased and adversarial. Moreover, their testimony is shaped and filtered by their lawyers, whose political and religious convictions and personal sensibilities tend to affect their presentation of cases. To win their suits, lawyers do not hesitate to distort the facts. When a judicial memoir was chosen for publication in a collection like Des Essarts's, further distortions were introduced by the editor's choice of excerpts and his commentary on the relative merits of the lawyers' arguments. When both sides of a case are presented, one has a better chance of understanding what went wrong in the marriage. But the truth is harder to uncover when only one spouse's side of the story is given or is strongly favored over the other (as in the judicial memoirs of individual lawyers or in some of Des Essarts's accounts). What emerges is at best an approximation of the truth.

Beyond the issue of veracity, there is the even thornier question of representativity and norms: To what extent are the cases in my course — or in any study — representative of prevailing attitudes and practices in the courts and in the private lives of couples? While it would be presumptuous to suggest that a handful of lawsuits can provide a comprehensive picture of the norms of the period, they do offer a representative sampling. Ranging in date from 1757 to 1805, the court cases involve couples from different social classes and regions of France exhibiting a variety of types of problems and abuse. Together, these six cases point to general shifts in attitudes, laws, and legal standards over the second half of the eighteenth century concerning the appropriate behavior of husbands toward wives. The four cases from Des Essarts's *Causes célèbres* (and various other cases we discuss in connection with them) reflect a gradual liberalization in attitudes and legal standards over the last five decades of the century. In contrast, Bellart's memoirs in the de l'Orme and Mandonnet cases reflect the conservative backlash against the progressive divorce law passed in 1792 and partially repealed in 1803 under pressure from Napoléon's conservative Catholic supporters.

Fictional Works

In the third part of the course, we explore how the issues of marital discord and spousal abuse foregrounded in these court cases are projected into the realm of fiction. To better understand the higher expectations for marital happiness that developed during the second half of the eighteenth century, I begin by having students read excerpts from Rousseau's novel *Julie, ou la Nouvelle Héloïse*, the first major literary work in French extolling companionate marriage. We then read two epistolary novels that challenge the ideal of companionate marriage set forth by Rousseau: Isabelle de Charrière's *Lettres de Mistress Henley* (1784; *Letters from Mistress Henley*) and excerpts from the autobiographical novel *Histoire de Madame de Montbrillant* ("The Story of Madame de Montbrillant"), by Louise Tardieu d'Esclavelles, marquise d'Épinay, published posthumously but written in the late 1750s. In a series of letters to a friend, Mrs. Henley seeks to explain her dissatisfaction with her marriage to a man whom others consider the ideal husband. Although he is in no way abusive, the incompatibility of their temperaments and views on parenting is a source of growing tension between them, which Mr. Henley chooses to ignore. As the birth of their first child approaches, Mrs. Henley's dissatisfaction gradually gives way to unhappiness and eventually to despair.

The conflicts in Mme de Montbrillant's marriage are more overt. D'Épinay's heroine ardently believes in the Christian ideal of conjugal fidelity and the newly evolving bourgeois ideal of domesticity that together were to find their most powerful expression in Rousseau's novel *Julie*. Her husband, on the other hand, belongs to the generation of financiers who attempt to rival the lifestyle of the French aristocracy through ostentatious spending and by publicly flaunting their affairs with richly kept courtesans. The incompatibility of the couple's views on marriage and family life soon becomes evident through the husband's flagrant love affairs, his virtual abandonment of his wife and their children, and his financial irresponsibility. Because of her husband's negligence, Mme de Montbrillant often finds herself unable to meet basic household expenses. After trying in vain to revive her husband's affections, she finally separates from him when he knowingly infects her with venereal disease. Only with the help of her father-in-law is she able to obtain a legal separation to protect her meager dowry and her children's inheritance. Drawn from her own experiences, d'Épinay's novel strikingly illustrates the legal and financial dependence of married women, even among those of the wealthiest and most prominent families.

We then read excerpts from two other epistolary novels by French women writers of the period. Like d'Épinay, Marie-Jeanne Riccoboni and Françoise de Graffigny both separated from abusive husbands. These experiences had a decisive influence on their development as writers and are clearly reflected in the stories they chose to tell. The earliest writings we have of Graffigny are three desperate letters to her father in which she begs him to save her from her husband's brutal beatings and to help her obtain a legal separation. In her best-selling novel *Lettres d'une Péruvienne* (1747; *Letters from a Peruvian Woman*), Graffigny reflects on the duplicity of faithless lovers, the injustice of the double standard, and the plight of women whose dowries are squandered by libertine husbands who mistreat and scorn them. Similarly, Riccoboni drew on the painful experiences in her marriage to give depth and poignancy to the heroines of her novels, which all deal in one way or another with the betrayal of women by the men they love. In *Lettres d'Adélaide de Dammartin, Comtesse de Sancerre* (1767; "Letters from Adélaide de Dammartin, Countess of Sancerre"), Riccoboni recounts the story of a woman who marries for love and then discovers that her husband had married her only for money and was involved in a long-standing affair. When she insists on a separation, he retaliates by turning family and friends against her through slander and innuendo to protect his financial interests. For Riccoboni and Graffigny, as for d'Épinay and Charrière, the decision to become a writer constituted a courageous act of self-affirmation in a period in which women writers were often mocked and scorned. Their writings constituted both a form of therapy and a means of protest against the condition of their female contemporaries—particularly the failure of society to protect women from abusive husbands.

Our exploration of marital discord and spousal abuse in eighteenth-century French fiction concludes with three fictional works (two written by men, one by a woman) based on true stories. The first two are gothic tales about women imprisoned by jealous husbands who unjustly accuse them of adultery: "Histoire de la Duchesse de C***" ("The Duchess of

C's Story"), by Stéphanie-Félicité Du Crest, comtesse de Genlis, embedded in her 1782 novel *Adèle et Théodore,* and the second-to-last novel of Donatien-Alphonse-François, marquis de Sade, *La Marquise de Gange,* published in 1813. Genlis's tale concerns a woman secretly confined by her husband for nine years in a dungeon under his palace after he drugs her and simulates her death and burial. In a footnote, Genlis explains that this is a true story based on the experiences of the Italian Duchess of Cerifalco [Girifalco], whom Genlis met in Rome in 1776—a meeting Genlis describes in her memoirs. Sade's novel, based on a famous 1667 court case, tells the story of a wealthy heiress held prisoner in her husband's castle and eventually murdered at his bidding by his two younger brothers. In contrast to the affectionate, harmonious family relations idealized in the sentimental novels of the period, gothic tales such as Genlis's and Sade's present abusive family relationships—a denaturing and defamiliarization of what the sentimental novel represents as natural and familiar. This defamiliarization of the familiar is particularly characteristic of gothic tales of conjugal violence, in which the husband, under the sway of jealousy or avarice, suddenly turns into a monster, transforming his home into a prison and the marriage into a waking nightmare. The gothic is, in a sense, the flip side of the sentimental novel—its seamy underside. The last work, Nicolas-Edme Rétif de La Bretonne's novel *Ingénue Saxancour,* is a thinly veiled account of his daughter's disastrous marriage. Published in 1789, Rétif's novel scandalized the public with its graphic descriptions of his son-in-law's sexual perversity and brutal violence. The novel remains shocking even two centuries later and continues to raise disturbing questions about power relations in abusive relationships.

All three novels are fictionalized versions of real-life events and, as such, provide insight into how incidents of spousal abuse were viewed and depicted in early modern France. Based on historical fact, these novels—like the court cases we examine—raise intriguing questions about the accuracy of the accounts they provide and the extent to which the marriages they depict were typical of the period. Whether partly or purely fictional, novels tend to feature larger-than-life characters and stories that are out of the ordinary. To a lesser extent, the same may be true of judicial memoirs, in which character traits and events are often exaggerated for polemical purposes. These distortions and magnifications are revealing in themselves. By drawing attention to what people perceived as abnormal and reprehensible, novels and judicial memoirs describing spousal abuse can tell us much about what was considered normal and acceptable.

In recent years, there has been much discussion among literary critics of the differences between male and female writing, whether in reference to the sex of the main characters or that of the authors. By comparing Sade's and Rétif's novels with Genlis's text, we explore how the sex of the author may influence the development of character, plot, tone, and narrative point of view. The comparison of these three texts ties in well with the comparison of Rousseau's *Julie* with the novels by Charrière and d'Épinay.

Stylistic Similarities between Judicial Memoirs and Fictional Works

In the final weeks of class, we further probe the connections between life and literature by comparing how spousal abuse is depicted in the novels and court cases and by delving more deeply into the stylistic parallels between these fictional works and judicial memoirs. Despite marked differences in genre, target audience, and the interests at stake in judicial memoirs and works of fiction, the narrative techniques and rhetorical devices used in the two kinds of texts are often strikingly similar. A trial lawyer's success, much like that of a novelist or dramatist, depends largely on his ability to tell a compelling story and to anticipate the reactions of his audience—his opponent, the courts, the legal community, the press, and the public. Indeed, the law is very much about conflicting stories molded into competing narratives by lawyers and submitted to the critical judgment of the judges, who must then produce a master narrative that will be retold and reinterpreted by legal commentators and by lawyers in subsequent cases.

To help convince the presiding judges to rule in favor of their clients, lawyers employed narrative devices (such as repetition, foreshadowing, and flashbacks) and various rhetorical styles (such as melodrama, sarcasm, and pathos) found in the novels and plays of the period. The use of these techniques is especially clear in the memoirs published for the wives in the Blé, Mézières, and de la Berge separation cases, which feature melodramatic tableaux and third-person narrative. Using the stock characters of the gothic and sentimental genres—virtuous heroine in distress, tyrannical husband, evil in-laws, devoted mother, faithful servant—these memoirs underscore the victimization of the plaintiffs by unscrupulous and abusive husbands. Like fiction writing, the composition of legal briefs was (and still is) highly self-conscious in the choice of tone and language. Like novelists, lawyers tend to both identify with and distance themselves from their subjects to present their story as effectively as possible. For example, in his judicial memoir for the marquise de Mézières, Delacroix switched to first-person confessional style and interjected dramatic dialogue in certain key passages, adopting his client's voice in an effort to appeal to the judges' compassion, but then returned to third-person narrative for most of his brief (Des Essarts, "Cause" [Mézières]). We find this same critical distance in Victor Avoyne de Chantereyne's portrayal of Mme Aubailly de La Berge's weakness and gullibility in dealing with her equally unscrupulous husband (Des Essarts, "Cause" [Aubailly de La Berge]). At times, both lawyers seem to be at pains to explain why these women stayed so long in abusive, life-threatening relationships. Through the artful use of melodrama, pathos, and other narrative devices drawn from popular fiction, they succeeded in overcoming the judges' skepticism and gaining a favorable outcome.

Besides being a carefully structured presentation of legal arguments and evidence, a trial lawyer's plea in a separation suit is a dramatic performance in which vivid human stories are played out, with momentous consequences for the spouses and their family. As Paul Gewirtz has observed, dramatic storytelling of this kind can help outsider groups such as women and minorities break through institutional barriers:

> Telling stories (rather than simply making arguments) . . . has a distinctive power to challenge and unsettle the legal status quo, because stories give uniquely vivid representation to particular voices, perspectives, and experiences of victimization traditionally . . . ignored when shaping legal rules. (5)

Through the engagement and empathy it generates, effective storytelling can win over an audience of insiders—judges, lawmakers, and legal commentators—who might be difficult to persuade otherwise. By giving voice to the concrete experiences of marginalized communities or individuals, such narratives can serve as a vehicle of dissent from mainstream legal thinking and a means of reform.

Just as lawyers often imitated the style and rhetoric used in the popular fiction of the day, so too novelists sometimes adopted the rhetorical techniques and legalistic language of jurists for dramatic effect. For example, we consider how in both Genlis's "Histoire de la Duchesse de C***" and Sade's *Marquise de Gange* the heroine is subjected to a summary trial in which her husband confronts her with evidence of her alleged adultery and then orders her to defend herself against his accusations. As is often the case in gothic tales, however, the trial serves not as a means for the accused to defend herself but as a way for the accuser to justify the punishment he has decided on in advance.

The Personal Is the Political

Feminist scholarship and pedagogy have played an important role in rescuing the seemingly trivial and marginal from obscurity and in bringing down conceptual barriers that traditionally have marked the divide between different realms of human experience. As Sarah Maza observes:

> Feminist thought has challenged us to rethink the division between public and private life and to question our society's implicit privileging of the public realm as the arena in which the really *important* things happen. (318)

While we tend today to separate the legal and political (the realm of reality and rationality) from the literary and familial (the realm of imagination and emotion), "eighteenth-century writers, including the authors of *mémoires judiciaires*, postulated the existence of an intimate connection between political norms (*la loi*) and social values (*les mœurs*)" (318).

The connection between public and private, *la loi* and *les mœurs*, the legal and the literary serves as a unifying theme in my course—a kind of *fil conducteur* through the labyrinth of our readings and discussions. In our study of troubled marriages in eighteenth-century France, we examine how accounts of spousal abuse in different types of texts vary in tone and perspective depending on the target audience and form adopted. But we also explore the similarities in style and content among these different kinds of texts. The success of judicial memoirs and causes célèbres collections depended in large part on their authors' ability to effectively employ narrative devices and various rhetorical styles and techniques found in popular novels and plays of the period. Lawyers used these literary techniques not only to help persuade the courts to rule in favor of their clients but also to convince the public—*le tribunal de la nation*—of the righteousness of their cause and the need for legal reform. This purpose was particularly true in the area of marital law, since judicial memoirs were, aside from plays and novels, one of the few ways that abuses in marriage could be brought to the public's attention.

The different accounts of spousal abuse we examine in this course point to the dynamic interplay among literature, law, and society. These interconnections are by no means clear-cut, however, and raise a number of intriguing questions: Did novels and judicial memoirs have any direct effect on social mores? Did women's lot improve as a result? Or did the condition of women improve primarily in response to changes in political and legal structures, such as passage of the divorce law and more egalitarian property laws in the early years of the French Revolution? There is evidence, for example, that by enabling women to leave troubled marriages, the legalization of divorce in 1792 led to a decline in marital discord and spousal abuse, whereas the law's partial repeal in 1803 under Napoléon and its total repeal in 1816 under the Bourbon restoration led to an increase in discord and abuse.

The effect of novels and judicial memoirs on attitudes and behaviors was no doubt less direct and more gradual. In the years leading up to the 1789 Revolution, debate intensified over the questions of what constituted acceptable behavior in marriage, whether the grounds for separation should be expanded, and if divorce should be permitted. Novels, judicial memoirs, and collections of causes célèbres played an important role in this debate by articulating the public implications of private conflicts and domestic abuses. By calling into question inequalities and abuses in marriage sanctioned by law and custom, novelists and jurists helped raise public awareness of these problems. They pointed to the pervasiveness of wife battering and other forms of spousal abuse across social classes as evidence of the need for a divorce law or more liberal separation laws that would permit otherwise defenseless women to escape brutal husbands. By politicizing the private and personalizing the political, these accounts of marital discord and spousal abuse had a significant impact on public opinion and served as an impetus for legal reform in the early years of the French Revolution. By bringing the traditionally private matter of spousal abuse into the public arena, these literary and legal texts began the arduous process of consciousness raising in which we are still engaged today.

Notes

1. All translations from the French are mine unless otherwise noted.

2. The Blé case is also available in Des Essarts on *Gallica* and, abridged with notes and commentary, in Vissière 269–84.

3. The Mézières case is also available, abridged with notes and commentary, in Vissière 225–45.

4. The Rouches case is available in microfiche from the Bibliothèque Nationale de France (MFICHE F-30961).

5. The Aubailly de La Berge case is also available in microfiche from the Bibliothèque Nationale de France (MFICHE F-31014).

Thomas M. Carr, Jr.

Convent Writing in Eighteenth-Century France

Although in Hispanic studies Teresa of Ávila and Juana Inéz de la Cruz have achieved canonical status (see Weber; Bergmann and Schlau), French nuns of the same period have been the province of historians or specialists in spirituality. Only the sixteenth-century poet Anne de Marquets and the Canadian missionary Marie de l'Incarnation have received recognition from literary scholars. For the last two decades, Hispanists such as Electa Arenal and Stacey Schlau (*Untold Sisters*) and Kathleen Ann Myers ("Crossing" and *Neither Saints*) have been engaged in rescuing the writings by the sisters of their two canonical nuns. In French studies, where the canonical women writers are laywomen, similar efforts have been directed at recovering women novelists, playwrights, and memorialists. Thus designing an early modern French literature course that includes nuns is almost as difficult as envisaging a Golden Age course without them. Of the fifteen authors anthologized in Bárbara Mujica's 2004 *Women Writers of Early Modern Spain: Sophia's Daughters*, seven are nuns.

Just the same, because my research has recently focused on ancien régime convent writing, I have made efforts to incorporate texts by nuns in my courses. In a survey of Canadian literature, selections of the letters of Marie de l'Incarnation (*Correspondance*) proved more effective as firsthand accounts of the colonial period than the extracts of the Jesuit relations I had previously used. In a thematic introduction to literature course, I taught Héloïse's letters to Abélard and sonnets by Anne de Marquets as texts by learned women, along with the memoirs of Marie-Jeanne Philipon Roland and Simone de Beauvoir.

The real challenge has been to work convent writing into my upper-level courses on the eighteenth-century novel and theater in a substantial way. As I considered options, I realized that many canonical texts already had convent episodes. This common characteristic probably reflects the increasingly realistic stance of eighteenth-century fiction: treating the convent was inescapable for writers of the period. The two respectable options for upper-class women at the time — entering a convent or marrying — can serve as the basis for an entire course. Furthermore, historians such as Elizabeth Rapley (*Social History*), Barbara B. Diefendorf (*From Penitence*), and Gwénaël Murphy have pointed toward a balanced view of the convent, which long had been treated either with extreme piety by apologists for the church or with the distaste that stemmed from the philosophes' campaigns against monasticism. Whence the organizing principle for the course I describe here: marriage or the convent.

This configuration leaves aside much valuable convent writing. Paul Scott's edition of La Chapelle's *L'Illustre Philosophe* makes available an example of convent theater, which seems to have been much less developed in France than in Italy, where Renaissance nuns published and performed religious plays. During the ancien régime, nuns were expected to eschew doctrinal controversy and largely did. The nuns of Port-Royal were the principal exception. The writings of Jacqueline Pascal, translated and introduced by John J. Conley, illustrate how theological issues became a source of personal anguish for a committed Jansenist. The examples of the routine convent preaching by three Port-Royal abbesses in my *Voix des abbesses* largely avoid doctrine in favor of the spirituality of ascetic monastic life. Samples of how to organize courses dealing with nuns around religious issues can be found in *Teaching Other Voices: Women and Religion in Early Modern Europe*, edited by Margaret L. King and Albert Rabil, Jr.

For my course, I revised the list of major literary texts to be studied to add a broader view of both the convent and the institution of marriage. Even though the portrait of convent life in *Les Lettres portugaises* is slight (Guilleragues), the novel is a must in this context. Instead of a *drame bourgeois* from the period of the high Enlightenment, I opted for Olympe de Gouges's thesis play *La Nécessité du divorce*, which was paired with selections from the relation of the Carmelite martyrs of Compiègne on which Francis Poulenc's opera *Dialogues des Carmélites* is based (Josephine-Marie de l'Incarnation). Just as divorce was in no way the end of marriage that some predicted, so the convent dissolutions under the Revolution were hardly the death of religious life for women. Beginning with Napoléon's reign, female religious orders were reborn in the nineteenth century at a rate even more accelerated than during the heyday of the Counter-Reformation in the first half of the seventeenth century. Finally, selections from Mme Roland's *Mémoires* are particularly valuable for their ability to offer an in-depth portrayal of various aspects of the life of an eighteenth-century woman. Roland recounts many of the experiences an eighteenth-century woman might know: sexual harassment, life in a convent boarding school, the negotiations of family and friends to find a suitable marriage partner, motherhood, and even finding passion with a man not her husband.

I chose texts by nuns that specifically complement the novels and plays. These texts resonate with some feature of the literary texts so that a nun's point of view can be contrasted with a point of view in the play or novel. Although literary works may leave aside much of real-life marital experience, fiction and the theater permit us to assess the expectations and social practices that surrounded marriage (see Trouille in this volume). Those characters who reject marriage — one thinks especially of the many seducers in libertine works — do so in the name of emotional or sensual pleasure that is antithetical to monastic life. Yet the values that underlie the convent are seldom presented positively in literature, where happiness is equated with worldly success, love, and passion.

The life path of a woman through marriage or the religious life is the organizing principle of this course. The first two texts, Robert Challe's "Histoire de Monsieur de Terny et de Mademoiselle de Bernay" from *Les Illustres Françaises* and Pierre Marivaux's *Le Jeu de l'amour et du hasard*, show the weight of parental pressure by contrasting a tyrannical father with an indulgent one. They are followed by Antoine-François Prévost's *Manon Lescaut* and *Les Lettres portugaises* (Guilleragues), where the lovers' very different expectations frustrate any desire for marriage. Denis Diderot's *La Religieuse*, narrated by Suzanne, a heroine who professes to be a devout Christian, details all the horrors that can befall a woman who is victim of a forced vocation. I use Pierre-Augustin Caron de Beaumarchais's *Le Mariage de Figaro* to illustrate the woes that novice mistresses congratulated their charges for avoiding by choosing virginity over marriage; the countess's libertine husband neglects her, and Marceline is an unwed mother. The last two works in the course, de Gouges's play and the Carmelite relation, feature the transformations the Revolution made in marriage and the convent: the introduction of divorce and the abolition of monastic vows. Roland's memoir, though written after the other texts we study, narrates her life from 1754 to 1793, and so I place it just before *La Religieuse* on the syllabus, to serve as a transition to the second half of the century.

My examples of convent writing roughly parallel a nun's life course as well. The account of Judith Moreau de Brésoles's (1620–87) vocation shows the numerous obstacles that young girls had to overcome to become nuns, not the least of which was parental objections (Morin). Marie-Madeleine de Saint-Stanislas's (1704?–60) narrative of her travels to New Orleans illustrates how the active orders of the teaching and nursing nuns became more prominent than the older ones devoted exclusively to prayer. The meditations of the Canadian missionary Marie de l'Incarnation (1599–1672) give students a taste of the prayer life of the devout nun. The letters of Anne-Julie Fraisse (1700–75?) offer an intimate view of affectionate bonds between nuns and their boarders (Coquerel). Angélique de Saint-Jean's (1624–84) captivity narrative portrays a nun standing up valiantly to the kind of pressure commonly brought by ecclesiastical superiors against nuns judged defiant. Finally, the Carmelites' similar refusal to conform to male requirements—this time those of revolutionary authorities—ends in real martyrdom (Josephine-Marie de l'Incarnation).

Anachronistic views that students are likely to hold on ancien régime marriage and on convent life must be dealt with. Students take for granted that marriage should be based on romantic passion. Their idea of convent life is formed by their experience of parochial schools or popular culture. Although some films such as *The Bells of Saint Mary's* and *Dead Man Walking* show nuns as strong women, others such as *Sister Act* portray them as incompetent, or even sadistic, as in *Agnes of God* and *The Magdalene Sisters*. The notion that passion is inimical to a successful marriage or that a conjugal union is an alliance of families is as foreign to students as the way the cloister limited a nun's contact with the outside world or the daily communal recitation of the divine office structured convent life. The absence of divorce and monastic enclosure make both marriage and convent life seem prisonlike to students. Here judiciously placed lectures and readings can initiate students to these realities. Dominique Godineau is particularly good on changes in marriage patterns. Diefendorf describes the wave of convent creation in the seventeenth century (*From Penitence*), and Rapley's *A Social History of the Cloister* provides a nuanced view of the patterns of convent life attuned to class and changes in the economy.

Since other essays in this volume treat marriage extensively (see esp. Trouille), I concentrate here on how the selected texts by nuns complement the novels and plays and bring to life the convent experience. The first nun narrative contrasts with Challe's dramatic tale of a young woman's rescue from a forced vocation imposed by her selfish father. Such extreme violence to a girl's wishes was, in fact, rare. More frequent was a subtle conditioning of girls destined to the cloister by their family. Parents placed the young girl in a convent boarding school at an early age; family expectations and the girl's experience of convent life converged in a vocation. Convent chronicles, on the other hand, highlight the heroic determination of girls who resisted parental opposition to their vocation (Diefendorf, "Give"). Marie Morin's (1649–1730) account of the vocation of Judith Moreau de Brésoles in the annals of the Hôtel-Dieu of Montreal has as many plot twists as Challe's tale (162–74). Judith was the favorite child of her wealthy and influential parents in Blois, who were distressed to learn that "cette amazone chrétienne" 'this Christian Amazon' wanted to become not only a nun but a lowly hospital one (162).[1] With the help of her confessor, Judith escaped from her parents' home at dawn and made her way secretly to La Flèche. Along the way, she stayed in convents that resembled stops of an underground railroad. She eventually became the superior of a hospital in Laval before leaving for Canada. The memoirs of Antoinette Micolon (1592–1659), who founded six Ursuline convents in Auvergne, also illustrate how determined nuns resorted to subterfuge, in conflicts not just with parents but also with secular and ecclesiastical authorities. Linda Lierheimer's bilingual edition *The Life of Antoinette Micolon* is particularly student-friendly.

Prévost's Manon Lescaut asserts to Des Grieux that her parents are sending her to Amiens to become a nun. Whether this is true or whether her parents were making use of the convent as a place of confinement and rehabilitation for wayward girls and wives, the claim permits Des Grieux to cast himself in the heroic role of saving Manon from a forced vocation. The convent text chosen to accompany the novel, however, complements its Louisiana episode. In 1728, just three years before *Manon Lescaut*'s publication in 1731, the travel narrative of eleven Ursulines who had crossed the Atlantic the previous year to found a hospital and school in New Orleans appeared in Rouen (Marie-Madeleine). Prévost only suggests the dangers of the crossing—including the threat of capture by pirates—in his brief account of his friend Tiberge's travels. For Des Grieux, the voyage is a delight since the captain allows him to be with Manon. Likewise Prévost's description of New Orleans is spare. The nuns, on the other hand, recount the hardships of the ocean journey and the laborious trip in a dug-out canoe up the Mississippi and describe the city's layout, buildings, and inhabitants. More pertinent to the convent theme is discussion of the new orders, such as the Ursulines, founded after the Council of Trent that emphasized service but still prescribed leading a cloistered life.

Compared with Suzanne in *La Religieuse*, the Portuguese nun in *Les Lettres portugaises* hardly invokes the routines of her convent life in Beja. Indeed, one can ask students how essential the monastic setting is to this painful display of unrequited passion. Despite Frédéric Deloffre's identification of Gabriel Joseph de Lavergne, comte de Guilleragues, as the novel's author (93), questions of voice continually resurface. Could only a woman have written these letters? Are they translations or adaptations of letters written by the real nun Mariana Alcoforado? Volker Schröder has shown that the Portuguese nun transposes into the register of romantic love forms of mental prayer made popular in seventeenth-century France by translations of Teresa of Ávila's works. Especially in the early letters, one finds traces of the recommended pattern of meditation that moves from preparatory invocations, through considerations of some religious truth, toward practical resolutions and an emotional response. Furthermore, meditation involves two forms of enunciation: an interior dialogue of self-examination and a dialogue of invocation, praise, and contrition directed toward God (284–97). Jacques Bénigne Bossuet acknowledged Marie de l'Incarnation as "la Thérèse de nos jours et du nouveau monde" 'the Saint Teresa of our day and of the New World' (343). Selections from her "Exclamations et elévations," "Entretien spirituel sur l'épouse des Cantiques" ("Spiritual Discussion on the Spouse of the Canticles"), and "Retraite de dix jours" ("Ten-Day Retreat") from volume 1 of her *Écrits spirituels et historiques*, give students examples of this form of prayer, which rivaled the traditional singing of the office among seventeenth-century nuns, and allow students to explore the parallels that Schröder has identified between the Portuguese nun's letters and mental prayer.

Many texts by nuns could accompany Roland's description in *Mémoires* of her year in a convent boarding school. Secretly Roland hoped to become a nun, but, aware that her parents would not consent, she gave as a pretext for her stay the need to prepare her First Communion (339). Convents were widely criticized even in the eighteenth century

for not giving girls a sound intellectual grounding and for not preparing them for life in the world. (Zilia's pointed critique in Graffigny's *Les
Lettres d'une Péruvienne* comes to mind, among others.) Thus Roland's
complaint she already knew what the nuns claimed to be teaching her is
not surprising (341), although it could reflect the admirable education
she had received at home, as much as the deficiency of the convent's curriculum. Pascal's *Règlement pour les enfants* (*A Rule for Children*) for the
boarding school at Port-Royal could be used to explore the priority given
to moral and spiritual formation over intellectual development in women's
education.

Instead, I prefer to develop a more cordial aspect of boarding school
life, focusing on the affectionate relationship Roland had with two nuns:
the choir sister Sainte-Sophie and the lay sister Angélique Boufflers, who
became a true friend. A collection of letters written by the Visitation nun
Anne-Julie Fraisse to Anne (Nanette) Calas shows the affectionate bonds
that could develop between the nuns and their wards (Coquerel). Nanette
was no ordinary boarder; she was in her early twenties when she was placed
in a Toulouse convent by royal order after her father, Jean Calas, accused
of murdering his son to prevent his conversion to Catholicism, was con-
victed, tortured, and executed. Unlike the painful experience of most
Protestant girls sent to convents to convert them, Nanette met a kindly
nun who became, according to the editor of the correspondence, "une
seconde mère" 'a second mother' to the young woman (Coquerel 312).
Quickly convinced of the innocence of the father, Anne-Julie solicited a
relative who was the son-in-law of Chancellor Guillaume de Lamoignon
on behalf of the family's appeal. Voltaire had the letter printed: "La sim-
plicité, la vertueuse indulgence de cette nonne de la Visitation, condamne
terriblement le fanatisme sanguinaire des assassins de Toulouse en robe"
'The simplicity and virtuous tolerance of this nun of the Visitation absolutely condemn the bloody fanaticism of the murderers in judicial robes
of Toulouse' (Letter). The nun's maternal instincts inform every letter
but are no where more apparent than when, on learning that Nanette is
pregnant, Anne-Julie suggests that the baby be named Anne or Julie if it
is a girl (431). To be sure, she entertains hopes that Nanette will convert.
But when the girl refuses, the nun assures Nanette that she respects her
frankness and integrity (422).

Reading extracts from Angélique de Saint-Jean's captivity narrative
with *La Religieuse* makes it clear that the tactics used to bring Suzanne to
submission in Longchamp were often used against nuns judged recalcitrant
by male ecclesiastics. Depriving nuns of the sacraments, deposing convent

officers, and exiling nuns to other houses or even convent prisons were not unheard of. Huguette Cohen has suggested that Diderot was thinking of the persecutions of the Port-Royal nuns in the mid seventeenth century and of eighteenth-century Jansenist nuns who refused to accept the papal bull *Unigenitus*. While Suzanne was defending her right to control her liberty, Angélique de Saint-Jean saw herself as a witness for the "truths" of Cornelius Jansenius's interpretation of grace. Just as Jeanne de Jussie (1503–61) recounts in her *Petite Chronique* (*Short Chronicle*) how she stood up to Protestant reformers in Geneva, Angélique portrays herself as victorious in theological debates on questions of grace and church authority (46–59), while being tempted with despair (60–68). Unlike Suzanne, who struggled to control her personal destiny, Angélique knew she had to remain true to her sister nuns at Port-Royal, who looked to her as a model.

The last example of convent writing, Josephine-Marie de l'Incarnation's *La Relation du martyre des seize carmélites de Compiègne* ("Account of the Martyrdom of Sixteen Carmelites of Compiègne"), is paired with de Gouges's *La Nécessité du divorce*, less as a supplement than a complement. *La Relation* illustrates admirably the transformation of the nun in public opinion from victim to counterrevolutionary fanatic, a transformation that Mita Choudhury has traced. The text itself is relatively short (forty-five pages in William Bush's edition) and also fragmentary. For this reason, I use it with Poulenc's *Dialogues des Carmélites*. The trial scene allows us to see how the revolutionary tribunal interpreted the nuns' rejection of the constitutional church as a dangerous act of treason. It also foregrounds a little-known aspect of convent culture: the writing of verse and hymns. While it is true, as in Poulenc's opera, that the nuns sang Latin chants on their way to the scaffold, the night before their execution one of them wrote a pious version of the "Marseillaise" to strengthen their resolve. Students can compare the chorus to the first stanza in this version with Claude-Joseph Rouget de Lisle's:

> Ranimons notre ardeur,
> Nos corps sont au Seigneur,
> Montons, montons à l'échafaud
> Et Dieu sera vainqueur (Josephine-Marie de l'Incarnation 111)

> Let us rekindle our ardor
> Our bodies belong to the Lord
> Let us ascend the scaffold
> And God will conquer

By presenting the configuration of this particular course, I hope to alert readers to the fascinating variety of nuns' voices that is available. (Approximately two hundred are included in my "Checklist.") We may not identify another Teresa of Ávila among them as we explore French convent writing, but we will certainly find many authors who can engage our students.

Note

1. All translations from the French are mine unless otherwise noted.

Suzan van Dijk

Female Variations on the Novel as Appreciated by Male Readers: Graffigny, Riccoboni, Charrière

The French eighteenth-century novel has been termed "feminocentric" (May 209; Fauchery 11; Miller, *French Dressing* 148)—a designation that must be seen in relation to the roles played by female characters in the novels, as reflected in many titles. Titles referring to women, such as *Les Illustres Françaises*, *La Religieuse,* or *La Nouvelle Héloïse*, are more common than those naming male figures, such as *Le Paysan parvenu* or the later *Adolphe* or *Le Père Goriot*. Some male authors of feminocentric works have even been considered as feminist *avant la lettre*; an example is Pierre Marivaux, the author of *La Vie de Marianne*, because of his theatrical work *La Colonie*. Usually, however, feminism is far removed from feminocentricity, as has been illustrated—intentionally or otherwise—by Pierre Fauchery. In his impressive study, *La Destinée féminine dans le roman européen* ("Women's Destiny in the European Novel"), women authors play a minor role, particularly for French literature: 38 French women novelists are included as opposed to 115 male novel writers. These proportions correspond, more or less, to Aurora Wolfgang's calculation that the average percentage of prose fiction published by women was about fifteen percent (*Gender* 8). However, German and English female novelists seem to have been relatively more numerous. Fauchery mentions 30 female versus

64 male German novelists and even 63 female versus 43 male English novelists (93–113). According to statistics presented by Angus Martin, "of all European countries, France produced (and exported) the most prose fiction" (103, 109).

But Fauchery's numbers are deceptive. If one looks at the names beginning with *B*, for example, minor women novelists such as Beauharnais, Benoist, Bodin de Boismortier, Boisgiroux, and Brayer de St. Léon are not mentioned, whereas equally minor (or even less significant) male writers such as Baret, Barrin, and Bernard are included in Fauchery's book. French women novelists are not only inadequately represented but also denied originality and presented as mere imitators of male initiative with regard to women's representation in fiction; some are even portrayed as narcissistic autobiographers (93).

Since Fauchery's study, a vast corpus of European women writers has been uncovered. According to the database for the project *New Approaches to European Women Writers*, there were 244 European women authors born between 1675 and 1775 alone (van Dijk, *Women Writers*). Further examination needs to be given to the number and gender of the readers of women writers and to the way in which they address their readership. Particularly intriguing is the question of feminocentricity in relation to female authorship. This question needs to be analyzed in comparison with male authors, whose example they might be supposed to have followed or been inspired by, and also with the reactions of male readers to these female novels. Indeed, many women engaged in dialogue with male authors, responding to propositions that their male counterparts presented in novel form and producing their own variations.

In this essay I would like to stress the interaction between female writers and male readers and focus on three major women novelists. These women are clearly not imitating but responding and reacting to previous male novelistic production, using these works as a starting point for the presentation of their own perspective on situations that had been envisaged from the "opposite" side by their male colleagues. I have chosen novels by Françoise de Graffigny (1695–1758), Marie-Jeanne Riccoboni (1714–92), and Isabelle de Charrière (1740–1805) as examples to illustrate these debates.

I do not, however, juxtapose the male and corresponding female novel—the "reading in pairs" advocated by Nancy K. Miller (*French Dressing* 3–42)—but consider this initial dialogue as the beginning of an ongoing debate, which often did not stop at the women's novelistic reaction.

Publication of these novels provoked new interventions with new readers—be it in private correspondence, in newspapers where critics may have
tried to influence public opinion, or in novels written in response. What
particularly interests me is the possibility that in these subsequent writings
gender may have determined readers' reactions. Since discussing complete
novels within this framework is impossible—and seems unnecessary—I
focus on specific gender-sensitive points, corresponding to several narrative topoi, that is, formative elements in fiction studied in the context of
the Société pour l'Analyse de la Topique Romanesque (SATOR; see www
.satorbase.org). The cases proposed here are suitable for use as examples
for students, who might be invited to select similar topoi and proceed to
comparative analyses on other, yet-to-be-created corpuses.

The three women discussed here were not equally well known in their
day. Graffigny and Riccoboni are among the most read of all eighteenth-
century novel writers, Graffigny as the author of one successful novel, *Lettres
d'une Péruvienne* (1747, partly rewritten in 1752), and Riccoboni with a
series of shorter, often epistolary works, published from 1757 onward.
Charrière's publishing career started in the Netherlands in 1763 with the
short story "Le Noble," but Charrière really became an author after moving to Switzerland in 1771, issuing publications from 1784 onward. She
arguably achieved the most success in the late twentieth century, following
the publication of her ten-volume *Œuvres complètes* (1979–84). Wealthier
than Riccoboni, Charrière was not dependent on the money earned by
her pen. She accordingly did not strive for the large-scale distribution of
her works, which were highly appreciated by her *intimi* but may have
been ahead of their time in their characteristic conciseness. When writing
about the "destinée féminine," however, Fauchery did include two of her
novels in his corpus, as well as Graffigny's novel and those of Riccoboni.

These three women's reactions to writing by men show them, on the
production side of their works, to be well inserted in the literary field. In
private life they were also in frequent contact with male authors, often very
famous ones. Graffigny was part of the famous Société du Bout du Banc,
which included Marivaux, Philippe Destouches, Antoine de Fériol de
Pont-de-Veyle, and Anne-Claude-Philippe de Tubières-Grimoard, comte
de Caylus, and she lived for several years in Cirey, in the company of Voltaire and Gabrielle-Émilie Du Châtelet. Moreover, she had an intense and
lengthy correspondence with her friend the poet François-Antoine Devaux,
in which she discussed her creative processes. Riccoboni frequently visited
Denis Diderot, who proposed narrative solutions for some of her novels,

with which she did not always agree. Her letters to the English actor David Garrick, on the other hand, reflect the disillusion she felt at her shabby
treatment by her publishers. Much less of Riccoboni's correspondence has
survived than has that of Graffigny and Charrière. Charrière met Diderot
in her youth and indirectly knew Voltaire, whom she did not appreciate
much, through David-Louis de Constant d'Hermenches. At the end of
the century, Charrière became an intimate friend of Benjamin Constant,
twenty years younger than she. With Constant and her German translator,
Ludwig Ferdinand Huber, she also discussed the treatment of her fictional
characters.

At the same time, these women were eager to declare their debt to
female predecessors. Graffigny had made her choice early: "Si j'avais une
ambition, ce ne serait pas d'être Mme Deshoulières, mais bien Mme de la
Fayette" 'If I had an ambition, it would be to be not Mme Deshoulières
but Mme de LaFayette' (*Correspondance* 1: 70; letter 37, Oct. 1738).[1]
Riccoboni is more emphatic:

> Madame de la Fayette fut toujours ma maîtresse et mon guide;
> l'honneur d'approcher d'elle, de la suivre, même à quelque distance,
> est la louange que je voudrais mériter, et serait un prix bien flatteur
> pour mes faibles essais. (Letter)

> Madame de la Fayette was always my teacher and my guide; the honor
> of approaching her, of following her, even at a certain distance, is the
> praise I would want to deserve. It would be a flattering prize for my
> feeble essays.

Charrière, who has also been termed "la Sévigné de notre siècle" 'the
Sévigné of our century' (B. Bray), was most enthusiastic about Wilhelmina
of Bayreuth, particularly in her letters to Voltaire:

> Je suis si vaine pour mon sexe des lettres de la margrave de Bayreuth que
> je les lis à tout le monde. Je n'ai jamais rien vu d'une femme qui prouve
> aussi complètement que nous pouvons être tout ce que sont les hommes.
> (*Correspondance* 3: 115; letter to Chambrier d'Oleyres, 6 Dec. 1788)

> I am so proud, for my sex, of the letters of Wilhelmina that I am read-
> ing them to everyone. I have never seen any woman who proves so
> completely that we can be what men are.

Inspired by their female predecessors, these three authors were also
surrounded by women who wrote, who tried to write, or who merely
claimed to do so. Riccoboni's daily life was much enlivened by her friend

Marie Thérèse Biancolelli, who was a translator: "Sans mon amie j'irais me pendre" 'Without this friend I would hang myself' (Letter). When in Cirey, Graffigny continually mocks Mme de Champbonin, one of the writing friends of "le Monstre" 'the monster' (the nickname Graffigny uses to designate Mme Du Châtelet), reproaching Devaux for comparing her with one of Champbonin's fictional characters: "Tu es bien impertinent de me dire que je vaux mieux que Mlle Datilly. Sais-tu que les comparaisons sont des injures?" 'Pardi, you are really insolent when you say that I am worth more than Mlle Datilly. Do you realize that such comparisons are insults?' (*Correspondance* 6: 484–87; July 1745). Even before her marriage and departure from the Netherlands, Charrière had been surrounded by young women who wrote and claimed to be her intimate friends, such as Mlle de Kinschot, completely forgotten now, the author of a stage play. Although Charrière considers their supposed friendship simply ridiculous (*Correspondance* 2: 83; 28 Apr. 1768), the young woman's claim illustrates Charrière's position as a role model and possible initiator into the literary world. She would continue to play this role later in Switzerland, when she encouraged young friends to take up writing. She even wrote some works together with Isabelle de Gélieu.

As for the novelistic responses of these three women to male novel writing and to existing conventions, their variations on the novel genre, I start with the well-established and well-documented facts that Graffigny's *Lettres d'une Péruvienne* was written in response to Charles de Secondat, baron de Montesquieu's *Lettres persanes*; that Riccoboni provided *Suite de Marianne* to Marivaux's (unfinished) *Vie de Marianne*; and that Charrière responded to Samuel de Constant's *Mari sentimental* with her *Lettres de Mistriss Henley*. These three works, as well as others by the same women, represent a tendency toward feminism that has been much appreciated by modern feminists—too much so, one might argue, but it must be stated that this tendency is not only in the eyes of modern beholders. It seems quite explicit in some of the letters that Graffigny added to her 1752 edition of the *Lettres d'une Péruvienne* and was also a pervading presence in Riccoboni's and Charrière's writing. More prolific as novelists than Graffigny, both Riccoboni and Charrière often used female narrators to represent female perspectives that were in contrast to the male point of view predominant in other novels. This technique appears in Riccoboni's *Lettres de Milady Juliette Catesby* (where the epistolary narrator is of course explicitly presented as female) and *Histoire du Marquis de Cressy* (where it is only implicit) and in Charrière's *Lettres écrites de Lausanne*, which is in some respects an answer to Pierre Choderlos de Laclos's *Liaisons dangereuses* (and also to Stéphanie de Genlis's *Adèle et Théodore*). These parallels have been suggested or developed amply elsewhere. I focus here on the context of the reception of these works. How did contemporary readers react to the adoption of these female positions, to the use of feminocentricity by a woman, in a way that might today be interpreted as feminist?

I use here as sources male critics, contemporaries of these three women, who comment on several narrative topoi. The topoi concerned are the unfaithfulness of the male lover, the (final) marriage of the heroine, and the death of the heroine. These topoi are current elements of the eighteenth-century novel, included by Fauchery in his overview of female destiny. In their own variations, for reasons not always easy to elucidate, the three women novelists choose either to replace these elements with the opposite narrative solution or to comment on and attack the elements through a female character, who serves as a spokeswoman.

Graffigny and the *Péruvienne*

In her *Lettres d'une Péruvienne*, Graffigny chose to attack marriage, not only through the critical remarks delivered by the Peruvian Zilia in her observations of married couples in Paris, but also by countering the novelistic law of the final marriage. Zilia's shocked comments on women's destiny and what we might call her protofeminism are illustrated at the plot level at the end of the novel, when Déterville wants to marry her. While it seems clear that her fiancé in Peru, Aza, is unfaithful, Zilia refuses to accept her suitor's proposition of marriage and offers Déterville friendship instead.

Although in the previous century Marie-Madeleine Pioche de la Vergne, comtesse de Lafayette, may be said to have set the example of having a heroine refuse marriage, the eighteenth-century press did not agree with Graffigny and reproached her for Zilia's refusal to marry Déterville. It is not always clear whether the norms that are implicitly referred to are novelistic conventions or those concerning the required attitudes for women in real life. One reviewer for *Les Cinq Années littéraires* is explicit on this point: the importance of the final scene (the preference is for the death of the heroine) is in the effect obtained: "Il faut la tuer, afin qu'elle vous intéresse encore davantage" '[Zilia] must be killed, so that she becomes still more interesting to the reader' (Clément 17). According to Joseph de La Porte, author of *Observations sur la littérature moderne*, Zilia should have entered into Déterville's proposition, in particular because of his being French: "Toute autre qu'elle, pour s'en consoler, eût écouté favorablement les propositions de Déterville . . . d'ailleurs il n'y avait qu'un Français, qui fût digne d'un cœur comme celui de Zilia" 'Any other woman than she would have been favorable to Déterville's propositions, if only to find consolation; and besides, only a Frenchman would have been worthy of such a heart as Zilia's' (La Porte, rev. of *Lettres d'une Péruvienne* 49). The reference is here more clearly to the period's reality and to French society, and La Porte is rather prescriptive: Zilia, for example, should have been familiar with the language of love that is, after all, the same the world over (51). His severity is addressed more to Zilia than to the author, whose exceptional talents are approved and applauded (54).

La Porte's knowledge that the novel had been written by a woman, whom the critic would have known by reputation or in person, may have occasioned his favorable appraisal of the author even as he rejected her narrative choices.[2] For the two other women novelists and the two novels selected here, this problem did not arise: Riccoboni's *Lettres de Milady Juliette Catesby* (1759) and Charrière's *Lettres de Mistriss Henley* (1784) were both published anonymously, and although some readers certainly knew about their female authorship, the critics consulted seem not to have been aware, or at least not certain, of this fact. So the reactions occasioned by some of the narrative topoi were probably not greatly influenced by indignation at, or admiration of, this particular example of female authorship.

Riccoboni and Juliette Catesby

The eponymous heroine of Riccoboni's *Lettres de Milady Juliette Catesby* was clearly voicing female irritation at male attitudes, suggesting that the conduct of her beloved but unfaithful Milord d'Ossery was characteristic of the whole male sex. Juliette and d'Ossery had been betrothed, but after his sudden disappearance she discovered that he had married the younger sister of a friend. In letters to her young friend Henriette Campley she expresses her sadness and indignation. In subsequent letters Henriette and the reader learn that Juliette has received an explanation from d'Ossery himself: after an unplanned encounter in a dark corner of his friend's house, the girl had become pregnant, and d'Ossery had felt obliged to marry her. When, as a widower, he comes back to Juliette, she refuses to forgive him for quite a long time. To Henriette, she writes, "Cet infidèle n'a point d'idée des chagrins qu'il m'a donnés. . . . Mais un homme comprend-il les peines qu'il peut causer?" 'This unfaithful man has no idea of the grief he has caused me. . . . But does any man understand the pain he may inflict?' (92; letter 21). She considers that men,

> [e]sclaves de leurs sens, lorsqu'ils paraissent l'être de nos charmes, c'est pour eux qu'ils nous cherchent, qu'ils nous servent; ils ne considèrent en nous que les plaisirs qu'ils espèrent de goûter par nous.
> (97; letter 22)

> slaves of their senses, while pretending to be enslaved by our charms, seek us out and serve us only for their own benefit, and value in us only the pleasures they hope to experience through us.

In the series of letters written by Juliette to her young friend, she repeatedly insists on the impossibility of "pardonner" what she experiences as insults by d'Ossery: the word "pardon" occurs thirty-eight times, generally accompanied by words such as "impossibilité" or "refus" (van Dijk, "Pardonner"). It is true, however, that the message of this spokeswoman is blurred by the ending of the novel, in which the conventional marriage takes place, but, significantly, this marriage is announced to Henriette not by Juliette herself, but by d'Ossery's male voice.

This novel, which was to enjoy considerable international success, received positive reviews and commentary in France. Yet the way in which the critics, in their summaries, present the story and the characters leaves us in doubt about what has been judged with so much enthusiasm. It seems abusive of the critics to easily dismiss Juliette's fears and indignation, which dominate the first part of the novel, the period during which Juliette is left in complete uncertainty about the reasons for d'Ossery's conduct. This dismissal is directly related to the critics' summarizing the story by reestablishing the chronological order, reassuring their audience of d'Ossery's excellent motives and noble character and accusing Juliette of exaggerating her case. D'Ossery has not really been unfaithful; she has only imagined him to be so (rev. in *Mercure* 74; rev. in *Journal* 123).[3] The affair with young Miss Jenny that led to his first marriage was nothing more than a little "aventure de l'après-dînée" 'after-dinner adventure' (La Porte, rev. of *Lettres de Milady Juliette Catesby* 332). The implicit reference is not only to novelistic conventions but to real life, where the events described are considered "très communs" 'very common' (315) and "simple" (rev. in *Année* 300). Such reactions illustrate male tolerance toward other males' conduct. Juliette's steadfast refusal to pardon is almost eliminated in these critiques, and the word "pardon," which Riccoboni clearly considered crucial, only occurs in a positive sentence such as, "she finally forgives" (rev. in *Journal* 123). This phrasing implies, at least, a consciousness that there is a case for forgiveness. The same consciousness transpires in the supposition of female authorship, voiced by two critics: ("Aux . . . distinctions injustes qu'ils établissent entre les deux sexes, . . . on croira que l'Auteur de ces lettres est une femme"; 'when considering the unjust distinctions established by men between the two sexes, one believes this novel to have been written by a woman' (rev. in *Journal* 127). The *Mercure de France* review quotes and comments on one of Juliette's exclamations:

> "J'oubliai mon amour, dit-il, . . . Ah! Oui, les hommes ont de ces oublis." . . . Cette réflexion est juste, naturelle et bien placée sous la plume d'une femme, si c'en est une en effet à qui nous devons ces agréables Lettres. (86)

> "I forgot my love," he said, . . . "Oh! Yes, men do forget their love." . . . This observation is correct, natural and well placed under a woman's pen—if indeed it is a woman to whom we owe these agreeable letters.

Such suppositions, probably occasioned by rumors about Riccoboni's authorship of the novel,[4] can also be considered as attesting to and accepting male culpability, which in the narrative summarizing the plot had been diminished or dismissed.

Charrière and Mistriss Henley

For Charrière's *Lettres de Mistriss Henley*, we have several comments by the author on the genesis of the novel: she declares that it constitutes an explicit reaction to Samuel de Constant's *Le Mari sentimental*, published the previous year (*Œuvres* 2: 402; letter to her brother Vincent, Apr. 1784; and 6: 559; letter to Taets van Amerongen, Jan. 1804). This novel is also mentioned and quoted at the beginning of the first letters by Mistress Henley, as having shocked her and prompted her letters to her female friend. Confronted by Constant's unhappy husband, who charges his wife with being the sole cause of his unhappiness because of her bad character, Mistress Henley feels compelled to react: she finds herself in an equally unhappy marriage and wishes to express her feelings and to warn other women at the same time. She is pregnant, and, in case she should die in childbirth, a death she expects and longs for, she asks her friend to be responsible for the dissemination of her message. The novel ends by strongly suggesting the death of the heroine but does not confirm or describe it.

One of the first, and immediate, reactions to Charrière's novel was an anonymous text entitled *Justification de Monsieur Henley.* Mr. Henley supposedly writes to his late wife's friend, asking her whether she had published the letters to take revenge. He then describes the end of his wife's life, his version of it, and fills in the blank left by Charrière. He emphasizes that his wife assured him that she was convinced of his love for her (306; 359). His version of the death of the heroine idealizes the closeness between the spouses just before her death. This response was published by the editor Buisson in an anonymous edition illustrating the two sides of unhappy marriage: *Le Mari sentimental* represents male discontent, while *Lettres de Mistriss Henley* together with *Justification* expresses the woman's perspective. The latter combination was completely against Charrière's intentions, as she explicitly stated in the *Journal de Paris* on 13 May 1786 (*Œuvres* 8: 98). The authors of the two critical reactions to Charrière's *Lettres de Mistriss Henley* discussed here comment on this edition and were misled by Buisson's suggestion that all three texts were by a single author whose intention was to show both sides of the unhappy marriage.

In 1785 the author of a piece in the *Année littéraire* approves of the innovation of starting this "double" novel with a marriage. He points out that Mistress Henley, although she had reason to be disappointed by her husband's coldness, complains only about herself and not about her husband. This is what the critic admires in her, but he notes that she has too much sensibility to endure life with this man. Without any transition, the critic then proceeds to discuss *Justification* and presents Mr. Henley as greatly admiring his deceased wife and regretting her death. He expresses no doubt about the author's intentions (rev. in *Année* 178). One year later, possibly influenced by rumors, the *Mercure de France* does make a distinction. The critic attributes the work (apparently both *Le Mari sentimental* and *Lettres de Mistriss Henley*) to "Mme de C . . . de Z." (192) but refuses to accept her authorship of *Justification*: it seems impossible that two writings so different in style could be by the same hand (192). As for Mistress Henley's inability to live with her husband and her longing for death, this critic remains unconvinced: "Elle nous peint M. Henley comme un homme plein de vertus, de sagesse et de mérite; de l'âme la plus noble" 'She portrays Mr. Henley as a virtuous, wise, and deserving man; a noble soul.' His "sang-froid inaltérable" 'unremitting sang-froid' is quite appreciated, although the critic agrees that it "contraste parfaitement avec les écarts de sa jeune épouse" 'contrasts perfectly with the excesses of his young wife.' Concerning the heroine's death, "c'est, à ce que nous croyons, un reproche à faire à l'Auteur, qui n'a pas assez motivé cette mort, et qui parait n'avoir tué son Héroïne que parce qu'il était pressé d'en finir" 'it is, in our view, a fault on the part of the author, who has not provided sufficient motivation for this death and who seems to have killed the heroine only in order to finish the book' (189). He considers that there was, in fact, no need for her to die, at least for the reasons mentioned, and accuses the author of exaggerating the seriousness of the heroine's problem. The year before, in the *Année littéraire*, the critic had not invoked any technical reasons but established a comparison with normal male and female reactions:

> Il n'y a pas dans tout ce que rapporte l'auteur de quoi se laisser mourir de chagrin. Quelle que soit la sensibilité, c'est la porter beaucoup trop loin; et je doute que les maris et les femmes de nos jours prennent les choses aussi vivement. (180)

> In all this there is nothing that justifies the character's dying of grief. Her sensibility has been exaggerated, and I doubt whether husbands and wives suffer so intensely nowadays.

The reference, again, is to the extratextual world and to the degree of probability conveyed by this comparison.

For these three women novelists, it seems clear that some of the variations they present on aspects of the female destiny are not fully recognized and appreciated by the critics. This negative reaction must have been foreseeable, which makes it plausible that the women's choices were made consciously. Illuminating the contemporary critical reception highlights the originality of these women's intervention in the literary field. In addition, this comparative approach provides a useful opportunity for measuring the importance to be attached to female variations of the eighteenth-century novel, which otherwise might be seen as too much subject to anachronistic interpretations.

    To arrive at a real understanding of the response to the work of these women, one needs to supplement the overview of contemporary reception with other documents: individual or private testimonies, such as Anne-Robert-Jacques Turgot's 1751 letter to Graffigny on *Lettres d'une Péruvienne* and Diderot's remarks concerning *Juliette Catesby* (*Correspondence* 89–102), and particularly women's reactions and comments, such as that of Germaine de Staël, who commented on Mistress Henley's "dégoût de la vie [et] son malheur . . . analysé avec une finesse d'esprit et de cœur étonnante" 'distaste for life and her unhappiness, which are so well presented and analyzed' (Letter to Charrière). Female reactions, however, are much more difficult to find. We must sift through private correspondence, translations, or intertextual references in other women's work, to find them.[5] The specificity of the periodical press as source lies in the fact that these evaluations, comments, and interpretations have often survived: many of them—particularly for French women's writing—have been copied and are in La Porte's *Histoire littéraire des femmes françaises*, which has been frequently used as a source during the nineteenth and even the beginning of the twentieth century (van Dijk, "L'Abbé").

Taking into account the false impressions of women's early writing that have long been produced by literary historians, we must decide on the need for comparative analysis: original texts should be juxtaposed with rewritings—on a larger scale than is possible here—to discover what the original message may have been. It is essential to include minor authors also, not only such celebrities as the three women presented here. There are many, often contrasting, ways in which women have provided variations on novelistic plots; there is not one specific female approach. Indeed, for whatever reason—financial, as in Riccoboni's finally marrying off Juliette and d'Ossery, or otherwise—not all women adopted Graffigny's provocative attitude (confirmed and reinforced in the second version of her novel) or Charrière's defense of women. It was also a woman, Mrs. R. Roberts, who in her 1774 translation of the *Lettres d'une Péruvienne* (*Peruvian Letters*) felt obliged to add a supplementary happy ending: the heroine's final marriage—"being desirous," as Roberts said in her preface, "that so generous a friend as Deterville might be as happy as his virtues deserved" (1: 4; see MacArthur on this point). Interestingly, the two final letters adopt the male perspective. Déterville writes to his friend, the chevalier Dubois: "Rejoice with me, my dear Dubois, for all is accomplished, and Zilia is mine" (2: 166). In her last letter, Zilia shows little concern for her own happiness: "If it will be any pleasure to my dear friend to hear that my wishes coincide with his, I frankly confess they do" (2: 159). Such attitudes as these, which are liable to be much less appealing to us today, also require analysis. One question that would then arise concerns the link between aesthetic value and ideological originality: can we find any justification for the elimination of minor women authors? There is still a lot that the field of reception has to offer us.

Notes

1. All translations from the French are mine unless otherwise attributed.

2. Some decades later La Porte would be responsible (in part) for *Histoire littéraire des femmes françaises*.

3. All anonymous reviews can be found under "Rev." in this volume's list of works cited.

4. In April 1759, *Correspondance littéraire* knew that the work had been written by Riccoboni. She had connections with Diderot, who was participating in this important, handwritten "newsletter," of which a new edition is currently being prepared by Ulla Kölving at the Centre d'Étude du XVIIIᵉ siècle in Ferney-Voltaire.

5. A digital framework concerning references to reception documents, male and female, that have been found up to now has been created at Utrecht University and is being further developed at Huygens Institute, The Hague, in the context of a European COST Action (2009–13) (see van Dijk, *Women Writers*).

Part II

Teaching Specific Texts

Kathleen Wine

Teaching Scudéry's *Clélie*: The Art of Romance

The first part of Madeleine de Scudéry's multivolume romance *Clélie* (1654–60) includes a foldout copy of the "Carte de Tendre" ("Map of the Realm of Tenderness"). The celebrated map of psychological terrain embodies a problematic feature of Scudéry's prodigious fictional output: its parts are perhaps too readily detachable from the whole. This detachability is fundamental to the practice of a writer who incorporated materials produced collectively in her salon into her romances and employed materials from the romances in her later volumes of autonomous *Conversations*. Yet it has encouraged an incoherent view of Scudéry (Coulet 175). Often dismissed as the creator of heroic romances doomed to extinction by their vast dimensions and conventional plots, she is also hailed as a trailblazer whose psychologically astute portraits, conversations, and intercalated stories anticipated the French novel's "interiority" and "psychological realism" (DeJean, *Tender Geographies* 82, 87), as well as its focus on contemporary high society (note the subtitle of Morlet-Chantalat's important study of *Clélie*: "de l'épopée à la gazette" 'from epic to gazette'). This dichotomy is unsatisfying on several counts. It exaggerates the distinctions between two genres, each of which blended varying degrees of psychological analysis and idealization. It ignores the extent to which the worldly society that Scudéry portrayed in her romances was shaped by and imitative of romance (Denis, "Romanesque" 108–13). And it fails to give Scudéry her due as a literary artist whose works of fiction merit consideration as compelling wholes, not as fitful harbingers of better things to come.

It must be admitted, though, that to read *Clélie*—2,500 dense pages in Chantal Morlet-Chantalat's recent critical edition (the edition referred to throughout this essay)—as a whole is not possible in the classroom. After various unsatisfactory attempts to communicate Scudéry's influence through a brief discussion of the "Carte de Tendre," I have twice included the first *livre* ("book") of the first of *Clélie*'s five parts in a course on fiction of the ancien régime. Although I asked my students to read only an excerpt, the part in question is not a single, subordinate one, taken out of context; it conveys the experience of reading the whole. Like subsequent *livres*, the first advances the primary plot, interrupts it by a novella-length *histoire* ("story") narrated by a character, and incorporates representative conversations at each level. Unlike later *histoires*, this first one, "Histoire d'Aronce et de Clélie," devoted to the life stories of Clélie and her lover Aronce before the work's opening, is in itself a complete romance. Yet it also contains the conversation about types of friendship that inspires Clélie to invent the map, supporting my point that the novel and the romance are one.

In devoting a substantial amount of class time to *Clélie*, I want to communicate not only Scudéry's contributions to the psychological vocabulary of the French novel but also the scope and playfulness of her fictional universe. I want students to take seriously the art of this highly stylized narrative, to recognize its aesthetic and psychological rewards, and to reflect on the special appeal these might have had for a woman writer. Finally, by identifying romance structures and themes, I want to prepare the class to examine the afterlife of these conventions in later novels, encouraging students to discard their naive preconceptions about the genre's realism in favor of a more mature consideration of its art.

The overt displays of artifice that typify *Clélie*'s "romanesque" dimension are more in tune with the baroque aesthetic prevalent during the first two-thirds of the seventeenth century than with the classicism anticipated in many of the work's parts. *Clélie* begins in medias res, perpetuating a tradition French romancers had borrowed from epic and from the so-called Greek romance of late antiquity (Plazenet, *L'Ebahissement*; Doody). On the eve of Clélie's marriage, an earthquake separates her from her betrothed: "la terre s'entrouvrant entre Aronce et Clélie . . . , il en sortit en un instant une flamme si épouvantable, qu'elle les déroba également à la vue l'un de l'autre" 'the earth opening up between Aronce and Clélie . . . , there instantly emerged a flame so terrible that it prevented each from seeing the other' (52).[1] After a night of apocalyptic upheavals, Aronce discovers that his rival, Horace, has abducted Clélie, initiating a series of mishaps that will postpone the marriage until the end of the work. Scudéry's virtuoso description of the earthquake and conflagration, cited by Jean Rousset as typifying the baroque preoccupation with movement (127), manifests an equally baroque fondness for ostentation (219–28), ceremonially heralding the importance of what is to come in the manner of fanfares or ornamental gateways.

Students need to appreciate that Scudéry is not simply following conventions but playfully emphasizing them, much as a filmmaker might craft a tribute to the car chase. To fulfill the romance plot's requirement that the lovers be separated, she cleaves the earth between them, flaunting her control over the fictional world rather than disguising it, in classical fashion, as nature. Students schooled to prefer the latter approach can reflect on the way Scudéry's flamboyantly baroque side complements the discretion required of women writers. Scudéry was practiced, like her fictional alter ego Sappho, in the social art of concealing her learning and talent (see "L'Histoire de Sapho" in *Artamène* 450–51) and regularly published her fiction under the name of her brother Georges (see Grande on the use of pseudonyms 283–304). Wouldn't she have reveled in the opportunity to show off?

Her showing off, moreover, has broader implications. According to Patricia Parker, romance "simultaneously quests for and postpones a particular end" (4; see also Schaeffer 299–300). Scudéry pushes this structural feature to the breaking point by beginning as the heroes have apparently reached the end of their romance, revealing her awareness that the genre's deferrals are potentially infinite: "[Aronce] s'imaginait toujours qu'il arriverait quelque accident qui retarderait encore son bonheur, comme il avait été retardé" 'Aronce was always imagining that some accident would happen that would further delay his satsisfaction, as it had already been delayed' (*Clélie* 50). Scudéry also raises the larger question of when any narrative begins: at what point does one draw a line through the seamless web connecting one event or one life to others? Margaret Anne Doody treats violent beginnings in the tradition of Greek romance as paradigmatic for the novel as a whole, signaling our need as readers to "cut ourselves off from our own life" (311). Scudéry's earthquake, which literally divides the characters from each other and from their pasts, is the ultimate novel beginning because it so forthrightly acknowledges that, for characters and readers, a narrative can only begin in medias res.

The new series of adventures that begins with the earthquake finds Aronce pursuing Clélie and her abductor until he is wounded. Aronce's convalescence at a nearby château will be the setting for the activities that occupy the characters' leisure time: conversation and narrative. The first conversation provides an excellent introduction to the work's psychological and analytical side, since it is a brief but searching discussion of *inclination* ("penchant"), a key concept in *Clélie* and in later novels. (See Paige in this volume for a discussion of this term.) The influential princesse des Léontins has learned of the recent arrival of Aronce and the prince de Numidie. Although she has heard favorable reports of each and respects the prince's superior rank, she feels an inexplicable urge to meet Aronce. With a group of friends, she debates the nature of this *inclination*. Is it dictated by minute but real differences, or is it totally irrational? Can one choose one's *inclinations*, or are they impervious to will (70–73)? While the group does not resolve this question, the princess's intuition is borne out when she meets Aronce. They instantly form a strong bond that is nonetheless distinct from love.

Students readily appreciate the importance of Scudéry's depiction of male-female friendship—a bond that, unlike marriage, women could choose. And students can be encouraged to consider the importance, in the hierarchical and rule-bound society of ancien régime France, of the *inclination*, which, like the related *je ne sais quoi*, emphasized inexplicable and intuitive kinds of knowing. Yet the next major plot twist offers us a challenge. Célère, having obtained Aronce's permission to entrust the princess with the politically delicate story of his life, begins with the news that Aronce, believed to be of unknown birth, is the son of Porsenna, king of Clusium. This development links one of Scudéry's admired conversations to a much-derided topos of romance—the recognition of identity. Why does Scudéry, having established a role for individual affinities that defy reason or social utility, make the princess's seemingly wayward *inclination* light on a person whose rank equals her own?

We will be in a better position to deal with this question when we have read the ensuing "Histoire d'Aronce et de Clélie" with an eye to the interaction of romance plot and psychological analysis. When Aronce was an infant, we learn, his mother placed him in the care of servants, hoping to conceal her clandestine marriage to the prince her father held prisoner.

Separated from his guardians during a storm at sea, the baby was rescued by Clélie's father, Clélius, and raised alongside Clélie during the family's exile from Rome. As a young man, Aronce, realizing that Clélius will never accept his daughter's marriage to a man of unknown birth, leaves home. But when chance reunites him with his adoptive family on the high seas, just in time to rescue them from pirates, he resolves to win Clélie's heart. He follows the instructions she inscribes on her "Carte de Tendre," eventually winning an affection that exceeds the *tendre amitié* ("tender friendship") she describes therein. But when Clélius becomes aware of his daughter's sentiments, he berates her for ignoring her duty to Rome and her lineage. Banishing Aronce, he orders her to marry the Roman Horace, although Clélie's mother believes her husband's youthful penchant for Horace's mother to have influenced his choice. But before Clélius can formalize the betrothal, Aronce foils a plot on his life, prompting Clélius to agree to "laisser Clélie maîtresse d'elle-même" 'allow Clélie to be her own mistress' (231).

The "Carte de Tendre" is immensely helpful in communicating to students the psychological import of this heroic storyline. In the conversation that precedes the map's invention, Clélie distinguishes the *tendre amitié* she reserves for an elect few from six other types of friendship (177)—a feat of analytical prowess students can compare with their rather less rigorous thinking about their "relationships." Responding to the query of a friend about where he stands with her, Clélie devises the map, which further distinguishes three types of tender friendship, based on esteem, gratitude, or *inclination*, and depicts the itineraries aspiring friends must follow to reach the three destinations (179). These types and their various stages are immediately applicable to the ongoing story. As we watch Aronce shower Clélie with favors directly recalling the map's "jolis vers" 'charming verses' and "petits soins" 'little gestures,' while Horace, sadly lacking in its recommended "complaisance" 'obliging spirit,' berates her about his rival's progress, we grasp that Clélie's growing feelings for Aronce are a complex mixture of incalculable attraction, gratitude, and esteem.

The map, moreover, turns out to be broadly applicable to other types of friendship. That of Aronce and Horace, for example, though solidly grounded in esteem and gratitude, does not survive their rivalry. On the other hand, Clélius's anger at Aronce's presumptuous love for Clélie cannot extinguish the "amitié fort tendre" 'very tender friendship' Clélius feels for his adoptive son (198). Only the extraordinary gratitude and respect Aronce inspires when he risks his life for Clélius, despite his impending banishment, can triumph over the latter's rigid Roman values, reinforced by the unacknowledged sentiments that incline Clélius in Horace's favor. Scudéry's analyses of friendship shed an interesting light on Clélie's subjection to her father's judgment in the choice of a spouse. This is no simple conflict between youthful desire and the paternal imperative to cement a sociopolitical alliance. The daughter's instinctive feelings are buttressed by rational and ethical considerations, while the father's reasons for rejecting her suitor are colored by his own earlier *inclination*. It is not at all clear whether Clélie was to be sacrificed to family and country or to paternal whims.

The romance thus turns out to have a psychological side. But Clélie's psychological map also draws heavily on romance. In charting itineraries to three allegorical destinations, Clélie offers a variant on the trials by which romance suitors traditionally won their ladies (Duggan 16; for a critique of the *Carte*'s courtly character, see Bassy 19–20). Like the romance lover, aspiring friends may fall into *error* ("ils s'égareraient" 'would go astray' [184; see Parker 17–31; Peters, *Mapping* 99]), leading, for example, to the "mer d'inimitié" 'sea of enmity,' whose stormy waters, "où tous les vaisseaux font naufrage" 'where all ships are wrecked' (184), recall the very accident that separated Aronce from his identity. Not exclusively internal or allegorical, the map connects the inner and the outer, the literal and the figurative. It wittily projects psychosocial tests befitting the salon habitué—"billet galant" 'galant note,' "assiduité" 'attentiveness,' "sensibilité" 'sensibility'—onto the archaic terrain of romance adventure. But tests like "Grand Cœur" 'Great Courage' or "Générosité" 'Magnanimity' confirm that the route to *amitié* opens out onto literal romance vistas. Clélie herself recalls that Aronce first won her esteem and gratitude in the old-fashioned way, by his timely appearance as the aforementioned pirates prepared to fling her overboard (187).

These observations can initiate a productive discussion of internalization, suggesting the relation of inner landscapes to archaic outer ones (but see also Peters on mapping 83–88) and paving our way for a later consideration of the way romance shapes the expectations of novel characters. But the difficulty of disentangling the novel and romance elements in the "Carte de Tendre" suggests that *Clélie* is more complex. As a roman à clef that transports Scudéry's contemporary acquaintances into the ancient Mediterranean world of Greek romance, it simultaneously modernizes the old and "antiques" the new.

Nevertheless, the "Histoire d'Aronce et de Clélie" culminates in a recognition scene that seems to partake exclusively of the second procedure. During a ceremonial procession in honor of her birthday, Clélie wears diamond jewelry, recovered by her father from the proverbial casket that floated alongside the baby Aronce at the time of the shipwreck. Two strangers recognize the ornaments and seek out the story of the rescue, which they determine to have happened at the very time and place they had lost their young charge. Convinced of Aronce's identity by a birthmark, they activate a hidden mechanism, which opens the diamond ornaments to reveal two miniature portraits—of a young woman and of a man who strongly resembles Aronce—final proof that he is the infant that Queen Galerite, the woman in the portrait, confided to them long ago (237–42).

Once again, rather than veil the conventional character of this recognition scene, Scudéry displays it, by describing Clélie's ornaments as "nœuds de diamants" (232). The knots that open to reveal Aronce's parents literally enact the undoing of the plot complication, or *nœud*, effected by the denouement, while symbolically evoking the idea of marriage or family ties. In this case, however, there would seem to be no complication, since Aronce has already won the right to wed Clélie, much as he wins the friendship of the princesse des Léontins, by sheer merit. The absence of an obstacle throws the social and psychological importance of recognition into bolder relief. Students are intrigued by the notion, common to many romances, that the main characters cannot marry until they know the identity of their parents and, hence, their own identity. Scudéry, however, gives this convention an interesting twist by setting Aronce's recognition during an ostentatious celebration of Clélie's birthday (Célère tells Aronce, "le jour de la naissance de Clélie . . . est destiné à vous apprendre la vôtre" 'the day of Clélie's birth . . . is destined to teach you yours' [236]). Scudéry thereby underscores the importance of birth. That she apparently considered her readers to be even more set on Clélie's marriage to a social equal than her hidebound father gives us an insight into the imaginative power of the social hierarchy, which will prove helpful when we deal with disastrously unequal relationships in novels like *Manon Lescaut*. And it can also prompt us to ask what sorts of equality we still demand between marriage partners.

Yet as those students who will confess to reading romance are quick to point out, the symmetrical coincidence also implies that Aronce and

Clélie are destined for each other, subordinating the role of parents to that of the higher forces that sanction the couple's wishes. This setup leads us to a significant generic difference: whereas many French novels are designed to demonstrate the destructive effects of love, romance often stages its vindication. Although Scudéry refused to marry and attributed her opinions about the oppressive character of contemporary marriage to more than one of her characters, she devoted considerable creative energy to the crafting of traditional marriage plots, which speak to the yearning that love and marriage might prove compatible. Her plots, moreover, vindicate women's preferences. In her fictional universe, the *inclinations* that predispose Clélie or the princesse des Léontins in Aronce's favor are not disruptive. Rather, they are proof of the powers of discernment that make the two women eminently capable of contracting their alliances and of participating in the social order. The ornaments that enhance Clélie's beauty and status on a day honoring her birth contain a secret she had already intuited. The disclosure of Aronce's identity elevates Clélie, showing her identity to be determined not only by her birth but also by the sureness of her choices.

The recognition scene may have been inscribed in the "Carte de Tendre" all along, in the form of a pun. The word *reconnaissance* means recognition as well as gratitude and was in the seventeenth century a term of art for an ending achieved through recognition of identity. When Aronce sets off for Tendre sur Reconnaissance, does he seek Clélie's gratitude or her recognition of his intrinsic nobility? (For a different view see Viala, "Racine" 374.) Does the recognition scene thus merely render official a knowledge already available to some? Or does Aronce's ritual separation from his parents betoken the insufficiency of birth unless confirmed by other forms of recognition? The "Carte de Tendre" points toward the cultural meaning of romance.

By the time we have worked our way to the end of our story, we are shocked to recall that we have only read the beginning of *Clélie*. Students can now more fully appreciate that the initial earthquake represents Scudéry's tip of the hat to the tradition of romance delay. They are better prepared to look at the sheer volume of pages that still separate the protagonists from their happy ending and to ask why the story should have to begin again. What *nœuds* have yet to be undone—the parents Aronce has never met, the baby brother lost at sea, the dozens of characters whose stories remain untold? If Aronce had to be reunited with his parents before he could marry, why must Clélie now be violently separated from hers?

Does she perhaps have tests of her own to undergo? We will not have time to pursue these questions very far. But if we consult our map once more, we can discern there too this structure of delay, as the "Carte de Tendre" comes to seem a *carte d'étendre* ("a map of drawing things out"). The three towns of Tendre are separated by a "mer dangereuse" 'dangerous sea' from distant "terres inconnues" 'unknown lands.' For Clélie, a lady of unimpeachable character, these "unknown lands" signify that tender friendship is a final destination: "elle n'a point eu d'amour, et . . . elle n'en peut avoir" 'she has never had a love affair and would never have one' (185). Her suitors, however, find it more difficult to ignore the "bien-heureuses Terres inconnues, qu'on ne voit qu'en éloignement" 'blessed unknown lands that one sees only in the distance' (189; see Guénoun 87–90). The rocky gulf that separates these destinations is not unlike the earthquake that opens a chasm between two lovers ostensibly at the end of their journey. One involves a woman's strategy for forestalling her admirers with an intermediate goal. The other involves a narrative strategy for diverting readers from an ultimate destination, identified in the opening paragraphs with the hero's erotic fulfillment, toward a series of secondary ones.

A consideration of the pleasures and risks of these strategies of suspense completes our reflections on *Clélie*. Later, it will ground our consideration of the erotic and narrative strategies to be found in novels. It will provide us with a valuable reference point, whether we are exploring Mme de Clèves's decision to deny Nemours his "bonheur" 'erotic fulfillment,' Voltaire's use of a famous earthquake to separate a group of characters he will later reunite, the abduction and sea voyage that open Françoise de Graffigny's *Lettres d'une Péruvienne*, the formal and philosophical playfulness of Denis Diderot's *Jacques le fataliste*, or Valmont's mocking abuse of an innocent "héroïne de roman" 'romance heroine' in *Les Liaisons dangereuses*. But to give Scudéry's art its due, we had first to suspend our desire to arrive too quickly at our destination, to linger with her in the liminal realms between novel and romance.

Note

1. All translations from the French are mine unless otherwise noted.

John D. Lyons

The Marquise de Sévigné: Philosophe

Marie de Rabutin-Chantal, marquise de Sévigné (1626–96), figures regularly in undergraduate and graduate courses on French literature and
culture. Students have heard her name and are well disposed to study an
author who breaks out of the mold of fixed genres like tragedy, comedy,
and fable. But in teaching her work, I have found a major, obvious challenge: how to give students a significant idea of Sévigné's style of thinking and writing, thematic breadth, and enduring relevance while selecting
passages from three thousand pages of her letters in the Pléiade edition of
Correspondance. Even though I recognize the powerful attraction of the
drama of maternal love and its implications for feminist and gender studies
(as laid out, for instance, in Farrell), the motherhood theme encompasses
almost all Sévigné's letters and could easily overwhelm an advanced survey
course on seventeenth-century culture. Over the years I have adopted an
approach that seems to surprise and interest students: I have them consider
Sévigné—in her correspondence with her daughter but also with others—
as a philosopher.

Sévigné is not read in many philosophy courses, since few women have
been admitted to the philosophers' club. But another, equally important
reason why this celebrated author of letters is generally unknown outside

the French literature classroom may be that what college and university teachers in America and Europe think of as philosophy is quite different from what an educated person in the seventeenth century would have understood by that term. The categories we use to read the past come from our present. Sometimes that is good. It permits us to recover the universe of women's writing. But sometimes the modern world imposes a narrower view of things, as it does for philosophy. This narrowing came home to me very dramatically when I was a young assistant professor at Dartmouth teaching a course on seventeenth-century French prose. A distinguished professor of philosophy, an eminent specialist of René Descartes, asked to audit my class to keep up his French. Tactfully, he agreed without hesitation to skip the week or so we were going to devote to Descartes. But while we were discussing a few essays of Michel de Montaigne, my senior colleague took copious notes and was beside himself with astonishment at the extent of Montaigne's influence on Descartes. His astonishment was dramatic evidence that departments of philosophy in the mid-twentieth century were devoted to reading the linear canon of philosophers. But these same philosophers were reading other writers whose thought seemed to them to be of great philosophical importance, whether or not they agreed with it. In short, we can access the writing of the past in greater depth and perceive its interconnections by accepting the broader use of the term *philosophy*.

Marie de Rabutin-Chantal, marquise de Sévigné, belongs to a tradition in which writers raise serious questions about life outside what we know as the professional framework of modern philosophy. In a tradition stretching back to antiquity, the pursuit of personal wisdom was the central task of the philosopher. Even Descartes, the early modern French philosopher who now appears to us most official or canonical, deliberately avoided the university and all other institutional ties in favor of undisturbed, self-directed inquiry, initially shared informally with friends in letters before presentation in a public mode. This tradition of personal inquiry includes Cicero, Seneca, Augustine, Boethius, Montaigne, Blaise Pascal, and Jean-Jacques Rousseau — to name only a few. It is a tradition in which the boundaries of rhetoric, ethics, epistemology, poetry, theology, and autobiography are not sharply drawn. The texts that constitute this tradition are often dialogues, letters, allegories, and novels, and for Sévigné, as for Madeleine de Scudéry and Paul Pellisson, these texts gave voice to "la philosophie comme une sagesse et non comme un système" 'philosophy as wisdom and not as system' (Viala, *France* 145).[1]

Sévigné's relation to philosophy manifests itself most strikingly in her denial. In the midst of a plangent expression of sorrow at her daughter's departure, she writes in August 1675, "L'amitié que j'ai pour vous ne cause pas une paix bien profonde à un cœur aussi dénué de philosophie que le mien; il faut passer sur ces endroits sans y séjourner" 'The friendship I have for you does not bestow a very deep peace on a heart so lacking in philosophy as mine' (*Correspondance* 2: 35). In this instance we see both a narrow and a broad significance in the term *philosophy*. At first glance, it seems that Sévigné is using the term in a reductive, colloquial sense to mean that she is not coolly above emotion and that she has not reached the Stoic ideal of *ataraxia*, or autonomy, that would make human attachments indifferent to her. *Philosophy*, then, would signify a vernacular understanding of Stoicism, which had experienced a huge revival a hundred years before but had recently foundered in the face of a withering critique in Sévigné's circle. But the writer's self-description as being without philosophy — and other negative self-descriptions in relation to philosophy, such as "je ne suis pas philosophe comme M. Descartes" 'I am not a philosopher like M. Descartes' (3: 396)—has many other interesting and important ramifications.

First of all, there is, in philosophy, a tradition of such denials, which seem, at least in part, to be based on a required humility. Only slightly before Sévigné, Descartes wrote in his *Discours de la méthode* (*Discourse on Method*) that he did not mean to teach people a method for thinking:

> [M]on dessein n'est pas d'enseigner icy la Methode que chascun doit suivre pour bien conduire sa raison, mais seulement de faire voir en quelle sorte j'ay tasché de conduire la miene. (4)

> My intention is not to teach here the method that everyone should follow to use his reason, but only to show in what way I have tried to use mine.

Descartes insists that his aim is to show in an autobiographical format examples of how he thinks, so that he can learn from rumors about his success or failure.

Another important implication of Sévigné's comment about "a heart . . . lacking in philosophy" concerns the specific occasion in which philosophy is introduced. It would take a certain quality of friendship, combined with a certain quantity of philosophy, to bring the author peace. This statement, then, is about the kind of friendship that Sévigné feels for her daughter as well as about the relation between philosophy and friendship.

This leads us to the established tradition of a relation between philosophy and friendship—*friendship* implying a much stronger, lifelong commitment than is perhaps understood when we say the word today (this topic is an excellent source of discussion in a French course, since students often remark that their French friends have different expectations in a friendship). It recalls Cicero (who is mentioned several times by Sévigné), whose *On Friendship* was an important reference for the complex interplay between philosophy and friendship: Cicero shows how a philosopher views friendship but also how philosophy comes to be known through conversation and letters exchanged among friends. We do not know whether Sévigné had direct knowledge of Cicero's *On Friendship* (she did write that one of her letters was like one of Cicero's [*Correspondance* 2: 900]), but it is clear that she would have disagreed passionately with several of the positions set forth by Laelius, the principal speaker in that dialogue. Laelius asserts that he rose above his personal sorrow at the death of his friend Scipio, that lamentation would be an unworthy act, that friends have "a complete identity of feeling about all things in heaven and earth," and that friendship is not based on need (187). In a certain sense Sévigné practices the same style of philosophizing as Cicero: informal exchanges among intimate friends on matters that concern the practical conduct of life, attitudes toward death, and the values that give meaning to our acts. She, however, rejects the content of the Stoic-inspired teaching of Cicero and Seneca and asserts the opposite: the value of sorrow and suffering, the differences in feelings and attitudes that arise in friendship but do not destroy it, and the imperfection of the self and with it the need and even neediness that she experienced in her love for her daughter.

Although I do not teach courses in the history of philosophy and do not think that a study of sources is appropriate in most of my courses, I do believe that it is important for students to realize how well versed Sévigné was in the philosophical tradition. Among the well-known philosophical writers she mentions are Plato, Aristotle, Seneca, Epictetus, Augustine, Thomas Aquinas, the Stoics generally (but, curiously, not Epicurus or Epicureans), and writers of her time such as Montaigne, Descartes, Pascal, Pierre Charron, Pierre Nicole, Fénelon, and Nicolas Malebranche. This is certainly not an insignificant survey of Western philosophy as it was conceived in her day. Some of these writers are referred to infrequently in passing, but others, particularly those from the Catholic tradition or among her contemporaries, appear repeatedly. In her *Correspondance* she mentions Augustine thirty-five times, Montaigne seven times, Malebranche at least ten times, Pascal at least twenty-seven times, and Descartes about three dozen times by name and many other times by allusion (in writing to her daughter she calls Descartes "votre *père*" 'your *father*' [2: 307]) or in terms of the Cartesian philosophy. The writer whose name appears most frequently in her correspondence is Nicole, who is not often noted in philosophy courses today but was celebrated in his day as the author (with Antoine Arnauld) of the Port-Royal *Logique ou l'art de bien penser* ("Logic; or, The Art of Thinking Well") and (with Pascal) of the *Lettres provinciales*. Sévigné mentions him directly dozens of times and refers frequently to his important multivolume book of religious and moral philosophy, *Essais de morale*.

How, then, does Sévigné relate to this mass of reading? As we look at her comments on what she has read or on discussions concerning these authors, we perceive easily that her aim was not to accumulate academic knowledge or even cultural literacy in the tradition but to clarify her views about life, time, friendship, will (especially the concept of *libre arbitre*, or free will), grace, providence, chance, beauty, suffering, and death. In a broad sense, we can call her an existential philosopher, though it is tempting to appropriate for Sévigné Ann Hartle's fitting description of Montaigne as "accidental philosopher," since there is so much in Sévigné that is reminiscent of his trial-and-error approach to formulating an evocation of the world as it is while keeping an eye on other writers' attempts to circumscribe it (4). Montaigne, just as Sévigné will do later, "presents himself as deficient and defective" and looks for truth "in the imprecision and richness of common language and opinion." And where Montaigne distinguishes himself constantly, according to Hartle, from Aristotle and his school, Sévigné distinguishes herself at every turn from the Stoics, on the one hand, and from Descartes, on the other.

Seventeenth-century philosophical thought grows out of the preceding century's two major enthusiasms: a practical morality based on Stoic principles and an epistemological problem growing out of the skepticism popularized by Montaigne. Pascal and Descartes react differently to these immediate influences, and Descartes starts his philosophy by trying to answer the problem of radical doubt, conceiving a very abstract, introspective system built around a disembodied self. Sévigné turns totally away from this Cartesian solution, opposes her daughter's devotion to Descartes, and sometimes refers to this abstractness as a form of Platonism. Sévigné casts herself as preferring Aristotle, using a rhetorical way to declare her preference for knowledge that derives from the senses and is based on experience and observation. Closer to Sévigné's actual practice is what Pascal called the "entretiens ordinaires de la vie" 'ordinary conversations of life' ([2004] 1159; fragment 618), a style of philosophizing he attributed to Epictetus and Montaigne. Like Pascal, Sévigné never considered Montaigne's skepticism worth rebutting in an extreme form. In other words, she never considered the hypothesis of the *malin génie* ("evil genius") who would dupe us all into systematic illusions about the evidence of our senses. Instead, she, like Pascal, is similar to Montaigne in basing her thought and writing on the observations of everyday experience. But she is closer to Montaigne than to Pascal both in taking a first-person approach to describing the world and in an exceptional attention to material detail and sense impressions.

Sévigné is a thinker who, like Montaigne and Pascal, is concerned with the human condition—the focus that characterized a loose category of French writers we call the *moralists*—and she focuses most intensely on life as it really is, rather than how it might be if we all mended our ways and lived up to rigorous standards of virtue. Using everyday life as the starting point for thought, Sévigné is keenly aware of her position in a life that includes boredom, frivolity, loss, longing, a range of physical sensations, enthusiasm, admiration, surprise, and death. For Sévigné, the goal of thinking is not to transcend this common lot of experience because this disorganized and unpredictable flux is the substance of human reality.

Sévigné's thought, as expressed in her writing, reveals its purpose in its characteristic format: the letter. She thinks in terms of this constant exchange wherein she conveys details of her daily life to her correspondent, usually her daughter, and she reviews and comments on what they have told her of their lives. This process quickly becomes vertiginous, since Sévigné imagines the reaction of her interlocutors as they imagine what she has described to them. The result is a complex form of imaginative meditation with many layers and many voices. This style of thought is similar to that of Pascal, who tried to assume dialogically the voice and attitude of his interlocutor with the goal of persuasion. Sévigné, however, has a different goal. She wants to interest her reader, and therefore she views the world with a dual perspective, conveying what she sees, hears, and feels but filtering it through her idea of what will appeal to her correspondent. It is appropriate that Sévigné has been described as "performing" motherhood (Farrell), because her work demonstrates the inescapably rhetorical nature of human discourse. We are always who we are for, or in the view of, someone else. Sévigné is, in fact, very modern, arguably much more so than Descartes, for she does not try to ground her being in an isolated, enclosed subject who thinks in solitude—though it takes some discussion for this notion to emerge, since students are generally already persuaded that Descartes represents the major turn toward philosophical modernity. By placing interest at the center of her thought, Sévigné stands at the threshold of the centuries of social thought in which human beings are described in terms of the interests they share, etymologically "what is between" (*inter est*). While *interest* as it is mobilized by political and economic philosophers after the seventeenth century (what is to our material advantage) seems at first glance to be radically different from the interest that Sévigné seeks (what attracts and holds our attention), the word reveals that there is something in common between the marketplace of economics and the sociability of the letter. Both are based in affect, and the rise of a politics of interest occurs precisely because of the shift in thinking from the heroic to the quotidian—from what we should do to what we really do—that so characterizes Sévigné (see Hirschman).

Sévigné is surely the seventeenth-century writer who made the strongest commitment to learning from and about everyday life. She combines a truly remarkable concreteness and sensuousness in all her descriptions, whether they concern sweating in a therapeutic spa bath at Vichy, purchasing lumber for rebuilding a roof, walking in a garden in the moonlight, or watching her only child leave in a coach. But this detail is always worked through a lively process of self-awareness. Sévigné unceasingly represents her own projection of memory and anticipation onto what she describes. Pascal famously said that we never live in the present; we only live in the past and future (*Pensées* [2004] 861; fragment 80). Yet for Pascal the present is an abstraction that he never tries to render. Although he theorizes it, Sévigné repeatedly tries to convey its concreteness while measuring it against remembered and anticipated moments. Only the constant perception of past or future loss seemed to endow things for Sévigné with an almost tragic sense of reality, as when she writes to her cousin:

> Pour ma vie, vous la connaissez aussi. On la passe avec cinq ou six amies dont la société plaît, et à mille devoirs à quoi l'on est obligé, et ce n'est pas une petite affaire. Mais ce qui me fâche, c'est qu'en ne faisant rien, les jours se passent, et notre pauvre vie est composée de ces jours, et l'on vieillit, et l'on meurt. (2: 32)

> As for my life, you know how it is. I spend it with five or six friends whose company I enjoy and in doing all the tasks that have to be done, and this is no small matter. But what bothers me is that while we do nothing the days pass, and our poor life is made up of these days, and we grow older, and we die.

In representing the human condition, Sévigné takes a leveling approach to things (juxtaposing a card game with news of a death) that also applies to people. This approach contrasts with the sharply hierarchical society in which she lived, where people paid attention to who got to sit on a stool and who got a chair. Sévigné sees a constant pattern of these things—what Pascal describes as "Vanité" (*Pensées* 847–64)—across the social spectrum. She fully accepts the centrality of the daily striving for status and recognition as a major human activity. She considered moralistic or philosophical pretensions to set oneself above human striving as irrelevant, and like Pascal she recognized that what is most frivolous contains the clues to true understanding of our existential situation. Her letters endlessly chronicle the bestowal and purchase of offices, ranks, and decorations and speculate on the way each death will redistribute standing among the survivors. But even though this central activity of striving in the context of the social structure depended on the existence of an infinite number of tiny distinctions in status, it ultimately made every person similar, rather than different. We are all inescapably bound to our personal perspective and longings, things that we cannot transcend. We cannot, with Stoic or Christian ascetic purity, transcend our lot in life. The story of the death of Vatel is the best-known instance of this theme in her work. She describes the challenge of this minor official who was the manager of the prince of Condé's chateau at Chantilly. Because of misinformation about the arrival of the seafood ordered for a dinner at which the king was being entertained, Vatel committed suicide as if he were a general who had lost a battle. Sévigné clearly relished the chance to show how little difference his suicide made in the order of things: "On dîna très bien, on fit collation, on soupa, on se promena, on joua, on fut à la chasse. Tout était parfumé de jonquilles" 'They dined very well, they snacked, they had supper, they strolled, they played games, they hunted. Everywhere there was the scent of daffodils' (1: 236).

The most original philosophical theme in Sévigné's work is her complete acceptance of suffering—but not in a Stoic mode of detachment. Although acceptance of reality and a life in harmony with nature in all its apparent harshness was a major Stoic theme, the Stoics taught a discipline of perception that would allow us to see the everyday surface of life as an illusion to be resisted to gain a transcendent tranquillity. For the Stoics, everything that can be taken away from us is mere appearance, not reality. In their view, if a loved one dies, we have lost nothing. Sévigné turns this doctrine upside down. She practiced and taught the humble lesson that we

are creatures made to be attached by love, need, and desire to other creatures; this world we share with them is the only reality we will know in life.
It is vain to try to rise above the world of experience. This view sets her
apart from all the philosophical and religious teachers she knew (with the
possible exception of Nicole). Pascal, picking and choosing among Stoic
doctrines and rejecting many, such as the importance of introspection,
taught rejection of human attachments. François de Sales, close friend and
spiritual adviser of Sévigné's grandmother Jeanne de Chantal, taught a
form of spiritual inwardness that transformed ordinary experience through
meditative imagination. Sévigné prefers instead to adhere to the suffering
that comes from human attachments, wishes, disappointments, and loss,
seeing in these the hand of God.

In terms of aesthetics, Sévigné is most known for her taste in drama—
she was an ardent fan of Pierre Corneille and lukewarm on Jean Racine.
How could she adopt a demystifying worldview based on everyday reality
filled with trivia and then praise enthusiastically the dramatist who most
stood for implausible heroism and villainy? There are two overlapping explanations. First, the everyday world is full of randomness, some of it spectacular and violent. A philosophy that accepts the real world must accept
the implausible and abnormal, rather than turn aside from what does not
fit what we would like to see. And Sévigné abounds in examples of things
strange and sudden, especially deaths. A second, converging reason is that
Corneille oriented his poetics toward implausible events based on history,
at a time when most dramatic theorists argued for eliminating from tragedy
incidents that were historically true but either too dependent on chance
or ideologically unacceptable. So Sévigné's adherence to interesting anecdotes from the everyday world fits logically with her dramatic taste. Sévigné teaches the paradox that the ordinary world includes chance, heroism,
and the sublime. This insight extends an invitation to all readers, including
students, to look at the life around them for similar incidents and to examine the way each of us decides to incorporate, connect, or package events
into various larger narratives—of religious belief, of relationships, of the
construction of a coherent sense of self, and so forth.

Finally, the underlying unity of Sévigné's thought can be found in her
commitment to a doctrine of Christian immanence. Sévigné accepted the
real, as she experienced it, because she identified the real with divine providence. God was, for her, what happened. Whatever caused her suffering,
including the absence of a daughter she loved (in her own view) far too
much, was the will of God. Rather than try to avoid suffering by reforming

herself or detaching herself from the world, Sévigné, in an original synthesis of her many influences (most notably Nicole), clung to the world and to her attachments — attachments that made her suffer — as the way to live a life of submission to a higher power.

Note

1. All translations from the French are mine unless otherwise indicated.

Richard E. Goodkin

Cartesian Lafayette: Clear and Distinct in *La Princesse de Clèves*

One of students' most accessible avenues of approach to Marie-Madeleine Pioche de la Vergne, comtesse de Lafayette, is through the titular heroine's protofeminist gesture of refusing marriage with M. de Nemours and her retreat into a solitary and reflective life that it is tempting to see as a forerunner of Virginia Woolf's "room of one's own." Such a reading of the novel's conclusion is well founded and compelling. The exercise I propose here, appropriate in either an undergraduate or a graduate literature course, is intended to supplement that interpretation by considering Mme de Clèves's departure from the social realm in parallel with René Descartes's famous contemplation of the world from the perspective of a small heated room, as alluded to in *Discours de la méthode* (*Discourse of the Method*). In addition to being readable as a sort of silent protest against the seductive but untrustworthy M. de Nemours or more generally against the morally bankrupt court, Mme de Clèves's withdrawal has larger philosophical resonances. It may thus be helpful for students to understand her story's conclusion both as the protest of a woman qua woman against a society run by and for the benefit of men and as a distancing from the world of the empirical. In this way Mme de Clèves's separation from society can be shown to be not only a movement away but also a movement toward, an attempt at forging a deeper and more stable understanding of the contingencies entailed in living in society than would be possible if Mme de Clèves were to remain in the domain to be subjected to her scrutiny.

I propose studying the central relationship in *La Princesse de Clèves*, the never-consummated desire of Mme de Clèves and M. de Nemours, in terms of Descartes's concepts of clarity and distinctness. These are words that Descartes famously uses with great frequency and that even two decades after his death had already begun to permeate French culture. In fact, Lafayette was quite familiar with Descartes's work,[1] and the two terms pepper her text. Moreover, our students have grown up in an age that has increased the ease and reduced the speed of transmitting knowledge and information so radically that they have trouble conceiving of a world in which writers and thinkers do not have immediate and unlimited access to one another's work and yet still are influenced by one another in sometimes surprising ways. This sort of conjunctive reading based on a small number of terms linking two writers might offer the instructor a rare opportunity to read the seventeenth century in terms of a many-layered zeitgeist.

One would begin with a presentation of Descartes's use of the terms *clear* and *distinct*. In his search for sound principles, Descartes repeats the refrain "clear and distinct": he can trust only perceptions that have both these features. The terms are often used interchangeably, but in *Principles of Philosophy* Descartes explains the difference between clarity and distinctness:

> A perception which can serve as the basis for a certain and indubitable judgement needs to be not merely clear [*clara*] but also distinct [*distincta*]. I call a perception "clear" when it is present and accessible to the attentive mind—just as we say that we see something clearly when it is present to the eye's gaze. . . . I call a perception "distinct" if, as well as being clear, it is so sharply separated from all other perceptions that it contains within itself only what is clear.
> (207–08, pt. 1, principle 45)

Clarity is defined by presence: at a single moment, if our senses are attentive, an object is made available to our perception. By contrast, distinct knowledge entails a process, a coming to awareness, that is, the exploration of relations between an object and other objects. In quite a different context Descartes implies that these two acts—perception of an isolated object and the qualification of objects by contrast to other objects—are the building blocks of cognition:

> It will be to the reader's advantage . . . to think of all knowledge what-
> ever—save knowledge obtained through simple and pure intuition of
> a single, solitary thing—as resulting from a comparison between two
> or more things. (*Rules* 57; rule 14)

Particularly important for *La Princesse de Clèves* is that clear cognition and distinct cognition have different relations to temporality. Clarity
is contained in a single moment. Distinction requires a series of steps,
since one can hardly conceptualize scrutinizing two objects and comparing them as taking place in a single moment of perception. Therein lies
one key advantage as well as a potential danger of clear cognition, for
Descartes recognizes that our minds are such that it is difficult not to give
ourselves over completely to the seductive perceptions of the present:

> [T]he minds of all of us have been so moulded by nature that whenever
> we perceive something clearly [*clarè*], we spontaneously give our assent
> to it and are quite unable to doubt its truth.
> (*Principles* 207; pt. 1, principle 43)

And yet Descartes states that we *must* doubt its truth-value in order to
seek knowledge through distinction as well as clarity. John Cottingham
has observed that in Descartes's writings one senses anxiety over the temporal disjunction thus created: intuitive thought, which founds the existence of the thinking self, takes place in a seamless present tense, whereas
deduction is a synthetic process implying duration:

> It is often said that Descartes, like other so-called "rationalist" philoso-
> phers, attaches great importance to deductive knowledge, and there is
> some truth in this. Yet . . . Descartes consistently regarded deduction as
> a second-best form of cognition. Intuition alone carries the self-evident
> certainty that arises when the mind's eye is directed towards a proposi-
> tion whose content is entirely clear and manifest. But because of the
> finite scope of the human mind, our ability to attend to a plurality of
> propositions at any one time is severely limited . . . ; hence the need for
> deduction, which involves temporarily leaving behind one proposition
> and moving on to the next, so that "in a certain sense deduction gets
> its certainty from memory."
> (46; concluding quot. from Descartes, *Rules*, rule 3)

How might the opposition between clarity and distinction help students interpret the love story between the princesse de Clèves and the
duc de Nemours that generally fascinates and perplexes them as much
as it does critics? In the novel's final direct quotation, Mme de Clèves,
after what seems to be her definitive refusal of Nemours, pronounces the

following words: "[A]ttendez ce que le temps pourra faire. Monsieur de Clèves ne fait encore que d'expirer, et cet objet funeste est trop proche pour me laisser des vues claires et distinctes" 'Wait and see what time may do. M. de Clèves has only just died, and that grim spectacle is still so close that I can as yet see nothing clearly and distinctly' (233; 151).[2] While we have no way of knowing whether this passage is an intentional echo of Descartes, the pairing of terms is suggestive: is Mme de Clèves expecting eventually to receive the kind of knowledge about Nemours that Descartes claims is possible if one abides by what is clear and distinct?[3] To answer that question, one could begin by scrutinizing the most puzzling object of knowledge in the novel, the duc de Nemours.

From the beginning of the narration, one can lead students to view Nemours as clear but not distinct, for he is a figure of pure, charismatic presence devoid of reference or comparability to others. While Mme de Clèves's husband, the anti-Nemours, is placed in a temporal context from his first mention—respectfully introduced after his father, identified as the middle of three sons, and characterized as having a precocious form of "prudence" 'discretion' that implies development across time—no information is given about the birth or lineage of the duc de Nemours: as "un chef-d'œuvre de la nature" 'nature's masterpiece' (72; 5), he seems to have sprung full-grown from the loins of some pagan divinity. Although an observer may see a "valeur incomparable" 'unparalleled valour' emanating from his person (72; 5), a moment of reflection suffices for that observer to realize that the phrase is as incoherent as Mme de Clèves's "exemples de vertu inimitables" 'inimitable examples of virtue' (239; 156): what is a value utterly unrelated to all other values? The infinitely attractive Nemours blocks out all else but himself:

> [Il avait] un agrément dans son esprit, dans son visage et dans ses actions, que l'on n'a jamais vu qu'à lui seul . . . un enjouement qui plaisait également aux hommes et aux femmes, . . . et enfin un air dans toute sa personne qui faisait qu'on ne pouvait regarder que lui dans tous les lieux où il paraissait. (72)

> [He had] something pleasing in his turn of mind, his expression, and his gestures, the like of which has never been seen . . . a light-hearted manner that was attractive to men and women alike, . . . a special air of distinction that made it impossible to look at anyone else when he was present. (5)

Nemours's personal magnetism is the source of his power. The surprise he expresses that the Queen of England, "qui ne m'a jamais vu" 'who

has never seen me' (75; 9), might wish to marry him implies he has reason to believe that, once seen, he cannot be resisted. And after sounding
out Elizabeth, Nemours's envoy informs him "qu'il était temps que sa
présence vînt achever ce qui était si bien commencé" 'it was time to go in
person and conclude an enterprise that had been so well begun' (90; 22).

Throughout the novel Nemours's presence casts a kind of spell over
Mme de Clèves:

> Elle ne pouvait s'empêcher d'être troublée de sa vue, et d'avoir pour-
> tant du plaisir à le voir; mais quand elle ne le voyait plus, et qu'elle pen-
> sait que ce charme qu'elle trouvait dans sa vue était le commencement
> des passions, il s'en fallait peu qu'elle ne crût le haïr par la douleur que
> lui donnait cette pensée. (107)

> She could not help being disturbed at the sight of him, and yet taking
> pleasure in seeing him; but when he was no longer before her eyes and
> she reflected that the enchantment she experienced when she saw him
> was the sign of a new-born passion, she came near to believing she
> hated him, so sharp was the pain this thought gave her. (39)

Nemours's presence alternates with reflection about him, the one preclud-
ing the other. Similarly, after the incident of the letter, the longest moment
of intimacy she shares with Nemours,

> Madame de Clèves demeura seule, et sitôt qu'elle ne fut plus soutenue
> par cette joie que donne la présence de ce que l'on aime, elle revint
> comme d'un songe, elle regarda avec étonnement la prodigieuse dif-
> férence de l'état où elle était le soir d'avec celui où elle se trouvait alors.
> (166)

> Mme de Cléves remained alone. As soon as she was no longer sustained
> by the joy of being with a person one loves, she awoke as from a dream.
> She contemplated with astonishment the immense difference between
> the way she had felt the previous evening and the way she felt now.
> (90)

As soon as the scene is over, the unmediated joy of seeing Nemours
is counteracted by the more abstract and disagreeable notion of Mme de
Clèves's moral slippage, her acute awareness of how quickly her virtuous
position is eroding. The opposition between Mme de Clèves's perception
of Nemours in his presence and in his absence underscores the problem
of judging him across time, the intermittency of her analytical powers caused
by Nemours's presence, which undermines the continuity and consistency
of her moral sense: "[J]e pensais hier tout ce que je pense aujourd'hui,

et je fais aujourd'hui tout le contraire de ce que je résolus hier; il faut m'arracher de la présence de monsieur de Nemours" '[M]y thoughts yesterday were no different from what I think today, yet today I do the very opposite of what I decided yesterday. I must tear myself away from M. de Nemours's presence' (167–68; 92).

With this idea of Nemours as a figure whose presence undermines Mme de Clèves's ability to make judgments outside the moment and whose effect on her is thus clear but indistinct, one can direct students toward a more specific examination of the use of the terms *clear* and *distinct* in the novel. While Nemours's effect on Mme de Clèves when they are together corresponds more closely to Descartes's depiction of the passions than to that of perception, Lafayette constantly evokes the problem of perceiving passion by the frequent use of various forms of the word *clair*, for example, *éclaircir*, *éclairer*, *clairement*, and *clairvoyant*. Lafayette uses these terms quite systematically in referring to the discovery and revelation of passion. The exposure of passion thus designated, however, is generally painful, dangerous, or deceptive.

When Mme de Clèves reappears at court after mourning her mother, her inability to hide signs of her passion from both Nemours and his rival the chevalier de Guise is described in these terms:

> Quelque application qu'elle eût à éviter ses regards et à lui parler moins qu'à un autre, il lui échappait de certaines choses qui partaient d'un premier mouvement, qui faisaient juger à ce prince qu'il ne lui était pas indifférent. . . . [L]e chevalier de Guise, . . . son rival, . . . était le seul homme de la Cour qui eût démêlé cette vérité; son intérêt l'avait rendu plus clairvoyant que les autres. (132)

> Try as she might to avoid his gaze and speak to him less than to others, she could not help making certain instinctive signs that gave him reason to believe she was not indifferent to him. . . . [T]he Chevalier de Guise [,] . . . his rival, . . . was the only man at court who had unravelled this secret; his own interest had made him more clear-sighted than the others. (60)

The "clairvoyance" of love gives the lover a kind of intuition: Mme de Clèves's involuntary reaction to Nemours is enough for her suitors to see into her heart, and the unfortunate suitor's clairvoyance only exacerbates his despair. The risks involved in perceiving passion are depicted in similar terms before Mlle de Chartres's marriage, when M. de Clèves and the chevalier de Guise, also rivals, first meet her:

Quoiqu'ils fussent amis, l'éloignement que donnent les mêmes préten-
tions ne leur avait pas permis de s'expliquer ensemble; et leur amitié
s'était refroidie sans qu'ils eussent eu la force de s'éclaircir. (80)

Although they were friends, the estrangement that occurs when two
men pursue the same object had prevented them from discussing the
matter; their friendship had grown cold without their having the courage to enlighten one another. (13)

Another example of the risks of clarity comes when Mme de Clèves,
taken by surprise, impulsively tells Nemours to leave her alone, prompting
him to express his feelings: "Madame de Clèves fut bien fâchée d'avoir
donné lieu à monsieur de Nemours de s'expliquer plus clairement qu'il
n'avait fait en toute sa vie" 'Mme de Clèves was sorry indeed that she had
given M. de Nemours cause to speak more openly than he had ever done
before' (180; 103). Even her recriminations of her husband when she
mistakenly believes that it is he who leaked the story of her *aveu* ("confession") so as to discover the identity of his rival is expressed in terms
of clarification: "Il faut que cet ami de monsieur de Nemours soit des
vôtres et que vous vous soyez fié à lui pour tâcher de vous éclaircir" 'This
friend of M. de Nemours must be a friend of yours, and you must have
confided in him in an attempt to find out the truth' (188; 110). M. de
Clèves's reply reinforces the shameful nature of such an *éclaircissement*:
"[V]oudrait-on éclaircir ses soupçons au prix d'apprendre à quelqu'un ce
que l'on souhaiterait de se cacher à soi-même?" 'Who would wish to set
his suspicions at rest at the cost of revealing to someone else what he
would like to be able to hide from himself?'(188; 110–11). The association
of clarity with dangerous revelation of passion extends to other characters
as well. Those who attempt to disabuse the king of his illusions about his
mistress's fidelity are punished—"Ceux qui ont voulu éclairer le roi sur
sa conduite ont péri dans cette entreprise" 'Those who have sought to
open the King's eyes to her conduct have been ruined in the attempt' (98;
30)—and when Sancerre first hears Estouteville reveal his love for Mme
de Tournon, Sancerre disbelieves his friend until he is finally forced to
demand clarification, however devastating, of his late mistress's infidelity:
"[J]'ai passé ensuite à vouloir m'éclaircir" 'I felt a desire to discover the
truth'(120; 49).

The potential dangers of "clarifying" passion can be used to draw out a
very important intellectual current that characterizes seventeenth-century
literature: the difficulty of knowing when and to whom to reveal one's
feelings and of reading those of other people. Students easily understand

the idea that appearances are often so deceptive that life in society can become a kind of game, a theme that permeates classical texts from Blaise Pascal's *Pensées* to Jean Racine's *Phèdre* to Jean de La Bruyère's *Caractères* and the *Maximes* of François, duc de La Rochefoucauld. What they have far greater difficulty accepting is that the revelation of the truth is not always desirable per se and that in certain circumstances one can be perfectly justified in not clarifying one's feelings. Indeed, a central lesson *La Princesse de Clèves* can teach students is that revelation and concealment of one's feelings can be veritable moral stances that go far beyond the realm of knowledge and into that of ethics. Students need not accept (or even be made aware of) Jansenist teachings about election and free will to understand that the passions are involuntary but that revealing or concealing them generally is not and that to judge Mme de Clèves on the basis of her lack of passion for her husband, for example, is less coherent than judging her on the basis of what she chooses to reveal to him, most notably her *aveu* about her love for another man. That passage can be justifiably called a scene of cruelty not because Mme de Clèves feels no passion for her worthy husband and does feel passion for a man who has done little to deserve it but because her choice of what to reveal and conceal from her husband about her passion for another only exacerbates M. de Clèves's suffering.

The most touching examples of excruciating clarification come in M. de Clèves's erroneous conclusions about Nemours's visit to the garden at Coulommiers while his wife was there. To the messenger who observed Nemours emerging from the garden at dawn M. de Clèves says, "C'est assez, . . . je n'ai pas besoin d'un plus grand éclaircissement" '[T]hat is enough: I need no further enlightenment' (215; 134). Trusting the deceptive clarity of the messenger's deluded expression of chagrin, M. de Clèves declines to demand the details. As he lies dying, still believing his wife unfaithful, he reproaches her—"Pourquoi m'éclairer sur la passion que vous aviez pour monsieur de Nemours, si votre vertu n'avait pas plus d'étendue pour y résister?" 'Why reveal to me your passion for M. de Nemours if your virtue was not better equipped to resist it?' (217; 136)— and after she reveals the truth of what happened that night, he concludes plaintively, "Vous m'avez éclairci trop tard" 'Your explanation comes too late' (219; 138).

The passages cited above allow students to arrive at the conclusion that *clarification* in this novel is associated with the seductive but deceptive promise of happiness through passion. If one instructs them to find examples of the use of *distinction*, they will discover that the term is associated with judgment that goes beyond the limits of the here and now and thus connotes a potential correction of that deceptiveness. Students should also be made aware of the conventional usage of the word in the vocabulary of courtship, which underlies the entire story: a woman who "distinguishes" a man implies that she has singled him out as at least potentially worthy of her, not in the moment but in the long run. Given the dearth of worthy suitors in the novel, distinction sometimes seems to be a category prominent by its absence, as when the vidame de Chartres narrates the queen's discreet overtures to him: "Enfin, il me sembla qu'elle souhaitait de s'assurer de mon secret, et qu'elle avait envie de me confier les siens. Cette pensée m'attacha à elle, je fus touché de cette distinction" 'It became apparent to me, in short, that she wanted to make sure of my ability to keep a secret and to entrust her own secrets to me. This notion drew me to her, I was touched by her favour' (150; 76); the problem here is that the queen's desire to distinguish the dastardly vidame is misplaced. Analogously, when the reine dauphine hands Mme de Clèves a letter supposedly written to Nemours, the princess's hitherto clear perception of his devotion to her becomes indistinct: "[E]lle tenait cette lettre avec une main tremblante; ses pensées étaient si confuses qu'elle n'en avait aucune distincte" 'She held the letter in a hand that trembled; her thoughts were so confused that not a single one was clear and distinct' (143; 70). Once the seductiveness of Nemours's presence is counteracted by a questioning of his reliability, his charm is no longer clear, but Mme de Clèves does not yet have any distinct revised judgment of him.

Throughout the novel, Mme de Clèves struggles to distinguish Nemours in the sense of a precise understanding of his moral worth. When she loses her husband, another man she has never managed to appreciate at his worth, her reaction to his death is again indistinct: "Madame de Clèves demeura dans une affliction si violente qu'elle perdit quasi l'usage de la raison. . . . [E]lle n'était pas encore en état de sentir distinctement sa douleur" 'Mme de Clèves was left in a state of such violent grief that it was as if she had lost the use of her reason. . . . [S]he was still not capable of discerning the true nature of her affliction' (219; 138). Students will be intrigued to discover that her grief over her husband's death does eventually become distinct, but only after she has finally distinguished Nemours from M. de Clèves.

Indeed, the opposition between clarity and distinction in the novel can be effectively used to study the final stages of Mme de Clèves's moral development. When Nemours decides to follow the princess to her country house, he first clarifies the lay of the land by questioning Mme de Martigues about Mme de Clèves's routines:

> Monsieur de Nemours . . . pensa qu'il n'était pas impossible qu'il y pût voir madame de Clèves sans être vu que d'elle. Il fit quelques questions à madame de Martigues pour s'en éclaircir encore; et monsieur de Clèves . . . crut voir dans ce moment ce qui lui passait dans l'esprit. . . .
>
> Monsieur de Clèves ne douta point du sujet de ce voyage; mais il résolut de s'éclaircir de la conduite de sa femme et de ne pas demeurer dans une cruelle incertitude. (207)

> M. de Nemours . . . reflected that it might not be impossible for him to see Mme de Clèves there without being seen by anyone but her. He asked Mme de Martigues some questions to be more certain. M. de Clèves . . . thought he saw what was going through his mind at that moment. . . .
>
> M. de Clèves did not doubt what the purpose of this journey was, but he resolved to inform himself of his wife's conduct and not to remain in such a cruel state of uncertainty. (126–27)

Nemours's "éclaircissements" about Mme de Clèves in the hope that she might agree to a romantic interlude are matched by M. de Clèves's desire to make clear his wife's conduct in the hope that she will not; when the moment of truth arrives, Mme de Clèves disappoints Nemours's expectations by a movement not of clarity but of distinction.

After Nemours makes a noise,

> Madame de Clèves tourna la tête, et, soit qu'elle eût l'esprit rempli de ce prince, ou qu'il fût dans un lieu où la lumière donnait assez pour qu'elle le pût distinguer, elle crut le reconnaître et, sans balancer ni se retourner du côté où il était, elle entra dans le lieu où étaient ses femmes. . . . [E]lle eut envie plusieurs fois de rentrer dans le cabinet et d'aller voir dans le jardin s'il y avait quelqu'un. Peut-être souhaitait-elle, autant qu'elle le craignait, d'y trouver monsieur de Nemours. Mais enfin la raison et la prudence l'emportèrent sur tous ses autres sentiments, et elle trouva qu'il valait mieux demeurer dans le doute où elle était que de prendre le hasard de s'en éclaircir. (210)

> Mme de Clèves turned her head. Whether because her mind was full of his image, or because he was in a spot where the light carried sufficiently for her to make him out, she thought she recognized him and, without hesitating or turning back in his direction, went to join her women in the other room. . . . Several times, the desire came over her to go back

into the side room and thence into the garden to see if anyone was there. Perhaps she wanted to find M. de Nemours there no less than she feared it. But at last good sense and prudence triumphed over all her other feelings, and she decided that it was better to remain in her present state of doubt than to take the risk of discovering the truth. (129–30)

If Mme de Clèves is able to distinguish Nemours in this failed consummation scene, distinction in this case indicates not the selection of a worthy suitor but the revelation of a hard-earned truth. What is being foreshadowed is the princess's ultimate perception of Nemours as less worthy of her than her husband; the *prudence* she uses to resist clarifying whether Nemours is present evokes the *prudence* that characterizes M. de Clèves from the very beginning of the story.

The second stage of Mme de Clèves's movement toward distinct knowledge takes place after M. de Clèves's death. M. de Nemours's decision to arrange a meeting with the princess and start things up again after a respectable amount of time has passed is, unsurprisingly, described in terms of clarification: "[I]l résolut de tenter quelque voie d'éclaircir sa destinée" '[H]e resolved at last to venture upon some course that would decide his destiny' (224; 143). But when the princess admits that she loves him but cannot accept him, it is finally a matter of distinction. Nemours protests:

> —Ah! Madame, vous oubliez que vous m'avez distingué du reste des hommes, ou plutôt vous ne m'en avez jamais distingué: vous vous êtes trompée et je me suis flatté.
>
> —Vous ne vous êtes point flatté, lui répondit-elle; les raisons de mon devoir ne me paraîtraient peut-être pas si fortes sans cette distinction dont vous vous doutez, et c'est elle qui me fait envisager des malheurs à m'attacher à vous. (230)
>
> "Ah! Madame, you forget that you singled me out from the rest of mankind—or perhaps you never did at all; you were mistaken, and I have been flattering myself."
>
> "You have not flattered yourself," she replied; "the reasons my duty dictates would perhaps not seem so persuasive were it not that I do indeed see in you qualities superior to those of other men, as you have guessed: that is what makes me see only unhappiness if I attach myself to you." (147)

What precisely is the princess saying? The term *distinction* first suggests that Nemours's courtship was successful and she has chosen him above all others. But in the light of the above analysis, does it not also imply, ironically, that she has understood him distinctly, exactly as he is, and that understanding, reached not by her heart but by her head, undermines her choice? In fact, if Mme de Clèves has distinguished Nemours as a suitor, it is her senses that have made that choice clear to her. The distinct knowledge of him brought to her by a more abstract form of cognition foretells only unhappiness:

> [L]a certitude de n'être plus aimée de vous comme je le suis me paraît un si horrible malheur que . . . je doute si je pourrais me résoudre à m'exposer à ce malheur. . . . [L]es hommes conservent-ils de la passion dans ces engagements éternels? (230–31)

> [T]he certainty that one day the love you feel for me now will die . . . seems to me so dreadful that. . . . I doubt whether I could bring myself to face such unhappiness. . . . [H]ow long does men's passion last when the bond is eternal? (148)

In concluding that Nemours is neither likely to change permanently nor more capable of fidelity than the category of all men to which he belongs, Mme de Clèves is using the kind of deductive process that underlies distinction, that is, a reasoning in steps: M. de Nemours is a man; men tire of women who return their love; Mme de Clèves returns Nemours's love; therefore Nemours will tire of her. Another way to approach the same problem would be to say that when Mme de Clèves is finally able to compare the "incomparable" Nemours with other men, she finds that in this way at least he is no different from them. Descartes put great stock in this kind of reasoning but sometimes expressed doubts about it because of the difficulty of assuring the truth of one's perceptions across time, that is, when one is no longer in the same moment in which a perception occurred. And yet being simply in the moment with Nemours makes for a clear perception of his irresistibility but not a distinct evaluation of his moral worth.

What does this conundrum imply about Mme de Clèves's final speech, the passage with which we opened, in which the princess speculates that her husband's death is too close for her to have "des vues claires et distinctes" about Nemours? One might argue that by this point her view of Nemours's effect on her is all too clear; as for distinction, will Mme de Clèves ever receive more distinct knowledge about his ability to diverge from the category of unfaithful men without actually putting her theory to the test? What seems to have sometimes given Descartes pause is that the reliance on perception across time implies the loss of a more direct perception based on presence. Perhaps the anxiety Mme de Clèves feels stems from a realization that, to test Nemours's fidelity, she would first need to accept his love but that she is unwilling to start the testing process without knowing its result.

If this is the case, distinct perception might be an epistemological analogue for conjugal fidelity, for however reliable they both may seem, it is impossible to guarantee that they will be true as long as the distinct knowledge that evaluates the prince as similar to or different from all other men remains open to presence and to the empirical. One might draw an analogy here to Phèdre, whose only surefire way of remaining faithful to Thésée is to put an end to her life and who, in the short time it takes to confess her love for Hippolyte before she dies, undermines that plan of artificial closure. If the subject of Lafayette's novel is Mme de Clèves's coming to understand the limitations of male fidelity, perhaps the mode of distinct perception by which she reaches her conclusion about Nemours has its limitations as well. On the one hand, one can hardly imagine a work of literature providing a more elegant conjunction between the means of knowledge (distinct perception) and its ends (the distinction of a worthy suitor). But on the other hand, such a conjunction of process and goal might encourage us to confuse the path with the destination, the method with the knowledge it aims to provide, and thus to go nowhere.

But in the end is that such a bad thing? What tells us that in her years of solitude Mme de Clèves does not go on testing Nemours? Perhaps having clearly understood the implications of his presence, she recognizes that the repercussions of his absence from her—the precondition of infidelity—are not yet distinct and never really could be distinct in the realm of experience, that is, until his or her literal death or the figurative death brought about by the loss of his love. Again, this lesson can be disquieting but also useful for students, many of whom hold the conviction that all conflicts are resolvable with time. To her dying day Mme de Clèves never voices a definitive decision about Nemours's trustworthiness or lack thereof. While she intones that her love for him will be eternal, she never explicitly draws a similar conclusion about his love for her; rather, she retreats into herself. She might have saved herself a lot of heartache, but would have deprived us of the pleasure of following her epistemological adventure, if at the age of sixteen she had avoided the court altogether and, like Descartes, taken up residence in a small heated room.

Notes

1. Among others, Mme de Lafayette frequented the salon of Mme de Sablé, who was a Cartesian. According to Eileen O'Neill, Cartesian doctrine was discussed in this salon ("Women Cartesians" 234).

2. I refer thoughout to Jean Mesnard's edition of *La Princesse de Clèves* and Terence Cave's English translation of the novel.

3. I am grateful to Nicholas Paige, who pointed out to me that the Cartesian resonance of this passage was observed by Pierre Force in "Doute métaphysique et vérité romanesque dans *La Princesse de Clèves* et *Zaïde*."

Louise K. Horowitz

Remembrance of Wars Past: Lafayette's Historical Hindsight

A critical tendency to minimize powerful historical and political realities, frequently subversive, when we consider the literature of seventeenth-century France results in a classroom focused on emotional or moralistic universalities. Affect is given priority in an essentialist, individual fashion, even when, as is the case for Marie-Madeleine Pioche de la Vergne, comtesse de Lafayette, the novellas are historically and politically driven. Lafayette focused in *La Princesse de Clèves* on the months immediately preceding the outbreak of civil warfare in the middle of the sixteenth century. In *La Princesse de Montpensier* the violent, cataclysmic events of the war years are forthrightly at the core of the work.

Scholarly analysis has clearly recognized and acknowledged Lafayette's interest in the sixteenth century's profound religious and political crises, but criticism has often viewed this material as primarily useful for discussing each novella's background or setting. In my classroom, I instead move history to the forefront, and I argue for the indivisibility of the tantalizing romantic adventures and the revealed or concealed historical underpinnings. One of my primary pedagogical tools is to consider specifically with students two major historical and political shifts that mark Lafayette's fiction, not as mere background, but rather as important foci of her work: the sixteenth century's Wars of Religion and the mid-seventeenth-century Fronde (the French civil war that overtly challenged the monarchy's claims and in which women played a central role).

I then concentrate on questions relating to the role of civil and affective transgression, especially on how these two domains are closely intertwined by the author as she presents and challenges patriarchal paradigms of control and power. Genealogy also comes to the forefront during our review of the prominent family names that Lafayette parades in her historical fiction yet that she also sometimes subtly conceals, as she creatively explores her century and its revealing ties to the preceding one. I have found that reading the texts in this fashion, both in the French literature and women's studies classrooms, permits a richer appraisal of Lafayette's role in early modern French literature; indeed, it is through the careful inclusion of political history that the ever-seductive "universal" is best appreciated.

Viewed in this fashion, the opening sentence of Lafayette's 1662 novella, *La Princesse de Montpensier*, is a hallmark of her literary corpus: "Pendant que la guerre civile déchirait la France sous le règne de Charles IX, l'amour ne laissait pas de trouver sa place parmi tant de désordres et d'en causer beaucoup dans son Empire" 'In the reign of Charles IX, when France was torn apart by civil war, Love continued to conduct his affairs amid the disorder and to cause many disorders in his own kingdom' (5; 159).[1] A critical commonplace suggests that Lafayette weaves a complex, interrelating pattern between, on the one hand, erotic passion, and, on the other, warfare. Scholarly studies often view this bond within the parameters of "l'histoire particulière," that is, the private history of significant personages on the world's stage. In this perspective, traditional and official historical writing fails to grasp the hidden causation behind well-noted public events, whereas a more personal or intimate narrative offers a complete and "true" account.

The celebrated story of Anne Boleyn, recounted in Lafayette's *La Princesse de Clèves* by Marie Stuart, includes references (many of whose sources were partisan Catholic historians) to Henry VIII's desire to wed Boleyn as his reason for separating from the Catholic Church. The English king's passionate attachment becomes the core explanation for his calculations, leading ultimately to schism, for Boleyn, while serving Marguerite de Valois at the French court, had been incited by the latter to adopt "les teintures de la religion nouvelle" 'the imprint of the new religion' and would have imparted her religious fervor to Henry VIII (133; 61).[2]

From a quite different vantage point, Lafayette in both *La Princesse de Montpensier* and *La Princesse de Clèves*, while indeed focusing on private history, was also reflecting and commenting directly on history. Pierre Malandain has suggested:

> [L]e *narré* romanesque dans cette oeuvre est un *dit* historique, c'est-à-dire, non seulement un discours situé très précisément *dans* l'histoire, mais surtout un discours *sur* l'histoire; un discours dont l'histoire est moins le référant que le signifié. (23)

> [T]he narrative in this novel is a historical *statement*, that is, not only a discourse *in* history but especially a discourse *on* history; a discourse where history is less the point of reference than its essential meaning. (my trans.)

Moreover, we no longer need to question whether this pattern was clear to Lafayette's contemporaries. Janet Letts, in her definitive study *Legendary Lives in* La Princesse de Clèves, persuasively demonstrates that the informed reading public of the seventeenth century would have readily grasped the historical base of a tale that took place only a century earlier, just as in our era we refer to the American Civil War in an effort to understand modern cultural patterns. Regarding Lafayette's fiction, however, a culturally informed interpretation is problematic because our students, even at an advanced level, lack a ready familiarity with the historically reverberating names that they either do not easily recognize or fail to interrogate for their full associative meanings. Instead, we embrace the seductive romance, while we also search for moralistic meanings concerning the princesse de Clèves's predicament. Despite Lafayette's carefully orchestrated codes, we cling to reading the novellas as moralistically driven tales portraying "exemples . . . inimitables" 'inimitable examples' of female virtue sullied or preserved (239; 156). I am not denying the appeal of this choice, since one of the most compelling novelistic aspects of Lafayette's work is the carefully drawn portrait of erotically charged relationships. Rather, in elucidating other compellingly suggestive aspects of Lafayette's writing, I seek to convey the parallel structures that compete with the love stories for readers interest, or at least competed with them in 1678. In fact, as I strive to convey to students, history, specifically the history of schism and civil war, cannot be separated from love, as the citation from *La Princesse de Montpensier* at the beginning of this study suggests. In Lafayette's universe, history and love find their genesis in the same predicaments and paradoxes that ostensibly herald the imprint of culture. Intertwined narratively, the one embedded in the other, turning in on themselves in the circular pattern announced by the opening sentence of *La Princesse de Montpensier*, libidinous energies emanate from one and the same source.

The novellas are the tale of the tale of history, and both are conditioned and framed by a specific, enduring memory and fear of civil war. They are haunted not only by the long-standing trauma of the preceding century's bitter struggle between Catholics and Protestants but equally, if not more significantly, by the mid-seventeenth-century struggle between the monarchy and prominent, powerful members of the French aristocracy. The Fronde was certainly no winner in the annals of official history. A voiding of its subversive political content was a commonplace for historical writers of the time. The sixteenth century's civil strife, grounded in political and economic realities that often are masked by religiously expressed disputes, serves as an original source for the memories of the intense internal friction of the late 1640s and early 1650s. In this sense, the Fronde becomes *le tracas*, the post-traumatic stress disorder that serves to convey an enduring fear of religious and political schism that had occurred in both France and England. It is this memory—but also therefore this projection—of the fundamental and atavistic division that conditions Lafayette's major writings. In Lafayette, as in Jean Racine, we are always in the time and space of *les frères ennemis* ("the enemy brothers").

Lafayette's two tales, however, separated by sixteen years, are scarcely clones, despite the surface similarity portraying an era of intense internal strife. Lafayette published *La Princesse de Montpensier* in 1662, centering this tale on the cataclysmic moments of Charles IX's reign. The time preceding and including the Saint Bartholomew Day's Massacre of August 1572 dominate the story, while the era's violent aggression parallels the abuse by the prince de Montpensier of his wife, for her tempestuous relationship with Henri de Lorraine, duc de Guise. Lafayette frequently composes without spacing and paragraphing, moving within one long paragraph that sometimes occupies several pages, from the intensity of passion to the spectacle of warfare and back. She names battles, and she names the Huguenots (this appellation per se never appears in *La Princesse de Clèves*), and she intermingles those references with sexually charged escapades, the "chose[s] de roman" 'something out of a romance' (10; 164). She parades sex and war, one libidinous mode commingling with the other in the violently patriarchal universe of the court. The comte de Chabannes desperately desires the princess; and he is thought to be a Huguenot. He indeed was a Huguenot until his return to the Catholic faction, which nonetheless slaughters him at the tale's end. Chabannes's wavering religious identity becomes the source, along with his transgressing sexual desire, of a challenge to the presumed stasis of the state and its fundamental unit, the family, dependent on monogamous standards for women.

It is no coincidence that, by choosing to name names, Lafayette created reverberating echoes among her seventeenth-century readers for whom the historical families were familiar, even intimately so. Embedded in the rivalry for the princesse de Clèves between the prince de Clèves and the duc de Nemours are discretely encoded signs of religious and political dissension, which may be interpreted only through the prism of history. Members of the Clèves family increasingly entered the fray on the Protestant side in the days after Lafayette's work concludes; the Savoie-Nemours clan, meanwhile, became ardent supporters of the Catholic League. Clèves's and Nemours's competition for the love of the princess heralds and mirrors the eventual political and religious division that would haunt France for decades to come. The evocative, spectacular memory of the violent English court becomes the anxious French projection of possible contamination. Civil war also haunts sixteenth-century Scotland, a state on the barbaric edge, whose brutal intrigues implicate and then doom Marie Stuart. Thus Lafayette scripts into her work another example of the competing forces of life and death, on the individual as well as the collective levels.

Following Micheline Cuénin and Chantal Morlet-Chantalat (118–21) and Faith E. Beasley (*Revising* 224–27), I have discussed the reverberating meanings of the château at Coulommiers constructed by the prince and princesse de Clèves (Horowitz, "Truly Inimitable?" 121–23). Many of the most dramatic scenes take place there: the infamous confession of the princess to her husband; his aggressive inquisition, as he demands from her ever more compromising details; Nemours's spying on the disheveled Mme de Clèves, a scene that becomes voyeuristic and phantasmal for both participants. Historically speaking, the residence at Coulommiers was built as a retreat by Catherine de Gonzague, daughter of Henriette de Clèves, although it did not yet exist in 1558–59, the temporal setting for *La Princesse de Clèves*. In 1678, the year of publication, the primary resident of Coulommiers was Marie d'Orléans Longueville, duchesse de Nemours, who had retreated there after her activity as a *frondeuse* ("member of the Fronde"). The duchesse de Nemours's involvement in the Fronde was exceeded among women probably only by "la Grande Mademoiselle," that is, the duchesse de Montpensier.

In psychological terms Lafayette's works tell the tale of the sundered self, trapped in the prison house of Eros and Thanatos. But the sundering, the schism to which I refer, occurs also within the collective body of culture. The fundamental dichotomy of individual existence between the forces of life and death, in Lafayette's perspective (matching Carl Jung's) applies also to the course of civilization and of specific cultures. Civil war, both in the form of the violent antagonisms of the sixteenth century (and yet an ongoing source of anxiety in the seventeenth) and the more recent traumas of the Fronde years, underlies her work.

La Princesse de Montpensier and *La Princesse de Clèves* present and explore this pattern in seemingly different manners. *La Princesse de Clèves*, Lafayette's most celebrated work, is a deeply encoded piece of fiction, dependent on the onomastic display, the vertiginous spilling of names, evident from its first pages. Romance is textually dominant, but, hidden within the tale of passion denied and censured, is the curious nomenclature that points directly to schism, as in the previously mentioned Nemours and Clèves divide (although, in romance terms, we should focus also on their dramatic similarity, for both are named Jacques). Likewise, the duc de Montgomery, who kills Henri II during the tournament celebrating the peace treaty of Cateau-Cambrésis and the double marriage of the king's daughter and sister, shortly thereafter, but beyond the pages of the novella, becomes a prominent figure in the Protestant cause. Montgomery's ultimate betrayal is not explicitly forecast by the narrator; but for readers then as now the slaying of the king is already an obvious symbol of transgression. The image and fear of regicide haunt Lafayette's work and explain her narrative fixation on England, emblem (for the French) of political choices gone haywire.

La Princesse de Montpensier, however, published in 1662 and probably composed in the preceding year, appears to be far more direct in its appraisal of psychic and social warfare. Lafayette structures the work so that passages of civil warfare of the 1570s alternate rapidly and regularly with romance. Descriptions of battles between Catholics and Huguenots are frequently interrupted, often without paragraphing, by overt romantic scenes and vice versa. Political transgressions are doubled by erotic ones, as the norms of patriarchy are twice challenged: the Huguenot rebellion is an attack on the body politic, while Mme de Montpensier's seductive maneuvers with both the duc de Guise and her husband's friend Chabannes are the result of an unhappy arranged marriage, against which her body and soul rebel. Lafayette seems not to be encoding, that is, not repressing narratively, as she does sixteen years later in her masterpiece. In *La Princesse de Montpensier*, students readily perceive that civil schism is brought to the narrative forefront, as is sexual desire: Mme de Montpensier, unlike the princesse de Clèves, is by the novel's last section fully accepting of a liaison with the duc de Guise. The repression that marks *La Princesse de Clèves* is absent in *La Princesse de Montpensier* at the level of the body and of the body politic. Yet the earlier work, while relentlessly depicting sensual passages alongside those concerning the sixteenth century's Wars of Religion, is also simultaneously masking and revealing the memory of the Fronde.

The ostensible "Publisher's Note to the Reader" is the earliest clue to Lafayette's project. This preface is a brief, tightly structured narrative of past and present, death and life:

> Le respect que l'on doit à l'illustre nom qui est à la tête de ce livre, et la considération que l'on doit avoir pour les éminentes personnes qui sont descendues de ceux qui l'ont porté, m'oblige de dire, pour ne pas manquer envers les uns ni les autres en donnant cette histoire au public, qu'elle n'a été tirée d'aucun manuscrit qui nous soit demeuré du temps des personnes dont elle parle. L'Auteur ayant voulu, pour son divertissement, écrire des aventures inventées à plaisir, a jugé plus à propos de prendre des noms connus dans nos histoires que de se servir de ceux que l'on trouve dans les romans, croyant bien que la réputation de Mme de Montpensier ne serait pas blessée par un récit effectivement fabuleux. S'il n'est pas de ce sentiment, j'y supplie par cet avertissement qui sera aussi avantageux à l'Auteur que respectueux pour moi envers les Morts qui y sont intéressés et envers les Vivants qui pourraient y prendre part. (5)

> The respect due to the illustrious name which appears in the title of this book, and the consideration one owes to the eminent descendants of those who have borne that name, requires me to say, if I am to avoid offending them in presenting this story to the public, that it has not been taken from any manuscript that has survived from the time of the persons who figure in it. The Author wished to amuse himself by composing entirely imaginary adventures, but he thought it better to take familiar names from our history than to use those one finds in romances; he judged that Mme de Montpensier's reputation could not

be damaged by a story which was in effect a fiction. If such was not his intention, allow me to make good the lapse by means of this notice, which will be to the Author's advantage and at the same time mark my respect towards the Dead who have an interest in the matter and towards the Living who might share that interest. (158)

According to the prefatory note, *La Princesse de Montpensier* is potentially grounded in confusing names. The heroine, Renée d'Anjou, Mlle de Mézières, is wed against her wishes to the prince de Montpensier, although she is in love with Henri de Lorraine, duc de Guise, the future head of the Catholic League. The novella was published only one decade following the end of the Fronde. For seventeenth-century readers, the name Montpensier, the precise appellation they were counseled by the publisher to ignore (which thereby ineluctably seduces them to heed), was impossible to repress. Lafayette assured through her choice of title that her readers would immediately mentally make the connection to "la Grande Mademoiselle," Louis XIV's cousin, Henri IV's granddaughter, and the ardent *frondeuse*. In Lafayette's first work we may already detect the pattern that ultimately marks and defines *La Princesse de Clèves*, where that other *frondeuse*, Mme de Longueville, the duchesse de Nemours, is "buried" and encoded in the name of Coulommiers. The reference to the other Mme de Montpensier, the unfortunate heroine of Lafayette's novella, cannot fail to evoke and memorialize the events of the Fronde and of its many forceful women participants, while clearly commemorating "la Grande Mademoiselle," whose life, like that of Lafayette's heroine, offered a decided challenge to the norms of patriarchy.

The note to the reader is a curious text. Denying, and thus paradoxically heralding, the connection between the title of the novella and one of the most prominent and subversive women of the seventeenth century, the ostensible publisher evokes a strong collective memory of civil turmoil and war, while focusing explicitly on issues of ancestry, lineage, and genealogy. The preface begs for "the consideration one owes to the eminent descendants of those who have born that name," thereby establishing a correspondence in culturally bound memory between the Wars of Religion and the more recently scarring Fronde. It concludes by emphasizing the hallmark of Lafayette's fiction: the civil wars that sundered French society, with a final signifying reference to "les Morts" 'the Dead' and "les Vivants" 'the Living,' drawing our attention once more to Lafayette's underlying pattern of an individual and collective struggle between the forces of life and death.

As the libidinous energy behind war and its attenuated twin, jealous male rivalry for women, flows through each work, much like the circulating desire that is the core of the lost letter in *La Princesse de Clèves*, the living and the dead are intimately entwined, the one the buried memory of the other, the one evoking the other, in forward and reverse motion. By naming names, Lafayette succeeds in speaking of the dead to the living, while the living are seized, refocused, and channeled through the prism of the dead. Montpensier is the suggestive name that permits this generational leap, but it signifies only social stasis, never progress. From one woman to the next, the same appellation evokes the double cultural fear of female desire and of political schism, the former causally linked, as in the memory of Anne Boleyn, to the latter. Scholars have interpreted Lafayette's choice to codify through nomenclature as a direct result of the changed historical climate that followed the Fronde. After 1661, Louis XIV and Jean-Baptiste Colbert began a fundamental transformation of history into propaganda for the purposes of glorifying the reign of the Sun King. The Fronde was basically erased from the accounts of French history. In Lafayette's time, the disturbing goals and complicated maneuvering that marked this period of civil strife needed to be cleansed, not only for the purposes of the monarchy but also to dampen the narrative of aristocratic rebellion when most of the active players, many from illustrious French families, were still alive. In a more personal fashion, as Alain Niderst has shown (Introduction xxx), Lafayette, in denying that she had any role in the composition of *La Princesse de Clèves* (even fifteen years after its publication) was adhering to some very clear restraints. The chevalier de Lescheraine, to whom she addressed the famous letter disclaiming authorship (*Correspondance* 2: 63–64), was secretary to Mme Royale, born Jeanne de Nemours, the regent of Savoy and a good friend of Lafayette's. Moreover, Lafayette's stepfather, Renaud-René de Sévigné, an active *frondeur*, was close to the court of Savoy through his participation in the Italian campaign, an important alliance that the novelist continued and maintained in later years (Horowitz, "Primary Sources" 172–73). These evident and powerful connections of ancestry are one of the most significant aspects of Lafayette's writing. Yet embedded in this perhaps careful consideration of family identity is, once more, the strikingly suggestive reminder of the Savoie-Nemours family's prominent role in the reverberating and haunting Catholic League, fundamental symbol of enduring schism. Collective cultural memory, which in Lafayette's universe reveals itself through love and war, obsessively returns to the sundering that lies at the genesis of civilization as the strategic rivalries within Henri II's court mirror those among the monarchs of sixteenth-century Europe.

Notes

1. Quotations from *La Princesse de Montpensier* are from Émile Magne's edition *Romans et nouvelles* and Terence Cave's translation.

2. Quotations from *La Princesse de Clèves* are from Jean Mesnard's edition and Terence Cave's translation.

Gabrielle Verdier

Mme d'Aulnoy as Historian and Travel Writer

Since the early 1980s, literary critics and historians have been revisiting early modern women writers of history and historical prose, challenging nineteenth-century positivist doctrines that deemed the so-called fair sex incapable by temperament and education of writing objective history. Groundbreaking research on both sides of the Atlantic has resulted in the inclusion of British writers of historical works such as Margaret Cavendish and Catherine Macaulay in literature and history courses. In France, the exclusion of women history writers has started to be questioned, and thanks to pioneering studies by critics beginning in the late twentieth century, teachers and students are now invited to consider as historical prose the memoirs and historical novels of Anne-Marie-Louise d'Orléans, duchesse de Montpensier; Marie-Madeleine Pioche de la Vergne, comtesse de Lafayette; and Mme de Villedieu.[1]

To this list I would add the travel writing of Marie-Catherine Le Jumel de Barneville, comtesse d'Aulnoy. The scandal surrounding d'Aulnoy's life and her legitimacy as historian is an extreme case of the literary misfortunes of many early modern women of letters: as late as 2009, editors continue to argue over the veracity and objectivity of her *Relation du voyage d'Espagne*, but these battles make the text all the more valuable for classroom use. We can read d'Aulnoy's historical works as entertaining milestones in the development of the novel, in France and in England, and as examples of both the opposition and the fusion of truth and fiction in seventeenth- and eighteenth-century historical narrative.

A successor to Montpensier, Lafayette and Villedieu, d'Aulnoy (1650/51–1705), expanded the range of French historical writing by publishing in 1690 *Mémoires de la cour d'Espagne* and in 1691 the first long travel account by a woman, *Relation du voyage d'Espagne*. It was translated the same year as *The Lady's Travels into Spain*, a title that calls attention to the author's gender. In 1698, the prestigious Ricrovrati Academy of Padua recognized her achievement by admitting d'Aulnoy as its seventh female member and naming her Clio, muse of history. Since she is known today as the most prominent female author of fairy tales of the late seventeenth century, modern readers may find this honor puzzling. D'Aulnoy, however, had earned an international reputation as the author of historical works well before the publication of her fairy tale collections in 1697 and 1698. Her court memoirs and historical novels, which focused on France's rivals, Spain and England, were translated into English, German, and Dutch. In England her reputation as female travel writer was used to launch her tales, published in 1707 as part 4 of *The Diverting Works of the Countess D'Anois, Author of Ladies* Travels to Spain.[2] D'Aulnoy's fame in England leads Melvin Palmer to conclude that this "Celebrated French Wit" as she was called was more popular than any of her French contemporaries in the first half of the eighteenth century ("Madame d'Aulnoy in England" 238).

As d'Aulnoy's fairy tales were adapted for a new audience of child readers, however, her life was scrutinized, with disapproval (Verdier, "Memoirs" and "Comment"). Certain readers began to doubt she had traveled to Spain, and her alleged involvement in a plot, probably hatched by her mother, to entrap her husband in the capital crime of *lèse majesté* was particularly damaging. A fantasy writer famous for her exuberant imagination could not be trusted to tell the truth, especially if she was an *aventurière* implicated in crimes. Thus, although d'Aulnoy's Spanish narratives had inspired Victor Hugo's romantic dramas *Hernani* and *Ruy Blas*, they were discredited in the late nineteenth century, and her other historical works forgotten.

Today, our nuanced understanding of the varieties of historical truth and gendered writing allows us to avoid black-and-white categories. Teachers are in an excellent position to help students appreciate d'Aulnoy's style in presenting personalities, situations, and events and understand the political implications of her textual strategies.[3]

D'Aulnoy's *Relation*

Relation du voyage d'Espagne best distinguishes d'Aulnoy from the previous generation of historical writers and is her most original work. Villedieu's fictional heroine in *Memoires de la vie de Henriette–Sylvie de Molière* and the Mancini sisters travel to flee aggressive males, a familiar romance emplotment (see Goldsmith, *Publishing*; Kuizenga's trans. [*Memoirs*]). D'Aulnoy, however, has a more mundane reason to travel—she is taking her daughter to live with her grandmother in Spain—and subordinates autobiography to observation as the enticing subtitle of the 1692 translation *The Lady's Travels into Spain* indicates: *Describing the Devotions, Nunneries, Humours, Customs, Laws, Militia, Trade, Diet and Recreations of That People. Intermixed with Great Variety of Modern Adventures and Surprising Accidents: Being the Truest and Best REMARKS Extant on That Court and Country.* The French permission to publish is in the name of Mme B*** D***, as for d'Aulnoy's Spanish memoirs, and the dedication to Louis XIV's nephew Philippe, duc de Chartres, future duc d'Orléans, is signed in the feminine. While many of her contemporaries published anonymously, d'Aulnoy announces her gender, an especially bold move when entering the male-dominated travel genre because the road was absolutely "no place for a lady" in the seventeenth century (Hodgson). The English titles further highlighted her gender, which very likely helped make *Lady's Travels* a best seller. By 1740, it had been reprinted eleven times in French and fourteen in English, including two serializations.

Several other reasons explain this phenomenal success. Exotic Spain, land of bullfights and inquisitions, was both intriguing and critically important in European power struggles.[4] Travel accounts were popular in general: the taste for movement and discovery over stability, expressed dramatically the European "crise de la conscience" 'crisis of consciousness' at the turn of the eighteenth century (Hazard). (Two centuries after that "crisis" we are still fascinated by the other discovered through travel, real or virtual.)[5] Dozens of male visitors had written about their travels in Spain before d'Aulnoy (see Foulché-Delbosc, *Bibliographie*), but Spain as experienced by a woman was doubly fascinating, especially because she could enter women's spaces from which men were excluded. *Relation* captivated new readers by its delightfully colorful and witty style as well as its timeliness. She "initiated a type of fiction in which the author tells . . . the story of a journey in a series of letters," leading, according to Robert Adams Day, to the epistolary novel in England (42–43) and appealing to readers' increasing preference for realism over historical romance (Palmer, "Madame d'Aulnoy in England" 240).

Controversies

Relation remained the most important source of information on Spain for nearly two centuries. The French historian Hippolyte Taine marveled: "You can see, you can touch" the strange customs; the figures painted by Félix Lope de Vega, Pedro Calderón de la Barca, Bartolomé Esteban Murillo, and Francisco de Zurbaran really did roam the roads of Spain (qtd. in Seguin 8). Some of d'Aulnoy's stories seemed exaggerated, but it was not until the later nineteenth century that her veracity was challenged. William Stirling discovered memoirs of the court of Spain covering the same period as d'Aulnoy's, 1679–81, and coinciding with the trip she relates in *Relation*. He attributed them to Pierre de Villars, French ambassador to Spain, whose wife had written lively letters describing the court of Carlos and his French bride. Noticing resemblances between d'Aulnoy's and Villars's memoirs, historians concluded that the countess drew most of her information from the ambassador. Although the lady was now somewhat discredited, Mme B. Carey felt that, for their style d'Aulnoy's Spanish works deserved a critical edition, which she published in two volumes in 1874 and 1876 as *La Cour et la ville de Madrid vers la fin du XVIIe siècle* ("The Court and City of Madrid toward the End of the Seventeenth Century"). In 1893, however, Alfred Morel-Fatio published a second edition of Villars's memoirs based on a longer manuscript and declared that d'Aulnoy merely elaborated on Villars.

The French Hispanist R. Foulché-Delbosc dealt the crowning blow in 1926. In his critical edition of *Relation*, he "demonstrated" that, in addition to Villars's memoirs (probably written by his secretary), d'Aulnoy's information came from published sources — earlier travel accounts, periodicals (e.g., *Mercure Galant* and *Gazette*) — and private letters and that her anecdotes were fiction, inspired by Spanish novels and plays. He removed the four inset stories because they are works "de pure imagination" and "d'une sensibilité écceurante" 'of nauseating sentimentality' like her 1692 Spanish novellas ("Madame d'Aulnoy" 19). While conceding that he was not able to find sources for many observations, he concluded that

Relation, too, was just a very clever compilation: "Mme d'Aulnoy n'est jamais allée en Espagne" 'Madame d'Aulnoy never went to Spain' (90; "Madame d'Aulnoy and Spain" lxi). Routledge used Foulché-Delbosc's article as the introduction to its 2004 reprint of the English translation. A publicity blurb features a quotation from the *Saturday Review*:

> Of all the literary fakes this is surely the most impudent, ingenious, and successful. The Comtesse d'Aulnoy was never in Spain (but) she was a born traveller. Not without reason have the editors of the Broadway Travellers included her fiction in their library of fact. For, despite its falseness, it is intellectually the real thing.

Other scholars are persuaded that d'Aulnoy did go to Spain. Her biography makes travels to Spain, Holland, and England plausible, and the readers of her day never doubted them. Born in Normandy around 1650 to a noble family, Marie-Catherine was married in March 1666 to a rich man nearly three times her age. Handsome François de La Motte, baron d'Aulnoy, had risen in the service of César de Vendôme as lover, *valet de chambre*, and finally comptroller general of his household.[6] By nineteen, pregnant with her fourth child, Marie-Catherine hated her husband, while her mother, Mme de Gudanne, was furious at his profligacy. The ladies (historians disagree on Marie-Catherine's involvement) hatched a plot with accomplices (lovers?) to entrap La Motte into bad-mouthing Louis XIV — *lèse majesté*, a capital offense. The plot failed: La Motte was exonerated, two male accomplices were executed, and the ladies disappeared. Gudanne fled to Italy, then to Madrid, becoming a pensioned personality at court while serving as a French spy. Marie-Catherine may have spent some time in prison or a convent with her newborn, Judith-Henriette (Roche-Mazon 143–50), but her whereabouts from 1670 to 1690 remain mysterious. In her English memoirs and Spanish travels, d'Aulnoy asserts that she sojourned in England and Spain and frequented the highest circles. Indeed, d'Aulnoy probably brought Judith-Henriette to Spain since Mme de Gudanne raised her granddaughter and married her handsomely. Foulché-Delbosc casts doubt on d'Aulnoy's word, arguing that her name does not appear in other accounts ("Madame d'Aulnoy" 14), but a document discovered in the Gironde archives in 1936 records a stopover d'Aulnoy made on her way to Spain (Palmer, "Madame d'Aulnoy's Pseudo-Autobiographical Works" 221). In his 1944 book on the "fantasies and realities" of her travelogue, the Spanish historian Gabriel Maura Gamazo concludes that d'Aulnoy resided in Madrid for twenty months and, when she observed closely, recorded with "fotográfica fidelidad" 'photographic accuracy' (341; my trans.).

Yet d'Aulnoy's reputation as a loose woman who framed her (abusive) husband continues to color reevaluation of her *Relation*. The Spanish editor Miguel Ángel Vega doubts d'Aulnoy went to Spain, stating that her true vocation was the fairy tale, and attacks "esta parricida frustrada" 'this frustrated husband-killer' (12; my trans.), this "Mata Hari *avant la lettre*" (14), for spreading "el cliché 'España, negra'" 'the "black legend" of Spain's decline' by her inventions and diatribes (40), judging her observations on high society in her anti-Spanish works worthy of the gossip magazine *Hola* (28). Taking the contrary position, the French editor Maria-Susana Seguin and the critic Fernande Gontier are convinced the voyage occurred. Gontier fills the biographical blanks in her 2005 novel, *Histoire de la comtesse d'Aulnoy*, with spying missions and glamorous liaisons inspired by Gudanne's life and d'Aulnoy's historical narratives. However gender may influence judgment, all critics agree that in 1690 d'Aulnoy burst on the French literary scene, opened a famous salon, and produced eleven best sellers in thirteen years.

Traveling in Spain with the Ingenious French Lady

History or hoax? Developments in historiography and literary criticism have discredited the dichotomies of nineteenth-century positivism separating scientific history from literature. No exact boundaries between these genres existed in the seventeenth century: history writing was governed by rhetoric, and the novel gained legitimacy by imitating history. Postmodern theorists expose the tropes and emplotment structuring even the most so-called objective history (White). Although Percy Adams classified d'Aulnoy as a "fireside" traveler, he showed that differences between the exaggerations of authentic travelers and their imitators the "travel liars," both of whom exploited the craze for travel accounts during the Enlightenment, are a matter of nuance (99). Indeed, the tradition of the "traveler as liar" is ancient, and authentic travel accounts studied by historians also follow narrative patterns. As basic facts about Europe became known, travel accounts were increasingly read for entertainment (Stagl).

Though there is no obvious plot, narrative conventions and symmetries abound in *Relation*. D'Aulnoy organizes her text into fifteen long letters to a female cousin in France: letters 1–7, 20 February–15 March 1679, recount the trip from Bayonne to Madrid and contain the novellas told by persons she meets; letters 8–14, 28 March–30 September 1679, describe events in Madrid, including preparations for the new queen; the shorter letter 15, dated 28 September 1680, summarizes Marie-Louise's arrival in Spain and refers to her own Spanish memoirs for details. Critics chide that it was impossible to write hundreds of pages in less than a month while traveling in a litter on mules and sleeping in awful Spanish inns. This observation is valid, of course, but the letter was a standard form of travel writing. Moreover, it allows d'Aulnoy to create a witty female narrator recounting her experiences to another woman, a device so successful that she used it again in the English memoirs. She thereby claims the authority that French women had gained by their writings (DeJean, *Tender Georgraphies*), which her English titles recognize. Yet other critics still consider that she was merely expressing the nationalistic prejudices of a French bluestocking (Vega 11).

D'Aulnoy's travel account thus invites students to explore the issues of bias, reliability, and originality. True, d'Aulnoy made mistakes and borrowed from previous accounts, especially Antoine de Brunel, *Voyage d'Espagne* (1655), and François Bertaut, *Journal du voyage d'Espagne* (1659). Her borrowings lend themselves to useful classroom activities: one can ask students to compare, for example, her description of Spanish inns and bullfights with Bertaut's (698, 780–82) and characterize her verve and point of view. D'Aulnoy's trip was limited to northwestern Spain and Madrid; yet to give readers a taste of other parts of the country, she invents traveling companions, four Spanish gentlemen who describe their compatriots and provinces (Toledo, Andalusia, Galicia, and Catalonia) and tell stories that capture the flavor of Spain. Unlike typical travelogues but like particular histories and novels, *Relation* is full of conversations with native informants she meets (or invents), giving an added air of authenticity to Spanish exotica. Again, these encounters can be compared with other travelers' descriptions of the regions (see the works in Bennassar and Bennassar). In her unusual preface introducing literary into historical vocabulary, d'Aulnoy justifies her method mixing observations and reports (Hester 92–94). To be believable, works must be true and also seem plausible ("vraisemblables"); yet she does not omit some "hyperboles" she heard from trustworthy persons (d'Aulnoy, *Relation* [2005] 31). Indeed, what seems extravagant in France may be common elsewhere. What better way to arouse interest in supposedly passionate Spain?

D'Aulnoy must have jotted notes, read earlier accounts, and kept her mother's letters, because when Spain was in the headlines again she produced the memoirs and travels in record time. After Marie-Louise's sudden death in February 1689, rumors of poisoning grew, especially since Carlos II was quickly remarried by proxy to Maria Ana of Neuberg in August 1689. In March 1690, the *Mercure Galant* began serializing anonymous memoirs on Spain. These correspond to the short version of the memoirs attributed to Villars. In April, the *Mercure* announced that serial publication would be interrupted because the author had agreed to publish the entire text. D'Aulnoy's *Memoires* appeared in November 1690, and *Relation*, dedicated to Marie-Louise's half-brother Philippe, in April 1691. Whether d'Aulnoy planted Villars's (stolen) manuscript (Foulché-Delbosc, "Madame d'Aulnoy") or used her own first draft (Gontier) to attract readers, the tactic was clever marketing, comparable to the publication strategies devised by Villedieu and Lafayette.

Relation is controversial, a literary gem, and a fascinating early example of ethnology and can be useful in a variety of courses: French literature, English literature, cross-cultural studies, early modern social history, travel writing, art and architecture, fashion and food, and women's studies. D'Aulnoy's observations reveal as much about France as they do Spain and even more about a woman's perspective as the author admires and criticizes things Spanish: excellent fruit, chocolate, and meat, but dishes ruined by all the garlic and saffron her Norman stomach cannot digest; beautiful and witty Spanish women who are compromised by skinniness, torturous fashions, toxic cosmetics, and lack of education; gallant but frightening courtship rituals—the most prized, flagellants spattering their lady with their blood. Born storyteller and *salonnière*, d'Aulnoy brings pathos and irony to dramatize the grand absurdity of bullfights and auto-da-fé stock travelogue topics: coquettish *mandarina* cows used to lure the wildest bulls and Carlos II fed raw garlic for stamina during fourteen-hour Inquisition ceremonies, followed by stomach-turning (for a Frenchwoman) blood and carnage. A brilliant blend of fact; often strange, exemplary fiction; and a seductive narrative voice, d'Aulnoy's *Relation* is the first masterpiece in the European travel genre written by a woman, and it raises fundamental stylistic, historical, and theoretical issues for teachers and students to consider, including national and gender biases, changing definitions of history and literature, and the ideological underpinnings of criticism.

Notes

1. Faith E. Beasley defines the ways in which women "revised" official male-authored history by stressing psychological causes in their "particular" histories, thus expanding the boundaries of historical truth (*Revising*). Elizabeth C. Goldsmith studies women's role in developing new types of life writing and the risks they took in publishing their stories (*Publishing*).

2. The following list of d'Aulnoy's historical works includes the publication dates of the French original and the translation and significant differences in the English titles.

> *Mémoires de la cour d'Espagne* (1690); *Memoirs . . . Written by an Ingenious French Lady* (1692)
>
> *Relation du voyage d'Espagne* (1691); *The Lady's Travels into Spain* (1691); *The Ingenious and Diverting Letters of the Lady's Travels into Spain* (1692)
>
> *Histoire de Jean de Bourbon, Prince de Carency* (1692; trans. 1719)
>
> *Nouvelles espagnoles* (1692) in *Diverting Works* (1707)
>
> *Nouvelles et mémoires historiques* (1693)
>
> *Mémoires de la cour d'Angleterre* (1695; trans. 1695)
>
> *Le Comte de Warwick* (1703; trans. 1707)

3. New technologies make d'Aulnoy's historical works accessible. Most of the French originals are digitized on the Bibliothèque Nationale de France site (http://www.bnf.fr/); English translations appear in microform collections (*Early British Fiction, Pre 1750*; *Early English Books, 1641–1700*) and on *Eighteenth Century Collections Online* (http://www.gale.com/EighteenthCentury/). We can now read *Relation* in a new critical edition by Maria-Susana Seguin (2005) or selections in the anthology of French travelers to Spain edited by Bartolomé Bennassar and Lucile Bennassar (1998) and in the Magellan series on cities (*Madrid* [2006]). A Spanish translation by Pilar Blanco and Miguel Ángel Vega (2000) is available in the Cómo nos vieron ("How They Saw Us") series. Routledge reprinted its expensive 1930 translation in 2004. A new English translation and introduction is forthcoming in the series The Other Voice in Early Modern Europe.

4. France and Spain had a centuries-old love-hate relationship (Shaub), fueled by wars ended by royal marriages to consolidate treaties. In 1559, Henri II's daughter Elizabeth of Valois was married to Philip II of Spain to seal the peace of Cateau-Cambresis. In 1615, the double marriages of the French and Spanish-Hapsburg royal siblings were arranged for political reasons: Anne of Austria wed Louis XIII, and his sister Elisabeth of Bourbon wed Anne's brother, Philip IV of Spain. The children of each royal couple, Louis XIV and Maria Teresa of Spain, twice first cousins, were married in 1660 to cement the treaty of Pyrenees. The chronology of d'Aulnoy's Spanish memoirs and travels coincides with the next royal marriage, in 1679, to seal the treaty of Nijmegen ending the Franco-Dutch war and advancing France's influence over Spain. Marie-Louise d'Orléans, daughter of Louis XIV's brother Philippe and Henrietta of England, was married to the "bewitched" Carlos II of Spain, disfigured and retarded because of Hapsburg inbreeding. Carlos was the son of Philip IV and his second wife, his niece Mariana

of Austria, also a Hapsburg. In 1689, the childless, twenty-seven-year-old Marie-Louise died and rumors of poisoning spread—again. Her mother, Henrietta, had also died suddenly at twenty-seven, in 1670, as had Elisabeth of Valois at twenty-one, in 1568, perhaps of poison. Declining Spain worried the rest of Europe. If Carlos did not produce an heir (likely) with his second wife, the Spanish Empire was up for grabs. Carlos named as successor Philippe of Anjou, his grand-nephew and Louis XIV's grandson, provoking the War of the Spanish Succession. Philippe V is the ancestor of Juan Carlos I, the present king of Spain. D'Aulnoy's Spanish works capitalized on this latest royal tragedy and international crisis.

5. See the *Huntington Library Quarterly's* 2007 special issue *Travel Writing in the Early Modern World*, which includes Nathalie Hester's provocative article on *Relation* as the "art of telling the truth."

6. César de Vendôme was the son of Henri IV and his mistress Gabrielle d'Estrées. His Hôtel de Vendôme in Paris was "popularly known as the Hôtel de Sodome" (Crompton 339).

Henriette Goldwyn

Mme Du Noyer's *Mémoires*: The Politics of Religion in the Ancien Régime

Anne-Marguerite Du Noyer's *Mémoires* chronicles a tragic turning point in European history and serves as critical and compelling reading for anyone interested in early modern France and Europe. The work illuminates issues that are at the heart of our multicultural and diverse societies, such as identity, persecution, displacement, immigration, exile, asylum, loss of mother tongue, and ultimately the obliquities of belonging in a new borderline culture. The travels and travails of a French Protestant at the end of the seventeenth and beginning of the eighteenth centuries pry open questions that resonate in a modern world increasingly dominated by the mass movement of peoples set adrift, wandering and in search of asylum. Mme Du Noyer's firsthand experience of exile after the revocation of the Edict of Nantes in 1685 presents, with poignancy and unfailing humor, a sense of the displacement and the fragmented psyche of the refugee and refugee community. As Charles Weiss indicates, the term *refugee* was in fact first coined in England to describe early French Huguenots who sought freedom of conscience and who began fleeing France in the sixteenth century after their religion came under attack there (1: x).

Mémoires also serves to reevaluate the contribution made by the French Protestant community in exile to the literature of testimony and protest after the revocation. Previously unexamined by literary critics, this area of study has drawn particular interest from cultural historians, sociologists, and historians of religion who have pondered the numerous ramifications of the revocation both in France and in the adopted Protestant countries where refugees finally settled. Therefore *Mémoires* provides today's readers with a unique voice and perspective on this watershed period in French political, intellectual, economic, and cultural life.

Historical Background

It would first be worthwhile to evoke for students and the reader in general the historical and cultural context of *Mémoires* and the respective importance of the Edict of Nantes and its revocation, the Edict of Fontainebleau, the two most crucial moments of the reformed church's destiny in France. Declared "perpéptuel et irrévocable," the Edict of Nantes—signed in April 1598 by Louis XIV's grandfather and converted Catholic, Henry IV— had granted Protestants equality and a degree of religious and political freedom. It proclaimed the legal recognition of the reformed church's privileges, including the freedom to hold public worship in cities and towns controlled by the reformed party. It also assured the right to uninhibited religious instruction and access to state offices for Protestants. The Edict of Nantes thus symbolically placed the kingdom of France at the forefront of religious tolerance by allowing religious pluralism; it was even called the first modern charter of liberty (Garrisson 16–21; Holt 164–66). However, for almost a century following the edict, the French Catholic Church worked unrelentingly to extirpate the heretics present in France, and on 22 October 1685 the Edict of Fontainebleau was proclaimed. Its preamble and twelve articles systematically revoked the Edict of Nantes and declared Protestantism illegal. As a result, approximately 150,000 to 200,000 Protestants fled France and sought asylum in surrounding Protestant countries—mainly in England, the United Provinces (the Netherlands), Switzerland, Germany, and Brandenburg (Prussia)—from 1680 to 1700. These countries came to be known as "refuges" (Le Goff 493; Bots 69; Yardéni 32).

As a member of an outlawed political-religious minority in France, Mme Du Noyer sheds a unique light on this pivotal moment. She produced a subversive text in a time of international war driven by Louis XIV's obsession with defining religious truth as part of an absolutist political project that sought to impose conformity and obedience from above. She chronicles life in France during and after the revocation and in the Netherlands and England where she lived as a Huguenot refugee. Her firsthand account of daily life in France and in the refuge details the acute identity crisis experienced by the community of refugees after their exodus from the homeland. The refuge constituted *un entre-deux culturel*, a cultural in-between, where the French Protestant community, torn from its roots, reconstituted itself and, as Mme Du Noyer points out, built a new identity different from the original one.

Biography: Becoming a Writer

Mme Du Noyer was born Anne-Marguerite Petit in Nîmes on 12 June 1663 to an upper-middle-class Calvinist family. Her mother died after giving birth to her, and her father relinquished her to her maternal aunt, in exchange for payment of his debts. Her aunt, the only person to whom Mme Du Noyer would remain profoundly attached all her life and whose death provoked a spiritual crisis, raised her niece in the strict Calvinist faith and gave her an outstanding education. Her *Mémoires* includes numerous literary and historical references. What predominates, however, is her extraordinary knowledge of the scriptures, which Mme Du Noyer quotes abundantly and from which she draws strength and solace in the bleakest moments of her life. After the revocation, she witnessed the cruelties perpetuated by the dragoons in their efforts to convert Protestant households but managed to resist all attempts of forced abjuration and subsequently escaped. She fled France twice in personally distressing circumstances and found refuge in Holland both times. She escaped first in 1686, disguised as a *marmiton*, or kitchen aide, and again in 1701 with her two young daughters, fleeing from her Catholic husband but obliged to leave her only son behind (she had promised her dying aunt to wed her daughters to Protestants only). In the Netherlands, a hotbed of oppositional propaganda journalism, Mme Du Noyer flirted with the most radical ideologies circulating in Europe at the time, ideas that ultimately led to rethinking the entire structure of the state and paved the way for a new political order.

Under these circumstances, Mme Du Noyer turned to writing. Her *Lettres historiques et galantes* (1707–17; "Historic and Gallant Letters"), which describes the main events of the end of Louis XIV's reign and the beginning of the regency, launched her as an author and established her reputation in her adopted country's literary community. Like most of the antimonarchical and antipapist Huguenot literature emanating from Holland, *Les Lettres historiques et galantes* was censored in France but widely distributed in Europe. This lampooning gazette in epistolary form—epistolary journalism—was a best seller and a controversial success in francophone circles and afforded Mme Du Noyer financial freedom until her death. Louis XIV is known to have avidly read some of the early letters that circulated separately and clandestinely in France. Mme Du Noyer was thus closely involved in the literary production of the refuge. In his dictionary entry, Alain Nabarra argues that exile provided her with the opportunity of becoming the first French female journalist and one of the most successful editors in chief, from 1711 to 1719, of the satirical periodical *La Quintessence des nouvelles* ("The Quintessence of News"), first founded in 1689 by other refugee authors (1: 360).

Mémoires

Mme Du Noyer started writing *Mémoires* in 1703 during her second exile. Originally published in Cologne in five volumes (2,159 pages) from 1710 to 1711, the work investigates the period of her life from 1663 to 1710. *Mémoires* can be divided into two parts. The first part mainly covers Mme Du Noyer's life in France before and during the revocation, the arrival of the royal dragoons in Nîmes, the faction between the various pastors, her first exile, her return, her incarcerations in Catholic institutions before abjuration, the restitution of her properties upon marrying a Catholic, and the birth of her children. The second part begins with her second escape accompanied by her daughters; her crisscrossing between the Netherlands, England, and the Spanish Netherlands (Belgium); her attempts to obtain aid from the government of host countries; making a living by sewing wigs; seeing her daughters married; settling down in The Hague to write *Mémoires*, and especially describing her two-timing coreligionists and such Protestant heroes as Jean Cavalier, the leader of the Camisards, and his consorts.

Why did she turn to autobiography at this particular moment? Mme Du Noyer insists in *Mémoires* that she took up her pen to refute pretense and gossip, to silence the slander she had met with during her life in Holland and England, and to incite the public's "compassion" (27).[1] Like women memorialists who preceded her—such as Mme de Villedieu, Hortense Mancini, and Henriette-Julie de Castelnau, comtesse de Murat— Mme Du Noyer turns to autobiography to clear her name from calumny. Her reputation had come under attack from several directions. First, she suffered the continual tongue-lashing of her paternal aunt in London, who considered her niece a burden and dismissed her claims of destitution, maintaining that Mme Du Noyer had left France with enough money and jewels not to be begging for assistance (212). Then Mme Du Noyer was reprehended by her husband, who in his own memoirs rebuffs her version of events and cruelly caricatures her. In a letter sent after her escape, he condemns her for having abducted his daughters over whom, he states, she has no legal rights (*Mémoires* 185). She was also judged severely as a mother by some members of the strict Calvinist community of the refuge for having made bad marriage matches for her daughters just to be rid of them; some were even shocked that she had taught her daughters how to sing, dance, and act and that she took pride in their beauty and public performances (181). Furthermore, they denounced the deterioration of her relationship with her daughters and ultimately blamed her for her oldest daughter's return to France and reconversion to Catholicism. Most tragic, it was a hostile Protestant community in exile, the same coreligionists Mme Du Noyer had longed to be reunited with in the land of freedom of conscience, that censured her and scrutinized her every move, going as far as admonishing her for not attending mass often enough. She discovered that these "faux-frères," or false brothers, revealed themselves to be most dangerous in their deceit, greed, envy, and hurtful gossip (196). Forced to establish itself on a new form of sociability, this community emphasized solidarity, mutual aid, and strict adherence to community regulations; those who, like Mme Du Noyer, fell outside its structure of Protestant solidarity found themselves ostracized. Deeply disillusioned, she writes, "J'avais compté sur la faim, la soif, le péril des voyages mais non pas sur celui des faux-frères" 'I had counted on hunger, thirst, and the dangers of travel, but not on those false brothers' (196). Inspired by Luke's famous "of one heart and soul" (Acts 4.32), she concludes on a bitter note, "J'avais cru que les réfugiés n'avaient qu'un cœur et qu'une âme" 'I had thought that my fellow refugees would all be of one heart and soul' (196). Faced with loneliness and the hostility from her fellow refugees, she especially feels this double loss of community (of a society of origin in France and the hoped-for community in the refuge), which prompts her to write her memoirs.

Historical Value

Mémoires contributes to the literature of testimony and protest after the promulgation of the Edict of Fontainebleau. First and foremost the work represents an indelible source of evidence of the exclusionary methods instituted against the reformed community before and after the revocation. Mme Du Noyer writes, "On disait hautement que le roi ne voulait qu'une religion dans son royaume et qu'il était résolu d'employer la force pour y réussir" 'It was openly reported that the king wanted only one religion in his kingdom and that he had resolved to use force to achieve his goal' (46). The mechanisms to eradicate heresy put in place by Louis XIV's government began with systematic regularity in 1681 and included persecutions, prosecutions, and forced abjurations. The infamously cruel "dragonnades," the practice of posting royal dragoons in the homes of recalcitrant Protestants to force them into abjuration by harassing and torturing them, culminated in an atmosphere of dread between 1685 and 1686 (46). Terrorized by the booted missionaries, the Huguenots turned to paid abjurations or the "caisse de conversion" 'conversion till,' which guaranteed a swift return to Catholicism (49).

Furthermore, *Mémoires* is a testimony to how certain articles of the revocation—such as those pertaining to the demolition of existing temples (art. 1), the forbidding of any public or private assembly of the reformed subjects (arts. 2 and 3), the banishment of Protestant ministers who refuse to abjure (art. 4), and the declaration that any child born to Protestant parents must be brought up in the Catholic faith (art. 8)—affected the core of the reformed faith transforming the life of the community forever (*Édit de Fontainebleau*). From the inception of her text, Mme Du Noyer specifically identifies freedom of conscience as an individual right (*Mémoires* 168). She champions the rights of Protestant mothers, including herself, to exercise the full powers and responsibilities of parenthood (185–86). In doing so, she defies the articles of the revocation that legalized, among other things, the removal of children from Huguenot parents for abjuration and sent many a reformed mother into exile without her children (76).

The memoirs also record the dangers and difficulties of illegal immigration, the long peregrinations of refugees in search of a new homeland, and their requisitions for financial help that proved to be a tremendous source of paranoia, creating insecurity and jealousy (174, 177, 191). In addition, they investigate life in the refuge and the institutions and networks that hosted asylum seekers. Mme Du Noyer especially describes life at the Schiedam Society, founded by the Princess of Orange in the Netherlands for Huguenot women of little means, where the memorialist spent six months with her daughters (181). Her sense of irony, expressed through her acerbic pen, intensifies criticism of the Sun King and his ministers, especially in contrast with her portrait of the hospitality and generosity found in the Dutch Republic and to a lesser degree in England's constitutional monarchy. Mme Du Noyer questions the legitimacy of absolute monarchy and lays bare the hypocrisy of religious leaders of all creeds (including Calvinists), as well as the lies of remunerated court historians. Ultimately taking aim at "un certain nombre de gens répandus dans le refuge et masqués même en réfugiés, qui sont proprement des émissaires de la France envoyés pour mettre la division et pour aigrir les gens . . . brouillent la mère avec l'enfant, la sœur avec le frère" 'those disguised as refugees who are emissaries of France sent to promote discord and dissension . . . pitting child against mother, sister against brother' (376), she deplores vehemently the use of spies sent by France to destabilize the newly formed community in exile. Her personal story is therefore closely intertwined with the documentary evidence of this intense historical moment and the life of her coreligionists. Mme Du Noyer is simultaneously author, narrator, heroine, and historical witness of events that she recounts.

Literary Value

In addition to their value as personal and historical memorial, these popular and widely read memoirs are of interest for their literary innovations. These are no longer memoirs presented as *appareils d'état*, or state documents, focusing on illustrious actors and their contribution to historical events. In this hybrid text with an exploded structure, Mme Du Noyer weaves her personal history into the official history. Thus the narrative is constantly interrupted and derailed by digressions and accumulations and interspersed with intercalated stories, letters, poems, conversations, and historical events. The structural dislocation of the text reflects the displaced self of the refugee (Goldwyn, Introduction 14). Against the accusation that her memoirs lacked verisimilitude—a charge that illustrates the seventeenth century's ongoing debate opposing *vérité*, or truth, and *vraisemblance*, or verisimilitude—Mme Du Noyer establishes their factual accuracy. In the foreword to her first volume, she argues with conviction that the province of memoirs is the recounting of unparalleled, extraordinary, and unique events that are nevertheless historically true ([1710–11] 1: 4–6).

Most important, this text, published during the final years of Louis XIV's reign, breaks with the established tradition of aristocratic memoirs. Mme Du Noyer does not write from an idyllic and privileged place as did, for example, Anne-Marie-Louise d'Orléans, duchesse de Montpensier, who began writing her memoirs while in exile at her château of Saint-Fargeau, with the hope of one day regaining her place at court. Rather, Mme Du Noyer wrote from a miserable room rented by the day and with no hope of ever returning to France. Far from marking a privileged situation of introspection and reflection, exile confronted her with the hard realities of being a refugee. Transforming a genre dominated by nostalgia for a courtly space under the gaze of the Sun King, she draws attention to the larger world outside the court and does not shy away from narrating the most shocking and sordid realities, including humiliations, inquisitions, prohibitions, confiscations, and the ever-present anxiety over financial destitution. Recounting the saddest period of her life, the second part of *Mémoires* thrusts the reader into a picaresque universe in which refugees are grappling with material, social, political, religious, and linguistic difficulties. Mme Du Noyer turns her attention to everyday life, the economy, the political misery of her coreligionists, and the practice of exile (planned itineraries, hiring guides, the cost of freedom). She discusses the sacrifice required for a meal of thirty *sous* (the equivalent of American pennies), the cost of shoes, gloves, ribbons, combs, and even pins (96). Most acute, she emphasizes the economic, cultural, and linguistic limbo in which the refugees existed and how they forged new identities that at times did not coincide with the originals. Her ruthlessly realistic viewpoint, her irreverence, and her scathing pen also focus on heroic ideals. In particular, Mme Du Noyer demystifies these ideals through her representation of figures like "le roi révocateur" (Louis XIV as betrayer) and Cavalier, "le héros imposteur" (19, 63), reducing the chief of the Camisard insurrection, a heroic figure of French Protestantism, to a vulgar "héros de Gonesse" (a reference to his origins as an apprentice bread baker [292]). Her vitriolic portraits put into relief the conventions and ideals of the age and the disillusionment experienced by those most affected by their violation.

Moreover, Mme Du Noyer's *Mémoires* foreshadows the travel accounts and travelers of the eighteenth century. She describes in great detail the regions and countries she visited. Yet these are not mere sentimental journeys, escapes from a jealous husband, or fictional wanderings where, under the guise of exoticism, the author hides a sociopolitical agenda. Mme Du Noyer, the heroine-narrator, is in constant motion: she must travel to preserve her moral, political, and personal freedom. For her, freedom of thought and existence constitute the imperative to flee and write. In a life marked by turmoil and movement, her traveling trunk, which she frequently loses, comes to symbolize her fragile link to the past, the umbilical cord between the mother country that has renounced her and her adopted country. It is the only object from her past that she cherishes, although its contents remain mysterious.

As a novelist, gazetteer, *épistolière* (letter writer), editor, and memorialist of the French Protestant diaspora and refuge, Mme Du Noyer enjoyed a certain degree of notoriety and success by scandal until the end of the eighteenth century. Two of the seven volumes of *Lettres historiques et galantes* (being reedited by Nancy O'Connor) were translated into English in 1716 (*Letters*). Cited by historians of Protestantism, partly because of her references to Cavalier and Voltaire, who had fallen in love with her youngest daughter, Pimpette, Mme Du Noyer's complete works have only received serious critical attention since the 1980s, mainly from historians of journalism of the ancien régime, historians of Protestantism, and gender scholars. This research has revived a body of work of lasting interest to scholars and students alike. The unique historical and literary value of *Mémoires*, and the timely issues it raises regarding exile, asylum, religious persecution, identity, and life writing, make Mme Du Noyer's work a valuable addition to syllabi of the early modern period.

Note

1. Unless otherwise specified, selections and citations of Mme Du Noyer's *Mémoires* are from my critical edition. All translations from the French are mine with the help of Cecilia Feilla.

Roxanne Decker Lalande

Mme de Villedieu and the Cornelian Paradigm: Problems of Gender and Genre in *Le Favori*

In this essay I propose an analytical reading of Mme de Villedieu's last play, *Le Favori* ("The Favorite"), that would encourage students to make useful comparisons between a female author's interpretation of authoritative rules and the canon, as embodied by Pierre Corneille. Such an approach has proved to stimulate classroom discussions encompassing historical, sociological, and cultural considerations on gender specificity in seventeenth-century France. My syllabus would necessarily include a close reading of Corneille's *Le Cid* and Molière's *Le Misanthrope*, which also bears striking resemblances to *Le Favori*. Villedieu's play would thus benefit from a careful comparison with tragic and comic conventions, as represented by the two male-authored plays.

Mme de Villedieu's brief but spectacular foray into the Parisian theater at the beginning of her authorial career can be seen as a challenge to the literary establishment. Tragedy was commonly considered male territory, requiring classical erudition generally unavailable to women of the time (see Gethner in this volume). Villedieu was the first woman author to have her plays professionally performed in the Hôtel de Bourgogne in Paris and the first to be at the core of a heated polemical dispute between her mentor, François Hédelin, abbé d'Aubignac, the foremost dramatic theorist of the time, and Corneille, her principal source. In June 1665 she received first billing for a command performance of *Le Favori*, which was staged by Molière in the gardens of Versailles. Although she has the merit of having collaborated more directly with Molière than with any other dramatist, it is ultimately Corneille's theater Villedieu chose to emulate. I attempt to reveal here the manner in which *Le Favori* echoes Corneille's early comedies as well as his great tragicomedies, while nonetheless deviating from the model and clouding generic distinctions even further in the process.

In the tragicomedy *Le Favori*, the problematic question of genre classification arises in much the same manner as it did with many of Corneille's greatest works. Perry Gethner ("Conspirators") and Henriette Goldwyn ("Men") have both examined the manner in which Mme de Villedieu patterned her dramatic works on the Cornelian paradigm, as well as her departures from that model. The playwright no doubt intended *Le Favori* to be a serious drama with a happy ending, in the vein of the Cornelian tetralogy. The author, though occasionally playful, was not a comic author and clearly did not want to be classified as one (Woodrough 44–45). Indeed, few of the scenes are laughable, the tone is generally serious, the style is elevated and in alexandrine verse form, and the characters are of noble birth. Though the subject matter is fictional rather than historical and based on a play by the Spanish playwright Tirso de Molina, the prevailing opinion is that the play serves as a thinly veiled reference to contemporary events, namely the condemnation of Louis XIV's finance minister Nicolas Fouquet four months before the staging of her play at Versailles (Hogg).

It is equally noteworthy that the previously mentioned collaboration between Villedieu and Molière began in 1660. On 14 April 1665 Molière chose *Le Favori* as one of the opening productions at the Théâtre du Palais-Royal. Contemporary reviews classified the play as a comedy, perhaps because of the intercalation of ballets or its pairing with comedies and farce. Goldwyn points out that the original title was *Le Favori ou la Coquette*, then changed to *La Coquette ou le Favori*, and finally became simply *Le Favori*. This change in title reflects the difficulty in making a clear-cut generic classification, as the coquette figure distinctly belongs to the realm of comedy. Despite the hero Moncade's proclivity for fits of melancholy and despair, the characters are unmistakably reminiscent of the comic tradition: the king is a deus ex machina, the favorite Moncade a misanthrope, Elvire a coquette, and Clotaire a vain and ridiculous courtier. Nevertheless, the play was finally published as a tragicomedy in 1665.

Thus from a purely formal point of view, the play straddles both genres: the idyllic setting—a country home in the kingdom of Barcelona—the novelistic names, and the fictional plot with its happy ending clearly pertain to the realm of comedy. The play's locale is Moncade's estate, which is described in the following terms:

> Vous êtes dans un lieu dont l'art et la nature
> Ont à l'envie formé l'admirable structure,
> Et le Roi, vous comblant d'un si rare bienfait,
> Vous fit le plus beau don que Prince ait jamais fait,
> Cette diversité de coteaux et de plaines,
> Ces superbes jardins, ces marbres, ces fontaines,
> Ces refuges sacrés de l'ombre et de l'effroi,
> Ces fertiles déserts . . .
>
> (act 1, sc. 1, lines 89–96)
>
> You are in a place whose magnificence has been fashioned by art and nature, and the king, your munificent benefactor, has given you the most beautiful gift ever bestowed by a prince: this varied landscape of hills and plains, these superb gardens, marble statues, and fountains, these sacred shelters from shadowy fears, these fertile deserts . . . [1]

This pleasure palace is indeed evocative of the gardens of Versailles themselves. In her account of the festivities at Versailles, Villedieu insists on the festive, comedic aspects of her play. It is framed by a comic prologue by Molière, includes interludes of ballet, and ends with the audience's coming on stage for a ball after the play. No doubt Molière's framing of the play was designed to downplay its subversive subtext.

To examine the historical antecedents of this play, one must begin by looking at two key components of Cornelian theater. As Serge Doubrovsky has pointed out, in Cornelian tragedy the relationship between the king and the hero (his favorite subject) is essential to the play's development and gives meaning and structure to its conclusion. It allows the play to end on a conciliatory note and thereby to fall short of pure tragedy. Essentially, the model relationship between hero and sovereign in Corneille's best-known works is the submission of the hero's quest for individual glory to the state and the monarch, whom the hero would potentially have the power to overthrow. Thus when the crown rests on the head of the monarch but depends on the arm of the hero, individualism is dangerously akin to subversion and mutiny and must be reigned in at all costs by a voluntary act of submission on the part of the hero. In exchange, the king has the power to immortalize the hero's achievements. The denouement points to a stable order in which everyone knows his place and in which the dialectic between sovereign and subject has, at least temporarily, been resolved.

Corneille's comedies, on the other hand, are marked by the shifting parameters of the love triangle, in which love is portrayed rarely as exclusive and eternal and usually as transitory and fickle, hence the continual need to put love to the test through duplicity and trickery. In Corneille's comedies, the issue at stake is to find stability and durability in a romantic relationship. The dynamic tension results from the imbalance of power between the object of desire and the desiring subject. Permanence, though desirable, is seldom obtained, and while it is not uncommon for lovers to unite, they often do so at the expense of rivals who are left to make do with an expedient but loveless match. Given the time constraints of the theatrical event, the best way to prove love's duration is through the test or trial, which serves to substantiate the degree of willingness to suffer for love and which in turn is often (mis)taken for a sign of durability and depth of feeling. In *Le Favori*, it is the monarch, not one of the lovers, who tests the loyalty of his favorite subject by arbitrarily withdrawing royal favor, thus mirroring the paradigm prevalent in Cornelian comedy and offering a remarkably original interpretation of the relationship between individual subjectivity and monarchy in the early modern period.

Goldwyn contrasts *Le Favori* to Cornelian drama by opposing the Cornelian *généreux* to the new order of the court chameleon ("Men").[2] Moncade has served the king on the battlefield, and his heroism is a source of pride, yet given the current social climate at court, royal favor has become a meaningless currency in an economy of flattery, where it no longer needs to be earned through noble deeds. Like Louis XIV, the king of Barcelona has formulated a politics of pleasure designed to ensure loyalty through a promise of affection (Peters, "Kingship" 263, 271). These conflicting values are in great part responsible for the perceived generic opposition between the realms of comedy and tragedy.

As the play begins, we are reminded of the monarch's indebtedness to Moncade. As in Corneille's great tragicomedies, the king's favorite is not only in command of the army but has also proved his loyalty to the sovereign through heroic bravery, and it is stated that the royal crown has been secured by the hero's courage in battle:

> Il est depuis dix ans l'appui de cet Etat;
> Deux fois nous avons vu Barcelone troublée,
> Et lui seul affermir la couronne ébranlée;
> Tant de fameux exploits parlent en sa faveur.
>
> (3.1.636–39)

For ten years now [Moncade] has been the backbone of this state; twice there have been disturbances in Barcelona and he alone has secured the teetering crown. So many famous deeds speak in his favor.

Whereas in Cornelian drama, the hero's quest for individual glory poses a serious threat to royal authority, which rests on the hero's valor and ability to defend the throne, that threat is never apparent in Villedieu's play, or rather it has already been resolved from the beginning at Moncade's expense:

> Il fut toujours soumis aux ordres de son Roi,
> Et de tous ses désirs il se fit une loi;
> Se peut-il que ce Prince ait perdu la mémoire
> De tant de grands exploits, de mérite et de gloire?
> (3.1.643–46)

> He was always submissive to his king's commands and ever at his beck and call. Can the prince have forgotten such great and commendable deeds of glory?

Moncade's submissiveness to the king is never at issue in Villedieu's play: even when the king seems to exert unjust tyrannical power, the absolutist doctrine is taken for granted. But this lack of challenge to the royal power ultimately leads to the feminization of Moncade. Moncade's submission to the king's desire is predicated on the eradication of a natural desire for personal recognition. This self-effacement has resulted in the hero's profound sense of alienation and in turn melancholy. In Cornelian drama, the hero's submission to the state is rewarded by the consecration of his glory through the king's memory. *Le Favori*, however, brings up the demoralizing possibility that a king might have a faulty memory.

Gethner observes that despite the king's sudden feigned displeasure and dismissal, neither Moncade nor Lindamire, the woman he loves, disputes the monarch's right to revoke his favor at any time ("Conspirators"). Though Lindamire and Moncade may have the right to remonstrate, they seem to hold the fundamental belief that the monarch owes his subjects nothing: "Quoique fasse un sujet, son Roi ne lui doit rien" 'Whatever a subject may do, his king owes him nothing' (3.1.647). Thus only the subject can be indebted, whereas the monarch's obligation is abolished a priori. The king's favor is perceived as a gratuitous reward, and therefore all the more magnanimous. Consequently, the cause for Moncade's insecurity and resentment stems primarily from his relationship to his sovereign.

In the economy of exchange, Moncade can own nothing because he owes everything to the king: "Mais ami, que me sert ce bien de ma fortune, / Si de tant de beautés je n'en possède aucune?" 'But friend, what good is good fortune, if I do not own a single one of these beautiful things?' (1.1.105–06). Moncade's melancholy arises from a deep-seated alienation deriving from his desire to be loved and admired for himself, not for his position of favorite to the monarch. This desire is based on an acute perception of the distinction between *être* and *paraître*, between essence and appearance. His power is illusory and he is dispossessed. He owns nothing, not even his honor, for the king is the source of his social stature and that favor can always be retracted arbitrarily: "les bontés du Roi sont mes plus grands appas" 'The king's favor is my greatest quality' (2.2.506). His value, in economic terms, is calculated solely on the basis of the monarch's investiture in him. It is not inherent, but temporarily bestowed:

> Et c'est d'un favori le plus pressant ennui,
> Que d'avoir comme il a, tant d'attraits *hors de lui*.
> Sa gloire a plus d'amis bien souvent que lui-même,
> Quelquefois on le hait en même temps qu'on l'aime.
> (1.4.234–37; my emphasis)

And the favorite subject's most compelling unease is to have so many *peripheral* assets. His credit often attracts more friends than he himself, and sometimes he is loved and hated simultaneously.

Moncade's essential internal value has been displaced by an honor and a presence that is alien to him; he has been reduced to a reflection of the king's presence. He has been seduced, if not physically, then at least by the material benefits afforded by his position as favorite. But by accepting these benefits, he has compromised his integrity and has to play the same game as the courtiers and flatterers he despises. There is a troubling loss of boundaries between the subject and his king revelatory of the tensions of defining the individual in an absolutist state. How can Moncade define himself when, as he claims, "On ne peut discerner de ce qu'il a d'appas / Ce qu'il a d'étranger, de ce qui ne l'est pas?" 'One cannot distinguish between (a favorite's) external and internal attributes' (1.4.239–40). The text reflects this internal division and reveals it as a form of paranoid schizophrenia: "Je suis jaloux de ma propre fortune, / Ce n'est pas moi qu'on aime, on aime vos faveurs, / Et vos bienfaits, Seigneur, m'enlèvent tous les cœurs 'I am envious of my own good fortune. It is your favor, not I, that is cherished, and your benevolence, my lord, leaves me bereft of the goodwill of others' (1.6.314–16). The hero is irreconcilably divided between a drive to individual independence and the imperative submission to the logic of absolutism (Peters, "Kingship" 265). Moncade reflects "Un homme qui parvient à ce degré suprême, / Doit se garder de tous, et surtout de lui-même" 'A man who has arrived at such heights must protect himself from everyone and above all from himself' (1.1.33–34).

Mitchell Greenberg argues that at the center of all melancholy is a loss, an essential void as elusive as it is pervasive. It is the inscrutability of this void that renders melancholia all the more opaque. In melancholia, the person lost always camouflages what has been lost (Greenberg 155). For Moncade, the problem is not so much the desire to be loved for himself as the subconscious realization that there is no self to be loved. What Moncade desires in wishing for autonomy is the eradication of the source of his being: the father-king: "Ah! Que je tiens, Ami, celui digne d'envie / Qui ne met qu'en lui seul le bonheur de sa vie; / Qui, fuyant des grandeurs les appas pernicieux" 'Ah! How I envy, dear friend, the man who finds life's happiness solely within himself and who flees the pernicious lure of greatness, trusting only his senses, his duty, and the gods' (2.6.581–83). Moncade would like to be empowered to reject the father's economy in which he lends himself to alienation in consumption. Although the favorite never bypasses the status of passive object, the sovereign interprets Moncade's resentment of his favors as a subconscious desire to eradicate (symbolically murder) the king to attain the right to self-determination.

Thus, to the monarch, Moncade's dissatisfaction is a form of sedition in its own right, a lack of gratitude and recognition of indebtedness, on the one hand, and the hero's apparent desire to separate his identity from that of the king, on the other. The king is jealous of this drive toward autonomy and, similar to a jilted lover, wishes for the impossible: total possession of the object of desire. More perceptive than his friend, Don Alvar perceives this trait in the king: "Les Princes sont jaloux de leur autorité, / Et veulent faire seuls notre félicité" 'Princes are jealous of their authority and want the exclusive right to make you happy' (3.1.623–24).

The subtext of the interchange between king and favorite is tinged with suggestiveness and couched in amorous terminology:

Le Roi: Quoi! Toute ma tendresse et toute ma faveur
   Ne sauraient l'emporter sur cette folle ardeur,
   Donc je ne puis *remplir* ce cœur insatiable
   .   .   .   .

> Quoi! je me donne tout entier à ce cœur téméraire,
> Et je suis moins pour lui qu'une vaine chimère,
> Qu'une vapeur d'amour dont il est enflammé?
> *Moncade*: Ah Seigneur! ah Seigneur! vous n'avez point aimé.
> *Le Roi*: Non, je n'aimais que toi, cruel, je te le confesse. (1.6.339–41, 345–49)

> *The King*: What! All of my tenderness and benevolence cannot conquer your
> mad obsession and I cannot satisfy your insatiable heart. . . . What! I give
> myself up entirely to this foolhardy soul and I am no more to him than a
> worthless fantasy, a vapor of love that has inflamed him.
> *Moncade*: Oh, Lord! Lord! One can tell that you have never loved.
> *The King*: That is not so, cruel-hearted one; I confess that I have loved only
> you.

The exchanges between Moncade and the king are remarkable for their
dramatic hyperbole: "The homosocial bond that characterizes the relationships of men in cultures of patriarchy is staged here as explicitly homo-
erotic" (Peters, "Kingship" 269). The monarch wishes to fill the favorite's
heart, to the exclusion of any other sentiment. The play thus reveals the
truth of tyranny: it desires dominion not only in the public but in the private sphere as well. The king's apparent bonhomie and benevolent affection is in reality a form of violence, a violation of the individual's intimacy,
stemming from his fear of the potential political menace of the private.

> Je savais qu'on doit craindre et qu'on doit obéir,
> Mais pour la liberté d'aimer et de haïr,
> Je croyais que les Rois la laissaient à nos âmes,
> Et que l'amour dut seul se mêler de nos flammes;
> Cette erreur se dissipe et je commence à voir
> Qu'un Roi peut ce qu'il veut et n'a qu'à tout vouloir.
> (3.1.627–32)

> I was aware that a king is to be feared and obeyed, but as for the free-
> dom to love and hate, I believed that to be a matter of choice and that
> love alone could determine our affection. This error has been dispelled
> and I have begun to see that a king can do as he wishes, and that he
> can wish for anything.

Interestingly, the accusations against Moncade are couched in terms
of sexual frigidity: "Chacun commence à voir avec quelle froideur, / Vous
recevez du Roi les pressantes caresses" 'Everyone is beginning to notice
that you shrink from the king's pressing embrace' (1.1.76–77). It is the
king's overbearing affection and invasiveness that Moncade finds insuffer-
able, and Clotaire's accusation that he is a fomenter of rebellion, though

never taken literally by the king, could nonetheless be seen as partially justified from an absolutist perspective. The individual is secret and therefore dangerous to the absolutist order, yet Villedieu treats this potentially serious threat by stressing the sentimental and quasi-amorous nature of the king's relationship with Moncade, thereby switching from the tragic to the comic register.

Whereas the relationship between Lindamire and Moncade is egalitarian and relatively undramatic, the bond between the king and his favorite is predicated on an imbalance of power. The king controls the market of sexual desire, in a society in which power and sexuality are openly linked: "Ce grand courroux du Roi, cet exil de la Cour / N'a pour tout fondement que cet effet d'amour?" 'What? The king's great anger and your exile from court are merely the effects of his love?' (3.1.615–16). Moncade is readily aware of the conflict between his love for Lindamire and his duty to the king: "Qu'on fait malaisément l'amour et son devoir, / Et qu'au cœur délicat se trouve de faiblesse, / Quand il sert à la fois son maître et sa maîtresse." 'How awkward it is to reconcile love and duty, and how weak the gentle heart that serves at once both master and mistress!' (1.5.264–66).

The hero's gaze is focused on a rival image, that of Lindamire, which distracts him from his adulation of the monarch. It is also narcissistically turned inward, as well as toward his reflection in like-minded others, rather than toward his sovereign.

The capricious actions of the king reveal him to be as much of a coquette as the flighty Elvire. This similarity brings us to a possible solution to the puzzling question of the play's original title: *La Coquette ou le Favori*. Despite Elvire's marginal role in the drama, her presence authorizes a lengthy definition and discussion of the term *coquette*. In response to her confidante Léonor's remonstrations, Elvire responds:

> Certes je ne sais pas si je la suis ou non;
> Mais je m'aime beaucoup et *j'aime fort à plaire*,
> J'aime assez le grand bruit et je hais le *mystère*,
> Je fais moins pour autrui que je ne fais pour moi,
> Et la *joie* est en tout et ma règle et ma loi.
> Si c'est ce qu'on appelle à présent des coquettes,
> Il est vrai, je la suis.
>
> (2.1.436–42; my emphasis)

In truth, I do not know whether or not I am (a coquette), but I do love myself above all others and I *love to be admired*. I enjoy great fanfare as much as I despise *mystery*. What I do for others is really for myself, and *fun* is my one true measure in life. If that is what people today call a coquette, then truly I am one.

In much the same manner and for the same reasons as Elvire, the king is jealous of Lindamire. For him, too, there is a pressing, self-centered need to be desired and an aversion to the mystery or secrecy of the individual. Most important, the king and the coquette are implicitly linked through their whimsical manipulation of sexual politics or the politics of pleasure; this link in turn ties the play to the comic register.

The bond between the king and his favorite derives from the exclusion of the feminine, articulating a false notion of male integrity that can be disrupted by the presence of the disunifying other: woman. Nonetheless, without the reassuring presence of Lindamire, the homosocial relationship between the king and Moncade has the potential to turn into a homo-erotic relationship in which the king dominates a submissive, feminized Moncade. This tension is resolved in due course by the king, whose coup de théâtre ultimately results in Lindamire's declaration of love for Moncade. Thus the king is able to satisfy his favorite by bestowing on him the woman of his choice as a sexual surrogate. He will be able to "gratifier sa création" 'gratify his own creation' (1.6.280). Ultimately, the sovereign's "generosity" reduces Moncade to silence, and, although he claims to be well enough rewarded with the proof of Lindamire's love, the outcome of events shows him to be even more heavily indebted than before, for now he owes Lindamire's love and ultimately his sentimental well-being to the king as well: "Eh bien! Après cela Moncade est-il heureux? / Goûtera-t-il encore une joie imparfaite, / Et son Roi lui sait-il donner ce qu'il souhaite?" 'Well now! Is Moncade finally happy? Will his joy remain bittersweet, and does his king understand how to grant his wishes?' (5.6.1392–94). The king's smug complacency is predicated on a complete misinterpretation of his favorite's dilemma. Moncade's discourse of disenfranchisement is suppressed, and his subsequent reply to the king is effectively interrupted. Moncade now has lost not only his sense of self but the ability to express that discontent as well. It would therefore be difficult to overlook the tragic overtones of the happy ending. Despite the happy ending of comedy, in which the lovers unite and the king's trust is restored, Moncade remains mute, cut off from transcendence, allowing history to continue without him. He is trapped in a play suspended between rival endings, at once comic and tragic, and caught in a contrived performance initiated by the king, who in the end rewrites his own play by "pardoning"

Moncade, thereby consolidating his own power. In the process, the king abdicates his desire for Moncade, thus becoming the embodiment of supreme reason, order, and light: civilized ideals in opposition to the murkiness of the disorder of the senses represented by the desiring monarch. Although Villedieu's play exploits the Cornelian model of tragicomedy by centering primarily on the hero-king relationship, her feminization of Moncade lends the play a lighter tone reminiscent of Cornelian comedy. Villedieu is known for having rewritten history by reinstating the feminine subtext, by disclosing the private sexual politics subtending major public decisions and events. That this relationship has sexual and homoerotic overtones is readily apparent. Villedieu's distinctly feminine plot twist consists in revealing the private sphere of male bonding as one that is potentially parallel in terms of its instability and exclusivity to that of lover and mistress. This twist is what brings the play to that slippery frontier between tragedy, serious drama, and comedy. The usefulness of teaching *Le Favori* today becomes apparent when one considers the subtle ways in which it deviates from canonical male-authored texts. Despite her desire to emulate Cornelian drama, Villedieu provides us with a distinctly feminine variant, which can help students of literature and literary history better understand the neoclassical paradigm through a comparative process.

Notes

1. All translations from the French are my own and based on Perry Gethner's 1993 edition of *Le Favori*.

2. The term *généreux* corresponds to the early-seventeenth-century ideal of a man with moral integrity who is willing to place love of country above love and love above self.

Volker Schröder

Verse and Versatility: The Poetry of Antoinette Deshoulières

From the late seventeenth to the early nineteenth century, Antoinette du Ligier de la Garde, dame Deshoulières,[1] was France's best-known and most widely published woman poet. Not only were her collected verses constantly reedited and extensive excerpts included in standard poetry anthologies; her prominence was also reflected in general reference works. The *Encyclopédie* discussed several of her poems and cited her to illustrate that the word *auteur* could be applied to women as well as men: Mme Dacier and Mme Deshoulières "tiennent rang parmi les bons *auteurs*" 'rank among the good *authors*.'[2] In 1798, she made her way into the dictionary of the Académie Française, whose fifth edition clarified the usage of *poète* and *poétesse* by referring to Sappho and Deshoulières (*Dictionnaire*). In the sixth edition (1835), she was again cited as example: "*Madame Deshoulières était un poète aimable*" 'Mme Deshoulières was an amiable poet'; the same sentence appeared in the subsequent editions, as well as in Émile Maximilien Paul Littré's dictionary ("the Littré"). Both Charles Batteux's *Cours de belles-lettres* ("A Course of the Belles-Lettres") and Jean-François de La Harpe's equally influential *Lycée, ou Cours de littérature ancienne et moderne* ("Lycaeum; or, Course of Lectures on Ancient and Modern Literature"), though generally dismissive of the female literary tradition, contained rather detailed and not entirely negative critiques of Deshoulières's poems, especially her famous idylls, which had achieved canonical status as models of French pastoral poetry.

In the course of the nineteenth century, however, Deshoulières's reputation underwent a dramatic reversal, leading from quasi-classical exemplarity to equivocal notoriety and, finally, almost utter obscurity. In 1839, Charles-Augustin Sainte-Beuve attributed her recent fall from favor to "un goût plus nouveau et dédaigneux" 'a more novel and disdainful taste' and undertook a nuanced reassessment of her case: "Elle vaut, elle valait beaucoup mieux que sa réputation aujourd'hui" 'She is, she was much better than her current reputation' (1310). Eight years later, Gustave Flaubert referred to "le talent si décrié et si peu connu de cette poète" 'this poet's talent, so much disparaged and so little known' (119). By the 1880s, only one of her poems—the melodious and melancholy "Vers allégoriques" to her children—had apparently survived in public memory, prompting one editor to rebut "ce triage sommaire et quelque peu brutal" 'this summary and somewhat brutal triage' through a new edition of selected works, the first to appear in over fifty years (Lescure ii). Yet the situation remained essentially unchanged throughout the twentieth century; Deshoulières was granted at most a few pages in various anthologies and manuals. No new edition appeared after 1924, when Frédéric Lachèvre included twenty-five of her poems in *Les Derniers Libertins*. The only comprehensive historical and critical study was George Borglum's unpublished Yale dissertation, completed in 1939. Whereas an ever-growing number of prerevolutionary women writers were progressively "resurrected," original scholarship on Deshoulières remained surprisingly sparse and yielded no more than a few scattered articles (Perkins, "Mme Deshoulières" and "Libertinage"; Kroll; Génetiot; for her fortune in eighteenth-century Germany and Russia, see K. Goodman and Klein, respectively).

The opportunity to pay renewed attention to this vanished *bon auteur* has thus been left almost entirely to the twenty-first century. Some progress was made in 2002, with Perry Gethner's edition of Deshoulières's tragedy *Genséric* (in the second volume of his *Femmes dramaturges*) and John J. Conley's discussion of her "naturalist creed" in *The Suspicion of Virtue: Women Philosophers in Neoclassical France* (45). While the dramatist and the "philosopher" were highlighted in America, the poet and lyricist caught the ear of the French singer-songwriter Jean-Louis Murat, who produced a CD featuring Isabelle Huppert as the voice of Antoinette, along with an attractive anthology and a (now defunct) Web site. In 2005, perhaps alerted by Murat's *coup de cœur*, the Parisian publishing house Bartillat issued a semischolarly edition of Deshoulières's *Poésies completes*; this 770-page volume (which includes the poems by her daughter Antoinette-Thérèse) presents much valuable historical material but is marred by countless textual errors and should be handled with caution (Hémon-Fabre and Leroy). A more thorough critical edition of Deshoulières's poetry, prepared by Sophie Tonolo, is forthcoming from Éditions Classiques Garnier; in the meantime, many of the earlier editions are easily accessible, in both print and digital form.

Today, after two centuries dominated by disdainful neglect and summary dismissal, teaching Deshoulières is once again a viable and worthwhile option. Over the past years, I have included selections from her poetry in undergraduate and graduate courses on French seventeenth-century women writers, where Deshoulières can be beneficially inserted in the vicinity of contemporaries such as Madeleine de Scudéry; Madeleine de Souvré, marquise de Sablé; or Marie de Rabutin-Chantal, marquise de Sévigné. But her work also lends itself to a variety of other teaching contexts, from poetry surveys and courses on classical *moralistes* to seminars on epistolarity or the representation of animals in literature and philosophy, among other possibilities.

To pursue this option successfully, we first need to confront the ingrained idea that French poetry went into hibernation at the end of the baroque era and that, with the sole exception of Jean de La Fontaine, no "true" poet survived the onset of classicism. More than any other woman writer of her time, Deshoulières compels us to reconsider the place and functions of poetry in the literary culture of the ancien régime, for her authorship and authority rested exclusively on her verse. She did attempt to conquer the stage, but *Genséric* was unsuccessful, leading her to abandon all further dramatic ventures; she published the play anonymously and did not include it in her collected *Poésies* (her daughter added it for the 1707 edition). By contrast, most of her female contemporaries with a substantial poetic output—Scudéry, Mme de Villedieu, Françoise Pascal, Catherine Bernard, Louise-Geneviève Gillot de Sainctonge, among others—also cultivated other genres and garnered the most enduring fame for drama or prose narrative; verse was relegated to a more marginal position or to specific stages of their careers. Among seventeenth- and eighteenth-century women writers, only Henriette de Coligny, comtesse de La Suze, attained comparable standing through poetry alone; but, unlike Deshoulières, La Suze never published a volume composed entirely of her own (rather slight) oeuvre and not augmented with texts by other authors.

By Deshoulières's own admission, "faire des vers" 'writing verse' was her "violent penchant," her innate and inescapable "maudit talent" 'cursed talent' (Deshoulières and Deshoulières 1: 110); this fateful obsession with poetry is one of the traits that Deshoulières shares with her counterpart and unfriendly adversary Nicolas Boileau (see his second satire, addressed to Molière). At the same time, she could have adopted La Fontaine's profession: "Diversité, c'est ma devise" 'Diversity, that is my motto' (*Œuvres* 1: 863). The great success and subsequent canonization of her idylls led to her being increasingly pigeonholed as a pastoral poet, but this label obscures the considerable variety of her poetry, which defies convenient classification. Throughout her thirty-five-year career as a published poet (from her debut in the 1659 *Recueil des portraits* to her death in 1694), Deshoulières continually expanded the range of her lyre, moving from small, modern "salon genres"—*madrigaux, airs, chansons, sonnets en bouts-rimés*—to longer, "classical" forms such as odes, idylls, and eclogues and, eventually, to somber "Réflexions morales" and "Paraphrases de psaumes." Her favorite genre, the verse epistle, provided a malleable medium for the discussion of a wide variety of subjects, both light and serious, ranging from the feelings of her devoted spaniel to the hypocrisy of the *faux dévots* ("false devotees") and, of course, the heroic exploits of Louis XIV. Like La Fontaine's, Deshoulières's verse is eminently *mêlé* and *libre* ("mixed" and "free"), not just in meter but also in tone and content. This versatility can be related to Scudéry's ideal of *galante* conversation in which everything, from trifles to elevated subjects, can be addressed as long as it is done in an appropriate and agreeable manner (Scudéry, "De la conversation" 72–74). Stylistically, too, Deshoulières's poetry strives to enact this conversational ideal by adopting a language that is flowing, *gracieux* and *naturel*. Once widely celebrated, the familiarity, orality, and (deceptive) simplicity of her style were sometimes mistaken for prosaicness by later critics; nowadays, they offer the advantage of making most of these poems quite accessible even to linguistically less-advanced students.

The protean diversity of Deshoulières's corpus is matched by the complexity of her historical position, first highlighted by Sainte-Beuve. On the one hand, her work shows strong roots in and nostalgia for the bygone era of the Hôtel de Rambouillet, which Deshoulières opposes to the "decadence" of the present. On the other hand, it announces in many ways the following century: her poetic "school," "un peu jetée de côté dans le dix-septième siècle, [semble avoir] eu sa revanche au dix-huitième" 'cast somewhat aside in the seventeenth century, seems to have got its revenge in the eighteenth' (Sainte-Beuve 1324). Deshoulières thus appears to be both behind her time and ahead of it; what's more, while she was critical of contemporary society and culture, she stayed intensely involved in the Parisian scene and intervened in current debates and quarrels, most (in)famously the cabal against Jean Racine's *Phèdre*. The tenth satire of Boileau (published two weeks after Deshoulières's death) lampoons her as a "reste" 'remnant' of the original *précieuses*, a "noble héritière" 'highborn heiress' who stubbornly upheld their "secte" 'sect' and used her salon to shape the public discourse on literature (134). This malicious caricature testifies to her central role as a link between generations, a relay more active and decisive, perhaps, than the foundational figure of Scudéry herself. In her poetry, Deshoulières did not simply preserve the legacy of her youth but adapted and modernized it, thus enabling her personal version of it to carry over well into the eighteenth century.

Pedagogically, this multifaceted and elusive character of Deshoulières's work presents both challenges and benefits:

> As it is her ambition to try every [poetic] genre, so her works will synthesize the multiple aspects of her age from the idyllic pastoral to satirical realism, from precious triviality to an almost romantic attitude toward nature, from subtle sensuality to philosophical mysticism. So persistent and successful are her efforts to be diverse, that the casual reader's attempts to fix her character are constantly frustrated. (Borglum 71)

Any selection and presentation for classroom purposes runs the risk of assigning reductive categories and overemphasizing one dimension at the expense of others. In particular, it is tempting to follow a long-standing tradition that has privileged among Deshoulières's poems those displaying supposedly "feminine" literary modes, such as the idyllic depiction of nature or the elegiac expression of sentiment ("Her heart belonged to nature, feeling, melancholy reverie" [Adam, *Grandeur* 188]). But a more diverse choice of texts can allow a fuller understanding, not only of the poetic avenues open to a classical woman writer, but also of the wide spectrum of poetry generally in the second half of the seventeenth century. To be representative, selections should also convey the role of poetry in the specific contexts of *mondain* ("worldly") sociability as well as its interaction with other literary and nonliterary discourses: indeed, far from being confined to lyric soliloquy, much of Deshoulières's oeuvre is (explicitly or implicitly) dialogic and dialectical. Reflecting and engaging in major social, moral, and philosophical debates of the time, it can be profitably paired with related works by other (male and female) writers.

One such grouping may focus on the poetic joust that took place in 1684, when the creation of Jean-Baptiste Lully and Philippe Quinault's opera *Amadis* prompted Deshoulières to publish a provocative *ballade* whose refrain would become almost proverbial: "On n'aime plus comme on aimait jadis" 'People no longer love as they did in times past' (Deshoulières and Deshoulières 1: 143). Written in mildly archaizing "langage marotique" (i.e., in the manner of Clément Marot), the poem deplores the decline of gallantry and attacks the disloyalty, brutality, and licentiousness of contemporary lovers. It sparked a protracted exchange of further ballads as well as madrigals, published for the most part in subsequent issues of the *Mercure galant* (see Tonolo for a full account). Among the men responding was La Fontaine, who wrote a ballad on the same rhymes to toss the argument back at its author: provided the lady is attractive, "On aime encor comme on aimait jadis" 'People still love as they did in times past' (*Œuvres* 2: 622–23). In the collected edition of her *Poésies*, Deshoulières underlined the dialogic character of her ballad by including the gallant responses written by the duc de Saint-Aignan and by addressing it to another old friend of hers, the duc de Montausier, in times past one of the key figures of the Hôtel de Rambouillet and the patient suitor of Julie d'Angennes. This dedicatory epistle renews and reinforces the indictment of "un siècle corrompu" 'a corrupt age' in which Montausier alone upholds "le vrai mérite, et l'antique vertu" 'true merit, and ancient virtue' (1: 141). It can be read alongside another of Deshoulières's epistles, this one addressed to a female friend living in the country, the "Épître chagrine" 'Ill-Humored Epistle' to Mlle de la Charce. Here too the poet blasts the insolence of "les jeunes gens" 'young men' and the decadence of "la nouvelle Cour" 'the new Court' but goes on to denounce the complicity of present-day women, who through their "indignes manières" 'unworthy manners' spoil the young fops instead of demanding respect and fidelity (1: 169–73).

This cluster of texts illustrates how "occasional" verse such as the balladic banter around *Amadis* can serve to expose and argue meaningful social issues: the relations between the sexes and the generations, the fate of *galanterie* and *politesse*, the status of the present as an age of progress or decline. It also shows Deshoulières's strategic appropriation of poetic genres and traditions: both thematically and formally, the *ballade* harks back not only to the age of Vincent Voiture and Rambouillet but also beyond, to the model of Marot and the mythical "siècle d'Amadis" 'age of Amadis.' As for "Épître chagrine," its generic designation is borrowed from Paul Scarron and allows Deshoulières to write indignant and mocking verse without having to use the title of "satire," which would have appeared indecent for a female author. Characteristically, in her exposition of the relations between men and women she refers to both male and female traditions and addresses both male and female interlocutors, thus realizing poetically the ideal of mutual attention and equality that has been lost in contemporary society.

Rich intertextual connections can also be drawn between Deshoulières's major poems and the moralistic and philosophical currents of her time. Her two sets of "Réflexions diverses" are made up of pithy epigrammatic stanzas that echo (sometimes literally) the *Pensées* of Blaise Pascal and the maxims of Sablé and François, duc de La Rochefoucauld. When the latter was tormented by old age and illness, Deshoulières composed the lengthy "Ode" exhorting him to despise death, about which nothing could be known, but to accept — rather than stoically suppress — the reality of physical pain, the only "vrai mal" 'true ill' intrinsic to human nature. The poem sets out to expound various philosophical views of death and the afterlife but then breaks off, acknowledging (and denouncing) that women are not supposed to probe these issues: "Il est un certain langage / Que je ne dois point parler" 'There is a certain language / That I must not speak' (1: 49; see also Timmermans 366). The passage points to the constraints that Deshoulières confronted when daring to write philosophical poems and that in turn complicate our attempts to find in them a clear-cut doctrine or system. This hermeneutic difficulty was first discussed by Pierre Bayle, who called Deshoulières "l'un des plus solides, et des plus brillants Esprits du XVIIe Siècle" 'one of the most solid and brilliant wits of the seventeenth century' and praised "l'élévation et la profondeur de sa Morale" 'the elevation and depth of her morality' (3: 560, 757). Replying to critics according to whom Deshoulières's idyll "Le Ruisseau" ("The Stream") negated the immortality of the soul and proved the author's *libertinage*, Bayle cautioned that as a poet Deshoulières was not speaking "dogmatiquement" 'dogmatically' and may have just been following "des Idées Poétiques qui ne tirent point à conséquence" 'poetical ideas that are of no consequence' (2: 721; see also Chométy 195–96, and 389–94 on Deshoulières's "Imitation de Lucrèce en galimatias fait exprès" 'Imitation of Lucretius in Intentional Gibberish').

A certain poetic vagueness, ambiguity, and playfulness must have been a prudent textual strategy for anyone tempted to articulate heterodox and materialist ideas, a fortiori for a woman writer; Bayle's caveat should be kept in mind when studying Deshoulières as a "philosopher" or "free-

thinker." In any event, her poems and especially her idylls, although sometimes seen as an expression of *quiétisme* (Adam, *Histoire* 3: 177), appear
strongly rooted in the tradition of epicurean naturalism revived by Pierre
Gassendi; here again, Deshoulières's proximity to La Fontaine is notable
and allows for manifold intertextual pairings (for a few comparisons, see
Collinet 449–52; Darmon 301–06). Even her frivolous and almost universally dismissed cat-and-dog epistles may warrant a closer look in this
context and are not devoid of anti-Cartesian overtones. In a diachronical
perspective, her idylls—opposing the pure, innocent state of nature to the
corruption of human society—can be read as a poetic preview of Jean-
Jacques Rousseau's *Discours sur les sciences et les arts.*

   In her "philosophical" but also her "sensual" poems, Deshoulières's
voice often sounds muted and leaves much unsaid or implied. What has
sometimes been criticized as intellectual or expressive feebleness seems to
proceed at least in part from deliberate self-restraint in an attempt to conform to standards of female discretion and modesty; we might note that
throughout her life she upheld a reputation as virtuous wife and mother,
unlike some of her notorious contemporaries (her fellow poet La Suze, for
example). Even so, Deshoulières was blamed for transgressing *bienséance*
and *pudeur* ("propriety" and "modesty"):

> On dit qu'elle a une facilité merveilleuse; mais que la bienséance devait
> la porter à mettre des bornes plus étroites à certaines libertés qu'elle a
> prises, et qui ne s'accordent point parfaitement avec la pudeur du Sexe.
> (Baillet 450)

> People say that she has a marvelous facility, but that propriety should
> have led her to set stricter limits to certain liberties which she has taken,
> and which are not in perfect harmony with the decency of her sex.

This judgment by a contemporary of Deshoulières's may help define two
main tasks implied in teaching her poetry: to trace the tension between
"limits" and "liberties" in the work of a classical woman writer and to
discern, through her manifold "talents" and "marvelous facility," the living presence of a strong personal voice, of a self that exists and persists in
verse.

Notes

   1. Deshoulières is pronounced "dézoulière."
   2. All translations are my own.

Donna Kuizenga

Villedieu and Manley: Teaching Early Modern Pseudo-Autobiographies

I have found that one of the most effective ways to teach French early modern women writers is to construct a course that combines their writings with texts by British women writers of the same period. This approach allows students to seize the particular features of a text more easily because the use of one or more companion texts provides them with context. In addition, it helps show that the concerns voiced by women writers of the early modern period are not unique to a single country but have a certain commonality. With this context, it is easier to help students see that many, indeed most, women writers positioned themselves as advocates for women and that they articulated their advocacy within the principal political frameworks of their time.

A persistent reading of women's texts is the autobiographical approach. Women, over many centuries, have been assumed to be incapable of thinking outside their personal experience, and thus works of fiction by women have often been read as disguised accounts of personal experience. Early modern women writers were aware of and resisted this kind of reading. This resistance is one of the ways in which they sought to find their voices in a world that would silence them. Pseudo-autobiographical texts are the locus of the most acute testing of the range of creative and authorial autonomy available to women in the early modern period. These texts are also appealing to students, initially because of their seemingly straightforward narrative stance and their adventure-filled plot lines. I have used the text-pairing method in both undergraduate and graduate courses, and while the graduate students tend to bring more sophisticated reading techniques to the works, the pairing is still an effective tool for identifying salient features of the works.

The pair of novels I have found most successful in the classroom is Mme de Villedieu's *The Memoirs of the Life of Henriette-Sylvie de Molière* (1672–74) and Delarivier Manley's *History of Rivella* (1714; later published as *Adventures of Rivella*). While there is no evidence that Manley was aware of Villedieu's work, the two writers have a great deal in common. Both women lived by the pen and sought to curry political favor to further their careers. Manley and Villedieu were the subject of extensive gossip and written up in scandal sheets. In response, both writers published autobiographical texts, works in which they took back power over their own life stories (cf. Showalter 57–58). In *Memoirs* and *Adventures*, Villedieu and Manley use multiple and often contrasting strategies to ensure their control of the power of representation. Because of these contrasting strategies, teaching the two texts together allows students to gain a clear picture of how each novel works and a more general understanding of what it meant for an early modern woman writer to assert her voice.

Sylvie, Villedieu's heroine, narrowly avoids rape at the hands of her foster father. Manley's young Rivella is tricked into a bigamous marriage by her guardian. The young women are ruined in the eyes of society and forced to seek their own ways in the world. Throughout their adventures, and despite a certain amount of double-dealing, both characters show themselves to be relatively disinterested and stoic in the face of reversals of fortune. In their love lives, both characters rise above the conventions of romance. Sylvie's tale underlines her lack of choice and economic dependence and her ingenuity in managing within that framework (DeJean, *Tender Geographies* 133). Rivella is, if anything, an even more active heroine. At the end of each novel, the heroine eludes the reader's grasp.

I begin with Villedieu's text, not only because it is chronologically first, but also, as a first-person text, it forces the reader to ask who the narrator is and thus to raise the question of pseudo-autobiography. How students approach the question of what is true depends on their depth of historical knowledge. Students of French literature may be more sensitive to the constant evocations of real people and incidents. For students in a course in translation or a comparative literature course, this point needs to be made through the use of examples such as the description of the royal festivities at Versailles. In both cases, however, without the aid of the instructor or the edition used, it is unlikely that students will be able to detect the places where Villedieu uses fact and where she alters it.

Sylvie's tale is told in six long letters to a female protector. It is the story of an abandoned infant of uncertain parentage, who is thrown out into the world on her own. Sylvie's trajectory includes encounters with libidinous and unreliable men and with both generous female protectors and ill-intentioned women enemies. Her life is marked by a grand passion for the young comte d'Englesac. Their often deferred and much opposed union turns out to be not the fitting ending of a romance, however, but the beginning of another series of troubles for the heroine as Englesac is, serially, impotent and unfaithful (see Démoris 137). Sylvie's struggles are as much economic battles as they are amorous ones. Over and over again she seeks economic security, struggling with constant assaults on her reputation, which block her economic objectives. While at the end of her tale she is sufficiently disgusted with the world to retire from it, Sylvie shows a remarkable ability to fend for herself. Her love for Englesac is great, but it is not naive. Sylvie does not present herself as a paragon of traditionally defined virtue. Rather, using a strategy that reappears in Manley's *Adventures of Rivella*, she defines her innocence situationally.

In initial discussions of *Memoirs*, I focus the students' attention on the character, her adventures, what they reveal about women's social situation, and the strategies used to cope with that situation. I then move the students to a discussion of the passages in the novel that address authorship, reading, and narrative voice. Sylvie is not just the writer of her own tale, however; she is also the subject of multiple readings. While the ostensible reason for telling her life story is her protector's request, Sylvie transforms herself into a textual commodity, a product designed to compete in the marketplace against the falsified versions of her life story. And it is in crafting Sylvie's narrative stance that Villedieu offers us lessons on how to read a woman writer's life story in a new way.

Most significant, Sylvie seeks to reassert her power over her tale by suggesting to her protector the appropriate reading of her text. Leading students through a systematic examination of the passages addressed to the reader helps them understand the complex way in which Villedieu is questioning both images and roles of women in her society and the way women's writings are read. This exercise can easily be made the subject of student presentations and thus empowers the students to undertake increasingly sophisticated readings of the novel. By means of Sylvie's ironic narration, Villedieu offers us the image of a woman who is not an object but a subject (DeJean, *Tender Geographies* 133–34; Hipp 80–81; Donovan 462). The mixture of real incidents from Villedieu's life and fictional events creates a distance between Villedieu and her text. Villedieu invites us to read her text and not her life. We can neither identify the author with her character nor deny that there are obvious parallels between them (cf. Boursier 278–79).

After studying Villedieu's text, for which I use one session in a weekly graduate seminar or a week to a week and a half in a traditional semester undergraduate course, I teach Manley's *Adventures*. Manley's heroine, Rivella, is also resilient, and she too explodes the virgin/whore dichotomy (cf. Ballaster 151; Spencer 58). The strategies that Manley uses to reassert control over the narrative of her life contrast instructively with Villedieu's. Where Sylvie relates her story in the first person, Rivella's story is told by a male narrator, Sir Charles Lovemore, to a male listener, the chevalier d'Aumont.

The tale Manley offers is not one of pure passion and idealized love but rather the adventures of a marginalized Tory woman writer who must fend for herself. In *Memoirs*, Villedieu uses Sylvie's comments on reading and textual reception to indicate how she would have her novel read. Manley allows us to watch her story being produced and consumed by two characters whose expectations and attitudes she exposes to our view.

Like Villedieu, Manley seeks to rectify false versions of her life. Her disguise as Rivella is always transparent since the character is identified as the author of Manley's *The New Atlantis*. While Villedieu uses her part-fictional, part-real alter ego to render impossible the reductive identification of author and text, Manley chooses to tell her story through one who would both defend and exploit her. For Sir Charles does indeed "love more." He has had an unrequited passion for Rivella from their youth. He admires and defends her, while presenting himself as an impartial historian who will judge Rivella's faults as well as her virtues. Her tale is told at the behest of the enthusiastic chevalier d'Aumont, freshly arrived in Britain and eager to make the acquaintance of Rivella.

While Sylvie's tale is shaped by her indications of how it is to be read, Rivella's is shaped by the attitudes and preconceptions of Lovemore and d'Aumont. For them, Rivella is a daunting mixture of intellectual and physical qualities, which make her desirable, if not in a conventional way.

While Sylvie bears the weight of a universally seductive beauty, Rivella's seduction comes rather from the combination of some good physical qualities with a superb knowledge of love and witty conversation. Sylvie's flirtation with her readers pales by comparison with the erotization that Rivella undergoes in Lovemore's presentation and d'Aumont's consumption of it. Indeed, critics have rightfully spoken of Lovemore's "pimping" Rivella (Ballaster 124, 147).

In the cool of the day, Sir Charles and the chevalier have retired into a garden whose gate they can close to prevent interruptions. D'Aumont begs Lovemore to keep his promise and tell the story of Rivella, whose character he longs to know before meeting her. I devote a good deal of time to the introduction, in which Lovemore and d'Aumont discuss sexual and textual pleasure. Students are immediately struck by the way this narrative approach contrasts with Villedieu's, and, because of the earlier discussion of addresses to the reader, they immediately question the opening of *Adventures*, asking what effects the change in narrative strategy will have and wondering why Manley chose to voice her tale through male narrators. This questioning allows students to identify the ways in which the narrative of *Adventures* differs from Sylvie's tale.

The introductory conversation between Lovemore and d'Aumont reproduces the kind of reading to which women's texts were subjected and against which Villedieu fights in *Memoirs*. It assumes an identity between writer and text, ties women's writing to the erotic, and eroticizes the woman writer, making her and her text objects for male consumption. The way in which Lovemore and d'Aumont eroticize Rivella seems different from the presentation of Sylvie, since plastic perfection is rejected as the sole criterion and erotic experience and sophistication are prized. In the end, however, all the wit and character of a woman who writes are made part and parcel of her erotic pull.

Both this thoroughgoing erotization of Rivella and the portrayal of Sylvie's magnetic beauty are revealing. In early modern society, women who became writers might well feel the need to mask excessive femininity, if not to satisfy some deep-seated anxiety as psychoanalysis would have it, then to ensure their continued viability in the marketplace that determined their livelihood (Riviere; Jensen, *Writing* 1–4; Todd 91; Démoris 138). Villedieu and Manley are able to exploit the trope of erotic desirability to double purpose, both using it to bolster readership and calling it into question through irony (see Todd 96; Gallagher 133). Having read both texts, students see the irony to which both writers subject the reduction of a woman to a beautiful and erotic object.

Sylvie's questioning of gender expectations is indirect. Her actions, her agency, speak for her (cf. Schwartz 79). Rivella confronts the issue head-on. Here, Lovemore speaks of her:

> Her Vertues are her own, her Vices occasion'd by her Misfortunes; and yet as I have often heard her say, *If she had been a Man, she had been without Fault*: But the Charter of that Sex being much more confin'd than ours, what is not a Crime in Men is scandalous and unpardonable in Woman, as she her self has very well observ'd in divers Places, throughout her own Writings. (8–9; references are to the 1725 ed.)

In addition to her clear recognition of the double standard and her transgressive position in relation to it, Rivella's other salient characteristics are her generosity and her truthfulness. The way in which Manley presents Rivella's truthfulness has complex implications for our reading of the text. From the beginning of Lovemore's narrative, Rivella is associated with truth telling and political engagement. If Rivella does not boast of the favor that she has won by her work and qualities, it is because "[s]he loves *Truth*, and has too often given her self the Liberty to *speak*, as well as *write* it" (14). When her publisher and his associates are arrested because of charges brought against her pro-Tory scandal chronicle, *The New Atlantis*, Rivella demonstrates her unselfishness by presenting herself for arrest so that the publisher and his associates may go free.

Rivella's defense of *The New Atlantis* elucidates the issue of truth and of how to read her *Adventures*. Questioned about her sources, Rivella first responds that she wrote only for her own amusement and was sorry to have offended anyone. When this tactic fails, she uses another. If what she has written resembles real people or events, "she said then it must be *Inspiration*, because knowing her own Innocence, she could account for it no other Way" (113). Rivella's argument does not deny *The New Atlantis*'s political allusions, but it does effectively make the question of their origin forever undecidable (cf. Gallagher 115–17). Like *The New Atlantis*, the first edition of Rivella's adventures carries as part of its title "secret memoirs." *Adventures* is thus placed under the same sign of indeterminacy as *The New Atlantis*. *Adventures* is truth clothed in fiction, but we cannot tell where the one ends and the other begins any better here than we could in reading Sylvie's story.

Having examined these features of *Adventures* with the students, often through student presentations focusing on particular aspects of the novel, I close this section of the course with a discussion of the way in which the authors choose to end their tales. As Villedieu and Manley blur the line between fiction and fact, so do they leave their narratives open-ended, allowing no easy conclusion, no pinning down of the heroine. A world-weary Sylvie will retire to a convent with her friend the abbess of Cologne. Given all that has gone before, it is difficult to see this retreat as a definitive one or to imagine that Sylvie will not return to the world.

The heroine's eclipse is even more striking in *Adventures*. As full as the portrait Lovemore provides is, he confesses to d'Aumont that "I never saw any of *Rivella*'s hidden Charms" (10). At the end of his tale, Lovemore tells d'Aumont that he has included only those events that caused the most scandal and that he has thus left much out for lack of time. Had this not been the case, he would have invited d'Aumont to Rivella's table, and

> [f]rom thence carried you (in the Heat of Summer after Dinner) within the Nymphs Alcove, to a Bed nicely sheeted and strow'd with *Roses, Jessamins* or *Orange-Flowers,* . . . and there given you leave to fancy your self the happy Man with whom she chose to repose her self, during the Heat of the Day, in a State of Sweetness and Tranquility: From thence conducted you towards the cool of the Evening, either upon the *Water,* or to the *Park* for Air with a Conversation always new, and which never cloys. (119–20)

The story ends here, however, on the image of Rivella's empty bed, the empty sign of her seduction. Rivella herself is nowhere to be seen.

Focusing on the denouements allows me to summarize the main issues raised by the two novels. While Villedieu constructs a reading of her text through Sylvie's apostrophes to her protector, Manley offers us an antireading. Lovemore and d'Aumont may well be sensible to Rivella's qualities, but they cannot and will not see her as other than an object of erotic desire. Lovemore turns Rivella into a commodity and sells her to d'Aumont, the eager consumer. But Manley pulls the strings and snatches Rivella from d'Aumont's grasp, leaving him only the empty bed. As Ros Ballaster has shown, "Manley's consummate irony is evident here. While the man appears to have 'authored' the perfect female object she is, in reality, elsewhere 'authoring' him" (150; cf. Todd 97–98).

Both Villedieu and Manley disrupt the presumed equivalence between author's life and text. They blur the line between fact and fiction

(Ballaster 151–52; DeJean, *Tender Geographies* 134) and create heroines who cannot be clearly defined. Villedieu and Manley provide expanded images of woman, for both Sylvie and Rivella survive their ruin and demand to be judged by new criteria. Through their creation of these writing heroines, Villedieu and Manley take for themselves the power to tell the stories of their lives, lives that have been turned into an appropriated and falsified public commodity (see Schwartz 83–84). When Sylvie takes on the task of representing herself to her protector, her gesture mimes but is not the same as Villedieu's. Manley, hidden in the wings, manipulates the manipulation of her story to reveal the preconceptions that structure it. And in the end she keeps Rivella and her "hidden Charms" for herself, refusing them to the prurient reader, as Villedieu makes Sylvie invisible in her convent. Villedieu and Manley do not lift the masks of womanliness, but instead selectively put them on to seize the power of the pen. The two texts have sufficient differences and similarities to allow students to examine the questions of women's agency and authorship in very rich ways. The Villedieu-Manley unit typically follows units on Madeleine de Scudéry and Marie-Madeleine Pioche de la Vergne, comtesse de Lafayette, and provides a good transition to the works of authors such as Aphra Behn; Marie-Catherine Le Jumel de Barneville, comtesse d'Aulnoy; Eliza Haywood; and Françoise de Graffigny..

Harriet Stone

Zoom Zoom: Focusing in on *La Princesse de Clèves* and *Lettres d'une Péruvienne*

La Princesse de Clèves and *Lettres d'une Péruvienne* are regular features in my French literature survey course. Typically, the subject of the evolution of the novel in early modern France engages students less than do the young heroines' plights depicted by Marie-Madeleine Pioche de la Vergne, comtesse de Lafayette, and Françoise de Graffigny. Yet these novels, especially when mediated by works of art, awaken students to narrative structure and thereby to some of the principal features of the novel genre; the art in turn reinforces the historical and social themes that each author highlights.[1]

I first teach each novel separately, focusing on the trajectory of the heroine in relation to the men who enter her life. In each case I highlight the triangular form that links the heroine to an "appropriate" mate (the prince de Clèves, Aza) and to an interloper (the duc de Nemours, Déterville). Class discussions are oriented around the critical questions of the heroine's choices in love and the idea of separation through marriage, death, and physical isolation, both voluntary and involuntary. For the princesse de Clèves, the mother's death, the husband's death, and the princess's successive retreats to Coulommiers structure both a linear and a thematic chain of separation that allows the class to appreciate the question of autonomy in the context of court life. The Peruvian princess's wrenching separation from her lover and country, her relative isolation in Paris, and Aza's remarriage punctuate a novel that similarly positions the heroine to reject expected endings for women.[2] We consider the denouement of each novel in the light of these losses. I often use a trial format, with students acting the parts of judge, attorneys, and witnesses for opposing critics, to debate whether the heroines have successfully negotiated the challenges they face and whether they experience any contentment as a result of their ultimate choice to remain alone.

The "zoom zoom" of my title refers, literally, to the focus of the next activity, which considers both novels together. I begin by having students describe what happens with a digital camera when we simulate movement rapidly away from or toward a subject using the zoom lens. Using our classroom as a model, I ask the students to explain the difference between a close-up portrait of one student using the zoom and a group portrait without the zoom that contains all the students. This easy technique allows the students to grasp the notion of simple and complex compositions, foreground and background, and to consider the different responses that each perspective cultivates.

I then show the class a copy of Nicolas Poussin's *Autoportrait* (1650; "Self-Portrait").[3] I present Poussin briefly, describing his artistic achievements, his contribution to French classicism, and his connections to the duc de Richelieu and the court of Louis XIII. I ask students how in his self-portrait Poussin encourages the reader to zoom in on the subject, his likeness as it appears in the foreground of the painting. We consider what the painting would look like if Poussin had done the equivalent of releasing the zoom lens to have the back wall be larger and more expansive and the figure of himself proportionately smaller. This exercise allows students to appreciate the choice that the artist has made in support of a representation that identifies him as an artist of prominence. If the foregrounded figure is the principal subject of the painting, the background, a series of framed canvases, is no less vital to our ability to identify this subject. Poussin presents three framed paintings with evidence of their canvases visible and a fourth painting, which we view only from behind. We analyze the inscription of the author's name on the first painting as it complements the visual image. This detail identifies Poussin's painted subject as himself and further establishes him as the creator of a work for posterity. It does more to reinforce his authority as an artist than does the goddess representing painting on the left of the second framed image. The third painting, completely obscured, meets the figure of Poussin at eye level, thereby accentuating the artist's vision. It emphasizes his ability to frame or conceptualize his subject, whether himself, as in this portrait, or nature and history, as in his other works.[4] As the fourth frame represents most emphatically by virtue of its being turned away from us, our view of the world depends on the artist's particular rendering of it, that is, the way in which he makes accessible certain meanings that would otherwise remain obscure.

Turning to *La Princesse de Clèves*, I explain that Lafayette's novel also depends on a deliberate framing of the heroine's story. Emphasizing a progression reminiscent of Poussin's frames, which take us deeper and deeper into the space of the painting, we discuss how the novel encourages us to see the princess against four distinct backdrops: the instruction to the princess provided through the novel's intercalated stories, the court of Henri II, this court as juxtaposed with the court of Queen Elizabeth in England, and finally Henri II's court as seen within the frame of the court of Louis XIV.

As with Poussin's framed paintings within the painting, Lafayette's four *mises en abyme* ("intercalated stories") help identify the princess as the primary subject of our attention. By framing a view of the court rife with intrigues, the individual stories create a sort of textual latticework through which the reader comes to measure the princess's growing knowledge and her responses to the challenges that face her. In the first instance, Mme de Chartres tells Mme de Clèves the history of Diane de Poitiers, the king's consort (93–99; 26–31).[5] The second story involves the prince de Clèves, who recounts to his wife the story of Mme de Tournon's betrayal of Sancerre, repeating the information Sancerre had told him (113–21; 42–51). In the third case Mme la Dauphine tells the princesse de Clèves the story of Anne Boleyn (133–35; 60–63). The fourth example relates the story that the vidame de Chartres tells Nemours about his connections to the queen, which story Nemours later relates to the princess (142–62; 70–87). An integral part of the princess's education, the four intercalated stories instill in her an inflexible standard of virtue by reinforcing the notion of the unstable relations at court and the potential for loss inflicted by gallantries of all sorts.

To this list of four *mises en abyme* we add the moment when the princess hears from Mme la Dauphine the story of her own confession to her husband, told as a third-person account of an anonymous "femme qui aime Monsieur de Nemours" 'woman who loves M. de Nemours' (182–83; 105–06). The princess famously pronounces this version of her story "guère vraisemblable" 'hardly . . . plausible' (183; 106). She has become the subject of a more elaborate intrigue involving the prince de Clèves; the eavesdropping duc de Nemours; his unreliable friend, her cousin the vidame de Chartres; and Mme la Dauphine. Or, more precisely, the performing subject, the princess who informs her husband of her feelings for another man, has become the narrated subject, part of the backdrop of court gossip. Referring once again to my demonstration of what happened when I released the zoom lens that highlighted one student in my image of the class, I suggest that the princess's individual portrait has been abandoned and merged into a group portrait, at a tremendous cost to her. By visualizing this process as a physical repositioning of the heroine within the narrative, students can understand the notion of the objectification of the subject and the loss that it implies. The princess has not only been betrayed by Nemours, who first spied on her and then told her story to the vidame de Chartres; she has also become an object of exchange, part of a larger story that refocuses her position and with it her identity as an autonomous subject. It transforms her, implausibly, from the woman who privately confessed to her husband into a novelistic persona, a woman whose story has become fodder for court gossip.

Moving to the second frame level, I ask the class to consider the princess's behavior as exceptional within the confines of the court. I direct the students' attention to the opening descriptions of the novel, beginning with the account of the king's relation to the queen and to his mistress, Diane de Poitiers (69–76; 3–10), and extending through the description of the court as a place dominated by "tant d'intérêts et tant de cabales différentes" 'countless interests at stake, countless different factions' (81; 14). We situate the princess within this dynamic world, underscoring how persistent changes of partners and alliances create a particularly precarious situation for a young woman anxious to maintain her virtue.[6]

Explaining that Lafayette has made the princess's private life the fictional centerpiece of an actual court facing real threats from abroad, I identify the history of relations between France and England as the novel's next frame. The historical dimension of this dilemma takes on added importance as we consider the political situation in England, where Elizabeth eventually ordered the beheading of her Catholic cousin Mary Stuart, Mme la Dauphine, who became queen of France following Henri II's death, as described in part 3 of the novel. Referring to France's violent religious wars, including the deaths of an estimated fifty thousand Huguenots in the Saint Bartholomew's Day Massacre of 1572, I explore with the class how the conflict that the princess feels between the prince de Clèves and the duc de Nemours, a potential king for Elizabeth, reflects the tensions being played out between Catholics and Protestants, French and English. While these historical details are embedded in the novel, my suggestion that they serve a function analogous to that of Poussin's third framed painting helps students appreciate how Lafayette invites them to zoom back and forth between the princess's trajectory and the more complex political and religious tensions of the period, which they might otherwise ignore.

Poussin's fourth frame, visible only from behind, allows a final link to Lafayette's invisible frame, which I define as the seventeenth-century court that is the ultimate context of her novel. The court of Louis XIV, as Lafayette's contemporary readers well knew, retained all the glitter, all the gallantry, and all the tensions between Catholics and Protestants that Lafayette uses to frame the princesse de Clèves's moral dilemma a century earlier. The Edict of Nantes, which Henry IV signed to bring an end to the Wars of Religion, would be revoked by Louis XIV, his grandson, just seven years after the publication of *La Princesse de Clèves* in 1678.

In the second part of this unit, devoted to the eighteenth century, I introduce François Boucher's *Déjeuner* (1739; "Breakfast")[7] to help situate Graffigny's novel. Representative of the rococo style, this painting depicts a wealthy bourgeois family at the breakfast table. Once again, I ask students to situate the figures in the foreground against the background. The rear wall includes several objects of interest, including a Buddha and teapot on shelves to the left of the fireplace mantel and, most striking, a framed mirror. Referring back to the framed paintings in Poussin's self-portrait, I ask the class to analyze the mirror's function in Boucher's painting. They note that it reflects the opposite wall, including the closed door, itself framed by the door frame and what appear to be curtains hanging on either side. The mirror draws the viewer's gaze back into the primary scene of the painting, that of the family gathered at the breakfast table. As framed by the mirror, however, this intimate scene assumes the attributes of highly stylized art. None of the figures or objects that we see in the room is reflected on the surface of the mirror, suggesting that the mirror functions like a framed canvas and that the figures and the objects in the foreground appear as elements of a painting. As a *mise en abyme* that displays the artist's framing of the image, the mirror points the viewer back into the breakfast scene to accentuate the painterly quality of all elements of the image and the ornamentalism of the objects that Boucher depicts.

Part of an ornate décor, these objects, I suggest, constitute the real background for the scene of the family's breakfast. The objects highlight the visual appeal of the painting and its function as a social portrait of a privileged class.

Boucher presents the high style of Parisian life in 1739, when he created the painting. The family setting—before a large fireplace in a room whose small dimensions contrast with the more expansive public spaces associated with the nobility and upper middle classes of the seventeenth century—suggests a certain intimacy. But if Boucher's *Déjeuner* celebrates the privacy of family life, it acknowledges the new fashions of the day with equal emphasis. Breakfast, Rose-Marie Hagen and Rainer Hagen note, was an innovation of the period:

> Louis XV was the first king to have bread or a roll in the morning with a hot drink. His royal predecessors had started the day with dinner around ten o'clock. Over the course of the decades, this large, hot meal moved closer and closer to midday and eventually became lunch. Louis XIV ate his dinner at one o'clock, but did not have breakfast. This was something only introduced by his descendants. (2: 282)

What lay behind the change was the new popularity of hot coffee, tea, and chocolate served in the home. Many art historians, including those responsible for the Louvre Web site, believe that the pot of hot liquid in Boucher's painting is coffee (Pomarède and Le Bourdellès). Hagen and Hagen argue, however, that the pot's shape suggests neither coffee nor tea but rather chocolate, with its distinctive slender body, broad handle, and short and wide spout that allows the thick chocolate to flow easily (2: 282). Chocolate was introduced in Spain from the American colonies in the sixteenth century. I remind the students that Graffigny built a bridge between the Inca civilization of the 1500s and eighteenth-century France. I focus the class's attention on the detail of the chocolate being served in the painting to introduce the concept of the novel's historical montage: its implausible blending of two civilizations that never actually encountered each other directly. The consistent historical detail, namely the enormous success of hot chocolate in France after Anne of Austria introduced it to the French court, also serves to open up the text for students. Made from cocoa, sugar, cinnamon, and vanilla, chocolate became a favorite drink of the French aristocracy in the eighteenth century (2: 282). Within the painting it evokes associations with other popular drinks of the period, coffee and tea, both of which were imported from abroad. The teapot and the

Buddha, the lacquer surface of the table, and the blue and white vase in
Boucher's boudoir extend the chain of exotic items that have been assimilated into the Parisian domestic sphere.

The presence of the two young children and the appealing gestures
through which the two women offer each of them a spoonful of the beverage add a strong dose of nature and nurture to this otherwise excessively polished scene.[8] The various objects associated with an exotic elsewhere, however, suggest through their status as privileged possessions the
prestige that French aristocrats and members of the upper middle class
acquired through trade, a process of cultural exchange that has far less
neutral implications. Boucher's cups without handles take their inspiration
from Chinese teacups, and the pattern of the cups, saucers, and sugar bowl
similarly imitates a Chinese model. To what extent does the other, exotic
culture exist authentically as an autonomous identity within this scene,
and to what extent does the painting instead suggest an other whose primary value is to empower the Europeans who have purchased it? Are the
exotic objects valued as foreign objects or as foreign objects assimilated
into French culture?[9]

Students readily note the dramatic difference between Graffigny's account of Zilia's abduction by the Spanish in the opening letters of the novel
and Boucher's quiet appropriation of the exotic in his painting. The violence with which Graffigny depicts the encounter of the Europeans with the
natives of the New World casts a very different light on the theme of cultural appropriation. In ways far less subtle than those employed by Boucher,
Graffigny suggests that imperialism—here, Europe's plundering of the
Incas—lies at the heart of their "cultural exchange" with the Spanish.

This discussion provides an excellent entry into the class's exploration of the underlying tensions in Graffigny's novel. We first consider how
the Inca culture, in addition to being a constitutive element of the plot,
constitutes a backdrop for Parisian culture. We then turn to Graffigny's
"publisher's preface,"[10] her fictional frame for the novel, to define the Eu-
rocentric perspective as one of cultural dominance. But we explore how,
through Zilia's letter writing, the European perspective comes under scrutiny. We define the reader's initial focus on Zilia, the Peruvian princess, as
the European reader's gaze on the exotic other deemed inferior (conquer-
able). This gaze shifts in the course of our reading as we share Zilia's perspective and read her critical examination of Europe's institutions and customs. I refer to this double perspective as a "double zoom" and encourage

students to consider how, by assigning the scriptoral role to Zilia, Graffigny does the equivalent of handing her a camera, allowing her to zoom in and record aspects of French culture that typically meld into the background and go largely unchallenged. I propose that Boucher's *Déjeuner* may be considered a case in point and ask students to consider whether they believe that the presence of exotic elements in the painting masks more exploitative East/West relations. I then ask the class to consider whether Graffigny's use of the Inca empire might also constitute an act of exploitation. While Graffigny uses the Inca culture to drive home her criticism of French society and although the Incas are safely removed from her French compatriots by two centuries, students generally believe that Graffigny's detailed ethnographic representation implies a genuine intellectual openness. They argue, moreover, that the novel demonstrates a clear protest of the violence committed against the Incas by the Europeans.

I find that the double zoom, the initial intense focus followed by a rapid shift in focus, helps students understand not just the presence of exotic elements in Graffigny's text but also the function of the exotic in the novel. To explore this idea further, we interrogate Zilia's relationship with Aza as mediated by events that inscribe her more deeply within European culture. We consider how, following Katharine Ann Jensen's reading, Zilia "imagines Aza's love to be a perfect mirror of her own," only to have that image shattered later when she learns that Aza had come to Spain and married a Spanish woman (*Writing* 109). This knowledge destroys Zilia's notion of her union with Aza as it does her idea that they are united within a culture that opposes them to the Europeans. With Aza allied through marriage to a European, Zilia is free to do the same. Nevertheless, she resists, and, through a gift of property that is more an act of restitution, Déterville sees to it that she acquires what had been taken from her in Peru. Graffigny does not allow her heroine simply to marry and live happily ever after, however. Zilia proposes to Déterville a trade that is, as Jensen explains, a genuine "cultural exchange": "He will teach her (French) science and art; she will teach him (Peruvian) virtue and the 'innocent and lasting' pleasures of friendship" (123). Zilia remains in Paris, but the novel presents no final assimilation of her life to Déterville's. Instead, Graffigny sustains the tension in a "fair trade agreement" between two people and two cultures, each with something to share and something to gain. This final agreement takes shape, moreover, without recourse either to physical violence or to plundering and in full recognition of cultural difference.

Bearing in mind the novel's denouement, the class returns to Zilia's account of her discovery of the mirror in letter 10:

> L'étonnement me tenait immobile, les yeux attachés sur cette ombre, quand Déterville m'a fait remarquer sa propre figure à côté de celle qui occupait toute mon attention: je le touchais, je lui parlais, et je le voyais en même temps fort près et fort loin de moi. (50)

> My amazement prevented me from moving, and my eyes were glued to this shadow when Déterville made me observe his own form next to the one that was so preoccupying me. I was touching him; I was speaking to him; and I could see him very close to me and at the same time very far from me. (my trans.)

Students note that, although Zilia's understanding has considerably expanded since her arrival in Paris, at the end of the novel she continues to see Déterville, to touch him, to speak to him, and also to perceive him to be at once very close and very removed. The novel sustains the double perspective, the double zoom so explicitly conveyed through the mirror in the initial description, by reinscribing it as a final cultural exchange. In this respect Graffigny and Boucher seem to have little in common. Recalling how the mirror in *Le Déjeuner* frames the scene in ways that emphasize a painterly surface, I conclude our discussion by expanding on the idea that in this painting the interior has become a place where art and ornament flourish. Boucher's image offers no way out of this décor into a harsher, less stylized reality. The family members are, consistent with Michael Fried's analysis of the figures in the eighteenth-century tableau, absorbed, so engrossed as to preclude the viewer's existence.[11] Furthermore, the ornament in Boucher's painting has become essential; we have the sense that the who's who of wealthy individuals requires that they partake of chocolate in appropriately ornate interiors with oriental touches. The artist blurs the line between functionality (liquids that nourish, pots that pour) and ornamentality (chocolate, served in pots modeled after oriental designs).

These observations lead the class to consider a fundamental, albeit complex, issue. Boucher's mirror, in which no object other than the closed door appears, seems literally to close the door on any reality other than that which we observe. Does it not then obscure the integrity of the other culture whose things (warm beverages, Buddhas, china) it assimilates? In contrast, Zilia's description of the mirror does not compress the narrated event into a single image. The text moves from her reflection in the mirror to her reflection beside Déterville and then to the couple's actual presence in the room. This dynamic is consistent with the ending that associates European and Peruvian gifts in an oath of friendship. Zooming in and then back from Zilia's image, which Zilia perceives as belonging to another and which Déterville teaches her to see as her own, Graffigny also describes an act of appropriation, but one that belongs to and authenticates the other (mirror image) as the self. Zilia comes to see herself as others see her, but they come to know her as she knows herself. The Peruvian other, doubly coded as female and exotic, is a subject whose agency the novel cultivates through a final refusal of a woman's conventional role. Zilia chooses to live in friendship but not love (which would subordinate her) with her French host.

Our final comparison of Lafayette's and Graffigny's heroines turns on this central point. In each novel the heroine's personal property allows her to live without integrating herself fully into society. The class considers to what degree wealth, specifically private property, provides the young women a source of contentment and to what degree it sustains their suffering. Expressed through the female protagonist, the social critique that emerges from these discussions benefits from feminist, orientalist, and colonialist discourses, but the broader goal remains for students to learn to navigate the complex terrain of desire, individual liberty, responsibility, and self-knowledge. By focusing on the various backdrops that the novels present as contexts for the heroines' experiences, I extend the idea of the zoom function to that of linear, or fixed-point, perspective. Recalling Leon Battista Alberti's definition of the picture as a framed surface situated at a certain distance from the viewer, we consider how the viewer function is inscribed in the texts, where "point of view" implies both angle of vision and critical interpretation. The princess, from her retreat in her home and the "maison religieuse" 'convent' (239; 156), and Zilia, in her own house, view society in ways that those who live within it are less inclined to recognize and to challenge. Each woman, moreover, chooses a path of virtue that is inseparable from isolation, a position outside that represents her sacrifice of a certain active engagement for a sustained ability to see, to meditate, and to know. Whether students interpret either novel's resolution as a defeat or a victory or something in-between, they appreciate the fact that Lafayette and Graffigny ascribe value to the external position, for it is there that the eyes of the reader come to rest.

Notes

1. Kafalenos offers excellent strategies for interpreting narratives.

2. DeJean, "Lafayette's Ellipses" and *Tender Geographies*, and Miller, *Subject to Change*, remain seminal texts for an appreciation of early modern fiction that privileges the female subject.

3. Poussin's *Autoportrait* can be viewed at the following sites: http://www.nicolas-poussin.com/tableaux/autoportrait-chantelou-1650-louvre.jpg; http://www.abcgallery.com/P/poussin/poussin75.html.

4. For discussion of these and other details about the painting, see the Louvre's excellent pedagogical volume by Revel.

5. I cite throughout Jean Mesnard's edition of *La Princesse de Clèves* and Terence Cave's English translation.

6. For more on the concept of framing in the novel, see Stone, *Classical Model* 150–69.

7. Boucher's *Le Déjeuner* can be viewed at the following sites: http://cartelfr.louvre.fr/cartelfr/visite?srv=obj_view_obj&objet=cartel_10254_12772_p0000199.001.jpg_obj.html&flag=true; http://www.abcgallery.com/B/boucher/boucher22.html.

8. Scholars have interpreted the painting as a portrait of the Boucher family, with the painter serving the hot beverage, his wife and son on the right, and his daughter and sister on the left.

9. I elaborate the function of the exotic other in my discussion of Racine's *Bérénice* (Stone, *Classical Model* 77–94) and of exotic objects in Dutch painting (Stone, *Tables* 34–36).

10. "Avertissement" in DeJean and Miller's edition of *Lettres d'une Péruvienne*, which is the edition I cite throughout.

11. Fried discusses other paintings by Boucher. See also Cuillé's analysis of the tableau in the eighteenth century.

Laure Marcellesi

Tahitian Voices: Mme de Monbart, Rousseau, and Diderot

In any exploration of the Enlightenment's engagement with the other, the fascination of late-eighteenth-century French authors with Tahiti is impossible to ignore. The philosophes saw the newly encountered island as the perfect crucible for their ongoing reflection on natural philosophy, faraway cultures, and colonial rule. In the three decades following Louis-Antoine de Bougainville's voyage to the South Pacific in 1769, Tahiti became a prevalent subject matter in French letters spanning a wide range of genres and perspectives. But in our courses on the Enlightenment's encounter with the other, we traditionally include only one text on Tahiti: Denis Diderot's canonical *Supplément au* Voyage *de Bougainville* ("Addendum to Bougainville's *Voyage*"). In doing so, we silence the plurality of voices heard in late-eighteenth-century France on the topic.

I propose to move beyond such a monolithic approach by integrating Marie-Josèphe de Monbart's *Lettres tahitiennes* ("Tahitian Letters") into our curriculum. Her 1784 novel expands our approach of the Tahitian theme in two ways. First, Monbart dramatizes the threat posed by European invaders of Tahiti, confronting the philosophes'—in particular Jean-Jacques Rousseau's—theories to the reality and urgency of the colonial situation of her time. Second, Monbart revisits the Enlightenment's anticolonial discourse by grounding it in the suffering of the female body. This relatively unknown, although once popular, novel sheds light on the blind spots of canonical works, prompting us to renew our approach to some of the most enduring texts on our syllabi.

Monbart was born Marie-Josèphe de Lescun in Paris around 1750 and was raised in Languedoc before she eloped with M. de Monbart to Germany. After their marriage ended in an annulment in 1785, she was briefly married to a German army officer by the name of von Sydow. Her solitary life on a remote Prussian estate was brightened by her friendship with the German author Jean Paul Friedrich Richter (Béguin). She died in Berlin in 1829. Her literary career dates from the time of her marriage to Monbart and is strongly influenced by Rousseau. Although she also wrote poetry, two treatises on female education, and a collection of short stories, *Lettres tahitiennes* is her most famous work. It was first published in Breslau in 1784, and its publication in two more editions in Brussels and Paris speaks to its Continental appeal.

A sentimental epistolary novel, *Lettres tahitiennes* chronicles the correspondence between Zeïr and Zulica, two young Tahitian lovers, after the departure of Zeïr on a French ship returning to Marseille. On arrival, Zeïr becomes acquainted with St. Val, an educated and virtuous young man, who tries to warn his Tahitian guest against the corruption of civilized society. But when Zeïr leaves for Paris, he too falls victim to the evils of the city and becomes as corrupted as the libertines with whom he associates.

In her letters from Tahiti, Zulica tells of the horrors brought upon the island by French and later British sailors. She is sold by her fellow Tahitians to an English captain and is taken to Europe against her will. When she escapes at last, she finds Zeïr tied by a promise to another woman, Mme de Germeuil, and persecuted by still another one of his lovers. Zulica, however, never falters in her love for Zeïr. After Mme de Germeuil's timely death, the lovers are reunited and move with St. Val to the south of France, where we expect them to live "happily ever after."

Lettres tahitiennes belongs to the vogue of works inspired by European contact with Tahiti, particularly the expedition by Bougainville, the name most associated with the French Pacific experience. In a two-year-long voyage around the world on the *Boudeuse*, Bougainville and his men spent only ten days on Tahiti in April 1768. Coming after long and hard months of navigation and characterized by abundance and sensuality, those ten days soon symbolized the whole expedition and founded the enduring myth of Tahiti in French culture. Bougainville was far more restrained in his enthusiasm than is commonly assumed. He delayed the publication of his journal until 1771, after he had had time to discuss Polynesian life and customs with a Tahitian man named Ahu-toru, whom he was taking back to France. Despite his caution, essays, pamphlets, plays, poems, novels, and treatises about Tahiti began to appear as soon as news of the island reached mainland France.

The first such text is a letter published in the French paper the *Mercure de France* in November 1769 by Philibert Commerson, the naturalist on board the *Boudeuse*. In his short travel account, part scientific anthropology, part quixotic philosophy, Commerson claims to have witnessed in Tahiti "l'état de l'homme naturel, né essentiellement bon" 'the state of natural man, born essentially good' and children of nature whose instinct "n'a pas encore dégénéré en raison" 'has not yet degenerated into reason' (qtd. in Bougainville 402–03).[1] These are Rousseauesque themes and rhetoric, and the encounter with Tahiti provided Enlightenment thinkers a perfect test case for Rousseau's theory of the noble savage. In 1770, for instance, Nicolas Bricaire de la Dixmérie uses the figure of a Tahitian *sauvage* ("savage"), a thinly veiled Ahu-toru, as the narrator for *Le Sauvage de Taïti aux Français* ("The Tahitian Savage's Address to the French"), which he follows by a rebuttal of Rousseau entitled "Envoi au philosophe ami des sauvages" 'Envoy to the philosopher, friend of the savage.' Monbart, too, sees in Bougainville's voyage and the Tahitian topos an opportunity to enter into dialogue with Rousseau but does so more persuasively than Bricaire de la Dixmérie. Her *Lettres tahitiennes* can therefore be read as an illustration of the theories presented in Rousseau's *Discours sur les sciences et les arts* (*Discourse on the Arts and Sciences*) and *Discours sur l'origine et les fondements de l'inégalité parmi les hommes* (*Discourse upon the Origin and the Foundation of the Inequality among Mankind*). As she puts into practice Rousseau's reflection on nature and human development in her novel, she both demonstrates how well she understands his philosophy and reveals its limits.

Not all texts inspired by Tahiti focused solely on Rousseau. In his collection of poems *Les Jardins* (1782; "The Gardens"), Abbot Jacques Delille portrays Ahu-toru wandering nostalgically in French gardens. Ahu-toru also appears the same year as the fictional author of *Histoire des révolutions de Taïti* ("History of the Revolutions of Tahiti"). The actual author, Jean-Charles Poncelin de la Roche-Tilhac, combines a fantastical account of the history of Tahiti with excerpts from travel narratives to better criticize the French society of his time. Within the diversity of genres and ideologies, three main themes emerge in late-eighteenth-century Tahitiana: nature's bounty on an island where work is superfluous; a peaceful political regime under a paternalistic leader; and an unconstrained, wholesome sexuality, free from old Europe's concepts of shame and decency. (These themes are, of course, intellectual constructions by French authors and should not be confused with a faithful representation of Polynesian life.) After all, the men on the *Boudeuse* name the island Nouvelle Cythère (New Cytherea) after the Greek island of love. This focus on love, understood as uninhibited sexuality, came to characterize most works inspired by Tahiti—and to supersede other aspects of the Tahitian theme.

Already in 1775, Voltaire uses accounts of Tahitian sexuality to motivate his call for philosophical relativism in his short story "Les Oreilles du comte de Chesterfield" ("The Ears of the Count of Chesterfield"). Tahitian sexuality is also the theme of *La Vierge d'Otaïti* ("The Tahitian Virgin"), a 1788 play by Jean-Baptiste-Claude Delisle de Sales with a moralist conclusion antithetical to Voltaire's. These two works are examples of a rich literary production that culminates in Diderot's *Supplément au Voyage de Bougainville*. Penned and circulated among friends in 1772 and published posthumously in 1796, *Supplément* depicts an idealized Tahitian society as the basis of a materialist philosophy and contestation of Eurocentrism. Gender and sexuality play a great part in this vision.

Monbart also writes about love and Tahitian sensuality, but as a critique of European invaders: sexual encounters become colonial encounters, uninhibited sexuality becomes coerced sexuality. As Monbart shifts the narrative focus from a male traveler to a Tahitian female main character with a prominent place and a forceful voice, she demystifies the male-centered fantasies of Tahiti.

In the second half of the eighteenth century, Rousseau's influential discourses—his 1750 *Discours sur les sciences et les arts* and his 1755 *Discours sur l'inégalité* —are the theoretical lens through which overseas travelers and mainland philosophes approach non-European peoples, especially during and after the encounter with the South Pacific. A self-proclaimed disciple of Rousseau, Monbart offers in *Lettres tahitiennes* a cogent illustration of the two *Discours*, dramatizing Rousseau's theories in her fiction. Zulica and Zeïr's story exemplifies the "civilizing" of natural societies in the course of human development as well as the tensions between nature and culture, tensions that Monbart tries to solve in a postlapsarian paradise organized around Rousseauesque ideals. She also brings to light other latent tensions in Rousseau's work: his silence on colonization and slavery.

In *Lettres tahitiennes*, one can follow the progress of the two Tahitian characters who, at the beginning, have not had "d'autre maître que la nature" 'a master other than nature' (1: vi), in the light of Rousseau's *Discours sur l'inégalité*. We can ask our students to map out Rousseau's theories in the novel. For instance, Zeïr's decision to board a ship bound for France, his thirst for knowledge, and his eagerness to emulate his French hosts demonstrate a crucial facet of human nature according to Rousseau: a sense of unrest and of amour propre natural to all men, the mark of their perfectibility and free will that led them to evolve. The novel then mirrors the three stages of human development put forward in *Discours sur l'inégalité*. Monbart places precontact Tahiti in the second phase, as St. Val, Zeïr's French mentor, tells his protégé that Tahiti represents not "l'état le plus parfait de la nature; mais seulement une des périodes des différentes gradations que vous parcourrez pour parvenir au point où nous sommes" 'the most perfect state of nature but only one of the periods in the various stages that you will go through to reach the state where we currently are' (1: 54). Unlike some of her contemporaries, Monbart does not confuse Rousseau's analysis of the state of nature with a naive primitivism and the dream of returning to a presocial state.

We can also ask students to examine in *Lettres tahitiennes* Rousseau's mistrust of civilization—even when it is deemed ineluctable. Zulica's reflection on writing, in particular, echoes a major statement of *Discours sur les sciences et les arts*, famously analyzed by Jacques Derrida in *De la grammatologie* (*Of Grammatology*). Zulica articulates a strong critique of modern civilization that has at its core not the bountiful harmony of precontact Tahiti but rather lack and loss. Even though Zulica considers Zeïr and herself to be fortunate to be able to communicate through writing, she soon reflects that writing is truly European, that is, civilized, because it is born out of suffering, loss, and separation, like all things civilized: "l'écriture ne peut avoir été inventée que par des aman[t]s malheureux" 'writing can only have been invented by unhappy lovers' (1: 6). In *Lettres tahitiennes*, parting and estrangement are not just a topic but an integral dimension of writing. Even though writing can suture the separation it manifests, it is only a last resort, a coping mechanism after the disaster brought on the island by the colonizers. In that perspective, all the luxury, including writing, introduced by the Europeans is but a consolation prize; it can never make up for what has been lost, for what was bountifully provided in the state of nature. Nevertheless, Monbart's main characters are aware that a return to Tahiti, to a precontact state of nature, at the end of their journey is as impossible for them as "retourner vivre à la forêt avec les Ours" 'going back to living in the woods with bears' is for Rousseau (*Discours sur l'origine* 207). The end of *Lettres tahitiennes* sees them establishing a small community in southern France and reconciling nature and culture in a postlapsarian utopia—a successful Clarens, as it were. In our classrooms, we can encourage students to analyze this final utopia, especially its hybrid combination of Rousseauesque ideals and elements from the Tahitian idyll that opens the novel.

Students can also be asked to pay attention to episodes in which Monbart diverges from Rousseau, addressing his blind spots. By dramatizing his philosophy, Monbart brings it to bear on issues that Rousseau only deals with in passing or metaphorically: colonization and slavery. The famous opening line of *Du contrat social* (*Social Contract*), "[l']homme est né libre et partout il est dans les fers" 'man is born free and yet everywhere he is in chains' (351), cannot be applied to Zulica even though she was born free and finds herself in chains halfway through the novel. Rousseau's statement is a political one and the *fers* a metaphor for deleterious political regimes, not a reflection on the human consequences of colonization and enslavement. Similarly, when his Émile is held in slavery in North Africa in *Émile et Sophie, ou les Solitaires* (*Émile and Sophia; or, The Solitaires*), he muses, "Émile esclave! . . . dans quel sens? Qu'ai-je perdu de ma liberté primitive? Ne naquis-je pas esclave de la nécessité? Quel nouveau joug peuvent m'imposer les hommes?" 'Émile, a slave! . . . how so? What have I lost of my original liberty? Was I not born a slave to necessity? What new yoke can men impose on me?' (916–17). On the contrary, Zulica's fate in *Lettres tahitiennes* shows that a "new yoke" can indeed be imposed on a human being by other human beings, especially in the double yoke of colonization and gendered power relations. For all his use of the concepts of slavery, Rousseau failed to fully address the moral issues at stake in such terms. *Lettres tahitiennes* can be used as a reality check for Rousseau's ideas as Monbart goes beyond his silences and metaphors and confronts his ideas with the realities of colonialism.

Lettres tahitiennes was not the only Tahiti-inspired work to express fear for the future of the island after the encounter with Europe and to present a strong anticolonial message. One can create a fruitful dialogue between Monbart's *Lettres tahitiennes* and Diderot's *Supplément*. Students can be encouraged to compare both texts with their common source, Bougainville's 1771 *Voyage autour du monde*, and reflect on what each author chose to foreground or forget; to reflect, that is, on each author's construction of an idiosyncratic literary representation of Tahiti. Students can also read side by side Zulica's letters and the famed "Adieux du vieillard" ("The Old Man's Farewell") in Diderot's *Supplément*. The most productive element in this dialogue is the representation of female sexuality, especially in relation to colonial violence. If Diderot's text is deeply anticolonial, his treatment of sexuality is dissociated from this critique. For Monbart, on the other hand, female sexuality is inextricable from colonial violence and lies at the very core of her anticolonialism.

Classroom discussions about *Supplément* never fail to touch on Diderot's imagined sexual utopia. Even if the text claims that men and women are both free to engage in sexual relationships, students are often struck by the emphasis laid on women's reproductive systems and how limiting the expectation of their fertility is: sterile and menstruating women are forbidden to engage in sexual intercourse and are ostracized by veils. Orou's description of sexual intercourse between French sailors and Tahitian women is particularly telling in this regard: he asserts that the offspring born of such unions are part of a plan to repopulate his island. Tahitian men first decide to test whether sterile Tahitian women could be succesfully impregnated by the newcomers and send them to satifisy the French sailors' sexual demands: "ce sont celles que nous avons exposées à vos premiers embrassements" 'these we exposed to your first embraces,' Orou explains (77). But in Diderot's text, when Tahitian men realize the intellectual superiority of Europeans, they put their most beautiful mates in the Frenchmen's beds: "nous vous avons destiné quelques-unes de nos femmes et de nos filles les plus belles à recueillir la semence d'une race meilleure que la nôtre" 'we sent to you some of our fairest wives and daughters to gather in the seed of a race that is better than our own' (77). The memorable *aumônier* ("chaplain") first turns down his host's offer to sleep with his wife and daughters but eventually gives in to their emotional pleas and converts to (Diderot's fictional) Tahitian mores, sleeping his way from Orou's youngest daughter to his wife. While Diderot's utopia has to be understood in the larger context of his materialist philosophy, the emphasis on women's reproductive system leaves no room for a portrayal of women as independent sexual agents. Rather, with the passive "exposées" and "destiné[es]," they are simply receptacles for male seed, pawns in a larger demographic plan designed by their male counterparts.

Monbart writes of the same encounter but from the viewpoint of a Tahitian woman. Monbart's imagined sexual utopia is a lost Tahitian paradise, where lovemaking used to be a religious act and gender relations were marked by perfect equality and mutual respect. This idyll vanishes as soon as European invaders set foot on the island. Far from the open arms of the Tahitian women Diderot imagines in *Supplément*, Monbart's female characters are appalled at the sexual impositions of the newcomers, who remain undeterred by Zulica's "larmes, répugnance, . . . continuels & humiliants refus, . . . résistance" 'tears, repugnance, . . . constant and humiliating refusals, . . . resistance' (1: 124–25). When Tahitian women refuse to indulge the sexual cravings of French sailors, the response is one of extreme violence: "ils ont osé violer l'asile que nous leur avions accordé; ils ont souillé de sang ces gazons consacrés aux plaisirs" 'they [the French sailors] have dared to violate the asylum we had given them; they have soiled with blood these lawns consecrated to pleasure' (1: 11–2). The verb *violer* is used metaphorically here to express the defilement of both the place and the laws of hospitality, but its literal meaning of physical rape is dominant.

This defilement culminates in Zulica's rape, which opens letter 21 and constitutes the turning point of the novel: "C'en est fait Zeïr, la malheureuse Zulica est devenue la proie d'un monstre" 'It is done, Zeïr, the miserable Zulica has become the prey of a monster' (1: 126). Zulica becomes the embodiment of the violent conquest of Tahiti. She no longer belongs to herself ("je ne m'appartiens plus" [1: 126]) and opens her letter in the third person. The tyrant she has denounced in previous letters is no longer the oppressor of an island but a personal tyrant, who has bought her and is taking her to England as one of his possessions. That Zulica is forced into the British captain's tent by her fellow Tahitians signals the destruction of the Tahitian society by mercantilism used as a colonial tool, a far cry from Orou's indigeneous collective plan in Diderot's *Supplément*. Where Orou saw the potential regeneration of his people, Zulica laments the loss of her friends, relatives, and homeland ("Je n'ai plus d'amis, plus de parents, plus de patrie" 'I no longer have friends, relatives, homeland' [1: 126]). The fate of the colonized woman both heralds and symbolizes the fate of the island.

With Zulica's rape at the heart of the encounter with Europe, the novel forces us to reconsider the traditional representation of Tahitian woman as sexually available. By giving Zulica a voice, by placing the emphasis on a Tahitian woman through Zulica's resistance, Monbart not only denounces the double oppression that Zulica endures as both other and woman but also challenges the dominant, male-oriented discourse on Tahiti and makes her reader reconsider the traditional representations of the lascivious Tahitian woman. Bringing *Lettres tahitiennes* to bear on our students' readings of *Supplément* thus offers a counterpoint to Diderot's discussion of sexuality. It also shows that analyzing the male fantasies underlying the common representation of Tahiti is not an anachronistic projection of our modern-day sensibility and feminism: as early as 1784, Monbart refused to accept the sexual stereotypes attached to Tahitian women in French fiction.

To recognize Monbart's exceptional voice, however, one has to break from the critical reception of her novel, which has traditionally shied away from addressing her analysis of the violence inflicted on Zulica as both colonized and woman. Critics either failed to mention Zulica's rape or interpreted it in unsettling ways, until Julia Douthwaite's *Exotic Women*. In her seminal study, Douthwaite analyzes the effects of the "heroine's rape and enslavement" on the Tahitian social order and on French discourse about Tahiti (167–68). Some critics simply allude to Zulica's voyage to Europe without dwelling on the circumstances: "[f]inalement, Zulica rejoint son amant," 'Zulica eventually joins her lover' (O'Reilly and Reitman 818). Most read the rape as a noble sacrifice on Zulica's part: "La mort dans l'âme, car infidèle à Zeïr, elle cède pour sauver ses compatriotes" 'With a heavy heart, since she has to be unfaithful to Zeïr, she gives in to save her fellow Tahitians' (Faessel 163). Here, she is forced by the fear of renewed violence against the islanders, not physical force; the choice is ultimately hers. The same idea presides over the statement, "Zulica rejoint son amant, en payant son passage à la façon de Sainte Marie l'Egyptienne" 'Zulica joins her lover, paying for her voyage in the way of Saint Mary of Egypt' (Chinard 421), as though Zulica had not been raped and abducted but had chosen to pay for her trip to Europe with her body. Such readings are completely unsubstantiated by the text: Zulica never envisages joining her lover in Europe but rather entreats him to come back to her; she writes of being dragged to the English captain against her will and placed on a boat bound for an unknown destination. It is as though two centuries of colonialism and postcolonialism were necessary to recognize what Monbart discerned in 1784: the dangers of exotic sexual stereotypes that draw a veil over the fate of the colonized woman.

Critics may have been confused by *Lettres tahitiennes*'s paradoxical feminist statement. Like Zilia in Françoise de Graffigny's *Lettres d'une Péruvienne* (*Letters from a Peruvian Woman*), Zulica demonstrates both heroic resistance in the face of male violence and moral steadfastness.[2] However, while *Lettres d'une Péruvienne* is a story of emancipation of a woman who, by the end of the narrative, leads an independent life on her own estate, Zulica never conceives of herself independently of Zeïr. Nevertheless, her story is a potentially empowering discourse for women. Confronted by male violence (at the hands of the British captain) and Zeïr's errings (both geographical and moral), Zulica is the moral anchor of the novel, as well as its structural backbone (her letters and actions shape the novel). As the heroine is elevated to a superior, almost saintly status, *Lettres tahitiennes* exemplifies one of the responses to women's condition in early modern France: advocating for women's rights by arguing women's moral superiority and leading role in moral reform. Even though Graffigny's Zilia may be more to our taste, Monbart's Zulica offers an opportunity to present our students with a more complete image of women's advocacy at the time.

In this perspective, Monbart's statement can be taken further and used to discuss the influence of Rousseauesque thought on feminism in the second half of the eighteenth century. In the wake of Rousseau's huge success among his women readers, especially after *Julie*, and because of his emphasis on sensibility, Rousseauesque thought was seen to advocate "a new moral order in which women could play a central role" (Trouille, *Sexual Politics* 4) and to offer a new dignity to women—as wives and mothers and moral models certainly. But Rousseau's influence does not mean uncritical adhesion to his pronouncements on women or on the topic of colonization. When Rousseau fails to provide Émile's female companion, Sophie, with a good education in *Émile, ou de l'éducation* (*Émile; or, Concerning Education*), Monbart feels compelled to offer her own treatise: *Sophie, ou de l'éducation des filles* ("Sophie; or, On the Education of Young Women"), in which she applies Rousseau's wisdom to Sophie's education, a work she later complements with *De l'éducation d'une princesse* ("On the Education of a Princess"). Monbart's project takes its place alongside important works such as *Adèle et Théodore*, by Stéphanie-Félicité Du Crest, comtesse de Genlis, and *Les Conversations d'Émilie*, by Louise Tardieu d'Esclavelles, marquise d'Épinay, and is bound to appear in courses on the Enlightenment.

Lettres tahitiennes is particularly distinctive among the literary works that followed Bougainville's voyage and can become a productive tool in our courses on the Enlightenment's encounter with the other. As the novel illustrates the inescapable Rousseauesque background to the topic, it offers students a chance to further their reflection on Rousseau's approach to nature versus culture, in all its subtleties and limits. If Monbart, like Rousseau, acknowledges that the state of nature belongs to the past and that the challenge lies in coming to terms with modern civilization, she does not hesitate to confront his discourse with the reality and urgency of the situation in Tahiti. Monbart's anticolonial critique stands in stark contrast to that of her contemporaries and, in particular, to Diderot's *Supplément*. Her novel is grounded in the suffering and resistance of the female body and articulated in a female voice. Not only does gender serve to denounce European crimes (here pillaging, bloodshed, and rape), it also questions the images that constitute the myth of Tahiti in the French *imaginaire* ("imagination"). The image of lascivious, scantily clad women, eager to offer their favors to any man, is denounced as a dangerous fantasy by Monbart as she revisits the discourse on Tahiti. Monbart sheds light on the women of the Enlightenment, revealing them to be not just passive victims of violence but also considerable moral anchors, active agents of resistence against colonization, and, by her own example, engaging and consequential writers.

Notes

1. All translations from the French are mine.

2. The two novels are often discussed together. In fact, Monbart's novel was marketed as a "suite aux *Lettres peruviennes*" 'sequel to the *Peruvian Letters*' on the front page of the Paris edition, probably in an attempt by the printer or bookseller to bolster sales.

Lisa Beckstrand

The Revolutionary Ideas
of Olympe de Gouges

The French Revolution, a fascinating and pivotal moment in history, continues to be a perennial favorite among students. Treatment of this foundational period finds its way into a variety of courses taught from various
disciplines. One cannot begin to understand the French Revolution without
examining the concept of individual rights and the ways in which citizenship came to be defined. While many textbooks on the Revolution discuss
the Déclaration des droits de l'homme et du citoyen (1789; "Declaration
of the Rights of Man and Citizen"), a seminal document that lays out
some of the most precious freedoms shared by French citizens today, few
analyses include a discussion of the constraints imposed by that document
on women and the ensuing controversy over definitions of citizenship at
that time. Olympe de Gouges's well-known text "Déclaration des droits
de la femme et de la citoyenne" (1791; "Declaration of the Rights of
Woman and Citizen"), a pastiche and development of the Déclaration des
droits de l'homme et du citoyen, is a quick read, is available in English,
and provides insights into the role that gender played in the development
of notions of citizenship and individual rights in the late eighteenth century. These two texts can be profitably paired.

In addition, a close reading of de Gouges's "Déclaration" also underscores the absurdity of any attempt on the part of France's National Assembly to discuss and define individual rights while fully condoning the practice of slavery. This paradox is further brought to bear in a short play by de Gouges entitled *L'Esclavage des noirs* ("The Slavery of Blacks"). While a comparison of de Gouges's "Déclaration" with the original Déclaration gives students insights into the complexity of social hierarchies of gender and race during the revolutionary period, an examination of de Gouges's play also illuminates the contradictions inherent in the philosophical arguments on individual rights that justified the exclusion of women and blacks. Both texts appeal to modern readers because of the way in which de Gouges redefines notions of individual rights and their role in the building of family and nation. This essay examines how cultural constructs of gender and race shaped by a newly forming political body affected de Gouges's understanding of cultural and social hierarchies of power. It seeks to understand how an unknown woman of little means was able to disrupt and transform scientific jargon and accepted philosophical truths to imagine and work toward a new model of society in which individual rights were extended to members of both sexes and all races. Finally, it looks at how de Gouges emphasizes the importance of human relationships to transform the prejudice inherent in the political thinking of her day.

The efforts by politicians to set forth in writing notions of individual rights, which would be universal and based on the idea of a social contract, failed to include all individuals. The Déclaration des droits de l'homme et du citoyen is just one expression of liberal political theory that proclaimed the sanctity of universal rights, grounded in nature, while neglecting to address the growing problems concerning the place of women in the public sphere and the morality of the slave trade. Many critics would argue that the discourse of citizenship and the construction of national identity were inextricably related to the process of exclusion (see Scott, "Woman"; Pateman; Hunt; Outram 124–52; see also Beckstrand, "Olympe de Gouges"). As scholars such as Lynn Hunt and Dorinda Outram have argued, it was women's exclusion from the political body that helped the revolutionary governing class legitimize its struggle for power. Outram states that the corruption of the ancien régime was ascribed to the agency of women; thus the developing governing class adopted an antifeminine rhetoric, thereby ensuring an all-male political embodiment (125). Feminists such as de Gouges, Anne-Josèphe Theroigne de Mericourt, and Etta Palm d'Aelders raised questions about the status of women, challenging liberal notions of the autonomous individual. Were women not considered citizens? As de Gouges wrote,"la femme naît libre et demeure égale à l'homme en droits" 'woman is born free and remains equal to man in her rights' and therefore ought to have the same privileges as men in education, employment, and political participation ("Déclaration" 207).[1]

Increasing focus on the female body as different and as suitable only for the maternal role made it difficult for women to assert themselves as individuals in the body politic. According to Thomas Laqueur ("Orgasm" 3) and Hunt (203), the mobilization of medical opinion occurred at the end of the eighteenth century as a result of concerns raised about women's participation. Londa Schiebinger notes the emergence of skeletal drawings during the same period, through which the scientific community determined a hierarchy of gender and race by skull and pelvic size (*Mind* 193). Schiebinger observes:

> [A]natomists, anthropologists, and natural historians, working under the banner of scientific neutrality, declared that, by nature, people with compressed crania (which included women of all races) or black skin were incapable of pursuing academic science. (*Nature's Body* 7)

While liberal political theorists and proponents of the social contract looked to nature as the supreme justification for women's difference and hence their subsequent exclusion from the public sphere, de Gouges looked to nature for inclusion. In the introduction to her "Déclaration," she appeals to the scientific method and challenges anyone to try to produce evidence of gendered hierarchies in the natural world. She writes:

> Remonte aux animaux, consulte les éléments, étudie les végétaux, jette enfin un coup d'oeil sur toutes les modifications de la matière organisée; et rends-toi à l'évidence quand je t'en offre les moyens; cherche, fouille et distingue, si tu le peux, les sexes dans l'administration de la nature. Partout tu les trouveras confondus, partout ils coopèrent avec un ensemble harmonieux à ce chef-d'œuvre immortel. (206)

> Go back to animals, consult the elements, study plants, finally glance at all the modifications of organic matter, and surrender to the evidence when I offer you the means; search, probe, and distinguish, if you can, the sexes in the administration of nature. Everywhere you will find them mingled; everywhere they cooperate in harmonious togetherness in this immortal masterpiece.

Equality between the sexes was founded in nature and thus required that women be assured the same inalienable rights bestowed on men.

Many of de Gouges's changes to the original declaration involved simply rewriting the articles to include women. These sections are characterized by appeals to equality between the sexes and emphasize rights to fair education, gainful employment, equitable job distribution, property ownership, participation in public administrative decisions and political processes, and legal representation. De Gouges points out the hypocrisies inherent in the original, namely, its pretensions of upholding the precepts of the social contract. Why were women subject to the laws applicable to all citizens when they were not really considered citizens? If women were equally punishable by law, they should also have a voice in the creation of those laws. She writes, "[L]a femme a le droit de monter sur l'échafaud; elle doit avoir également celui de monter à la Tribune" '[W]oman has the right to mount the scaffold; she must equally have the right to mount the rostrum' (208). While many of the articles are transformed into clever turns of phrase emphasizing women's equality with men, de Gouges develops other sections, adding completely new information and emphasizing women's difference from men. In these sections she focuses on the female body, demanding special rights for women, rewriting biological theories about female nature, and redefining notions of family (see also Tucker in this volume).

Article 11 of the Déclaration, citing freedom of speech as one of the most precious rights of man, is particularly interesting with regard to de Gouges's text. Rather than merely appealing to equality, de Gouges demands certain rights for unmarried mothers and raises the issue of paternal obligation. Freedom of speech is not intrinsically a precious right of women: it is precious because it helps enforce the responsibility of fathers toward their children:

> La libre communication des pensées et des opinions est un des droits les plus précieux de la femme, puisque cette liberté assure la légitimité des pères envers les enfants. Toute Citoyenne peut donc dire librement, *je suis mère d'un enfant qui vous appartient*, sans qu'un préjugé barbare la force à dissimuler la vérité. (208)

> The free communication of thoughts and opinions is one of the most precious rights of woman, since that liberty assures the recognition of children by their fathers. Any female citizen thus may freely say, *I am the mother of a child that belongs to you*, without being forced by a barbarous prejudice to hide the truth.

Here de Gouges appeals to notions of women's difference, underscoring the Rousseauesque ideals of mothering (i.e., child bearing and child rearing; see also Marcellesi and Jensen in this volume). Philosophers' focus on the female body as only suitable for the maternal role made women's participation in the political sphere impossible. In the words of Carol Pateman, women were seen as "incapable of entering the original contract and transforming themselves into the civil individuals who uphold its terms" because of their unusual relation to nature through childbirth (96). De Gouges, in her version of the declaration, uses the idea of women's difference for her own purposes, redefining women's nature as strength rather than weakness.

Women's specific relation to nature inspired de Gouges to demand special rights for mothers. In "Projet d'un second théâtre et d'une maternité," she proposed the construction of maternity hospitals as a way to address the unhygienic conditions of existing hospitals where one out of four women died in childbirth. While she demanded special rights for mothers, she reminded men of their responsibilities as fathers. By consistently referring to paternal obligation in her text, de Gouges suggests to her readers that, although child bearing had to do with women's difference, child rearing did not. She makes it clear that the business of raising children was not necessarily gender specific and that fathers had a place in the care of their children as well.

The responsibilities of fathers and the rights of single mothers are underscored further in de Gouges's "Forme du contrat social de l'homme et de la femme" ("Form of the Social Contract for Men and Women"), at the end of "Déclaration." Her idea of a social contract within marriage proposed that both husband and wife were equal and that their property and assets would be communally owned. Children would inherit equally, regardless of gender, and could take the name of the father and mother who acknowledged them. Again, her text emphasizes the importance of parental (and especially paternal) obligation, addressing the subject of fathers who abandon or deny the existence of their children: "et nous imposons de souscrire à la loi qui punit l'abnégation de son propre sang" 'and we are charged to subscribe to the law that punishes the renunciation of one's own blood' (211). The contract also insists on the creation of laws to protect unmarried women from abandonment by their fiancés and widows from being denied spousal inheritance. It allows for adoption of poor children by rich families, to alleviate the situation of mothers who have no means to care for their children. De Gouges further argues for the protection of prostitutes, the marriage of priests, the abolition of slavery in the colonies, and the restoration of the king to the throne. The precepts of de Gouges's contract emphasize the importance of the family, ensuring that women and children (as well as blacks, priests, the subjects of the king) do not fall prey to the abuses of patriarchal authority. It attempts to restore the rights denied by unequal power relations.

Most striking, and central to her philosophy, is the connection de Gouge draws between the process of constructing a nation, that is, national and political identities, and the business of building and maintaining a family (see Beckstrand, *Deviant Women*). The third article of de Gouges's declaration defines the nation as the marriage of man and woman:

> Le principe de toute souveraineté réside essentiellement dans la Nation, qui n'est que la réunion de la femme et de l'homme: nul corps, nul individu, ne peut exercer d'autorité qui n'en émane expressément. (207)

> The principle of all sovereignty rests essentially with the nation, which is nothing other than the union of woman and man; no body and no individual can exercise any authority that does not come expressly from [the nation].

By mingling the ideas of nation and family, de Gouges blurs the line between public and private, bringing women into the realm of politics and redefining *universal* and *political* as non–gender specific. Again in her social contract, de Gouges mentions the importance of uniting the executive and legislative powers of government, comparing them to the marriage of man and woman: "Je considère ces deux pouvoirs, comme l'homme et la femme qui doivent être unis, mais égaux en force et en vertu, pour faire un bon ménage" 'I consider these two powers to be like man and woman who must be united but equal in force and virtue to make a good household' (213). De Gouges saw the Revolution as an opportunity to restore the power imbalances that an unjust society had permitted. A constitutional monarchy would eradicate the tyrannical abuses of power by the king, just as de Gouges's "Déclaration" and social contract, by making women citizens, would erase the patriarchal abuses of power by husbands and fathers. Her text is strikingly appealing to the modern reader because of the way in which it calls on men to be primary participants in the familial realm and on women to play a central role in the political realm.

De Gouges's interest in establishing individual rights was not limited to the defense of women alone but extended to questions about the status of blacks in society as well. Although de Gouges addressed the issue of slavery only briefly in "Déclaration," she wrote a play in which she brought the issue of slavery to center stage. But sympathizing with the abolitionist movement proved to be a dangerous position for de Gouges. First performed in 1789, *L'Esclavage des noirs* was bitterly attacked by colonialists and their lobbyists in France as an antislavery tract, inciting sympathy for the slaves and portraying colonialists as inhumane and unreasonable. De Gouges's questioning of gender and race-biased social institutions prompted the mayor of Paris to censor her controversial work.[2] The play centers on the search for and trial of a fugitive slave, Zamor, who has murdered his master and fled to a nearby island. In hiding, Zamor witnesses a shipwreck and saves a young French couple from drowning, befriends them, and recounts his story of defending his fiancée (also a slave) from the sexual, violent abuses of his master. Zamor confesses that his attempt to thwart those abuses resulted in his accidentally killing his master. The young French couple believe that Zamor would be found innocent (since he killed in self-defense); however, authorities and the local populace were clamoring for an execution to set an example to all other slaves of the consequences of challenging those in authority.

It is not hard to understand why the play created controversy. It may have been against the proprieties of the period to portray a hero who commits murder; moreover, de Gouges's hero and murderer was a semieducated black slave who evoked sympathy from spectators and readers of the play. The depiction of his innocence raised questions about whether blacks had the right to defend themselves. This issue is reflected in scene 2 of the second act, in which a group of black slaves, Zamor and his fiancée's friends, discuss human rights. On learning that Zamor and his fiancée, Mirza, have been arrested and are awaiting execution, their friend Betzi asks how it is possible that they could be executed without a trial or without ever having the opportunity to tell their side of the story. It is ironic that this is how de Gouges (a white woman writing about the rights of blacks) met her own fate: de Gouges's portrayal of blacks in this play resulted in a lettre de cachet demanding her immediate imprisonment.

In the discussion that ensues, de Gouges uses the voice of Coraline, a wise black woman who is one of the governor's slaves, to undermine racial and gender-related stereotypes. Coraline replies, "Jugés! il nous est défendu d'être innocents et de nous justifier" 'Judged! It is forbidden for us to be innocent and to defend ourselves' (75). After the slaves relate their family histories, about which they know very little (other than that they have all been bought and sold in the market), Coraline reassures the others that they will not remain in chains forever. It is interesting that de Gouges uses a masculine voice, Azor's, to express the point that black slaves may one day overturn the master/slave hierarchy and a black female voice to reinvent the system. Coraline responds to Azor, "Tiens, pour être bon, il ne faut être ni maître ni esclave" 'Say, to be good one must be neither slave nor master' (76). Azor believes that the power imbalance can only be remedied by being inverted, and he informs Coraline that her idea of a society without masters or servants is pure nonsense. She responds by informing the others that she has read in a book that to be happy one needs to be "libre et bon cultivatieur" 'free and a good laborer.' Since liberty is the only thing missing from their lives, once it is given, "il n'y aura ni maître ni esclave" 'there will be neither master nor slave' (77). Among the books that come to mind here are Jean-Jacques Rousseau's *Discours sur l'origine et les fondements de l'inégalité parmi les hommes* (*Discourse upon the Origin and the Foundation of the Inequality among Men*) and his *Contrat social* (*Social Contract*), which put forth the enlightened ideal that no man has any natural authority over another and that social inequalities are contrary to the laws of nature. While Rousseau believed this ideal in principle, he also took great pains to write that women were inferior to men when it came to governing and consequently needed to be subject to men's authority in the public realm. Like Rousseau, de Gouges held that the authority of one person over another was not natural but a result of social corruption. Unlike Rousseau, de Gouges applied this thinking to all parts of society, including women and blacks.

The above-quoted exchange in *Esclavage* contradicts ideologies emphasizing binary oppositions and problematizes a hierarchical view of the world. It is the black female character who challenges the system of unequal power relations and imagines a utopia in which there would be neither slaves nor masters. The male voice, which represents the voice of society, desires that such hierarchies be maintained, albeit inverted.

The denouement of the play brings together other textual strategies that break down racial barriers and gender stereotypes and undermine the master/slave hierarchy. Like "Déclaration," *Esclavage* magisterially interweaves the injustice of slavery with the theme of the global family, forcing the issue of the liberation of slaves to be felt as an immediate imperative. Although Zamor's pardon comes, in part, as a result of the governor's reconciliation with a biological daughter that he had abandoned at birth, de Gouges's text underlines the importance of looking beyond the limitations of biology to understand the human family. The filial relationship between Zamor and the governor serves to break down racial barriers and imbues state honor with familial honor. M. de Saint-Frémont is torn between his duty to the state and his desire to protect Zamor because of the relationship between them. The governor had not only raised and educated Zamor from infancy but adored him "comme son enfant" 'like his child' (43). And Zamor reveals that he has faithfully carried out his duties to the governor more out of "la tendresse de son fils" 'the tenderness of a son' than by "le dévouement d'un esclave" 'the duty of a slave' (46). The destruction of the other becomes synonymous with the destruction of one's own, as boundaries between the powerful and the powerless are weakened. The transformation of relationships from those of violence (white master / black slave, colonizer/colonized) to those of familial love (father/son) coincides with the process of liberation. As in de Gouges's other texts (and consistent with Coraline's ideas), this transformation enables the power brokers to effect change and restore the natural rights of human beings. The play ends with a discourse on liberty, in which the governor emphasizes the importance of "l'amour du bien public" 'love of the common good' and the need for wise laws to prevent excesses and protect human rights (133).

L'Esclavage des noirs stands alone as one of the few attempts to confront boldly the racial and gender-related bigotry that had been sanctioned by the authority of science. De Gouges used the play as a vehicle to criticize the physiological and biological rationale employed to justify the exclusion of women and blacks from the universal rights accorded to European men. Her play undermined the common stereotypes of the colonized (i.e., the black slaves) as unintelligent, inarticulate, biologically inferior, and capable of committing senseless acts of violence. At the same time, her emphasis on the notion of a global family as a means of approaching the subject of individual rights weakened, or threatened to weaken, political and nationalistic tendencies toward racist and sexist abuses of power. While late-eighteenth-century France was not ready to restore the natural rights of freedom and equality to all individuals, de Gouges would be remembered by some as one of the courageous few who dared to plead the cause of women and blacks through writing, despite the violent hostility that led to her execution. A closer examination of her work will give students of any course on the Revolution or the history of political thought insights into the complexities of the gender and race-related prejudice that served to define the discourse on individual rights during that pivotal period.

Examining the ways in which individual rights were being defined when constitutions were being crafted over two hundred years ago could not be more pertinent to our culture today. To get undergraduate students to think about this subject, an instructor could ask the following questions: What constitutes citizenship today? What rights are afforded to citizens? Is there evidence in our society today that would suggest a two-tiered society of first- and second-class citizens, like the one de Gouges decried, in which women and blacks were not given the same basic rights and freedoms as others? How and by whom is this tier system defined or communicated? Such current issues as racial profiling, unequal pay for equal work, bans on gay marriage, refusal of medical care to undocumented workers, or failure to provide a living wage to many of our citizens echo eerily, to a certain degree, the societal ills that plagued de Gouges and her contemporaries in late-eighteenth-century France. Examining in detail de Gouges's efforts and strategies to transform the prejudicial thinking that permeated the original documents defining citizenship in her historical context can give today's students a greater appreciation of their role in defining individual rights and engaging with democracy in present-day society.

Notes

Portions of this essay are adapted from material that appeared in *Deviant Women of the French Revolution and the Rise of Feminism* (Fairleigh Dickinson UP, 2009) and are published with permission.

1. All translations from the French are mine unless otherwise noted.

2. For a detailed account of political reactions to the play, see Olivier Blanc's biography *Olympe de Gouges*.

Part III

Teaching Specific Courses

Chloé Hogg

Early Modern Women and the Philosophical Tradition

My teaching contribution stems from a conversation I had some years ago with a professor of philosophy. We were discussing René Descartes, when it struck me that his Descartes and mine barely knew each other. His Descartes was a philosopher who had never been challenged by Madeleine de Scudéry (refuting his belief in animal machines and radical doubt) or championed by the Cartésiennes. Mine was a writer, who delighted me with the clear prose and shifty rhetoric of his 1637 *Discours de la méthode* (*Discourse on the Method*). Talk faltered. A few years later, I found myself thinking of this exchange as I planned an undergraduate seminar on seventeenth- and eighteenth-century French literature and philosophy, taught in translation to a group of mostly nonmajors. I wanted to make my failed conversation with the philosophy professor work—this time with students. The course focuses on women's participation in early modern philosophy, the dissemination of texts and ideas, and the rhetorical and literary strategies used by writers to present ideas and persuade readers. To address these topics, I organize my teaching around pairs of writers, two of which—Elisabeth of Bohemia and Descartes, Scudéry and Blaise Pascal—I present in this essay.

The growing interest in early modern women philosophers, combined with recent editions and translations of key works, promises to make Elisabeth and Scudéry increasingly familiar names on course syllabi, with or without an illustrious male counterpart (see O'Neill, "Early Modern Women"; Conley; Lyons, Cherbuliez, and Goodkin in this volume). Yet by bringing together philosophy and literature, the old and the new canons, writers familiar in English (Descartes, Pascal) and a major early modern author taught primarily in French (Scudéry), the pairs have great crossover appeal. They can be successfully incorporated into courses on literature, history, philosophy, women's studies, and general European civilization surveys. These pairings also lead us, as French scholars, to think about the writers outside expected disciplines and contexts. Consider, for example, the master rhetoricians Scudéry and Pascal taught in a composition and rhetoric course or a discussion of early modern friendship taking up Descartes and Elisabeth's model of personal intellectual exchange.

Here I speak to these diverse teaching possibilities by sharing my own experience and by suggesting general ideas and themes for approaching these writers in the classroom. I begin with a selection of the letters of Elisabeth of Bohemia and Descartes, which my students read after studying *Discours de la méthode* and discussing an excerpt from Erica Harth's *Cartesian Women: Versions and Subversions of Rational Discourse in the Old Regime*. I then introduce Scudéry's *Conversations* and present strategies for pairing her texts with Pascal's *Pensées* as a contrasting study in the rhetoric of conversation and conversion. In each case, I opt for a back-and-forth approach, using one text to better read another rather than structuring the pairs as inevitably oppositional.

Elisabeth and Descartes

The correspondence between Princess Elisabeth of Bohemia (1618–80) and René Descartes (1596–1650) began in 1643 and continued until Descartes's death. Commonly read as a key source for Descartes's thinking on the mind-body problem and the passions (Descartes wrote *Les Passions de l'âme* [1649; *The Passions of the Soul*] in response to his exchanges with Elisabeth), the letters range over topics of political, moral, and natural philosophy. Elisabeth's critique of Cartesian dualism, articulated in her correspondence, establishes her as "a precursor to modern feminist philosophers" (Broad 15; see also Wartenberg). The pair's intellectual exchange was well known in the seventeenth century; Descartes dedicated his *Principles of Philosophy* (1644) to Elisabeth, and his letters to her were included in the first edition of his correspondence (1657–67). Yet Elisabeth's letters were not published until 1879, the princess having refused requests to make public her end of the correspondence after Descartes's death.

This epistolary conversation—arguably one of the founding texts of feminist philosophy—has only recently become convenient to teach. *The Correspondence between Princess Elisabeth of Bohemia and René Descartes*, edited and translated by Lisa Shapiro, provides the entire exchange with notes, biographical information, and a presentation of the philosophical questions covered in the letters. Andrea Nye's *The Princess and the Philosopher* mixes the letters with commentary; Jacqueline Broad offers a useful introduction to Elisabeth's philosophy and a bibliography in *Women Philosophers of the Seventeenth Century*; and Margaret Atherton excerpts the letters on the mind-body connection in *Women Philosophers of the Early Modern Period*. Flammarion publishes an inexpensive edition of Descartes's *Correspondance avec Élisabeth*, edited by Jean-Marie Beyssade and Michelle Beyssade.

The publication history of the letters brings home to students the point that we should not take the availability of the books we read for granted—a reminder of the course's ongoing investigation into the dissemination of texts and ideas. More generally, the correspondence helps us appreciate the stakes of philosophy, not only Descartes read in a book, but Descartes's philosophy questioned, discussed, and lived. On a practical level, the medium of Elisabeth and Descartes's conversation asserts itself in the material problems of managing a correspondence, making the urgency of their engagement felt as the writers apologize for messy drafts and worry about letters going astray. Students trace the correspondents' search for the terms of engagement, even the language, on which to build one of the seventeenth century's most productive "cross-sex intellectual friendships" (Perry 173).

While the correspondence as a whole merits study, one can handily supplement a text by Descartes with a short selection of letters; I assign the *Discours*, although Elisabeth refers frequently to his *Meditations on First Philosophy* (1641).[1] We read the first five letters of the exchange, which lay the groundwork of Elisabeth's philosophical interrogations and the pair's epistolary negotiations (6 May, 21 May, 10 June, 28 June, and 1 July 1643). Students find Elisabeth's writing difficult to follow, even in English. Luckily, this initial difficulty opens up a useful contrast with rhetorical strategies in the *Discours*, emphasizing just how readable Descartes made this text, which my students declare "much easier" than Elisabeth's letters. A brief introduction to the Cartesian concept of the mind-body connection is helpful; for students reading in French, it may be enough to have them begin by recognizing the philosophical parts of the letters while you summarize Elisabeth's critiques, focused in this selection on Descartes's explanation of the action of the mind on the body.

As a further preparation for reading, I ask students how they would write to a princess or to a philosopher. Moving into the letters, I rephrase the question: In what language, style, and tone does each correspondent speak to the other? This question guides students to identify key rhetorical strategies as Elisabeth and Descartes negotiate the language and the terms of their exchange. I prepare students for the conventions of seventeenth-century letter writing by reminding them of the formality of French salutations and closings even today. In the first letter, students remark a change in language and tone from the first paragraph—Elisabeth presents herself as "une personne ignorante et indocile" 'an ignorant and intractable person,' ashamed of "un style si déréglé" 'so disordered a style'—to the second, in which she briskly poses her challenge, "Pourquoi je vous demande une définition de l'âme plus particulière qu'en votre Métaphysique, c'est-à-dire de sa substance, séparée de son action, de la pensée" 'This is why I ask you for a more precise definition of the soul than the one you give in your *Metaphysics*, that is to say, of its substance separate from its action, that is, from thought' (65; 61–62; 6 May 1643).[2] I prompt students to articulate their responses in general terms: What kind of voice do you hear in the first paragraph? the second? (On Elisabeth's "two voices," see Nye 11.) Pushing the discussion, I ask the class to consider how Elisabeth uses these different voices to communicate her questions to Descartes.

We then examine how Elisabeth defines the exchange with Descartes, or, how the correspondents describe their letters. The letter stands in for an earlier attempt at meeting, "une conversation si profitable" 'such a profitable conversation,' that, in the opening of her letter, Elisabeth regrets having missed (65; 61). In her closing, Elisabeth figures Descartes as "le meilleur médecin pour [mon âme]" 'the best doctor for [her] soul,' whose "remèdes" 'remedies' she seeks (66; 62). Thus the stakes of the correspondence are high. Three years into their friendship, Elisabeth writes movingly of the importance of Descartes as interlocutor: without the assistance of his letters, she fears, her surroundings and the lack of intelligent conversation "éteindraient ce petit rayon de sens commun que je tiens de la nature, et dont je reconnais l'usage par votre méthode" 'would extinguish the small ray of common sense that I take from nature and which I remember how to use by your method' (173; 139; July 1646). We reconsider the Cartesian cogito in the context of such urgently expressed desire for intellectual discourse. "I think, therefore I am" is no abstraction for Elisabeth, whose letters are filled with references to the gender, social, political, and familial constraints that limit her opportunity for study and reflection. Elisabeth seeks the time and space to think but also to converse freely and without interruption: I speak with you, therefore I am.

We don't spend a lot of time on the content of Descartes's response to Elisabeth's repeated queries on the mind-body connection, which readers, starting with Elisabeth, have not found convincing. Instead, we pursue the questions that structured our reading of the first letter: How do the correspondents speak to each other? How do they define their exchange? Students have difficulty wending their way through the elaborately drawn-out compliment that begins Descartes's letter of 21 May 1643 but easily recognize the hyperbolic quality of the praise. It is worth paraphrasing, if necessary, to discuss the striking imagery by which Descartes represents the supernatural experience of a woman speaking philosophy. Had he been privileged to see Elisabeth, he declares, the sight of "des discours plus qu'humains [sortir] d'un corps si semblable à ceux que les peintres donnent aux anges" 'superhuman discourse emerging from a body so similar to those painters give to angels' would have rendered him as amazed as someone who has died and gone to heaven (67; 63). Standing in for this ethereal vision is something more material: Elisabeth's letter and ideas, or, as Descartes writes, "les traces de vos pensées sur un papier" 'the traces of your thoughts on a paper' (67; 63). In contrast to Elisabeth, who describes her recourse to writing as a replacement for conversation, Descartes insists on the materiality of paper and ink. Only the mediation of the letter makes the conversation possible.

After analyzing the opening selection together, students can be divided into pairs and assigned specific exchanges to explore the correspondence on their own. One topic that garners the interest of students and scholars alike is Elisabeth's attention to the embodied, material, and gendered aspects of experience. Elisabeth's experience as a woman, a feeling subject, and an ailing body offers a powerful counterpoint to Descartes's claims of unperturbed rationality and detachment. Yet we soon discover how embodied Descartes becomes in the correspondence. While Elisabeth reads Descartes's texts with care, citing specific pages and figures, Descartes reads her body. Elisabeth's depressed spirits and physical ailments become matter for discussion and dissent between the two friends; the soul doctor gives medical advice as well. The pair's personal exchanges inspire their philosophical reflections on the influence of mind on body and body on mind. Thus I end the discussion by asking students if we should read Elisabeth's correspondence "just as we would any other philosophical work" (Shapiro 4). Or do the letters, as a medium and a genre, make a difference?

Scudéry and Pascal

Given the central position of Scudéry (1607–1701) in the early modern literary and intellectual scene, it seems hard to imagine not teaching her in courses on literature, history, and philosophy. Scudéry's extensive corpus spans almost all genres of the seventeenth century, including rhetorical speeches, letters, poetry, novels, and conversations. Her literary career stretches from the reign of Louis XIII through the civil unrest of the Fronde and the early years of Louis XIV to the Sun King's triumphs and decline. Scudéry addresses the major intellectual, political, and literary questions of her day: her writings contain not only the celebrated "Carte de Tendre" 'Map of Tenderness' but also discussions of political theory, history, natural science, philosophy, and morality and the ongoing meditation on gender relations and the place of women in seventeenth-century society for which she is best known.

Scudéry's *Conversations* are the work of an established author, published late in her career in the 1680s and 1690s.[3] They are increasingly easy to find and include texts of readable length and vocabulary. Delphine Denis and Phillip J. Wolfe have edited selected conversations in French. Jane Donawerth and Julie Strongson include four conversations in their edition and translation, *Selected Letters, Orations, and Rhetorical Dialogues*. All of Scudéry's conversations can be downloaded from the Bibliothèque Nationale de France's *Gallica* site, and a seventeenth-century translation, *Conversations upon Several Subjects in Two Tomes*, is available from *Early English Books Online*. On the literary conversation, I consult Elizabeth C. Goldsmith's *Exclusive Conversations: The Art of Interaction in Seventeenth-Century France*, which analyzes Scudéry's texts in the context of theories of social interaction and seventeenth-century forms of sociability. Selecting from the impressive range of subjects covered in Scudéry's five volumes of conversations can be difficult. For the seminar, I assign "De la conversation" ("On Conversation") and "De parler trop, ou trop peu, et comment il faut parler" ("On Speaking Too Much or Too Little, and How to Speak Well").[4]

Each conversation stages a group of cultivated men and women discussing a topic of moral and social relevance. Through the conversational process, Scudéry's ideal interlocutors explore beliefs and conventions—correcting, if necessary, a behavior or opinion—and define, as they perform, the rules of polite society. Goldsmith points to the dynamics of closure/interiority and openness/exteriority that regulate the ideal salon conversation and Scudéry's print versions: participants form an exclusive coterie founded on the equality of all members, a group separate from yet oriented toward the society around them (*Exclusive* 44–51). The *Conversations*' focus on celebration of Louis XIV and consensus among participants, the unifying centripetal force, competes against more centrifugal pulls toward diversity and dissent.

This centripetal-centrifugal tension structures our approach to the *Conversations* from the start. Students analyze the frontispiece to *Conversations nouvelles sur divers sujets* ("New Conversations on Diverse Subjects") reproduced in Donawerth and Strongson, noting the association of the author's name ("Conversations par Mademoiselle de Scudéry") with the royal space of Versailles's Galerie des Glaces ("Hall of Mirrors") depicted above this inscription.[5] We describe the *Conversations* using information gleaned from the image (a public, royal, and recognizably French space, peopled by well-dressed upper-class men and women). Students then contrast this scene with the different settings described in the texts (usually an idyllic retreat in a private home or garden), not to mention the sustained exchange of talk that requires more attention and comfort than that afforded by the public throng in the Galerie. The image installs Scudéry's conversations at the heart of Versailles—but is Versailles, the symbol of Louis XIV's absolutism, conducive to conversation?

As we discuss Scudéry's theory of civility—conversation as "le lien de la société de tous les hommes" 'the bond of society for all humanity'—I ask students to pay attention to possibilities of breakdown in conversational and social cohesion ("De la conversation" [Denis] 305; "On Conversation" 96). Despite the group's exclusivity, Scudéry's elite conversationalists face the threats of bad conversation, ill-mannered people, unwanted visitors, and the moral and social vices they confront in talk. They probe social conventions and uncover prejudice, injustice, immorality, and weakness at the heart of the Sun King's glittering reign. Understanding this, students can make sense of Scudéry's insistence on speaking well. Talk matters, for the conversational process restores, even as it dissects, consensus and civility.

Readers of Scudéry commonly focus on her presentation of civility and *galanterie* ("gallantry"). The *Conversations*, however, examines forces of disequilibrium and disproportion more readily associated with the austere philosophy of Pascal (1623–62). I bring these two writers together through the framework of conversion and conversation when reading a selection of Pascal's *Pensées* (1670), followed by "De la conversation" and "De parler trop." A comparative approach focused on rhetorical and formal analysis helps students handle these texts with more confidence. I start by asking the class to compare a page from the *Pensées* with a page from a conversation, moving from obvious differences (short versus long, fragmented versus flowing) to resemblances (e.g., the dialogic form of many Pascalian fragments). Consulting the *Oxford English Dictionary* online, students discuss the meanings and etymology of *converse* ("to pass one's life, live, dwell in or with") and *convert* ("to turn about, turn in character or nature"). We then connect this discussion to Pascal's description of his project in the "Ordre" fragment and Scudéry's definition of *conversation* at the beginning of "De la conversation." Throughout our reading of the texts, we work to link rhetorical strategies to the goals of conversion and conversation as defined in our discussions.

In an earlier activity, groups of students work on a selection of fragments from different sections of Pascal's text to create and justify their own order for the *pensées*. I ask students if the same could be done with Scudéry's texts—can a conversation be cut up? This exercise both acknowledges the specific challenges of reading the text (students have trouble keeping track of speakers and the flow of talk) and focuses our attention on the structure of the conversation. We refine this focus by drawing up a conversational code of conduct as presented by the interlocutors. Since the rules are as much performed as presented, I ask the class how the men and women in Scudéry's conversations show their conversation skills. It is also helpful to gather some basic information: Who starts the conversation? How are topics developed? Who manages the conversation? How does it end? Questions on the conversation lead us into the conversation: for instance, we discuss the contradiction between the role of women as conversation arbiters in both "De la conversation" and "De parler trop" and the critique of certain types of women's speech in "De la conversation."

Thinking about how Scudéry translates common Pascalian themes such as *ennui* and *divertissement* into conversation underscores Scudéry's interest in sociability, the here-and-now possibilities of women and men's living together in social, affective, and gendered relations (on Scudéry's treatment of *ennui* compared with Pascal's, see Goldsmith, *Exclusive* 51–54). Pascal's "Wager" fragment ("Infini-Rien") might be compared with "Contre ceux qui parlent peu sérieusement de la religion" ("Against Those Who Speak Disrespectfully of Religion"), in which Scudéry has a Persian speaker make the wager argument in favor of belief in God. This conversation ranges beyond the problem of the "libertin," the object of Pascal's attention, to explore the condition of the "libertine." Scudéry's female libertine, in fact, wagers more than the male, since her freethinking jeopardizes her reputation and renders her vulnerable to unpleasant treatment from men. Hence for Scudéry, the conversion conversation has stakes in this life as well as in the next.

In "De la raillerie" ("On Wit"), Scudéry positions her conversations as the modern equivalent of Plato's and Xenophon's dialogues while expressing the fear that her dialogues might not be taken seriously by her contemporaries. Taking the *Conversations* seriously yields teaching opportunities far beyond what this essay presents. A consideration of Cartesian doubt might include Scudéry's critique of radical doubt and its resolution in the mock-serious treaty concluded between doubters and nondoubters in "De l'incertitude" ("On Incertitude"). Political theorists will be intrigued by Scudéry's description of the "passion sans nom" 'passion without a name' that binds subject to sovereign in "Des passions que les hommes ont inventées" ("On the Passions Invented by Men") (277; my trans.). More modern connections can be made, too. Students reading "De la conversation" and "De parler trop" are surprised to find that the preoccupations of a seventeenth-century Frenchwoman feel relevant to them. As a useful, enjoyable, and very Scudérian way of exploring these connections, I propose another conversation—this one organized and animated by students after Scudéry's model. We have heard countless commentators bemoan the loss of public dialogue and civility. What better response than a conversation on conversation in the age of smart phones and text messaging?

Notes

1. I point out to students that Elisabeth, as royalty, is referred to by her first name, to explain the Elisabeth/Descartes nomenclature.

2. All quotations from *Correspondance* are from Beyssade and Beyssade's edition and Shapiro's translation.

3. They include both new and previously published conversations (the latter excerpted from her novels with some modifications): *Conversations sur divers*

sujets; Conversations nouvelles sur divers sujets; La Morale du monde, ou Conversations; Nouvelles Conversations de morale; and *Entretiens de morale.*

4. All quotations from *Conversations* are from *Conversations sur divers sujets* (1680) and Donawerth and Strongson's *Selected Letters*, unless otherwise indicated.

5. The frontispiece appears to represent the Galerie des Glaces. The Galerie des Glaces was completed in 1684, the same year as the publication of *Conversations nouvelles sur divers sujets*, and is featured in one of the conversations from this collection, "De la magnificence et de la magnanimité" ("On Magnificence and Magnanimity").

David Harrison

The Politics of Politesse

Madeleine de Scudéry's *Conversations* are significant not only for their form—the conversation being a key mode of literary and philosophical expression in the seventeenth century—but also for their content. Scudéry's conversations define the rules of sociability for the worldly classes (*les honnêtes gens*) under Louis XIV. As such, they are perfect texts to use in a course unit focusing on French society during the classical era, particularly as a counterpoint to the texts commonly employed in such a unit (e.g., La Bruyère, Saint-Simon) written by male authors. In this essay, I focus on Scudéry's conversation on politeness ("De la politesse") and how it can be used by itself and in combination with other texts to examine the complexity of court society and to raise important questions about the politics of politeness.

Context: The French Civilization Course

My French civilization course, taught at the undergraduate level, spans the period of the Gauls to the Revolution, with about three weeks (or nine fifty-minute course sessions) devoted to the seventeenth century. The course serves as an introduction to the major political and cultural events of the period, while developing the students' skills in reading and critical analysis. I use the Larousse *Histoire de France* to provide historical background, but I focus our class discussions on specific literary and philosophical texts as well as visual material. The seventeenth-century unit concentrates on different aspects of court society: the iconography of Versailles and Louis XIV, celebration and condemnation of centralized authority, the training of the courtier, and the ethics of the new social hierarchy. Because of the difficulty of the original texts, I often use excerpts, selecting particular passages for close study in class.

Since the theme of politeness runs through the seventeenth-century material, Scudéry's "De la politesse" is especially germane. The dialogue is currently available only in French in Delphine Denis's collection of Scudéry's conversations. The conversation brings together two women (Clarinte, Fénice) and three men (Théanor, Cléonte, Clitandre) who attempt to answer the following questions: What is politeness? What causes people to be polite? Why is the court the center of politeness? Along the way, the conversants, or "devisants," also discuss the relation between politeness and virtue, as well as men's frequent impoliteness toward women. While their voices tend to resemble one another, there are a few clearly established roles: Clarinte is the hostess of the conversation, Théanor the erudite sage, and Clitandre the young man, or "galant," in need of a lesson in manners.

Strategies for Discussion of the Text

I open the discussion of the text by reviewing the various ways that the idea of politeness has appeared in the course, such as medieval chivalry and Renaissance education, codes of honor and of piety. I sometimes ask whether the notion of "civilization" (an anachronistic term from the nineteenth century) is related to the idea of politeness, and I may mention the "civilizing process" that Norbert Elias uses to portray the early modern period. By opening with these general review questions, I wish to remind students that rules of behavior exist in all of French history, that these rules embody certain social values that are frequently contested, and that Scudéry's ideas can be understood in relation to other texts.

I then divide students into small groups and have each group pick out the various terms that Scudéry's conversants use to define "politesse." The dialogue does not give a single definition of the idea, but instead employs several parallel terms: "savoir vivre" ("to know how to live"), "parler à propos" ("to speak at the right time and on the subject at hand"), "le bel usage" ("good usage"), "l'esprit" ("wit, intelligence"), "la raison" ("reason"), and "l'exactitude" ("precision, correctness").[1] Each of these terms denotes a different quality, and I ask students to imagine the ways a person would ideally display each quality. For example, "le bel usage" and "parler à propos" indicate verbal skill: politeness is a way of speaking, and thus conversation, such as Scudéry's, is the perfect medium for its expression. But "savoir vivre" suggests talent that can be expressed nonverbally; it might be shown in the way one dresses or the dinner that one offers to one's friends. In any case, all these terms demonstrate that politeness is a social value—to show one's wit and intelligence, one must be surrounded by equally intelligent and witty people—and thus requires the space of urban elites. Students can connect this idea to the rise of Paris, and ultimately Versailles, as the center of power. Scudéry's "politesse" indicates a certain disdain for the provinces and therefore underscores the difference between the traditional, landholding aristocracy and the new, court-bound aristocracy.

In the space of court there is no clear boundary between public and private information, and Scudéry's multiple definitions of "politesse" prove this point. On the one hand, politeness means never saying anything that would possibly hurt or embarrass one's interlocutor, part of the meaning of speaking thoughtfully ("parler à propos"). On the other hand, to have the "exactitude" of knowing what subjects to avoid, one must have extensive background knowledge of one's interlocutor—his or her likes and dislikes, relations to other people in society, ambitions. In other words, politeness appears to respect the privacy of the other while in fact requiring that private matters be shared in advance. Curiously, politeness feeds on gossip, since gossip provides the necessary facts that can then be studiously avoided in polite conversation. While Scudéry's conversants may not admit to it, they require a network of information gatherers—people like Louis de Rouvroy, duc de Saint-Simon; Gédéon Tallemant des Réaux; or Célimène and the "petits marquis" in Molière's *Le Misanthrope*—to be polite.

Scudéry distinguishes politeness from virtue, and thus the text raises questions about the role of traditional Christian morality within court society. Théanor notes that politeness makes virtue more pleasurable, but why does virtue need the polish provided by politeness? Are biblical teachings insufficient for the proper sociability of court society, and, if so, is it possible to imagine a form of sociability that would be divorced from the Bible altogether? Asking these questions allows students to compare Scudéry's text with texts written in earlier periods that stress the role of Christianity in social relations, such as Jean de Joinville's *Vie de Saint-Louis* or the letter from Gargantua to Pantagruel in François Rabelais's *Pantagruel* (ch. 8). The instructor can then also evoke the quarrels over religious piety that marked the seventeenth century. Indeed, a character like Molière's Tartuffe would condemn the sinfulness of Scudéry's characters, just as Jansenists condemned the worldly values of the court.

In the same way that politeness reflects changing social mores, it shows the changing role of the aristocracy. Scudéry's Fénice brings forward the example of a soldier who is impolite because he maintains his military air at court: when he enters mixed company, "il a une démarche trop guerrière et son action a quelque chose de trop fier" 'his bearing is too warriorlike and his acts too proud' (126).[2] What better example than this to talk about the domestication of *la noblesse d'épée* ("the nobility of the sword") under Louis XIV? I ask students to imagine how such a soldier would be judged in other historical moments and why his militarism needs to be attenuated for him to be socially acceptable in the new regime.

But the most interesting facet of Scudéry's dialogue concerns men's impoliteness toward women. Clarinte notes that young men only wish to converse with beautiful women but do not hesitate to socialize with ugly men. Women's intelligence is therefore judged according to women's looks, but this standard does not apply for men's intelligence. The discussion continues for about three pages and has Clitandre receiving a good scolding for his prejudices. This section of the dialogue is an excellent point of departure for discussing how Scudéry views politeness as a factor in male-female relations. Polite men treat women as intellectual equals, no matter their appearance, hence politeness as a social value frees women from the restrictions imposed by age and physical beauty. Moreover, women are the implicit arbiters of politeness, since the dialogue occurs within the space of the salon and is mediated by the hostess, Clarinte. Thus politeness is doubly in the service of women's power, both as a critique of the male gaze and as a source of female social authority.

Regardless of how an instructor chooses to explore Scudéry's dialogue, it is beneficial to end the discussion of the text by asking students to give a personal reaction to the conversation. Are Scudéry's ideas still valuable today as a definition of politeness? Are they too restrictive or too far removed from modern forms of sociability? I ask my students who have spent time in France whether any of Scudéry's ideas hold true today, and inevitably some remark that conversation (especially around the dinner table) remains an important factor in French life.

Even negative reactions to the text (and there are many) are peda- gogically useful. The students who criticize Scudéry's conversants for their elitism are preparing the class for a discussion of texts that take a different approach toward politeness. It is easy to disparage Scudéry's view of po- liteness, but students are ultimately surprised when they discover that the authors who share their scorn often express conservative views of sexual relations. Does abandoning Scudéry also mean jettisoning her view of male-female equality?

Combining Scudéry's Dialogue with Other Texts (and a Film)

Scudéry's conversation on politeness works well in combination with the following texts: selections from Saint-Simon's *Mémoires*, Jean de La Bru- yère's discussion of the court in *Les Caractères*, and especially Jean-Jacques Rousseau's *Discours sur les sciences et les arts*. I also like to show Patrice Leconte's film *Ridicule* (1996) to compare its views of politeness with those of the four authors.

Saint-Simon's verbal portrait of Louis XIV, included in the Flamma- rion pocket anthology of Saint-Simon's *Mémoires*, places "politesse" in op- position to "noblesse" to criticize the king (234–71). According to the memorialist, a youthful Louis XIV learned politeness in the salon of the comtesse de Soissons (249), but this education distracted the king from learning history—that is, the family history of the old nobility (235). In other words, "politesse" is a diversion from genealogical knowledge, which is seen by Saint-Simon as essential to the proper functioning of the monarchy, and the king is therefore vulnerable to forgetting aristocratic traditions and bestowing too much power on his bourgeois ministers.

Students generally enjoy Saint-Simon's energetic skewering of Louis XIV: sentences like, "L'esprit du roi était au-dessous du médiocre" 'The king's intelligence was below average' always produce smiles from under- graduates who are used to laudatory portraits of the Sun King (234). But Saint-Simon's view of politeness is troubling when discussed in combina- tion with Scudéry's text. Is Louis XIV ignorant because he has spent too much time with polite women? Would Saint-Simon say that Scudéry's sa- lon hostess, Clarinte, is similar to the comtesse de Soissons and that a good leader should avoid her company? Is politeness a ruse in the service of so- cial mobility, and should polite commoners be prevented from advancing into positions of power? Students who may agree with Saint-Simon's satire of court sociability are forced, through Scudéry, to ask whether his critique is motivated in part by a fear of women's social power and whether rules of politeness underscore or obfuscate differences in social class.

In a similar vein, La Bruyère's depiction of the court in section 8 of *Les Caractères* becomes more complex when preceded by Scudéry's dialogue. Like Saint-Simon, La Bruyère views politeness as a courtly vice—a social mask that covers limitless individual ambition. La Bruyère's anecdotes, particularly their use of pseudo-Greek names like Cimon and Clitandre (fragment 19), evoke the world of Scudéry's conversants. Indeed, it can be useful to have students find an anecdote with a character who seems to embody Scudéry's notions of "bel usage" or "exactitude": how do Scudéry's terms of refinement look perverse or ridiculous when illustrated by La Bruyère? But before letting La Bruyère have the last word on politeness, I like to remark on how the "vice" of courtly sociability is viewed by the moralist as a feminine trait. In fragment 18, in particular, La Bruyère describes certain courtiers whose success comes from their extreme politeness toward women. These "hommes flatteurs, complaisants" 'smooth-talking men' are "dévoués aux femmes" 'devoted to women' and "flattent toutes les passions" 'fawn on women's obsessions,' but from this effort they arrive at the highest offices of the kingdom. Once again, the sexuality of politeness comes forward: Is courtly sociability a threat to masculinity? Are Scudéry's men—especially Théanor, the exponent of civil behavior—less manly for being polite?

Rousseau's first discourse, *Discours sur les sciences et les arts,* is the most explicit at linking politeness to masculine infirmity. In the first ten paragraphs of the opening section of the discourse (30–34), Rousseau equates politeness with indecency, insincerity, loss of individuality, and, most dramatically, repression of natural male strength: "L'homme de bien est un athlète qui se plaît à combattre nu: il méprise tous ces vils ornements qui gêneraient l'usage de ses forces" 'The man of virtue is an athlete who takes pleasure in fighting naked; he detests all these vile embellishments that hamper the use of his strength' (32). Students find Rousseau's argument against civil society even more extreme than Scudéry's argument in favor of it—all the more reason, then, to place these authors in tandem on the syllabus. How might Clarinte defend her position to Rousseau? What could Théanor say to dispute Rousseau's conclusions?

For a modern-day take on this debate, it is useful to discuss *Ridicule,* Leconte's enjoyable film about fictional intrigue at the court of Louis XVI.

As the film's title suggests, the courtiers display a refined sense of wit—the ability to politely mock their peers—to maintain influence. Power derives from conversation, and at the center of power is the recently widowed Mme de Blayac, played with a discreet but unambiguous eroticism by Fanny Ardant. Here, then, is a tale that combines all the elements of the texts that I have discussed: Scudéry's conversants are placed in La Bruyère's world of ambition, overseen by a woman like Saint-Simon's comtesse de Soissons. Is the result of this mix the moral turpitude described by Rousseau? Students can decide this question for themselves, but it is interesting that the protagonist of Leconte's film, the marquis Ponceludon de Malavoy (Charles Berling), ultimately rejects Ardant for the less worldly and more natural Mathilde de Bellegarde (Judith Godrèche), who lives outside court. Courtly wit may be fun to flirt with, but the ingenue makes a better wife.

The joy of teaching Scudéry's "De la politesse" in a French civilization course comes, in part, from the still-relevant questions the text raises when linked with other classical authors. Is politeness an asset, a ploy, or a vice? To what degree do we view politeness today as a female quality? How does political discourse tend, like Rousseau, to equate politeness with male weakness? Is social harmony, founded on intellectual equality and the art of conversation, an illusion? If so, on what other basis should individuals—especially political elites—seek to engage with the world? The politics of politeness may be especially relevant to the period of Louis XIV, but, in the absence of lasting tolerance and social concord, it seems no less important today.

Notes

1. For a discussion of the French lexicon during this period, see Paige in this volume.

2. All translations from the French are mine unless otherwise noted.

Deborah Steinberger

Women and Men Writing about Love: An Approach to Teaching Seventeenth-Century Literature

As those who teach it know, the French seventeenth century is often perceived by students as uncomfortably distant and even intimidating. Many of the themes and concepts attached to the period are foreign to students: salon society, collaborative writing, *préciosité*. The widespread practice of organizing seventeenth-century survey courses by genre does not help matters. Because theater flourished in France during this period and the great plays of Molière (and to a lesser extent, those of Jean Racine and Pierre Corneille) are still performed around the world, dramatic literature is often granted a survey course, while the many other genres of this period are often relegated to a second catchall survey. In my university's course catalog the nondramatic (and generally less familiar) canonical authors of the period were lumped together in one course and labeled "critics and moralists." I suspected that few students would gravitate to such a course, whose title failed to convey the richness and excitement of this literature. Having decided that the course needed a more precise focus, I chose a theme certain to appeal to most students and developed the erstwhile prose and poetry survey into a seminar called Writing about Love.

Course Overview

One of my main objectives was to diversify the list of authors normally taught in a seventeenth-century survey course. I added works by canonical and noncanonical women writers to more traditional offerings by François, due de La Rochefoucauld; Charles Perrault; and Jean de La Fontaine, to feature a roughly equal number of male and female authors. The principal works on the syllabus are by Honoré d'Urfé (*L'Astrée*); Molière (*Les Précieuses ridicules* ["Precious Provincials"] and *L'École des femmes* ["The School for Wives"]); Madeleine de Scudéry (excerpts from *Clélie*); Marie-Catherine Le Jumel de Barneville, comtesse d'Aulnoy ("L'Ile de la félicité" ["The Island of Felicity"]); Perrault ("Peau d'âne" ["Donkey Skin"] and, with François-Timoléon de Choisy and Marie-Jeanne Lhéritier, *Histoire de la Marquise-Marquis de Banneville*); Gabriel Joseph de Lavergne, vicomte de Guilleragues (*Lettres portugaises*); Françoise Pascal (*Le Commerce du Parnasse* [*Letters from Parnassus*]); La Fontaine (selected fables); La Rochefoucauld (*Maximes*); Marie-Madeleine Pioche de la Vergne, comtesse de Lafayette (*La Princesse de Clèves*), and Marie de Rabutin-Chantal, marquise de Sévigné (selected letters from *Correspondance*). To privilege the dialogues among the works, I eliminated the strict division by genre previously in place. It makes sense, for example, to study Molière's satire *Les Précieuses ridicules* along with selections from the influential works that so delighted his young protagonists Madelon and Cathos: *L'Astrée* and the "Carte de Tendre," the celebrated roadmap to love from Scudéry's novel *Clélie*.

The texts we study represent a rich variety of genres: there are novels, comedies, fairy tales, letters, poems, fables, maxims, and portraits. This eclectic approach is further justified by the fact that during the seventeenth century in France, authors and readers reveled in genre blending: they enjoyed producing and reading collections of very diverse texts. Excellent and entertaining examples of works that defy classification abound, particularly in the popular literature of the time. From the October 1678 issue of the periodical *Le Mercure galant*, my students examine an intricate diagram depicting arguments for and against the princesse de Clèves's famous confession ("Dissertation" 138–39), and from the best-selling anthology *Poésies de Madame la Comtesse de la Suze*, we read Roger de Bussy-Rabutin's humorous "Almanach pour l'année 1665," where the phases of passion are compared to the seasons of the year. Among the authors on the course syllabus is the dramatist, poet, epistolarian, painter, and musician Françoise Pascal. Pascal was a distinguished playwright, the author of three one-act comedies and three full-length tragicomedies, one of which is a *pièce à machines*, a dramatic work employing spectacular mechanical special effects. Her religious poetry ranges from book-length dramatic monologues and dialogues to *Noëls*, popular tunes transformed into sacred songs. Her innovative *Le Commerce du Parnasse* is an *œuvre mêlée* (in prose and verse) that is part letter collection and part novel.

On the first day of class, I present a brief overview of the different characterizations of love and ways of writing about love that influenced seventeenth-century authors. Students work in groups to analyze the style, imagery, and meaning of selections from Plato (the story of the androgyne from the *Symposium*), the troubadours, Petrarch, Louise Labé, and Pierre de Ronsard. After this introduction, we begin our studies of seventeenth-century literature with the first book of d'Urfé's *L'Astrée*. Though brief, the excerpt exposes the students to the style and themes of this work that influenced writers and readers for centuries.

From there we proceed to study the concept of *préciosité* and the salons of Catherine de Vivonne, marquise de Rambouillet, and Mlle de Scudéry. Once the class is acquainted with the contributions of these women, we turn to Molière's *Précieuses ridicules*. I emphasize the play's commentary on the role of literature in the creation of desire and its parody of the language of the *précieuses*. I have found that students often struggle to understand the work's numerous literary allusions and can lose sight of the play's message and its humor. I therefore highlight Scudéry's "Carte de Tendre" (*Clélie* [Morlet-Chantalat] 1: 178–87), which we interpret in class, and I distribute impromptus and *bouts-rimés* from Scudéry's contemporaries. To enhance students' understanding of the play as a performance text, I show the televised version of Georges Bensoussan's production of *Les Précieuses ridicules*. Although Bensoussan's sympathetic portrayal of Madelon and Cathos and his decidedly noncomic emphasis on the young women's disappointed ambitions do not seem to me faithful to the spirit of Molière's satire, this production inspires animated student discussion about what the play means and interesting debate about whether Molière can be considered a protofeminist. Women's rights and the rites of love are also central concerns in Molière's *L'École des femmes*, the next work we study. I ask the students to characterize the different types of love depicted in the play, as well as the conflicting views on marriage expressed by the main characters. At this point in the course I assign an excerpt from a special issue (*Extraordinaire*) of the *Mercure galant* from April 1679, which presents arguments for and against marriage, from both male and female perspectives ("Si un homme").

Love Letters

In her conversation dealing with epistolary practices, "De la manière d'écrire des lettres" ("On the Manner of Writing Letters"), Scudéry distinguishes between gallant letters and love letters: *lettres galantes* are written to be shown to others, while intimate *lettres d'amour* are meant to be hidden and if made public would bring shame to those who receive them (155). When we study *L'École des femmes*, we pay special attention to a text that appears in act 3, scene 4, of the play: Agnès's love letter to Horace, a private, secret text publicized by its proud recipient, who unwittingly reads it to his jealous rival. Our discussion is enhanced by Barbara Johnson's illuminating analysis of the deceptively simple letter. The next two works we study, Guilleragues's *Lettres portugaises* and Pascal's *Le Commerce du Parnasse*, are likewise useful for exploring the categories of public and private writing. Both first published in 1669 by the editor Claude Barbin, these two epistolary works complement each other. The first, generally thought to have been written by a man appropriating a female voice, appears to reveal intimate correspondence intended for private consumption: a Portuguese nun writes passionate prose to the French officer who seduced and abandoned her. *Le Commerce du Parnasse* is a prose and verse work by a woman writing in her own voice and eager to be read by the public. In fact, I believe that Pascal's small collection of letters may be a response to *Les Lettres portugaises* (Steinberger xv–xviii). In *Le Commerce du Parnasse*, Pascal replaces the image of the suffering, passionate female writer of letters with that of a witty, wise, self-reliant woman of letters who declares that passion has no place in her life. Her collection consists of playful rejections of a stubborn suitor's repeated declarations of love and criticism of his stilted expressions. This contrast between the two works is significant even if, as Myriam Cyr has sought to show, a real Portuguese nun did write the letters attributed to Guilleragues. A third letter collection published by Barbin in 1669, Mme de Villedieu's *Lettres et billets galants*, may also be studied in this context: these private letters were sold to Barbin by Villedieu's lover and initially published without her consent (see Jensen, *Writing*).

As with the letter collections, I stress the ties between the authors of other types of works we study. We read La Fontaine's fable dedicated to

La Rochefoucauld, "L'Homme et son image" ("The Man and His Image"), as well as Mme de Lafayette's portrait of Mme de Sévigné (Montpensier, *Divers Portraits* 313–17). After these units and one on La Fontaine in which we analyze selected fables dealing with love and marriage, we turn to expressions of maternal love, as seen in Mme de Sévigné's letters to her daughter. Finally, as a counterpoint to the fairy tales studied earlier in the semester, we end with a novella attributed to Perrault, the abbé de Choisy, and Lhéritier, *Histoire de la Marquise-Marquis de Banneville*, an astoundingly modern tale of the love of two young cross-dressers.

Course Methods: Simulating the Salon

To the extent possible, I aim to simulate a literary salon in the classroom, for students to learn by doing and to appreciate the conditions of production of many of the texts. Students create, collaborate, converse, and critique one another's work. After reading examples of *énigmes* ("verse riddles") by Charles Cotin, I ask students to compose similar riddles for their classmates to solve. After studying the "Carte de Tendre," students design their own "geographies" of modern love and present them to their classmates. After reading La Rochefoucauld's *Maximes*, students compose and present their own maxims and analyze and critique those of their classmates. And once the students have studied Mme de Lafayette's anonymous portrait of Mme de Sévigné, as well as La Rochefoucauld's self-portrait, they are asked to write their own self-portraits, signed with a pseudonym. These portraits are randomly distributed to classmates, who read them aloud; the students then try to guess the identity of the author of each piece.

Like the maxim, the *question d'amour* is a seventeenth-century salon activity that involves both introspection and social commentary and is eminently suited to the college classroom. In the *Recueil de pièces galantes en prose et en vers de Madame la Comtesse de la Suze* ("Collection of Gallant Works in Prose and in Verse by Madame the Countess de la Suze"), I found several discussion-provoking questions that, when asked in the salon, were meant to challenge those present to compose answers in verse:

Savoir s'il y a des secrets pour être aimé (157)

Are there secrets for being loved?[1]

Savoir si l'on peut avoir un amour tout désintéressé (162)

Is there such a thing as selfless love?

Savoir si les grands plaisirs de l'amour sont dans la tête ou dans les sens (158)

Are the greatest pleasures of love situated in the mind or the senses?

Savoir qui aime mieux des hommes et des femmes (162)

Who loves better, men or women?

Savoir ce qui est plus difficile, de retourner de l'amour à l'amitié, ou de passer de l'amitié à l'amour (159)

Is it easier to go from love to friendship or from friendship to love?

Aside from being great fun, the questions work beautifully to pave the way for two of the texts on the syllabus, La Rochefoucauld's *Maximes* and Lafayette's *La Princesse de Clèves*. Students recognize the debate in the novel's first book, over whether a man should want the lady he loves to go to the ball, as a *question d'amour* for which Mme de Lafayette and her circle might have composed responses. In fact, in the *Mercure galant*'s publicity campaign for the novel, the newspaper presented Lafayette's work itself as a *question galante*, which it posed to readers: "Je demande si une femme de vertu . . . fait mieux de faire confidence de sa passion à [son] mari, que de la taire" 'I am asking whether a virtuous wife . . . does better to confide her passion [for another man] to her husband or to say nothing of it' (Apr. 1678 [298–300]; qtd. in Laugaa 27). Finally, these *questions d'amour* help familiarize students with seventeenth-century euphemisms, as in, "Savoir si l'on peut toujours aimer une femme sans recevoir les dernières faveurs" 'Can one remain steadfastly in love with a woman without "going all the way"?' (La Suze, *Recueil* 157) After I read to my students a selection of *questions d'amour* from the *Recueil de pièces galantes*, I have them choose together the one they find the most interesting, and I invite them to compose their own answers, in verse. We then publish a class anthology.

Along with these individual writing projects, I assign one major group project, which involves the *conte de fées* ("fairy tale"). We study together Perrault's "Peau d'âne" and Mme d'Aulnoy's "L'Île de la Félicité," the first fairy tale published in France. Students work in groups to analyze the tales, their structure, and their essential features. They are asked to compare the two fairy tales, noting any differences they find between a fairy tale written by a man and one written by a woman. They remark, for instance, that the perfect union that the lovers enjoy in Mme d'Aulnoy's tale does not involve marriage. They also analyze the contrasting representations of male and female desire in these stories. Then, using what they have learned, in small groups they compose their own fairy tales, which they read aloud to their classmates the following week.

I have taught Writing about Love to both graduate students and undergraduates, and it has worked well at both levels. I have additional requirements for graduate students. Over the course of the semester, they must make oral presentations from critical articles. The selections I propose vary from year to year, but I consistently assign the penetrating analyses of Barbara Johnson (on *L'École des femmes*), Domna Stanton (on *préciosité* ["Fiction"]), and Volker Schröder (on *Les Lettres portugaises*). On the final day of class, I ask graduate students to present their term-paper research. This research day leads to lively discussion and to the salonlike atmosphere I try to create in the classroom. Overall, I find the course accomplishes its chief goals: it brings out students' creativity and helps them develop their critical skills while introducing them to gender studies in the context of some of the important and exciting literary and intellectual movements of seventeenth-century France.

Note

1. All translations from the French are mine unless otherwise noted.

Francis Mathieu

Early Modern Women Writers in a History of Ideas Survey Course

Courses focusing on or including the so-called *moralistes* of the early modern period tend to focus solely on the works of celebrated male authors who have long achieved canonical status, such as Michel de Montaigne, René Descartes, and François, duc de La Rochefoucauld. My aim here is to provide an alternative approach to teaching moralist literature by incorporating works by French women writers. Rather than outline a rigid syllabus, I describe a methodology and illustrate it with a detailed example. I suggest pulling together the following authors, spanning the sixteenth and seventeenth centuries, whose works are closely interconnected: Montaigne; Marguerite de Navarre; Louise Labé; Marie de Gournay; Descartes; Blaise Pascal; La Rochefoucauld; Madeleine de Souvré, marquise de Sablé; Marie-Madeleine Pioche de la Vergne, comtesse de Lafayette; Jean de La Bruyère; and Fénelon. My main objective is to explore the essential concerns and issues that male and female moralists, philosophers, and writers voice in their works.

I propose mapping out the evolution of thought throughout the works studied and emphasizing the intertextual elements that link many of the authors listed above. This methodology shows how female writers engage in a dialogue with their male counterparts, and vice versa. Strategic prereading activities are a decisive factor in the success of such a course, since it is crucial to point out to students the notions and lexicon that they should be looking for as they study the texts. The methodology would be suitable for a range of teaching contexts and levels, a general education class such as a freshman seminar in a liberal arts college, an advanced undergraduate course, or a graduate seminar.

My approach is designed to avoid two traps that can undermine the academic success and intellectual usefulness of studying noncanonical works. First, tagging unfamiliar female writers onto a typical survey of prominent male authors to fulfill a political obligation overshadows the intellectual value of the lesser-known works. Second, crafting a syllabus exclusively dedicated to works written by women not only leaves students with a significant information gap but also fails to illustrate that female writers can be considered on a par with their male contemporaries. In both cases students are left with only a partial understanding of the philosophical thinking of the period and the false impression that the ideas of women were either disconnected or tangential to their male peers. Instead, women writers are presented naturally, in their original literary contexts, so that their works and those of the standard male writers complement each other. In this way, instructors can provide students with a more complete understanding of the era (see Beasley's introduction to this volume). A course that integrates women's texts and ideas allows us to highlight how these works differ or agree with those of the male canon and helps students see how women influenced literary, philosophical, cultural, and social developments. It also aims to enhance students' interest in the early modern period, an era that may seem remote and unfamiliar to them. I suggest fulfilling this goal by concentrating on key topics of the early modern period that are still relevant in the twenty-first century—topics like the insights that male and female authors provide on the human condition, education, or the place of women in society. Given its interdisciplinary underpinnings, a course designed around the authors listed above would be best described as an early modern history-of-ideas survey course.

One philosophical concept that can be found in Montaigne, Pascal, and Lafayette is *divertissement* ("diversion"). Montaigne expresses his insights and ideas on this topic in his *Essais*. Montaigne's treatment evolves into *divertissement* in Pascal's *Pensées*. In what follows, I propose that *divertissement* be studied as the most prominent aspect of Pascal's philosophy on the human condition. I show how to teach the ways in which

Lafayette turns herself into a philosophical and spiritual authority by exemplifying Pascal's *divertissement* in her novel *La Princesse de Clèves*. I believe this topic is particularly pertinent to today's students. When asked, students usually come up with consumerism or workaholism among the forms *divertissement* takes in the twenty-first century. Diversion works wonders in making these three writers, otherwise known for being difficult to teach, accessible to students. This strategy provides an excellent context in which to teach *La Princesse de Clèves*, while underlining that women, overshadowed in intellectual history, were actively engaged in the circulation of innovative philosophical ideas through an erudite literary interchange with male writers.

Lafayette's role in moralist literature has been obscured by the attention paid to her male counterparts. Yet her biographers have shown that Lafayette was a great admirer of Pascal's works (Pingaud 43; Duchêne, *Madame de Lafayette* 96), and many scholars have reflected on the general influence of the philosopher's *Pensées* on her novel *La Princesse de Clèves* (see Mesnard 38; Laudy 126; Francillon 201). In my course, students study Pascal before Lafayette and know that the philosopher believed that human beings fall prey to *divertissement* because of the unconscious need to keep their minds stimulated. According to Pascal, without *divertissement*, ennui (or boredom ensuing from idleness) leaves people face-to-face with themselves and their human condition. This state of mind is unbearable because of the prospect of death that is so convenient to forget. As Pascal states, however, *divertissement* is deceptive because it leads people to be less devoted to their faith in God, which he considered the only genuine source of *repos* (tranquility or peace of mind).

After students have examined Pascal's general concept of *divertissement*, we turn to the intertextual elements that connect *Les Pensées* to *La Princesse de Clèves*. First, I direct students to examine the ways in which *divertissement* is rewritten in the novel by focusing on Lafayette's depiction of court society. The lengthy opening passage, with its elaborate depiction of Henri II's court, its world of visual facades, and its historical accounts, unfortunately tends to confuse and alienate students (Laden 54; Pósfay 102). But a careful coaching of students and a prereading activity that puts this challenging passage in the light of Pascal's *divertissement* can help alleviate students' resistance, awaken their interest, and put their analytical skills on the right track. The prereading activity might include a review of the appropriate Pascalian lexicon (such as *divertissement, ennui, obstacle, repos, chasse, insensiblement*). Students can then look for these terms in the opening passage of *La Princesse de Clèves* and in the rest of the work as their reading progresses (see Paige in this volume). At this point I remind students that Pascal identifies Lafayette's chosen setting, the court, as the quintessential location of *divertissement*.

Let me note here that translation issues present challenges (see Beasley, "Teaching"; Paige in this volume). Terence Cave has provided the best translation of Lafayette's novel (Beasley, "Teaching" 137), but he did not always translate the Pascalian lexicon of *divertissement* as accurately as he could have. For instance, Cave often chose to translate *divertissement* and *divertir* as "entertainment" and "entertain," losing the Pascalian slant of the French text somewhat. Students working with translated texts should be informed about the Pascalian interpretation that can be associated with "entertainment" and "entertain" in the prereading activity.

Students will be able to see that Lafayette employed Pascal's key words to depict the world of court from the first page of the novel, when the court is set against the backdrop of *divertissement*: "C'était tous les jours des parties de chasse et de paume, des ballets, des courses de bagues, ou de semblables divertissements" 'Not a day passed without hunting parties, tennis games, ballets, tilting at the ring, and other similar diversions' (69; 3).[1] It is no coincidence that hunting is listed as the first activity associated with *divertissement*. This placement echoes Pascal's use of hunting as the main allegory for his theory of *divertissement* and foreshadows a fuller treatment of the topic. Moreover, much like hunting, ball games (including tennis, to which Pascal refers directly in his *Pensées*), and by extension the other recreational activities mentioned by the novel's narrator, all allude to *divertissement*. The presence of Pascal's *divertissement* confirms that the hyperboles and superlatives that saturate the opening passage ought to be read as ironic. Thus students should come to the realization that the author's depiction of court society's "magnificence" is meant as a wry reflection on courtiers' "paraître" ("physical and social appearance").

Lafayette's word choices later include another noteworthy reference to Pascal's *divertissement*:

> Personne n'était tranquille, ni indifférent; on songeait à s'élever, à plaire, à servir, ou à nuire; on ne connaissait ni l'ennui ni l'oisiveté, et on était toujours occupé des plaisirs ou des intrigues. (81)

> No one was tranquil or indifferent; all thoughts were on seeking advancement, gaining favor, helping, or harming; boredom and idleness were unknown, everyone was kept busy by pleasure or intrigue. (14)

A Pascalian reading of this essential passage reveals that Lafayette describes courtiers as people whose lives are so full of activities that they never have to endure the Pascalian ennui.

In the next step of our analysis, we focus on the duc de Nemours. This character embodies not only the quintessential courtier but also a soul enslaved by amorous passion. Since Pascal's *divertissement* gives a new dimension to Nemours's passion, it may be helpful to reread in class the key passages from *Les Pensées* in which Pascal explains what motivates people to pursue their obsessions (in Sellier's edition, see thoughts 33, 70, 73, 134, 165–71, and 686; in Eliot's English edition, see thoughts 139–43, 168, 170). Students need to keep in mind that Pascal believed the hunt is more important than the catch as far as *divertissement* is concerned. As students reflect on this character as well as the manner in which love is depicted in the novel, they might be reminded that, for Pascal, the passions constitute the most significant form of *divertissement*. It is also crucial to ask students to pay close attention to how Pascal's psychological and moral analysis of *divertissement* is exemplified in most passages dealing with Nemours's passion for Mme de Clèves. This hermeneutical guidance, coupled with intertextual elements that support this reading, helps students see that Nemours is more obsessed with the obstacles to his love than with the object of his desire, much like the allegorical Pascalian hunter who enjoys the chase more than the catch.

Hunting, an ancestral symbol of amorous pursuits with which Nemours is associated twice in the novel, provides an ideal starting point for analyzing this character's amorous passion in the light of *divertissement*. In addition to remaining true to the traditional symbolism of hunting, Lafayette incorporates an allusion to *divertissement* whenever Nemours is aggressively pursuing the heroine. Thus soon after he has given in to his passion, the duke disappears from court, pretends to have "une grande passion pour la chasse" 'a great passion for the chase,' and arranges hunting parties, just as the narrator mentions that the court has assembled for "divertissement" (129; 57). Again, when Nemours acts as if he were lost, so that he can discreetly make his way to Mme de Clèves's place in the countryside, he happens to be hunting (169; 93). Strikingly, the narrator had just alluded to *divertissement* by indicating that when the duke is received by his sister, she gives herself up to "entertaining" him. It is no coincidence that this juxtaposition of hunting and *divertissement* happens twice, and this repetition is worth underscoring for students.

Eventually, enough clues should accumulate to let students conclude for themselves that Nemours is probably not seeking the conquest of the heroine but relishing the hunt or chase triggered by his desire. Students will be able to deduce that Lafayette alludes to Pascal's teachings to suggest that Nemours may just be looking for the thrills and hurdles inherent in a passionate pursuit. When the duke seeks these exciting challenges, he could be unconsciously seeking *divertissement* and avoiding facing himself and dealing with the human condition.

Students' attention may be drawn to the role played by obstacles in *La Princesse de Clèves*. Obstacles are a hallmark of Pascal's *divertissement*, since they delay the catch indefinitely through their perpetuation of the chase. Students can be asked to analyze the function of obstacles in the novel in the light of their Pascalian meaning. Students will see that obstacles act as a powerful sort of narcotic, intoxicating and addicting individuals to *divertissement*. Throughout the plot, this addiction to obstacles gives structure to Nemours's pursuit of love. The first illustration of his addiction is a recurring story within the main plot whose purpose has left many critics puzzled: Nemours's flirtation with the idea of seducing Queen Elizabeth I of England. In fact, its telling concluding passage leaves no ambiguity:

> Son esprit s'était insensiblement accoutumé à la grandeur de cette fortune et, au lieu qu'il l'avait rejetée d'abord comme une chose où il ne pouvait parvenir, les difficultés s'étaient effacées de son imagination, et il ne voyait plus d'obstacles. (90)

> His mind had imperceptibly become accustomed to the idea of this great fortune; whereas he had at first rejected it as something unattainable, the difficulties had been erased from his imagination, and he no longer saw any obstacles. (23)

It is right then, once all obstacles have been overcome, that the duke abandons this scheme to focus on Mme de Clèves, a new target that comes with the promise of formidable obstacles (see the description of her upbringing and how she appears to be unassailable).

A Pascalian reading of Lafayette also allows us to reconcile students with the unsettling conclusion of the novel. More accustomed to Hollywood's happy endings, most students have trouble accepting that the heroine refuses to marry her beloved Nemours and opts instead for social exile. This resistance can be assuaged if students are encouraged to entertain the idea that Mme de Clèves makes these controversial choices because she realizes that the man she loves is perverted by *divertissement*. In fact, the text indicates that Mme de Clèves not only insightfully identifies the telltale symptoms of Nemours's addiction but also uses those warning signs as irrefutable arguments when she refuses to engage in any sort of liaison with him. Students will have an easier time analyzing the ending if they are prepared to find the Pascalian facets through a prereading activity that directs their attention to these signs and how Mme de Clèves perceives them.

For example, the heroine contends that, once married, men are incapable of conserving the passion that inspires fidelity. During the private meeting when the two protagonists are at last free to express their love to each other, the princess argues that marriage brings obstacles to an end, therefore smothering passion. She claims that, hitherto, only the trial of obstacles has accounted for Nemours's fidelity (231; 148–49). The lucidity of the heroine's analysis had in fact been foreshadowed or corroborated by a revealing piece of narration that can be brought to light for students in the prereading activity, a homework assignment, or in class: "peut-être que des regards et des paroles obligeantes n'eussent pas tant augmenté l'amour de M. de Nemours que faisait [la] conduite austère [de Mme de Clèves]" 'indulgent words and glances would not, perhaps, have increased Nemours's love as effectively as [Mme de Clèves's] austere conduct' (178; 102). Mme de Clèves also rightly attributes her deceased husband's enduring love to her lack of reciprocal feelings, which created just the obstacle necessary to allow his passion to survive marriage: "peut-être aussi que sa passion n'avait subsisté que parce qu'il n'en aurait pas trouvé en moi" 'perhaps, too, his passion only endured because he found no answering passion in me' (231; 148). Again, the heroine's analysis had been validated earlier on by the narrator:

> La qualité de mari lui donna de plus grand privilèges, mais elle ne lui donna pas une autre place dans le cœur de sa femme. . . . [P]our être son mari, il ne laissa pas d'être son amant, parce qu'il avait toujours quelque chose à souhaiter au-delà de sa possession. (89)
>
> The status of husband gave him greater privileges, but the place he held in his wife's heart was no different . . . [A]lthough he was her husband, he did not cease to be her lover, since he always had something to desire beyond possession. (22)

Following Pascal's theory of *divertissement*, which parallels Mme de Clèves's logic, Nemours's amorous passion would indeed die if a total victory, such as marriage, annihilated all the obstacles that had kept him from being with the object of his desire. Nemours would then feel compelled to seek other challenges elsewhere, like those furnished by a new object of desire. Hence the heroine decides to protect herself by saying no to Nemours.

By tracing the presence of Pascal's *divertissement* in Lafayette's *La Princesse de Clèves*, students can easily see how the main characters can be read as allegories for the human condition as seen in the philosopher's work. This interpretation strengthens the heroine's controversial choices by unveiling their psychological and spiritual magnitude. It also demonstrates that the choices were both rational and inevitable conclusions to her quest for the Pascalian repose she finds in the last pages of the novel. Awareness that Lafayette imbued her text with a level of meaning drawing on Pascal's work gives students a renewed understanding of both the novel and the philosophical text.[2] Finally, I suggest reinforcing students' understanding of why Lafayette draws on Pascal. As a female novelist, Lafayette uses Pascal's lexicon and philosophy to foster edification, understanding, and communication with a community of readers. Through the moral dilemma of her female character and the faithful reference to Pascal's thinking on the human condition, she employs the medium most readily available to women in the seventeenth century, the novel, to participate in the intellectual movements of her time.

Another pertinent topic that would enable students to study contrasting ideas found in the works of male and female authors is the place of women in early modern society and the thorny question of their education. Several seventeenth-century authors take up this topic, including Montaigne, Labé, Marguerite de Navarre, Lafayette, La Bruyère, La Rochefoucauld, and Fénelon (*De l'éducation des femmes*, ch. 1). I also strongly recommend including two short protofeminist texts by Gournay that are strikingly avant-garde: *Égalité des hommes et des femmes* (1622; "The Equality of Men and Women") and *Grief des dames* (1626; "The Ladies' Grievance").

I hope the ideas suggested here illustrate how scholars can incorporate works by women in the curricula while continuing to teach the more traditional topics of a *moraliste* course. Extremely relevant in the works of Marguerite de Navarre, Pascal, Lafayette, La Rochefoucauld, La Bruyère, and Sablé, the struggle between the passions (especially love and self-love) and reason, as well as the notions of civility, worldliness, social mores, and court society, is essential to understanding the period and the role played by women, both as authors and active participants in the civilization process. Finally, the theme of cultural relativity (particularly in Montaigne and Descartes) invites an exploration of the foundation of anthropological thought, starting with travel's capacity to inspire personal growth and a new perspective on other cultures, leading to an ability to understand and question one's own culture.

Notes

1. All quotations from *La Princesse de Clèves* are from Jean Mesnard's edition and Terence Cave's English translation.

2. Additional Pascalian elements in Lafayette's text that merit examination, but that I cannot develop here, include the teachings on passion as a *divertissement* that all the inserted narratives provide; the heroine's ceaseless penchant for repose and her opposition to *divertissement*; the four mentions of *course de bagues* ("tilting at the ring") in the context of love and *divertissement*.

Katherine Montwieler

French Women Writers
in a World Literature Survey

For two years, I had the opportunity to teach in the pilot program Learning Communities at the University of North Carolina, Wilmington. Currently, around eleven thousand students are enrolled at the university, and in an attempt to create the kind of academic environment found at small liberal arts colleges, the College of Arts and Sciences started the Learning Communities program in fall 2003. When incoming first-year students enroll in this program, they take three classes together, two devoted to conventional curricular offerings and Introduction to University Life, a one-credit-hour class. A colleague in the history department and I designed a sequence that focused on European history and literature since 1660, and in both classes we included texts by seventeenth-, eighteenth-, and nineteenth-century French women writers. Although we changed the name of the sequence each time we taught it (e.g., Monsters, Madmen, and Monarchs; Revolutionary Sensibility), we always organized the class chronologically around absolutism, the Enlightenment, industrial and social revolutions, and the rise of empire. While I taught this particular version of the class as part of an interdisciplinary sequence, I am aware that similar courses are generally taught as independent, discrete English or comparative literature classes. So although I describe my pedagogical experience, I would encourage readers to try out comparable classes or assignments even if they do not have the formalized interdisciplinary context that I had. Up until the teaching of this class, my research and pedagogical interests had focused on eighteenth- and nineteenth-century British women writers; prompted by my colleague in history, Lynn Mollenauer, a sixteenth- and seventeenth-century French historian, we included Marie-Madeleine Pioche de la Vergne, comtesse de Lafayette; Françoise de Graffigny, and Claire de Duras in our sequence. We found that they paired beautifully with the canonical British women writers Aphra Behn, Mary Wollstonecraft, and Mary Shelley and complicated the perspectives offered by the usual (male) suspects included in such courses.

Given that many undergraduate students have not read literature before 1850 or studied another language, I begin the course with a lure. After lecturing on the historical and social context of mid-seventeenth-century Europe, I lead the class in a symptomatic, deconstructive reading of a selection from Samuel Pepys's diary. The passage is devoted to Charles II's triumphant return to England and neatly crystallizes the peculiarly Restoration-era yoking of the sacred and the profane, the sublime and the scatological (Charles II holds a Bible while his dog relieves himself on the boat). Not surprisingly, students recognize and delight in Charles's performances and Pepys's rendering of events. While exploring images, tone, and historical details, students are also encountering some of the skills I am attempting to teach them—how to look at a text closely and critically and to ask and answer questions of it. If on the first day I can reach students through image and theme—if they can realize the preoccupations of seventeenth-century denizens were not that different from their own and in some ways even more profane and outlandish—then they will be much more likely to be open to the other, more challenging texts we read throughout the semester.

The first of five units in the class is "Absolutism and Society." We follow our reading of Pepys with Behn's *Oroonoko* (1688), which tells the story of an African prince who is captured and enslaved in his native Coramantien (modern Ghana) and taken to Suriname before attempting an unsuccessful rebellion that leads to his death. Part romance, part travelogue, part antiracist tract, the text elicits a host of subjects for class discussion: the rise of colonialism, the construction of the other, and our narrative expectations as twenty-first-century readers, among others. Behn deliberately troubles her racist readers with her ennobling of an African. In addition, the royal prince is a thinly veiled portrait of Charles II, and the portrayal of his corrupt grandfather's court in Coramantien recalls those of England and Europe. As students learn to recognize these similarities, we begin our semester-long discussion of constructions of national identity, race, and gender, as they see (most for the first time) such concepts as historically constructed and not biologically determined.

Following *Oroonoko*, we backtrack to Lafayette's *The Princesse de Clèves* (1678). The students find Behn considerably more accessible than Lafayette, which is why I begin with Behn. Having one, much briefer, seventeenth-century novel under their belt, students are more confident about approaching another. Lafayette of course more clearly describes European court culture, and we compare the novels stylistically and thematically, trying to untangle how genre (the ostensible personal confession) relates to plot (the tragic love story). I draw my students' attention to representations of sensibility in both texts to show how the phenomenon is a marker for seventeenth-century writers of our shared humanity and a sign that paradoxically indicates women's power and powerlessness. We discover that women are empowered by their bodies and by their emotions—and yet those bodies and emotions also limit their position in their individual societies, since the women cannot escape their societies. Despite crossing oceans, they are unable to change or break away from the powerful social structures that surround them.

This introduction to sensibility provides a good introduction to the second section of the class, "The Enlightenment: Reason, Logic, Our Rights and Obligations," in which I show my students that reason and rationality are not as distinct from sensibility as they might appear. "The First Evening" of Bernard Le Bouvier de Fontenelle's *Conversations on the Plurality of Worlds* (1686; 9–22) establishes this link, as the intellectual astronomer engages a sharp-witted female aristocrat in flirtatious banter about the position of the planets and the order of the universe (see also Beasley and Cherbuliez in this volume). The students here learn that science is not as dry as some textbooks would suggest and become aware of the importance of metaphors in conceptualizing natural phenomena. I have been consistently surprised at how positively students respond to Fontenelle—their pleasure in reading comes from how different they find *Conversations* from any other text they have read, whether literary or scientific. This recognition leads to a conversation about interdisciplinarity in general and how subjects that might appear distinct can illuminate each other.

I follow *Conversations* with "Epistle I" from Alexander Pope's *An Essay on Man* (1733), another text that crosses disciplinary boundaries. This is the class's first exposure to poetry: Pope's heroic couplets tend to satisfy students' expectations about what a poem looks like, but they find his discussion of the universe and his tone refreshing. I also like following Behn and Lafayette with Fontenelle and Pope because students see that the physical and the emotional are not solely feminine concerns and that men are not more interested in cerebral matters than women; rather, students observe that in the seventeenth and eighteenth centuries such gender stereotypes were not so firmly rooted in culture—that in some ways some people in earlier centuries were freer than people living today.

We continue to explore rationality and reason by reading the last part of Jonathan Swift's novel *Gulliver's Travels, a Voyage to the Land of the Houyhnhnms* (1735). Swift appears to appreciate the rationality of the Houyhnhnms, but, by the text's end, when Gulliver is unable to communicate kindly with his fellow men and his family, it is clear to the students that the writer is showing the limitations of reason and the necessity for compassion. As another piece of travel writing, *Gulliver's Travels* sets the stage for Graffigny's *Letters from a Peruvian Woman* (1747). Whereas Fontenelle and Pope show how sensibility informs our understanding of science and Swift emphasizes its importance to personal relationships, Graffigny uses sensibility as a critique of slavery and nascent imperialism. Adopting the voice of Zilia, Graffigny takes her critique of racism a step further than Behn by showing an Indian woman as fully human, fully loving, and fully rational—characteristics that Pope suggests belong primarily to Europeans. I ask the students how the novel differs from others they have read, and they come to recognize the significance of Graffigny's portrayal of Zilia as narrator: the subaltern has a voice in this text. In addition to portraying the violence wrought by European expansion, Graffigny condemns European practices at home in her portrayal of the insipidness of women's education, anticipating Wollstonecraft's *Vindication of the Rights of Woman*, which we read in the next section of the class, "Revolutions: The Factories, the French, the Feminine."

We begin the Industrial Revolution with a selection of poems by William Blake, Mary Darby Robinson, and William Wordsworth. Again, I lecture on historical events before leading the class in analytical discussions of the texts. Any number of Blake's poems could be included as outcries against industrialism—I choose "London," both versions of "The Chimney Sweeper," and "Holy Thursday" because they are pithy and dense. Robinson's poem "A London Summer Morning" offers a counterpoint to the most common perception of Romantic-era writers as damning all things industrial and praising poetry as a sanctuary from the working world in her depiction of the labor of writing in the context of a deafening London day. Wordsworth's hostility toward the Industrial Revolution is articulated in "Composed upon Westminster Bridge" and his pastoral alternative in "Lines Written in Early Spring," "Expostulation and Reply," and "The Tables Turned." Throughout our discussions of these poems, I again point out how the poets use and manipulate sensibility.

We explore literary responses to the French Revolution with Anna Seward's "Sonnet: To France on Her Present Exertions" and excerpts from Edmund Burke's "Reflections on the Revolution in France" and Wordsworth's *Prelude* (books 9 and 10). All these works, although by British citizens, are profoundly invested in the French cause and offer a compelling portrait of the connections between emotions and politics. Seward's sonnet personifies the abstract concepts of revolution and justice. The selections I choose by Burke and Wordsworth emphasize the effect of revolution on human beings—whether royalty in Burke or the poor in Wordsworth. We conclude the unit by reading a few chapters from *Vindication of the Rights of Woman*, in which Wollstonecraft, like Graffigny, argues for women's education. Claiming to use the French Revolution as inspiration, Wollstonecraft contends that the rights and gains made by men must extend to women citizens as well. According to her, current social mores encourage women to privilege love, sensuality, and beauty over their intellectual capabilities. Like Burke, Wollstonecraft makes her argument so passionately that she seems at odds with the points she makes regarding rationality and reason—her ideals in tension with her feelings—once again exemplifying the rhetoric of sensibility.

The penultimate section, "European Encounters with the Other," explores the lingering effects of revolution. We read Shelley's *Frankenstein* (1818) and Duras's *Ourika* (1823). I particularly like the pairing of these works because they show how Europeans set themselves against other people, portraying them literally (Shelley) and figuratively (Duras) as monsters. When we discuss *Ourika*, I ask the students to conceptualize an alternative ending to the novel (e.g., Could Ourika move to England and become an abolitionist? Could she be involved in a successful slave revolt?). I ask students why Duras chooses the ending she does and what the ending of the novel reveals about Duras and the limits of her imagination. As these texts look back to the French Revolution, we explore how the writers recontextualize revolution in the context of the world, portraying creatively (rather than polemically, the way that Wollstonecraft does) how those ideals change when we take gender and race into consideration.

The course concludes with the section "The Modern Empire and Its Monsters." A selection from Friedrich Engels's *The Conditions of the Working Class in England* (1845) marks our return to industrialism, and Charles Dickens's *Hard Times* (1854) is a sensible response to it. Engels provides an objective portrayal of the poverty that accompanies industry, while Dickens creates a human story out of the misery to which both writers compellingly bear witness. By this point in the semester the students recognize how words color and shape our response to a situation. That awareness is a key lesson that I want them to take from the class, so that when confronted with representations of their reality or historical moment, students can analyze how they are being primed for a particular response as well as what is missing from an exploration of events. They understand the impact and significance of sensibility. I follow Dickens with Robert Louis Stevenson's *The Strange Case of Dr. Jekyll and Mr. Hyde* (1886). Stevenson's text exemplifies the moment at which the European recognizes the monster within himself—the Mr. Hyde lurking in Henry Jekyll is variously aligned with animals, the poor, the Irish, and women—and yet, as Stevenson accurately anticipates Sigmund Freud (a discussion for another class), the monster is lurking within every respectable human being. Christina Rossetti's "Goblin Market" (1862) recalls Engels in an imaginative context suggesting that the real monsters are capitalists exploiting country innocents, and Rudyard Kipling's short story "The Mark of the Beast" (1899) figures the European male as hysterical, monstrous, and other when he is set loose in India.

Lafayette, Graffigny, and Duras provide vital structural support to this class. The literary tropes (sensibility, gender, love, and violence) and historical frameworks (court politics, slavery, colonialism, and empire) that they discuss offer a foundation for a course devoted to European literature. They are integral to this particular expression of a course, though they would be wonderful additions to a more advanced class devoted to sensibility that could also include Samuel Richardson's *Clarissa*, Frances Sheridan's *The Memoirs of Miss Sidney Bidulph*, Henry Mackenzie's *The Man of Feeling*, Johann Wolfgang von Goethe's *The Sorrows of Young Werther*, and Germaine de Staël's *Corinne*. That my first-year students wind up enjoying the novels and their challenges, however, suggests not only that the texts are just as useful and important to an introductory level class but also that they are lively, engaging, accessible, and appreciated by young readers facing a plethora of distractions.

Notes on Contributors

Faith E. Beasley is professor of French at Dartmouth College and editor of *Cahiers du dix-septième*. She is the author of *Revising Memory: Women's Fiction and Memoirs in Seventeenth-Century France* and *Salons and the Creation of Seventeenth-Century France: Mastering Memory* and editor, with Katharine Ann Jensen, of *Approaches to Teaching* The Princess of Clèves. She is working on a book-length study of the influence contact with India had on France's Grand Siècle.

Lisa Beckstrand, academic planner in academic affairs for the University of Wisconsin, has taught graduate and undergraduate French literature, language, and culture at Montclair State University and French and women's studies at Concordia College. She is the author of *Deviant Women of the French Revolution*, which examines the writings of Olympe de Gouges and Manon Roland.

Mary Ellen Birkett is professor of French studies at Smith College. She is the author of *Lamartine and the Poetics of Landscape* and editor, with Denis Hudson, of *Religious Tolerance and Intolerance in Ancient and Modern Worlds* and, with Christopher Rivers, of *Approaches to Teaching Duras's* Ourika. She is studying the formation of French colonial policy in the first half of the nineteenth century.

Thomas M. Carr, Jr., is professor of French at the University of Nebraska, Lincoln. In addition to articles on Voltaire, Malebrache, and Marivaux, he is the author of *Descartes and the Resilience of Rhetoric* and *Voix des abbesses du Grand Siècle: La Prédication au féminin à Port-Royal* and the editor of Antoine Arnaud's *Réflections sur l'éloquence des prédicateurs*.

Juliette Cherbuliez is associate professor of French and a co-organizer of the collaborative research group TEMS, at the University of Minnesota. She is the author of *The Place of Exile: Leisure Literature and the Limits of Absolutism* and the editor of Anne de la Roche-Guilhen's *Rare-en-Tout*. She is finishing a book project called "The Medean Presence," on the destructive powers of early modern literature.

Suzan van Dijk is a specialist of French and comparative literature. She has developed the online database and virtual collaboration Women Writers' Networks (www.womenwriters.nl) and created the international network New Approaches to European Women's Writing. She is founding editor of the Cahiers Isabelle de Charrière / Belle de Zuylen Papers and is currently preparing a book on Dutch discourse about women's writing from 1770 to 1870.

Perry Gethner is Norris Professor of French and head of the Department of Foreign Languages at Oklahoma State University. He has published articles on the history of seventeenth-century French drama and opera and critical editions and translations of numerous plays, including a two-volume anthology of works by women playwrights.

Elizabeth C. Goldsmith is professor of French literature at Boston University. She has published widely on French women writers and is a specialist of the epistolary genre. Her recent books include *Lettres de femmes, textes inédits et oubliés du XVIe au XVIIIe siècles* (edited with Colette Winn) and *Publishing Women's Life Stories in France, 1642–1720: From Voice to Print*. She is working on a book about early modern women and travel.

Claire Goldstein is associate professor in the Department of French and Italian at Miami University in Oxford. Her interests include seventeenth- and eighteenth-century literature, material culture, gardens, and natural philosophy. She is the author of *Vaux and Versailles: The Appropriations, Erasures, and Accidents That Made Modern France*. Her new project examines comets in the age of Louis XIV.

Henriette Goldwyn is professor of French at New York University and the New York director of NYU in Paris. She has published widely on French women writers and is the editor of Mme Du Noyer's *Mémoires* and the co-editor of the five-volume *Théâtre de femmes de l'ancien régime, XVIe, XVIIe et XVIIIe siècles*. She is working on the Huguenot literary production of the diaspora and the religious and political impact of female prophesying, memoirs, periodicals, essays, and polemical letters, written and published in serial form.

Richard E. Goodkin is professor of French and senior fellow at the Institute for Research in the Humanities at the University of Wisconsin, Madison. His books include *The Tragic Middle: Racine, Aristotle, Euripides, Around Proust*; and *Birth Marks: The Tragedy of Primogeniture in Pierre Corneille, Thomas Corneille, and Jean Racine*. He is the editor of *Autour de Racine: Studies in Intertextuality* and *In Memory of Elaine Marks: Life Writing, Writing Death*. His contribution to this volume is adapted from a project for which he received a Guggenheim Fellowship in 2005–06.

David Harrison is associate professor of French and director of the Center for International Studies at Grinnell College. He has written on Saint-Simon, Molière, and Ninon de Lenclos. His work has appeared in *Dalhousie French Studies, French Review, Papers on French Seventeenth-Century Literature*, and *Seventeenth-Century French Studies*.

Chloé Hogg is assistant professor of French at the University of Pittsburgh. She has completed a book, "Absolutist Affections: Love and War in Louis XIV's France," and is working on a project on material and political culture in the writings of Madeleine de Scudéry. Her publications include articles on Graffigny, Scudéry, and Villedieu.

Louise K. Horowitz is professor of French at Rutgers University, Camden, and a member of the Rutgers, New Brunswick, graduate faculty. She is the author of *Love and Language: A Study of the Classical French Moralist Writers* and of *Honore d'Urfé*. Her most recent publications have focused on specific historical and political tensions underlying seventeenth-century French literature, particularly concerning Lafayette and Racine.

Katharine Ann Jensen is associate professor of French at Louisiana State University. She is the author of *Writing Love: Letters, Women, and the Novel in France, 1605–1776* and *Uneasy Possessions: The Mother-Daughter Dilemma in France, 1671–1928*. She is also the editor, with Faith E. Beasley, of *Approaches to Teaching Lafayette's* The Princess of Clèves.

Donna Kuizenga is dean of the College of Liberal Arts and professor of French at the University of Massachusetts, Boston. Her publications include a new translation of Villedieu's *The Memoirs of Henriette-Sylvie de Molière* and *Women Writers in Pre-revolutionary France: Strategies of Emancipation*, which she edited with Colette Winn. Her other publications include works on Lafayette, Claire Goll, Pierre Le Moyne, and Cureau de La Chambre.

Roxanne Decker Lalande is professor of French at Lafayette College. Her main areas of research include seventeenth-century drama, comic theory, and women writers of the classical period. She is the author of *Intruders in the Play World: The Dynamics of Gender in Molière's Comedies* and the editor of *A Labor of Love: Critical Reflections on the Writings of Marie-Catherine Desjardins (Mme de Villedieu)* and has translated into English Villedieu's *Le Portefeuille* and her *Lettres et billets galants*.

Ann Leone is professor of French studies and landscape studies at Smith College. She has written about the narrative functions of gardens and other landscapes in the works of Colette, Alice Walker, Chekhov, Mme de Lafayette, and Goethe, among others. She is working on vernacular gardens in Northampton, Massachusetts.

John D. Lyons is Commonwealth Professor of French at the University of Virginia and Chevalier de la Légion d'Honneur. He has published extensively on sixteenth- and seventeenth-century French literature. His books include *Exemplum; The Tragedy of Origins; Before Imagination;* and *Chance, Literature, and Culture in Early Modern France*, edited with Kathleen Wine.

Laure Marcellesi is assistant professor of French at Dartmouth College. Her research focuses on travel literature in the French Enlightenment and on gender and colonization. She is working on "Literary Encounters," a book exploring representations of Tahiti in late-eighteenth-century France.

Francis Mathieu is assistant professor of French at Southwestern University. His main research interests include the deployment of rhetoric in seventeenth- and eighteenth-century novelistic forms, gender-centered studies, and intertextuality. He has published articles in the *French Review* and *Cahiers du dix-septième*.

Katherine Montwieler teaches English and women's studies at the University of North Carolina, Wilmington. Her articles have appeared in *Tulsa Studies in Women's Literature, Women's Writing, Romanticism on the Net, Nineteenth-Century Feminisms,* and *Dickens Studies Annual.* She is studying the role of sensibility in nineteenth-century women's poetry.

Nicholas Paige is professor of French at the University of California, Berkeley. He is the author of *Being Interior: Autobiography and the Contradictions of Modernity in Seventeenth-Century France* and *Before Fiction: The Ancien Régime of the Novel* (forthcoming) and has translated Lafayette's *Zayde: A Spanish Romance*.

Volker Schröder is associate professor of French at Princeton University. Among his publications are an in-depth study of Racine's *Britannicus, La Tragédie du sang d'Auguste*; the essay collection *Présences de Racine,* and an annotated critical edition of Marie-Anne Barbier's tragedy *Cornélie, mère des Gracques.* His current work focuses on civility and verbal violence in the age of Louis XIV.

Allison Stedman is associate professor of French at the University of North Carolina, Charlotte. She is the author of the forthcoming book *Rococo Fiction in the Age of Louis XIV (1650–1715): Seditious Frivolity* and the co-editor of an English translation of the *Voyage de Campagne par Madame la comtesse de M**** by Henriette-Julie de Castelnau, comtesse de Murat, also forthcoming.

Deborah Steinberger is associate professor of French and comparative literature at the University of Delaware. She has published articles on seventeenth- and eighteenth-century French theater, writing by early modern women, and early modern French journalism, with an emphasis on Donneau de Visé and the *Mercure galant,* and is the editor of critical editions of theater and other works by Françoise Pascal.

Harriet Stone is chair of the Department of Romance Languages and Literatures and professor of French and comparative literature at Washington University in St. Louis. Her publications include *Tables of Knowledge: Descartes in Vermeer's Studio; The Classical Model: Literature and Knowledge in Seventeenth-Century France; Royal Disclosure: Problematics of Representation in French Classical Tragedy*; and a special issue of *L'Esprit Créateur* on Racine. Her current work focuses on the interplay of texts and images.

Mary Trouille is professor of French and women's studies at Illinois State University. She is the author of *Sexual Politics in the Enlightenment: Women Writers Read Rousseau* and *Wife-Abuse in Eighteenth-Century France.* Trouille is also the translator of *Rethinking France: Les Lieux de Mémoire*, volume 1, and the editor and translator of Stéphanie de Genlis's 1782 novella *Histoire de la Duchesse de C****. She is preparing a critical edition of Rétif de La Bretonne's novel *Ingénue Saxancour.*

Holly Tucker is associate professor of French and Italian and medicine, health, and society at Vanderbilt University. Her books include *Pregnant Fictions: Childbirth and the Fairy Tale in Early-Modern France; SLA and the Literature Classroom: Fostering Dialogues* (with V. Scott); and *Blood Work.* She has published articles on seventeenth-century literature and on medicine in its historical and cultural contexts.

Gabrielle Verdier is professor of French at the University of Wisconsin, Milwaukee. Her research has focused principally on writers and genres considered marginal. The author of a book and articles on Charles Sorel, she has also written numerous articles on fairy tales and women writers, among them Montpensier, Lenclos, d'Aulnoy, Staal-Delaunay, and Olympe de Gouges. She is working on an English translation of d'Aulnoy's *Travels into Spain.*

Caroline Weber is associate professor of French and comparative literature at Barnard College. She is the author of *Terror and Its Discontents: Suspect Words in Revolutionary France* and *Queen of Fashion: What Marie Antoinette Wore to the Revolution*, which was named a *New York Times* Notable Book and a *Washington Post* Best Book of the Year. She is a regular contributor to the *New York Times Book Review.*

Kathleen Wine is associate professor of French at Dartmouth College. She is the author of *Forgotten Virgo: Humanism and Absolutism in Honoré d'Urfé's* L'Astrée and the editor, with Claire Carlin, of *Theatrum mundi: Essays in Honor of Ronald W. Tobin* and, with John D. Lyons, of *Chance, Literature, and Culture in Early Modern France.* She is working on a book on the relationship between print and oral culture in baroque romance.

Abby Zanger is a specialist of early modern French literature and history who has taught at Harvard University, Yale University, Tufts University, and Boston University. She is the author of *Scenes from the Marriage of Louis XIV: Gender and the Making of Absolutist Power*, editor of a special edition of *L'Esprit Créateur* on sexuality in early modern France, and coeditor of the Ashgate Press book series Women and Gender in the Early Modern World. She is researching print culture and early modern French political allegory.

Works Cited

Aarne, Antti, and Stith Thompson. *The Types of the Folktale: A Classification and Bibliography*. Helsinki: Acad. Scientarum Fennica, 1961. Print.

Abélard and Héloïse. *Correspondance*. Ed. Edouard Bouyé. Paris: Gallimard, 2000. Print.

Adam, Antoine. *Grandeur and Illusion: French Literature and Society, 1600–1715*. London: Weidenfeld, 1972. Print.

———. *Histoire de la littérature française au XVIIe siècle*. 5 vols. Paris: Domat, 1948–56. Print.

Adams, Percy G. *Travelers and Travel Liars, 1660–1800*. Berkeley: U of California P, 1962. Print.

Adams, William Howard. *The French Garden, 1500–1800*. New York: Braziller, 1979. Print.

Agnes of God. Dir. Norman Jewison. Columbia Pictures, 1985. Film.

Altman, Janet Gurkin. "The Letter Book as a Literary Institution, 1539–1789: Toward a Cultural History of Published Correspondences in France." *Yale French Studies* 71 (1986): 17–62. Print.

Anatomy of Gender. Northwestern U, 2005. Web. 29 Apr. 2010.

Anderson, Elizabeth. "Le Jardin révélateur: Louis XIV, Madame de Lafayette, Madame de Sévigné." BA thesis. Smith Coll., 2004. Print.

Angélique de Saint-Jean. *Relation de captivité de la Mère Angélique de Saint-Jean*. Ed. Louis Cognet. Paris: Table Ronde, 2005. Print.

Anne de Marquets. *Sonets spirituels*. Ed. Gary Ferguson. Geneva: Droz, 1997. Print.

Apostolidès, Jean-Marie. *Le Prince sacrifié: Théâtre et politique au temps de Louis XIV*. Paris: Minuit, 1985. Print.

———. *Le Roi-machine: Spectacle et politique au temps de Louis XIV*. Paris: Minuit, 1981. Print.

Arenal, Electa, and Stacey Schlau, eds. *Untold Sisters: Hispanic Nuns in Their Own Works*. Albuquerque: U of New Mexico P, 1989. Print.

Aronson, Nicole. *Madame de Rambouillet ou la magicienne de la Chambre Bleue*. Paris: Fayard, 1988. Print.

———. *Mademoiselle de Scudéry ou le voyage au pays de Tendre*. Paris: Fayard, 1986. Print.

Atherton, Margaret, ed. *Women Philosophers of the Early Modern Period*. Indianapolis: Hackett, 1994. Print.

Aulnoy, Marie-Catherine Le Jumel de Barneville, comtesse d'. "La Chatte blanche." *Contes de Madame d'Aulnoy*. Paris: Garnier, 1882. 63–77. *Gallica*. Web. 3 Dec. 2010.

———. *La Cour et la ville de Madrid vers la fin du XVIIe siècle*. Ed. B. Carey. 2 vols. Paris: Plon, 1874, 1876. *Bibliothèque Nationale de France*. Web. 27 July 2010.

————. "L'Ile de la Félicité." *Contes I: Les Contes de fées.* Ed. Philippe Hourcade. Paris: Société des Textes Français Modernes, 1997. 9–26. Print.

————. *Madrid.* Paris: Magellan, 2006. Print. Heureux Qui Comme Ulysse 43.

————. *Relación del viage de España.* By d'Aulnoy. Introd. Miguel Ángel Vega. Trans. Pilar Blanco and Vega. Madrid: Cátedra, 2000. Print. Como nos vieron 5.

————. *Relation du voyage d'Espagne.* Ed. R. Foulché-Delbosc. Paris: Klincksieck, 1926. Print.

————. *Relation du voyage d'Espagne.* Ed. Maria-Susana Seguin. Paris: Desjonquères, 2005. Print.

————. *Travels into Spain.* Introd. R. Foulché-Delbosc. 1930. London: Routledge, 2004. Print. The Broadway Travellers.

————. *Travels to Spain.* Ed. and trans. Gabrielle Verdier. Chicago: U of Chicago P, forthcoming. The Other Voice in Early Modern Europe.

Baillet, Adrien. *Jugemens des savans sur les principaux ouvrages des auteurs.* Vol. 4, pt. 5. Paris: Dezallier, 1686. Print.

Ballaster, Ros. *Seductive Forms: Women's Amatory Fiction from 1684 to 1740.* Oxford: Clarendon; New York: Oxford UP, 1992. Print.

Barbier, Marie-Anne. *Arrie et Pétus.* Gethner, *Femmes dramaturges* 1: 243–314.

————. *Cornélie mère des Gracques.* Ed. Alicia Montoya and Volker Schröder. Toulouse: Société de Littératures Classiques, 2005. Print.

Baridon, Michel. *Jardins de Versailles.* Photographs by Jean-Baptiste Leroux. Arles: Actes Sud; Versailles: École Nationale Supérieure du Paysage; Milan: Motta, 2001. Print.

Barthes, Roland. *Mythologies.* Ed. and trans. Annette Lavers. New York: Noonday, 1972. Print.

Bassy, Alain-Marie. "Supplément au voyage du Tendre." *Bulletin du bibliophile* 1 (1982): 13–33. Print.

Batteux, Charles. *Cours de belles-lettres, ou Principes de la litterature.* Paris: Desaint and Saillant, 1753. Print.

Bayle, Pierre. *Dictionnaire historique et critique.* 5th ed. 4 vols. Amsterdam: Brunel, 1740. Print.

Beasley, Faith E. "Molière's Precious Women." Gaines and Koppisch 59–66.

————. *Revising Memory: Women's Fiction and Memoirs in Seventeenth-Century France.* New Brunswick: Rutgers UP, 1990. Print.

————. *Salons, History and the Creation of Seventeenth-Century France: Mastering Memory.* Aldershot: Ashgate, 2006. Print.

————. "Teaching *La Princesse de Clèves* in Translation." Beasley and Jensen 127–38.

————. "Versailles Meets the Taj Mahal." *French Global: A New Approach to Literary History.* Ed. Christie McDonald and Susan Rubin Suleiman. New York: Columbia UP, 2010. 207–22. Print.

Beasley, Faith E., and Katharine Ann Jensen, eds. *Approaches to Teaching Lafayette's* The Princess of Clèves. New York: MLA, 1998. Print.

Beaumarchais, Pierre-Augustin Caron de. *Le Mariage de Figaro.* Ed. Antonia Zagamé. Paris: Flammarion, 2010. Print. Étonnants Classiques.

Beauvoir, Simone de. *Mémoires d'une jeune fille rangée*. Paris: Gallimard, 1992. Print.

Beckstrand, Lisa. *Deviant Women of the French Revolution*. Madison: Fairleigh Dickinson UP, 2009. Print.

———. "Olympe de Gouges: Feminine Sensibility and Political Posturing." *Intertexts* 6.2 (2002): 185–202. Print.

Beebee, Thomas. *Epistolary Fiction in Europe, 1500–1850*. Cambridge: Cambridge UP, 1999. Print.

Béguin, Albert. "Une Amie française de Jean-Paul: Madame de Monbart (Joséphine de Sydow)." *Revue de littérature comparée* 15 (1935): 30–59. Print.

Behn, Aphra. *The Fair Jilt*. London: R. Holt, 1688. Print.

———. *Love Letters between a Nobleman and His Sister*. London: Virago, 1987. Print.

———. *Oroonoko and Other Writings*. Ed. Paul Salzman. Oxford: Oxford UP, 1994. Print.

Bellart, Nicolas-François. "Mémoire pour Madame de l'Orme contre M. de l'Orme, son mari." Bellart, *Œuvres* 3: 64–91.

———. *Œuvres. Mémoires et plaidoyers*. 6 vols. Paris: J.-L. Brière, 1827. Print.

———. "Réflexions rapides pour M. M . . . contre sa femme." Bellart, *Œuvres* 3: 504–36.

The Bells of Saint Mary's. Dir. Leo McCary. Rainbow Productions, 1945. Film.

Bennassar, Bartolomé, and Lucile Bennassar, eds. *Le Voyage en Espagne. Anthologie des voyageurs français et francophones du XVIe au XIXe siècle*. Paris: Laffont, 1998. Print.

Bérenguier, Nadine. "Victorious Victims: Women and Publicity in *Mémoires Judiciaires*." *Going Public: Women and Publishing in Early Modern France*. Ed. Elizabeth C. Goldsmith and Dena Goodman. Ithaca: Cornell UP, 1995. 62–78. Print.

Bergmann, Emilie L., and Stacey Schlau, eds. *Approaches to Teaching the Works of Sor Juana Inés de la Cruz*. New York: MLA, 2007. Print.

Bernard, Catherine. *Laodamie reine d'Epire*. Gethner, *Femmes dramaturges* 1: 181–242.

Bernier, François. *Histoire de la dernière révolution des états du Grand Mogol*. Paris: Barbin, 1670. Print.

———. *Un Libertin dans l'Inde Moghole: Les voyages de François Bernier*. Ed. Frédéric Tinguely. Paris: Chandeigne, 2008. Print.

Berrall, Julia S. *The Garden*. New York: Viking, 1966. Print.

Bertaut, François. *Journal du voyage d'Espagne*. Paris: Claude Barbin, 1659. Excerpts rpt. in Bennassar and Bennassar.

Bertière, Simone. *Marie Antoinette, l'insoumise*. Paris: Fallois, 2002. Print. Vol. 4 of *Les Reines de France au temps des Bourbons*.

Besenval, Pierre de. *Mémoires sur la cour de France*. 1805. Ed. Ghislaine de Diesbach. Paris: Mercure de France, 1987. Print.

Beugnot, Bernard. *Le Discours de la retraite au XVIIe siècle: Loin du monde et du bruit*. Paris: PUF, 1996. Print.

Birkett, Mary Ellen. "Gardening and Poetry: The Languages of Love in *La Nouvelle Héloïse* IV, 11." *Romance Notes* 26.2 (1985): 115–19. Print.

Birkett, Mary Ellen, and Christopher Rivers, eds. *Approaches to Teaching Duras's Ourika.* New York: MLA, 2009. Print.

Blake, William. *Songs of Innocence and of Experience.* Oxford: Oxford UP, 1967. Print.

Blanc, Olivier. *Olympe de Gouges.* Paris: Syro, 1981. Print.

Blanchard, Antoine. *Essay d'exhortation pour les états différens des malades . . . [et] un examen général sur tous les commandements et sur les péchés de plusieurs états.* 2 vols. Paris, 1713. Print.

———. "Péchés de l'épouse à l'égard de son mary." Blanchard, *Essay* 2: 198–99.

———. "Péchés des maris à l'égard de leurs femmes." Blanchard, *Essay* 2: 195–98.

Boileau, Nicolas. *Satires, épîtres, art poétique.* Ed. Jean-Pierre Collinet. Paris: Gallimard, 1985. Print.

Bordo, Susan, ed. *Feminist Interpretations of René Descartes.* University Park: Penn State UP, 1999. Print. Re-reading the Canon.

Borglum, George Paul. "Madame Deshoulières (1638–1694)." Diss. Yale U, 1939. Print.

Bossuet, Jacques Bénigne. *Instruction sur les états d'oraison.* 2nd ed. Paris: Jean Anisson, 1697. Print.

Bots, Hans. "Le Refuge dans les Provinces Unies." *La Diaspora des Huguenots.* Paris: Champion, 2001. 63–74. Print.

Boucher, François. *Le Déjeuner.* 1739. Oil on canvas. Musée du Louvre, Paris.

Bougainville, Louis-Antoine de. *Voyage autour du monde.* Ed. Michel Bideaux and Sonia Faessel. Paris: PU Paris-Sorbonne, 2001. Print.

Bouhours, Dominique. *Les Entretiens d'Ariste et d'Eugène.* Paris: Mabre-Cramoisy, 1673. Print.

Bourassin, Emmanuel, ed. *Page à la cour de Louis XVI: Mémoires du comte d'Hézècques.* 1804. Paris: Tallandier, 1987. Print.

Bourgeois, Louise. *Recueil des secrets de Louyse Bourgeois . . . ses plus rares expériences pour diverses maladies, principalement des femmes, avec leurs embellissemens.* Paris: M. Mondière, 1635. *Gallica.* Web. 29 Apr. 2010.

Boursier, Nicole. "Le Corps de Henriette-Sylvie." *Le Corps au XVIIe siècle.* Ed. Ronald W. Tobin. Paris: PFSCL, 1995. 271–80. Print. Biblio 17, 89.

Bray, Alan. *The Friend.* Chicago: U of Chicago P, 2003. Print.

Bray, Bernard. "Belle épistolière, ou 'la Sévigné de notre siècle.'" *Lettre de Zuylen et du Pontet* 22 (1997): 4–11. Print.

Bricaire de la Dixmérie, Nicolas. Le Sauvage de Taïti aux Français, *avec* Un Envoi au philosophe ami des sauvages. Paris: Lejay, 1770. Print.

Broad, Jacqueline. *Women Philosophers of the Seventeenth Century.* Cambridge: Cambridge UP, 2002. Print.

Broomhall, Susan. *Women and the Book Trade in Sixteenth-Century France.* Aldershot: Ashgate, 2002. Print.

Brunel, Antoine de. *Voyage d'Espagne.* Paris: Charles de Sercy, 1655. Excerpts rpt. in Bennassar and Bennassar.

Brunot, Ferdinand. *Histoire de la langue française des origines à nos jours.* 1905. 13 vols. Paris: Colin, 1966. Print.

Buffet, Marguerite. *Nouvelles Observations sur la langue française . . . avec* Les Éloges des illustres sçavantes. Paris: Cusson, 1668. Print.

Burke, Edmund. "Reflections on the Revolution in France." *Burke, Paine, Godwin, and the Revolution Controversy.* Ed. Marilyn Butler. Cambridge: Cambridge UP, 1984. 33–48. Print.

Burke, Peter. *The Fabrication of Louis XIV.* New Haven: Yale UP, 1992. Print.

Burney, Fanny. *Camilla; or, A Picture of Youth.* Ed. Edward A. Bloom and Lillian D. Bloom. Oxford: Oxford UP, 2009. Print.

———. *Cecilia; or, Memoirs of an Heiress.* Ed. Peter Sabor and Margaret Anne Doody. Oxford: Oxford UP, 2008. Print.

Bussy-Rabutin, Roger de. "Almanach pour l'année 1665." La Suze, *Poésies* 88–116.

Butler, Judith. *Gender Trouble: Feminism and the Subversion of Identity.* London: Routledge, 1990. Print.

———. *Undoing Gender.* New York: Routledge, 2004. Print.

Cadden, Joan. *Meanings of Sex Difference in the Middle Ages.* Cambridge: Cambridge UP, 1993. Print.

Cailli, Mme de. *Griefs et plaintes des femmes malmariées.* Paris, 1789. Print.

Campan, Mme. *Mémoires de Madame Campan: Première femme de chambre de Marie Antoinette.* 1822. Ed. Jean Chalon. Paris: Mercure de France, 1988. Print.

Carr, Thomas M., Jr. "A Checklist of Published Writings in French by Early Modern Nuns." *The Cloister and the World: Early Modern Convent Voices.* Ed. Carr. Spec. issue of *EMF: Studies in Early Modern France* 11 (2007): 231–57. Print.

———. "From the Cloister to the World: Mainstreaming Early Modern French Convent Writing—an État Présent." *The Cloister and the World: Early Modern Convent Voices.* Ed. Carr. Spec. issue of *EMF: Studies in Early Modern France* 11 (2007): 7–26. Print.

———. *Voix des abbesses du Grand Siècle: La Prédication au féminin à Port-Royal.* Tübingen: Narr, 2006. Print.

Castelot, André. *Le Procès de Marie-Antoinette.* Paris: Perrin, 1993. Print.

Castiglione, Baldesar. *The Book of the Courtier.* Trans. George Bull. Harmondsworth: Penguin, 1967. Print.

Certeau, Michel de. *La Fable mystique: XVIe–XVIIe siècles.* Paris: Gallimard, 1982. Print.

Challe, Robert. "Histoire de Monsieur de Terny et de Mademoiselle de Bernay." *Les Illustres Françaises.* Ed. Jacques Cormier and Frédéric Deloffre. Paris: Poche, 1996. 199–246. Print.

Chalon, Jean. Preface. Campan 7–12.

Chang, Leah. "Clothing 'Dame Hélisenne': The Stage of Female Authorship and the Production of the 1538 *Angoysses Douloureuses qui procèdent d'amours.*" *Romanic Review* 92.4 (2001): 381–403. Print.

———. *Into Print: The Production of Female Authorship in Early Modern France.* Newark: U of Delaware P, 2009. Print.

Chantal, Jeanne de. *Correspondance.* Ed. Marie-Patricia Burns. 6 vols. Paris: Du Cerf, 1986–96. Print.

Charnes, Jean-Antoine, abbé de. *Conversations sur la critique de* La Princesse de Clèves. 1679. Ed. François Weil et al. Tours: U de Tours, 1973. Print.

Charrière, Isabelle de. *Caliste ou Lettres écrites de Lausanne*. Ed. Claudine Herrmann. Paris: Des Femmes, 1980. Print.

———. *Correspondance*. Charrière, *Œuvres*, vols. 1–6.

———. *Letters of Mistress Henley Published by Her Friend*. Trans. Philip Stewart and Jean Vaché. New York: MLA, 1993. Print. MLA Text and Translations 1.

———. *Lettres de Mistress Henley*. 1784. Ed. Joan Hinde Stewart and Philip Stewart. New York: MLA, 1993. Print. MLA Text and Translations 1.

———. *Œuvres complètes*. Ed. Jean-Daniel Candaux et al. 10 vols. Amsterdam: Oorschot, 1979–84. Print.

Chartier, Roger, and Henri Jean Martin. *Le Livre triomphant*. Paris: Promodis, 1984. Print. Vol. 2 of *Histoire de l'édition française*.

Cherbuliez, Juliette. *The Place of Exile: Leisure, Literature, and the Limits of Absolutism*. Lewisburg: Bucknell UP, 2005. Print.

Chéron, Elizabeth Sophie. "La Coupe du Val-de-Grâce." Ed. Jean-Marc Poiron. Démoris and Delpierre, *Homage* 28–53.

Chinard, Gilbert. *L'Amérique et le rêve exotique*. 1913. Paris: Droz, 1934. Print.

Chodorow, Nancy. *The Reproduction of Mothering: Psychoanalysis and the Sociology of Gender*. Berkeley: U of California P, 1978. Print.

Chométy, Philippe. *"Philosopher en langage des dieux": La Poésie d'idées en France au siècle de Louis XIV*. Paris: Champion, 2006. Print.

Choudhury, Mita. *Convents and Nuns in Eighteenth-Century French Politics and Culture*. Ithaca: Cornell UP, 2004. Print.

Cicero, Marcus Tullius. *Laelius: On Friendship. On the Good Life*. Ed. and trans. Michael Grant. Harmondsworth: Penguin, 1971. 172–227. Print.

Clément, Pierre. Rev. of *Lettres d'une Péruvienne*, by Françoise de Graffigny. *Les Cinq Années littéraires* 10 Feb. 1748: 13–19. Print. Rpt. in Graffigny, *Lettres* [2002] 251–53.

Cobbe, Frances Power. "Wife-Torture in England." *Contemporary Review* 32.2 (1878): 55–87. Print.

Cohen, Huguette. "Jansenism in Diderot's *La Religieuse*." *Studies in Eighteenth-Century Culture* 11 (1982): 75–91. Print.

Cojannot–Le Blanc, Marianne. *D'Acide et d'encre: Abraham Bosse (1604?–1676) et son siècle en perspectives*. Paris: Centre National de la Recherche Scientifique, 2004. Print.

Collinet, Jean-Pierre. *Le Monde littéraire de La Fontaine*. Paris: PUF, 1970. Print.

Conley, John J. *The Suspicion of Virtue: Women Philosophers in Neoclassical France*. Ithaca: Cornell UP, 2002. Print.

Connell, Raewyn. *Masculinities*. Berkeley: U of California P, 1995. Print.

Constant, Samuel de. *Le Mari sentimental ou le mariage comme il y en a quelques-uns*. 1783. Milan: Cisalpino-Goliardica, 1975. Print.

Cook, Elizabeth Heckendorn. *Epistolary Bodies: Gender and Genre in the Eighteenth-Century Republic of Letters*. Palo Alto: Stanford UP, 1996. Print.

Coppola, Sofia. "French Royalty as Seen by Hollywood Royalty." Interview by Kristin Hohenadel. *New York Times*. New York Times, 10 Sept. 2006. Web. 7 Feb. 2011.

Coquerel, Athanase-Josué. *Jean Calas et sa famille, étude historique d'après les documents originaux, suivie des dépêches du Cte de Saint-Florentin et des lettres de la sœur A.-J. Fraisse de la Visitation à Mlle Anne Calas*. 1858. Geneva: Slatkine, 1970. Print.

Corneille, Pierre. *Le Cid*. Ed. Georges Forestier. Paris: Magnard, 1988. Print.

———. *Cinna*. Corneille, *Œuvres* 1: 903–69.

———. "Excuse à Ariste." Gasté 64–72.

———. *Œuvres complètes*. Ed. Georges Couton. 3 vols. Paris: Gallimard, 1980. Print.

———. *Polyeucte*. Corneille, *Œuvres* 1: 971–1050.

Cotin, Charles. *Les Énigmes de ce temps*. Ed. Florence Vuilleumier. Paris: Société des Textes Français Modernes, 2003. Print.

Cottin, Sophie. *Claire d'Albe*. Ed. Margaret Cohen. New York: MLA, 2002. Print. MLA Texts and Translations 13.

Cottingham, John. *A Descartes Dictionary*. London: Wiley-Blackwell, 1993. Print.

Coulet, Henri. *Le Roman jusqu'à la révolution*. Paris: Colin, 1967. Print. Vol. 1 of *Histoire du roman en France*.

Craveri, Bernadetta. *L'Age de la conversation*. Paris: Broché, 2002. Print.

———. *The Age of Conversation*. Trans. Teresa Waugh. New York: New York Review of Books, 2006. Print.

Crawford, Katherine. *Perilous Performances: Gender and Regency in Early Modern France*. Cambridge: Harvard UP, 2004. Print.

Crenne, Hélisenne de. *Les Angoisses douloureuses qui procèdent d'amour*. 1538. Ed. Jean-Philippe Beaulieu. Saint-Étienne: U de Saint-Étienne, 2005. Print.

———. *Les Angoysses douloureuses qui procèdent d'amours*. 1538. Ed. Christine de Buzon. Paris: Champion, 1997. Print.

———. *Les Épistres familières et invectives*. 1539. Ed. Jerry C. Nash. Paris: Champion, 1996. Print.

———. *A Renaissance Woman: Hélisenne's Personal and Invective Letters*. Trans. Marianna M. Mustacchi and Paul J. Archambault. Syracuse: Syracuse UP, 1986. Print.

———. *Le Songe de Madame Hélisenne*. Ed. Jean-Philippe Beaulieu and Diane Desrosiers-Bonin. Paris: Champion, 2007. Print.

———. *The Torments of Love*. Trans. Lisa Neal and Steven Rendall. Minneapolis: U of Minnesota P, 1996. Print.

Crompton, Louis. *Homosexuality and Civilization*. Cambridge: Belknap–Harvard UP, 2003. Print.

Cuénin, Micheline. *Roman et société sous Louis XIV: Mme de Villedieu*. Paris: Champion, 1979. Print.

Cuénin, Micheline, and Chantal Morlet-Chantalat. "Châteaux et romans du XVIIe siècle." *Dix-septième siècle* 118–19 (1978): 101–23. Print.

Cuillé, Tili Boon. *Narrative Interludes: Musical Tableaux in Eighteenth-Century French Texts*. Toronto: U of Toronto P, 2006. Print.

Cyr, Myriam. *Letters of a Portuguese Nun: Uncovering the Mystery behind a Seventeenth-Century Forbidden Love*. New York: Miramax, 2006. Print.

Dabbs, Julia K. "Not Mere Child's Play: Jacques Stella's *Jeux et plaisirs de l'enfance*." *Gazette des Beaux Arts* 125 (1995): 303–12. Print.

Dangerous Liaisons. Dir. Stephen Frears. Lorimar Film Entertainment, 1988. Film.

Darmon, Jean-Charles. *Philosophie épicurienne et littérature au XVIIe siècle en France: Études sur Gassendi, Cyrano de Bergerac, La Fontaine, Saint-Evremond.* Paris: PUF, 1988. Print.

Darnton, Robert. *Forbidden Bestsellers of Pre-revolutionary France.* New York: Norton, 1995. Print.

Davis, Natalie Zemon. "Women on Top: Symbolic Sexual Inversion and Political Disorder in Early Modern Europe." *The Reversible World: Symbolic Inversion in Art and Society.* Ed. Barbara A. Babcock. Ithaca: Cornell UP, 1978. 147–90. Print.

Day, Robert Adams. *Told in Letters: Epistolary Fiction before Richardson.* Ann Arbor: U of Michigan P, 1966. Print.

Dayton, Cornelia Hughes. *Women before the Bar: Gender, Law, and Society in Connecticut, 1639–1789.* Chapel Hill: U of North Carolina P, 1995. Print.

Dead Man Walking. Dir. Tim Robbins. Havoc, 1995. Film.

Déclaration des droits de l'homme et du citoyen. *The Age of Enlightenment.* Ed. Otis E. Fellows and Norman Lewis Torrey. Upper Saddle River: Prentice, 1971. 675–77. Print.

Declercq, Gilles, and Michel Murat, eds. *Le Romanesque.* Paris: P de la Sorbonne Nouvelle, 2004. Print.

DeJean, Joan. *Ancients against Moderns: Culture Wars and the Making of a Fin de Siècle.* Chicago: U of Chicago P, 1997. Print.

———. "Classical Reeducation: Decanonizing the Feminine." DeJean and Miller 22–36.

———. "Lafayette's Ellipses: The Privileges of Anonymity." *PMLA* 99.5 (1984): 884–902. Print.

———. *Tender Geographies: Women and the Origins of the Novel in France.* New York: Columbia UP, 1991. Print.

DeJean, Joan, and Nancy K. Miller, eds. *Displacements: Women, Tradition, Literatures in French.* Baltimore: Johns Hopkins UP, 1991. Print.

Delille, Jacques. *Les Jardins.* Paris: F.-A. Didot l'aîné, 1782. Print.

Delisle de Sales, Jean-Baptiste-Claude. *La Vierge d'Otaïti. Théâtre d'un poète de Sybaris, traduit pour la première fois du grec, avec des commentaires, des variantes et des notes, pour servir de supplément au "Théâtre des Grecs."* Orléans: Couret de Villeneuve, 1788. 1–103. Print.

Deloffre, Frédéric. Notice. Guilleragues 61–144.

Delon, Michel. "La Marquise et le philosophe." *Revue des sciences humaines* 54.182 (1981): 65–78. Print.

De Man, Paul. *Aesthetic Ideology.* Ed. Andrzej Warminski. Minneapolis: U of Minnesota P, 1996. Print.

———. *The Resistance to Theory.* Minneapolis: U of Minnesota P, 1986. Print.

Démoris, René. *Le Roman à la première personne.* Paris: Colin, 1975. Print.

Démoris, René, and Gilles Delpierre. "Les Femmes à l'Académie de Peinture sous l'Ancien Régime." Démoris and Delpierre, *Homage* 112–14.

———, eds. *Homage à Elisabeth Sophie Chéron: Texte et peinture à l'âge classique.* Paris: P de la Sorbonne Nouvelle, 1992. Print.

Denis, Delphine. *Le Parnasse galant: Institution d'une catégorie littéraire au XVIIe siècle.* Paris: Champion, 2001. Print.

———. "Romanesque et galanterie au XVIIe siècle." Declercq and Murat 105–17.

Desan, Suzanne. *The Family on Trial in Revolutionary France.* Berkeley: U of California P, 2004. Print.

Descartes, René. *Correspondance avec Élisabeth et autres lettres.* Ed. Jean-Marie Beyssade and Michelle Beyssade. Paris: Flammarion, 1989. Print.

———. *Discours de la méthode. Œuvres complètes.* Ed. Charles Adam and Paul Tannery. Vol. 6. Paris: Vrin, 1996. 1–78. Print. 11 vols.

———. *Meditations on First Philosophy.* Descartes, *Philosophical Writings* 2: 1–62.

———. *Les Passions de l'âme.* Paris: Flammarion, 1996. Print.

———. *Passions of the Soul.* Descartes, *Philosophical Writings* 1: 325–404.

———. *The Philosophical Writings of Descartes.* Trans. John Cottingham, Robert Stoothoff, and Dugald Murdoch. 3 vols. Cambridge: Cambridge UP, 2006. Print.

———. *Principles of Philosophy.* Descartes, *Philosophical Writings* 1: 193–291.

———. *Rules for the Direction of the Mind.* Descartes, *Philosophical Writings* 1: 9–76.

———. *Traité de l'homme.* Ed. A. Bitbol-Hespéridès. Paris: Seuil, 1996. Print.

Des Essarts, Nicolas-Toussaint. "Cause de séparation: Faits singuliers." [Mézières case, cause 93]. Des Essarts, *Causes* 35: 95–132.

———, ed. *Causes célèbres, curieuses et intéressantes, de toutes les cours souveraines du royaume avec les jugemens qui les ont décidées.* 165 vols. Paris: P. C. Simon, 1773–87. Print.

———. "Demande en séparation de corps et de biens." [Aubailly de La Berge case, cause 577]. Des Essarts, *Causes* 158: 97–207.

———. "Demande en séparation de corps et de biens." [Rouches case, cause 341]. Des Essarts, *Causes* 105: 3–126.

———. "Le Mal vénérien est-il une cause de séparation?" [Blé case, cause 2]. Des Essarts, *Causes* 1: 135–83.

Deshoulières, Antoinette. *Genséric.* Gethner, *Femmes dramaturges* 2: 157–234.

Deshoulières, Antoinette, and Antoinette-Thérèse Deshoulières. *Œuvres de Madame et Mademoiselle Deshoulières.* 2 vols. Paris: Libraires Associés, 1764. Print.

Desprechins, Anne. "Regard de Madame de Sévigné sur le jardin." *Correspondances: Mélanges offerts à Roger Duchêne.* Ed. Roger Duchêne, Wolfgang Leiner, and Pierre Ronzeaud. Aix-en-Provence: U de Provence, 1992. 395–404. Print.

Desrochers, Étienne. *Portrait de Mlle L'Héritier. Contes de Fées. Expositions.* Bibliothèque Nationale de France, n.d. Web. 20 May 2010.

Des Roches, Madeleine, and Catherine Des Roches. *Les Missives.* Paris: Abel Angelier, 1586. Print.

Diaz, Brigitte. "De la lettre aux *Mémoires*: Les Fonctions autobiographiques de la lettres dans la correspondance de jeunesse de Mme Roland (1767–1780)." *Femmes en toutes lettres: Les Épistolières du XVIIIe siècle.* Ed. Marie-France Silver and Marie-Laure Girou Swiderski. Oxford: Voltaire Foundation, 2000. 211–27. Print.

Dickens, Charles. *Hard Times*. Ed. George Ford and Sylvere Monod. New York: Norton, 1990. Print.

Dictionnaire de l'Académie Française. Dictionnaires d'autrefois. The ARTFL Project. ARTFL Project, U of Chicago, n.d. Web. 19 Mar. 2010.

Diderot, Denis. *Correspondance: Décembre 1757–Novembre 1759*. Ed. Georges Roth. Vol. 2. Paris: Minuit, 1956. Print.

———. *La Religieuse*. Ed. Annie Collognat-Barès. Paris: Pocket, 1997. Print.

———. *Supplément au* Voyage de Bougainville. Ed. Michel Delon. Paris: Folio Classique, 2002. Print.

Diefendorf, Barbara B. *From Penitence to Charity: Pious Women and the Catholic Reformation in Paris*. Oxford: Oxford UP, 2004. Print.

———. "Give Us Back Our Children: Patriarchal Authority and Parental Consent to Religious Vocations in Early Counter-Reformation France." *Journal of Modern History* 68.2 (1996): 265–307. Print.

van Dijk, Suzan. "L'Abbé de La Porte et la canonisation des romancières du XVIIIe siècle. Le cas de Françoise de Graffigny." *Romanistische Zeitschrift für Literaturgeschichte* 1997 (21): 43–54. Print.

———. "Pardonner à un homme? Attitudes de l'écrivaine et de ses personnages dans les lettres authentiques et fictionnelles." *Madame Riccoboni, une diversité décontractée*. Ed. Jan Herman and Paul Pelckmans. Paris: Peeters, 2008. 47–61. Print.

———. *WomenWriters*. Huygens Instituut, 2009. Web. 17 June 2010.

"Dissertation sur la question proposée dans le second Extraordinaire du *Mercure*." *Mercure galant* Oct. 1678: 135–50. *Gallica*. Bibliothèque Nationale de France. Web. 9 Sept. 2010.

Donovan, Josephine. "Women and the Rise of the Novel: A Feminist-Marxist Theory." *Signs* 16.3 (1991): 441–62. Print.

Doody, Margaret Anne. *The True Story of the Novel*. New Brunswick: Rutgers UP, 1997. Print.

Doubrovsky, Serge. *Corneille ou la dialectique du héros*. Paris: Gallimard, 1963. Print.

Douthwaite, Julia V. *Exotic Women: Literary Heroines and Cultural Strategies in Ancien Régime France*. Philadelphia: U of Pennsylvania P, 1992. Print.

Dream Anatomy. National Library of Medicine. US Natl. Lib. of Medicine, Natl. Insts. of Health, 9 July 2009. Web. 28 Apr. 2010.

Du Boccage, Anne-Marie. *Les Amazones*. Gethner, *Femmes dramaturges* 2: 371–445.

Du Bosc, Jacques. *Nouveau Recueil de lettres des dames de ce temps*. Paris: Augustin Courbé, 1635. Print.

Du Châtelet, Gabrielle-Emilie. *Le Discours sur le bonheur*. Paris: Payot-Rivages, 1997. Print.

Duchêne, Roger. *Écrire au temps de Madame de Sévigné: Lettres et textes littéraires*. Paris: Vrin, 1982. Print.

———. *Madame de Lafayette*. Paris: Fayard, 1988. Print.

Du Deffand, Marie. *Lettres de la marquise Du Deffand à Horace Walpole (1766–1780)*. Ed. Paget Toynbee. 3 vols. London: Methuen, 1912. Print.

Duggan, Anne E. "Lovers, Salon, and State: *La Carte de Tendre* and the Mapping of Socio-political Relations." *Dalhousie French Studies* 39 (1996): 15–22. Print.

Du Noyer, Anne-Marguerite. *Letters from a Lady at Paris to a Lady at Avignon, Containing a Particular Account of the City, the Politicks, Intrigues, Gallantry, and Secret History of Persons of the First Quality in France.* 2 vols. London: W. Means and J. Browne, 1716–17. Print.

———. *Lettres historiques et galantes de deux dames de condition.* Cologne: Pierre Marteau, 1713. Print.

———. *Mémoires.* Ed. Henriette Goldwyn. Paris: Mercure de France, 2005. Print.

———. *Mémoires de Mme Du N*** écrits par elle-même.* 5 vols. Cologne: Pierre Marteau, 1710–11. Print.

Durand, Catherine. *Comédies en proverbes.* Gethner, *Femmes dramaturges* 2: 235–318.

Duras, Claire de. *Ourika, an English Translation.* Trans. John Fowles. New York: MLA, 1994. Print.

Du Rousseaud de La Combe, Guy. "De la séparation entre mari et femme." *Recueil de jurisprudence civile.* 1st ed. Paris: Mesnier, 1736. 346–47. Print.

———. "De la séparation entre mari et femme." *Recueil de jurisprudence civile.* 4th ed. Paris: Knapen, 1769. Sec. 9, 639. Print.

L'Édit de Fontainebleau ou la Révocation (1685). Musée Virtuel du Protestantisme Français. Musée Virtuel du Protestantisme Français, 1994. Web. 25 Dec. 2006.

L'Édit de Nantes. 1598. *Centre d'Édition de Textes Électroniques.* U de Nantes, n.d. Web. 17 Nov. 2010.

Elias, Norbert. *The Civilizing Process.* Trans. Edmund Jephcott. Oxford: Blackwell, 1994. Print.

———. *The Court Society.* Ed. Stephen Mennell. Trans. Edmund Jephcott. Dublin: U Coll. Dublin P, 2006. Print.

Elisabeth of Bohemia and René Descartes. *The Correspondence between Princess Elisabeth of Bohemia and René Descartes.* Ed. and trans. Lisa Shapiro. Chicago: U of Chicago P, 2007. Print. The Other Voice in Early Modern Europe.

Encyclopédie, ou Dictionnaire raisonné des sciences, des arts et des métiers. 1751–80. Stuttgart-Bad Cannstatt: Frommann, 1966. Print.

Engels, Friedrich. *The Condition of the Working Class in England.* Ed. David McLellan. Oxford: Oxford UP, 1993. Print.

Épinay, Louise Tardieu d'Esclavelles, marquise d'. *Les Contre-confessions: Histoire de Madame de Montbrillant.* [1818]. Pref. Elisabeth Badinter. Notes by Georges Roth. Paris: Mercure de France, 1989. Print.

———. *Les Conversations d'Émilie.* Paris: Bélin, 1783. Print.

———. *Memoirs and Correspondence of Madame d'Épinay.* Trans. J. H. Freese. London: H. S. Nichols, 1899. Microfilm. Research Publications, 1977, reel 539, no. 4140.

Evain, Aurore, Perry Gethner, and Henriette Goldwyn, eds. *Théâtre de femmes de l'Ancien Régime.* 2 vols. to date. Saint-Étienne: U de Saint-Étienne, 2006– . Print.

Faessel, Sonia. *Visions des îles: Tahiti et l'imaginaire européen. Du mythe à son exploitation littéraire (XVIIIe–XXe siècles).* Paris: L'Harmattan, 2006. Print.

Farrell, Michèle Longino (*see also* Longino, Michèle). *Performing Motherhood: The Sévigné Correspondence.* Hanover: UP of New England, 1991. Print.

Fauchery, Pierre. *La Destinée féminine dans le roman européen du dix-huitième siècle, 1713–1807. Essai de gynécomythie romanesque.* Paris: Colin, 1972. Print.

Flaubert, Gustave. *Par les champs et par les grèves.* Ed. Adrianne J. Tooke. Geneva: Droz, 1987. Print.

Flax, Jane. "The Conflict between Nurturance and Autonomy in Mother-Daughter Relationships and within Feminism." *Feminist Studies* 4.2 (1978): 171–89. Print.

Foley, Helene, ed. *The Homeric Hymn to Demeter.* Bloomington: Indiana UP, 1989. Print.

Fontenelle, Bernard Le Bouvier de. *Conversations on the Plurality of Worlds.* 1686. Ed. and introd. Nina Rattner Gelbart. Trans. H. A. Hargreaves. Berkeley: U of California P, 1990. Print.

———. *Les Entretiens sur la pluralité des mondes.* 1686. Ed. Christophe Martin. Paris: Flammarion, 1998. Print.

———. "Lettre d'un géometre de Guyenne." 1678. Laugaa 22–25.

Force, Pierre. "Doute métaphysique et vérité romanesque dans *La Princesse de Clèves* et *Zaïde.*" *Romantic Review* 83.2 (1992): 161–76. Print.

Foulché-Delbosc, R. *Bibliographie des voyages en Espagne et en Portugal.* Paris: Welter, 1896. Print.

———. "Madame d'Aulnoy." Aulnoy, *Relation* [1926] 6–22.

———. "Madame d'Aulnoy and Spain." Aulnoy, *Travels* [2004] i–lxxiv.

Fouquet, Françoise. *Les Remèdes charitables de Madame Fouquet, pour guérir à peu de frais toute forme de maux tant internes qu'externes, invéterez, et qui ont passé jusques à présent pour incurables, experimentez par la meme.* Lyon: Jean Certes, 1685. *Gallica.* Web. 29 Apr. 2010.

The Four Seasons. Duke University Medical Center Library. History of Medicine Collections, Duke U, 2010. Web. 28 Apr. 2010.

Francillon, Roger. *L'Œuvre romanesque de Madame de Lafayette.* Paris: Corti, 1973. Print.

François, Alexis. *Histoire de la langue française cultivée des origins à nos jours.* 2 vols. Geneva: Julien, 1959. Print.

Frappat, Bruno. "Un Fléau social: Les Femmes battues." *Le Monde* 4 Nov. 1975: 10. Print.

Fraser, Antonia. *Marie Antoinette: The Journey.* New York: Nan A. Talese–Doubleday, 2001. Print.

French, Roger. *Dissection and Vivisection in the European Renaissance.* Aldershot: Ashgate, 1999. Print.

Fried, Michael. *Absorption and Theatricality: Painting and Beholder in the Age of Diderot.* Chicago: U of Chicago P, 1980. Print.

Fryberger, Betsy G. *The Changing Garden: Four Centuries of European and American Art.* Berkeley: U of California P, 2003. Print.

Furetière, Antoine. *Dictionnaire universel.* 1690. 3 vols. Ed. Alain Rey. Paris: SNL–Le Robert, 1978. Print.

———. *Le Roman bourgeois.* 1666. Ed. Marine Roy-Garibal. Paris: Flammarion, 2001. Print.

Gaines, James F., and Michael S. Koppisch, eds. *Approaches to Teaching Molière's Tartuffe and Other Plays.* New York: MLA, 1995. Print.

Galen. *On the Usefulness of the Parts of the Body.* Ed. and trans. Margaret Tallmadge May. Ithaca: Cornell UP, 1968. Print.

Gallagher, Catherine. *Nobody's Story: The Vanishing Acts of Women Writers in the Marketplace, 1670–1820.* Berkeley: U of California P, 1994. Print.

Garrisson, Janine. *L'Édit de Nantes et sa révocation: Histoire d'une intolérance.* Paris: Seuil, 1985. Print.

Gasté, Armand, ed. *La Querelle du Cid: Pièces et pamphlets.* Paris: H. Welter, 1899. Print.

Gelbart, Nina Rattner. Introduction. Fontenelle, *Conversations* vii–xxxii.

Génetiot, Alain. "L'Épître en vers mondaine de Voiture à Mme Deshoulières." *Littératures classiques* 18 (1993): 103–14. Print.

Genlis, Stéphanie-Félicité Du Crest, comtesse de. *Adèle et Théodore, ou Lettres sur l'éducation.* Paris: Lecointe and Durey, 1827. Print.

———. *De l'esprit des étiquettes de l'ancienne cour et des usages du monde de ce temps.* Paris: Mercure de France, 1996. Print.

———. "Histoire de la Duchesse de C***." *Adèle et Théodore, ou Lettres sur l'éducation.* 1782. Paris: Maradan, 1804. 3: 96–193. Print.

———. *Histoire de la Duchesse de C***.* Ed. Mary Trouille. Critical ed. with orig. English trans. Oxford: Mod. Humanities Research Assn., 2010. Print. Critical Texts Ser.

———. *Les Petits Émigrés, ou Correspondance de quelques enfans.* Paris: Maredan, 1803. Print.

Gethner, Perry. "Conspirators and Tyrants in the Plays of Villedieu." Lalande 31–42.

———, ed. *Femmes dramaturges en France (1650–1750): Pièces choisies.* 2 vols. Tübingen: Narr, 1993, 2002. Print. Biblio 17.

Gewirtz, Paul. "Narrative and Rhetoric in the Law." *Law's Stories: Narrative and Rhetoric in the Law.* Ed. Peter Brooks and Gewirtz. New Haven: Yale UP, 1996. 2–13. Print.

Girard, Quentin. "'La Princesse de Clèves,' un livre pour Sarkozy." *Slate* 18 Mar. 2009. Web. 9 June 2011.

Godineau, Dominique. *Les Femmes dans la société française. 16e–18e siècle.* Paris: Colin, 2003. Print.

Goldsmith, Elizabeth C. *Exclusive Conversations: The Art of Interaction in Seventeenth-Century France.* Philadelphia: U of Pennsylvania P, 1988. Print.

———. *Publishing Women's Life Stories in France, 1647–1720.* Aldershot: Ashgate, 2001. Print.

———. "The Quarrel over *La Princesse de Clèves.*" Beasley and Jensen 30–37.

———, ed. *Writing the Female Voice: Essays on Epistolary Literature.* Boston: Northeastern UP, 1989. Print.

Goldsmith, Elizabeth C., and Dena Goodman, eds. *Going Public: Women and Publishing in Early Modern France.* Ithaca: Cornell UP, 1995. Print.

Goldsmith, Elizabeth C., and Colette H. Winn, eds. *Lettres des femmes: Textes inédits et oubliés du XVIe au XVIIIe siècles.* Paris: Champion, 2005. Print.

Goldwyn, Henriette. Introduction. Du Noyer, *Mémoires* [2005] 7–24.

———. "Men in Love in the Plays of Madame de Villedieu." Lalande 64–83.

Gomez, Madeleine-Angélique de. *Marsidie reine des Cimbres.* Evain, Gethner, and Goldwyn 3: forthcoming.

Goncourt, Edmond de, and Jules de Goncourt. *La Femme au XVIIIe siècle*. Paris: Charpentier, 1882. Print.

Gontier, Fernande. *Histoire de la comtesse d'Aulnoy*. Paris: Perrin, 2005. Print.

Goodman, Dena. *Becoming a Woman in the Age of Letters*. Ithaca: Cornell UP, 2009. Print.

———. "Letter Writing and the Emergence of Gendered Subjectivity in Eighteenth-Century France." *Journal of Women's History* 17.2 (2005): 9–37. Print.

———. *Marie-Antoinette: Writings on the Body of a Queen*. New York: Routledge, 2003. Print.

———. *The Republic of Letters: A Cultural History of the French Enlightenment*. Ithaca: Cornell UP, 1994. Print.

Goodman, Katherine R. "Klein Paris and Women's Writing: Luise Gottsched's Unknown Complaints." *Daphnis* 25.4 (1996): 695–711. Print.

Gothein, Marie Luise Schroeter. *A History of Garden Art*. Ed. Walter P. Wright. Trans. Mrs. Archer-Hind. Vol. 2. London: Dent; New York: Dutton, 1928. Print.

Gouges, Olympe de. "Déclaration des droits de la femme et de la citoyenne." 1791. *Écrits politiques*. Ed. Olivier Blanc. Paris: Côté-Femmes, 1993. 1: 205–15. Print.

———. *L'Entrée de Dumouriez à Bruxelles*. de Gouges, *Théâtre* 1: 131–244.

———. *L'Esclavage des noirs*. 1789. Paris: Côté-Femmes, 1991. Print.

———. *Molière chez Ninon, ou le siècle des grands hommes*. Paris: L'Auteur et Cailleau, 1788. Print.

———. *La Nécessité du divorce*. de Gouges, *Théâtre* 2: 145–81.

———. *Théâtre politique*. Paris: Côté-Femmes, 1991. Print.

Gournay, Marie de. *Égalité des hommes et des femmes; suivi de* Grief des dames. Ed. Claude Pinganaud. Paris: Arléa, 2008. Print.

Graffigny, Françoise de. *Cenia*. The Lunatic Lover *and Other Plays by French Women of the Seventeenth and Eighteenth Centuries*. Ed. Perry Gethner. Portsmouth: Heineman, 1994. 269–330. Print.

———. *Cénie*. Gethner, *Femmes dramaturges* 1: 315–72.

———. *Correspondance*. Ed. English Showalter et al. 13 vols. to date. Oxford: Voltaire Foundation, 1985– . Print.

———. *Letters from a Peruvian Woman*. Trans. David Kornacker. New York: MLA, 1993. Print. MLA Texts and Translations 2.

———. *Lettres d'une Péruvienne*. 1747. Ed. Joan DeJean and Nancy K. Miller. New York: MLA, 1993. Print. MLA Texts and Translations 2.

———. *Lettres d'une Péruvienne*. Ed. Jonathan Mallinson. Oxford: Voltaire Foundation, 2002. Print.

———. *The Peruvian Letters*. Trans. R. Roberts. 2 vols. London: T. Cadell, 1774. Print.

Grande, Nathalie. *Stratégies de romancières: De* Clélie *à* La Princesse de Clèves *(1654–1678)*. Paris: Champion, 1999. Print.

Greenberg, Mitchell. *Corneille, Classicism, and the Ruses of Symmetry*. Cambridge: Cambridge UP, 1986. Print.

Grenaille, François de. *L'Honnête Fille*. Paris: Jean Paslé, 1640. Print.

Groult, Benoîte. Preface. *Crie moins fort, les voisins vont t'entendre*. By Erin Pizzey. Trans. Collectif de Traduction des Éditions des Femmes. Paris: Des Femmes, 1975. 7–14. Print.

Guénoun, Solange. "*Clélie*: Terres inconnues et imaginaires. Pour une épistémologie du transport." *Papers on French Seventeenth-Century Literature* 16 (1984): 81–100. Print.

Guilleragues, Gabriel Joseph de Lavergne, vicomte de. *Lettres portugaises. Chansons et bons mots, Valentins*, Lettres portugaises. Ed. Frédéric Deloffre and Jacques Rougeot. Geneva: Droz, 1972. 61–177. Print.

Guyon, Jeanne-Marie. *Correspondance*. Paris: Champion, 2003. Print.

———. *Le "Moyen court" et autres récits*. Ed. Marie-Louise Gondal. Grenoble: Millon, 1992. Print.

———. *La Vie par elle-même et autres écrits biographiques*. Ed. Dominique Tronc. Paris: Champion, 2001. Print.

Guyot, Joseph-Nicolas. *Répertoire universel et raisonné de jurisprudence*. Paris: Visse, 1785. Print.

Hagen, Rose-Marie, and Rainer Hagen. *What Great Paintings Say*. 2 vols. Cologne: Taschen, 2003. Print.

Haraway, Donna. *Simians, Cyborgs, and Women: The Reinvention of Nature*. London: Routledge, 1991. Print.

Harrison, Jane E. *Until Next Year: Letter-Writing and the Mails in the Canadas, 1640–1830*. Quebec: Canadian Museum of Civilization, 1997. Print.

Harth, Erica. *Cartesian Women: Versions and Subversions of Rational Discourse in the Old Regime*. Ithaca: Cornell UP, 1992. Print.

———. *Ideology and Culture in Seventeenth-Century France*. Ithaca: Cornell UP, 1983. Print.

Hartle, Ann. *Michel de Montaigne: Accidental Philosopher*. Cambridge: Cambridge UP, 2003. Print.

Hazard, Paul. *La Crise de la conscience européenne, 1680–1715*. 1935. Paris: Fayard, 1961. Print. Trans. as *The European Mind, the Critical Years, 1680–1715*.

Hazlehurst, F. Hamilton. *Gardens of Illusion: The Genius of André Le Nôtre*. Nashville: Vanderbilt UP, 1980. Print.

Heise, Ursula K. "The Hitchhiker's Guide to Ecocriticism." *PMLA* 121.2 (2006): 503–16. Print.

Hémon-Fabre, Catherine, and Pierre-Eugène Leroy, eds. *Antoinette Des Houlières: L'Enchantement des chagrins*. Paris: Bartillat, 2005. Print.

Hepp, Noémi. "L'Arrière-saison, 1685–1715." *Précis de littérature française du XVIIe siècle*. Ed. Jean Mesnard. Paris: PUF, 1990. 309–425. Print.

Hesse, Carla. *The Other Enlightenment: How French Women Became Modern*. Princeton: Princeton UP, 2001. Print.

Hester, Nathalie. "Travel and the Art of Telling the Truth: Marie-Catherine d'Aulnoy's *Travels to Spain*." *Huntington Library Quarterly* 70.1 (2007): 87–102. Print.

Hipp, Marie-Thérèse. *Mythes et réalités, enquête sur le roman et les mémoires, 1660–1700*. Paris: Klincksieck, 1976. Print.

Hirschman, Albert O. *The Passions and the Interests: Political Arguments for Capitalism before Its Triumph*. Princeton: Princeton UP, 1977. Print.

Histoire de France. Paris: Larousse, 2002. Print.

Hodgson, Barbara. *No Place for a Lady: Tales of Adventurous Women Travelers.* Berkeley: Ten Speed, 2002. Print.

Hoffmann, Kathryn A. *Society of Pleasures: Interdisciplinary Readings in Pleasure and Power during the Reign of Louis XIV*. New York: St. Martin's, 1997. Print.

Hogg, Chloé. "Staging Fouquet: Historical and Theatrical Contexts of Villedieu's *Le Favori*." Lalande 43–63.

Holt, Mack P. *The French Wars of Religion, 1562–1629*. Cambridge: Cambridge UP, 1995. Print.

Horowitz, Louise K. "Primary Sources: *La Princesse de Clèves.*" *French Forum* 25.2 (2000): 165–75. Print.

———. "Truly Inimitable? Repetition in *La Princesse de Clèves*." Beasley and Jensen 120–26.

Hunt, Lynn. *The Family Romance of the French Revolution*. Berkeley: U of California P, 1992. Print.

Jackson, J. B. *Discovering the Vernacular Landscape*. New Haven: Yale UP, 1984. Print.

Jensen, Katharine Ann. "Making Sense of the Ending: Passion, Virtue, and Female Subjectivity." Beasley and Jensen 68–75.

———. *Uneasy Possessions: The Mother-Daughter Dilemma in French Women's Writings, 1671–1928*. Newark: U of Delaware P, 2011. Print.

———. *Writing Love: Letters, Women, and the Novel in France, 1605–1776*. Carbondale: Southern Illinois UP, 1995. Print.

Johnson, Barbara. "Teaching Ignorance: *L'École des femmes.*" *Yale French Studies* 63 (1982): 165–82. Print.

Join-Lambert, Sophie, and Maxime Préaud, eds. *Abraham Bosse: Savant Graveur: Tours, vers 1604–1676, Paris*. Paris: Bibliothèque Nationale de Paris, 2004. Print.

Joinville, Jean de. *La Vie de Saint-Louis*. Paris: Livre de Poche–Lettres Gothiques, 2002. Print.

Josephine-Marie de l'Incarnation. *La Relation du martyre des seize Carmélites de Compiègne: Aux sources de Bernanos et de Gertrud von Le Fort*. Ed. William Bush. Paris: Du Cerf, 1993. Print.

Joubert, Laurent. *Popular Errors*. Trans. Gregory David de Rocher. Tuscaloosa: U of Alabama P, 1989. Print. Trans of *Erreurs populaires*.

Jussie, Jeanne de. *Petite Chronique*. Ed. Helmut Feld. Mainz: Von Zabern, 1996. Print.

———. *The Short Chronicle: A Poor Clare's Account of the Reformation of Geneva*. Ed. and trans. Carrie F. Klaus. Chicago: U of Chicago P, 2006. Print.

Justification de Monsieur Henley. Le Mari sentimental, Lettres de Mistriss Henley, Justification de Mr Henley. Genève: Buisson, 1785. 303–60. Print.

Kafalenos, Emma. *Narrative Causalities*. Columbus: Ohio UP, 2006. Print.

Kaplan, E. Ann. *Motherhood and Representation: The Mother in Popular Culture and Melodrama*. New York: Routledge, 1992. Print.

Keller-Rahbé, Edwige, and Nathalie Grande, eds. *Madame de Villedieu et le théâtre*. Tübingen: Narr, 2009. Print. Biblio 17.

King, Margaret L., and Albert Rabil, Jr. "Editors' Introduction to the Series." *Declamation on the Nobility and Preeminence of the Female Sex.* By Henricus Cornelius Agrippa. Ed. and trans. Rabil. Chicago: U of Chicago P, 1996. i–xxviii. Print.

———, eds. *Teaching Other Voices: Women and Religion in Early Modern Europe.* Chicago: U of Chicago P, 2007. Print.

Kipling, Rudyard. "The Mark of the Beast." *"The Mark of the Beast" and Other Horror Tales.* Ed. S. T. Joshi. New York: Dover, 2000. 70–80. Print.

Klein, Joachim. "Französische Gedichte in russischen Übersetzungen der 1760er Jahre (mit einem Seitenblick auf die russische Rousseau-Rezeption)." *Semiosis: Semiotics and the History of Culture.* Ann Arbor: U of Michigan P, 1984. 359–75. Print.

Kroll, Renate. "La Chanson des femmes poètes au XVIIe siècle: Mme de La Suze et Mme Deshoulières." *La Chanson française et son histoire.* Ed. Dietmar Rieger. Tübingen: Narr, 1988. 27–45. Print.

Kuizenga, Donna. "Espaces féminins? La topique des lieux dans les *Nouvelles Afriquaines* et les *Mémoires de la vie de Henriette-Sylvie de Molière* de Mme de Villedieu." *Locus in Fabula: La Topique de l'espace dans les fictions françaises d'Ancien Régime.* Ed. Nathalie Ferrand. Louvain: Peeters, 2004. 407–18. Print.

La Bruyère, Jean de. *Les Caractères.* Ed. Robert Pignarre. Paris: Flammarion, 1996. Print.

La Chapelle. *L'Illustre Philosophe ou l'histoire de sainte Catherine d'Alexandrie.* Ed. Paul Scott. Evain, Gethner, and Goldwyn 2: 223–315.

Lachèvre, Frédéric. *Les Derniers Libertins.* Paris: Champion, 1924. Print.

Laclos, Pierre Choderlos de. *Dangerous Liaisons.* Trans. Douglas Parmée. New York: Oxford UP, 1999. Print.

———. *Les Liaisons dangereuses.* 1782. Ed. René Pomeau. Paris: Flammarion, 1996. Print.

Laden, Marie-Paule. "Virtue and Civility in *La Princesse de Clèves.*" Beasley and Jensen 54–59.

Lafayette, Marie-Madeleine Pioche de la Vergne, comtesse de. *Correspondance.* Ed. André Beaunier. 2 vols. Paris: Gallimard, 1942. Print.

———. *La Princesse de Clèves.* Ed. Dorian Astor. Paris: Gallimard, 2005. Print. Folioplus Classiques.

———. *La Princesse de Clèves. Œuvres complètes.* Ed. Roger Duchêne. Paris: Bourin, 1990. Print.

———. *La Princesse de Clèves.* 1678. Ed. Jean Mesnard. Paris: Flammarion, 1996. Print.

———. *The Princesse de Clèves.* Lafayette, *The Princesse de Clèves* 1–156.

———. *The Princesse de Clèves.* Trans. Terence Cave. Oxford: Oxford UP, 1992. Print.

———. *La Princesse de Montpensier.* Lafayette, *Romans* 1–33.

———. *The Princesse de Montpensier.* Lafayette, *The Princesse de Clèves* 157–88.

———. *Romans et nouvelles.* Ed. Émile Magne. Introd. Alain Niderst. Paris: Garnier, 1970. Print.

———. *Zayde: A Spanish Romance.* Ed. and trans. Nicholas Paige. Chicago: U of Chicago P, 2006. Print. The Other Voice in Early Modern Europe.

————. *Zayde, histoire espagnole*. Ed. Camille Esmein-Sarrazin. Paris: Flammarion, 2006. Print.

La Fontaine, Jean de. *Fables*. Paris: Flammarion, 2004. Print.

————. *Œuvres complètes*. Ed. Jean-Pierre Collinet and Pierre Clarac. 2 vols. Paris: Gallimard, 1958–91. Print.

Lagniet, Jacques. *Recueil des plus illustres proverbes divisés en trois livres*. Paris, 1663. Print.

La Harpe, Jean-François de. *Lycée, ou Cours de littérature ancienne et moderne*. Paris: Crapelet, 1816. Print.

Lalande, Roxanne, ed. *A Labor of Love: Critical Reflections on the Writings of Marie-Catherine Desjardins (Mme de Villedieu)*. Madison: Fairleigh Dickinson UP, 2000. Print.

Lambert, Anne-Thérèse de Marguenat de Courcelles, marquise de. *Réflexions nouvelles sur les femmes*. 1727. Paris: Côté-Femmes, 1989. Print.

————. *Réflexions sur le goût*. *Œuvres*. Paris: Veuve Ganeau, 1748. 1: 141–47. Print.

Lamorlière, Rosalie. *La Dernière Prison de Marie-Antoinette*. Paris: H. Gautier, 1897. Print.

"Landscape." *Oxford English Dictionary*. Reissued 1st ed. 1933. Print.

La Porte, Joseph de. *Histoire littéraire des femmes françaises*. Paris: Lacombe, 1769. Print.

————. Rev. of *Lettres de Milady Juliette Catesby*, by Marie-Jeanne Riccoboni. *Observateur littéraire* 1 (1759): 314–37. Print.

————. Rev. of *Lettres d'une Péruvienne*, by Françoise de Graffigny. *Observations sur la littérature moderne*. Vol. 1. Paris: La Haye, 1749. 33–54. Print. 9 vols. Rpt. in Graffigny, *Lettres* [2002] 267–76.

Laqueur, Thomas. *Making Sex: Body and Gender from the Greeks to Freud*. Cambridge: Harvard UP, 1992. Print.

————. "Orgasm, Generation, and the Politics of Reproductive Biology." *Representations* 14 (1986): 3–23. Print.

————. "Sex in the Flesh." *Isis* 94.2 (2003): 300–06. Print.

La Rochefoucauld, François de. *Maximes et réflexions diverses*. Paris: Flammarion, 1999. Print.

————. *Portrait de La Rochefoucauld par lui-même*. *Encyclopédie de L'Agora*. Encyclopédie de L'Agora, 2000. Web. 28 Jan. 2011.

La Roche-Guilhen, Anne de. *Rare-en-tout*. Gethner, *Femmes dramaturges* 1: 127–80.

La Rochejacquelein, Marie de Donnissan, marquise de. *Mémoires de la marquise de La Rochejacquelein*. Ed. André Sarazin. Paris: Mercure de France, 1984. Print.

La Suze, Henriette de Coligny, comtesse de. *Poésies de Madame la Comtesse de la Suze*. Paris: Charles de Sercy, 1666. Print.

————. *Recueil de pièces galantes en prose et en vers de Madame la Comtesse de la Suze, comme aussi de plusieurs autres auteurs*. Vol. 4. Paris: Gabriel Quinet, 1680. Print.

Lathuillère, Roger. *La Préciosité: Étude historique et linguistique*. Geneva: Droz, 1969. Print.

La Tour Du Pin, Henriette-Lucy Pillon, marquise de. *Mémoires de la Marquise de La Tour Du Pin: Journal d'une femme de cinquante ans.* Paris: Mercure de France, 1989. Print.

Laudy, Bernard. "La Vision tragique de Madame de Lafayette, ou un jansénisme athée." *Revue de l'Institut de Sociologie* 3 (1969): 121–34. Print.

Laugaa, Maurice. *Lectures de Madame de Lafayette.* Paris: Colin, 1971. Print.

Lauzun, Armand-Louis Gontaut, duc de. *Mémoires du duc de Lauzun.* Ed. Georges d'Heylli. Paris: Edouard Rouveyre, 1880. Print.

Le Goff, Jacques. *Histoire de la France religieuse.* Paris: Seuil, 1988. Print.

Lennox, Charlotte. *The Female Quixote; or, The Adventures of Arabella.* 1799. Ed. Margaret Dalziel. Oxford: Oxford UP, 2008. Print.

Leone, Ann. "*La Princesse de Clèves* and the Politics of Versailles Garden Design." *Mosaic* 27.2 (1994): 25–48. Print.

Lescure, Mathurin de. "Madame des Houllières: Sa vie et ses ouvrages." *Œuvres choisies de Mme des Houllières.* Paris: Librairie des Bibliophiles, 1882. i–xxii. Print.

Lettres portugaises et suites. Ed. Anne-Marie Clin-Lalande. Paris: Hachette, 2001. Print.

Letts, Janet. *Legendary Lives in* La Princesse de Clèves. Charlottesville: Rookwood, 1998. Print.

Lhéritier de Villandon, Marie-Jeanne. "Les Enchantements de l'éloquence." *Les Contes de fées du XVIIème siècle.* Ed. Christine Rousseau. Rousseau, n.d. Web. 24 Mar. 2010.

———. "Les Enchantements de l'éloquence." Perrault, *Contes* 239–70.

———. *Œuvres meslées, contenant L'innocente tromperie, L'avare puni, Les enchantemens de l'éloquence, Les aventures de Finette, nouvelles et autres ouvrages, en vers et en prose, de Mlle L'H*** [L'Héritier de Villandon], avec le Triomphe de Mme Des Houlières, tel qu'il a été composé par Mlle L'H***.* Paris: J. Guignard, 1696. *Gallica.* Bibliothèque Nationale de France. Web. 20 May 2010.

Lilti, Antoine. *Le Monde des salons: Sociabilité et mondanité à Paris au XVIIIe siècle.* Paris: Fayard, 2005. Print.

Linguet, Simon-Nicolas-Henri. *Lettre du marquis de C*** au comte de F*** contre le divorce.* Paris: Desenne, 1790. Print.

Littré, Émile. *Dictionnaire de la langue française.* Paris: Hachette, 1863–72. Print.

Longino, Michèle (*see also* Farrell, Michèle Longino). "The Mother-Daughter Subtext in *La Princesse de Clèves.*" Beasley and Jensen 76–84.

Loskoutoff, Yvan. *La Sainte et la fée: Dévotion à l'enfant Jésus et mode des contes merveilleux à la fin du règne de Louis XIV.* Geneva: Droz, 1987. Print.

Lougee, Carolyn. *Le Paradis des Femmes: Women, Salons, and Social Stratification in Seventeenth-Century France.* Princeton: Princeton UP, 1976. Print.

Louis XIV. *Manière de montrer les jardins de Versailles.* Paris: Plon, 1951. Print.

———. *The Way to Present the Gardens of Versailles.* Trans. John F. Stewart. 1982. Paris: Réunion des Musées Nationaux, 1992. Print.

Lully, Jean-Baptiste, and Philippe Quinault. *Amadis.* Paris: Christophe Ballard, 1684. Print.

MacArthur, Elizabeth J. *Extravagant Narratives: Closure and Dynamics in the Epistolary Form.* Princeton: Princeton UP, 1990. Print.

Maclean, Ian. *Woman Triumphant, 1610–52.* Oxford: Oxford UP, 1977. Print.

The Magdalene Sisters. Dir. Peter Mullan. Scottish Screen, 2002. Film.

Maintenon, Françoise d'Aubigné, marquise de. *Correspondance de Mme de Maintenon et de la Princesse des Ursins, 1709: Une Année tragique.* Ed. Marcel Loyau. Paris: Mercure de France, 2002. Print.

Maison, André, ed. *Anthologie de la correspondance française.* 7 vols. Lausanne: Rencontres, 1969. Print.

Malandain, Pierre. "L'Écriture de l'histoire dans *La Princesse de Clèves.*" *Littérature* 36 (1979): 19–36. Print.

Manley, Delarivier. *The Adventures of Rivella.* Ed. Katherine Zelinsky. Peterborough: Broadview, 1999. Print.

———. [*The Adventures of Rivella.*] *Mrs. Manley's History of Her Own Life and Times. Published from Her Original Manuscript.* 4th ed. London: E. Curll and J. Pemberton, 1725. Print.

———. *The New Atlantis.* Ed. Rosalind Ballaster. New York: New York UP, 1992. Print.

Marie Antoinette. Dir. Sofia Coppola. Columbia Pictures, 2006. Film.

Marie de l'Incarnation. *Correspondance.* Solesmes: Abbaye Saint-Pierre, 1971. Print.

———. *Écrits spirituels et historiques.* Ed. Albert Jamet. 2 vols. Québec: Ursulines de Québec, 1985. Print.

Marie-Madeleine de Saint-Stanislas. *Relation du voyage des Dames religieuses ursulines de Rouen à la Nouvelle Orléans.* 1728. Rouen: Cahiers des Études Normandes, PU de Rouen, 1988. Print.

Mariette, Pierre-Jean. *Abécedario de P. J. Mariette [texte imprimé], et autres notes inédites de cet amateur sur les arts et les artistes, ouvrage publié d'après les manuscrits autographes.* 1851–60. Ed. Charles-Philippe de Chennevières and Anatole de Courde de Montaiglon. Paris: Nobele, 1966. Print.

Marin, Louis. *Le Portrait du roi.* Paris: Minuit, 1981. Print.

Marivaux, Pierre Carlet de Chamblain de. *Le Jeu de l'amour et du hasard.* Ed. Marie-Thérèse Ligot. Paris: Pocket, 1998. Print.

———. *La Vie de Marianne.* 1731. Ed. Frédéric Deloffre. Paris: Garnier, 1957. Print.

Martin, Angus A. "Le Roman européen au 18e siècle et la statistique bibliographique." *Dix-huitième siècle* 25 (1993): 101–14. Print.

Martin, Christophe. "Présentation." Fontenelle, *Entretiens* 21–45.

Martin, Claude. *La Vie de la venerable Mère Marie de l'Incarnation, première supérieure des Ursulines de la Nouvelle France. Tirée de ses lettres et de ses écrits.* Paris: Louis Billaine, 1677. Print.

Mathiex, Jean. *Histoire de France.* Paris: Hachette, 1996. Print.

Matthews-Grieco, Sara F. *Ange ou diablesse. La Représentation de la femme au XVIe siècle.* Paris: Flammarion, 1991. Print.

Maura Gamazo, Gabriel. *Fantasías y realidades del viaje a Madrid de la condesa d'Aulnoy.* Madrid: Calleja, 1944. Print.

Mauriceau, François. *Diseases of Women with Child and in Child-Bed.* London: Darby, 1983. Print.

May, Georges. *Le Dilemme du roman au XVIIIe siècle. Étude sur les rapports du roman et de la critique (1715–1761).* Paris: PUF, 1963. Print.

Maza, Sarah. *Private Lives and Public Affairs: The "Causes Célèbres" of Prerevolutionary France.* Berkeley: U of California P, 1993. Print.

Merlin-Kajman, Hélène. *Public et littérature en France au XVIIe siècle.* Paris: Belles Lettres, 1994. Print.

Mesnard, Jean. Introduction. Lafayette, *La Princesse de Clèves* [Mesnard] 37–39.

Meurdrac, Marie de. *La Chymie charitable et facile, en faveur des dames.* 2nd ed. Paris: Jean d'Hoüry, 1674. *Gallica.* Web. 29 Apr. 2010.

Michelet, Jules. *Histoire de la Révolution Françoise.* Paris: Laffont, 1979. Print.

Micolon, Antoinette. *The Life of Antoinette Micolon.* Ed. and trans. Linda Lierheimer. Milwaukee: Marquette UP, 2004. Print.

Mignot, Claude. *Le Val-De-Grâce: L'Ermitage d'une Reine.* Paris: Centre National de la Recherche Publique, 1994. Print.

Miller, Nancy K. *French Dressing: Women, Men, and Fiction in the Ancien Régime.* New York: Routledge, 1995. Print.

———. *Subject to Change: Reading Feminist Writing.* New York: Columbia UP, 1990. Print.

Molière. *Les Amants magnifiques.* Molière, *Œuvres* 2: 645–92.

———. *Dom Juan.* Molière, *Œuvres* 2: 1–85.

———. *L'École des femmes.* Paris: Larousse, 2003. Print.

———. *Les Femmes savantes.* Ed. Thanh-Vân Ton-That. Paris: Larousse, 2007. Print.

———. *Georges Dandin.* Ed. Patrick Dandrey. Paris: Klincksieck, 2007. Print.

———. *La Gloire du Val-de-Grace.* Paris: Jean Ribou, 1669. Print.

———. "La Gloire de Val-de-Grace." *La Vie de Pierre Mignaud, premier peintre du roy.* Paris: J. Boudot, 1730. N. pag. *Gallica.* Web. 27 Apr. 2010.

———. *Le Médecin malgré lui.* 1666. Ed. Philippe Labaune. Rev. ed. Paris: Flammarion, 2007. Print.

———. *Le Misanthrope.* Molière, *Œuvres* 2: 121–218.

———. *Le Misanthrope.* Ed. Jacques Chupeau. Paris: Gallimard, 2000. Print.

———. *Œuvres complètes.* Ed. George Couton. 2 vols. Paris: Gallimard, 1971. Print.

———. *Les Précieuses ridicules.* Paris: Larousse, 2003. Print.

———. *Le Tartuffe.* Paris: Larousse, 2002. Print.

Monbart, Marie-Josèphe de. *De l'éducation d'une princesse.* Berlin, 1781. Print.

———. *Lettres taïtiennes.* 2 vols. Paris, [1784]. Print.

———. *Sophie, ou de l'éducation des filles.* Berlin, 1777. Print.

Montagu, Mary Wortley. *The Letters and Works of Lady Mary Wortley Montagu.* London: Henry G. Bohn, 1861. Print.

Montaigne, Michel de. "De la solitude." *Essais.* Ed. Alexandre Micha. 3 vols. Paris: Flammarion, 1969. 1: 289–99. Print.

Montesquieu, Charles de Secondat, baron de. *Lettres persanes.* Oxford: Voltaire Foundation, 2004. Print.

Montpensier, Anne-Marie-Louise d'Orléans, duchesse de. *Against Marriage: The Correspondence of La Grande Mademoiselle.* Ed. and trans. Joan DeJean. Chicago: U of Chicago P, 2002. Print. The Other Voice in Early Modern Europe.

———. *Divers Portraits.* Caen, 1659. Print.

———. *Mémoires de Mlle de Montpensier, petite-fille de Henri IV.* 4 vols. Paris: Charpentier, 1858–68. Print.

Morin, Marie. *Histoire simple et véritable: Annales de l'Hôtel de Dieu de Montréal, 1659–1725.* Ed. Ghislaine Legendre. Montréal: PU de Montréal, 1979. Print.

Morlet-Chantalat, Chantal. *La Clélie de Mademoiselle de Scudéry: De l'épopée à la gazette: Un Discours féminin de la gloire.* Paris: Champion, 1994. Print.

Mortimer, Ruth, comp. *French Sixteenth-Century Books.* 2 vols. Cambridge: Belknap–Harvard UP, 1964. Print. Pt. 1 of *Catalogue of Books and Manuscripts: Harvard College Library Department of Printing and Graphic Arts.*

Motteville, Françoise Bertaut de. *Mémoires pour servir à l'histoire d'Anne d'Autriche.* Paris: Fontaine, 1982. Print.

Mujica, Bárbara. *Women Writers of Early Modern Spain: Sophia's Daughters.* New Haven: Yale UP, 2004. Print.

Murat, Henriette-Julie de Castelnau, comtesse de. *A Trip to the Country.* Ed. and trans. Allison Stedman and Perry Gethner. Wayne State UP, forthcoming.

Murat, Jean-Louis. *Madame Deshoulières.* LABELS/Virgin France, 2001. CD.

Murphy, Gwénaël. *Le Peuple des couvents. Poitou. XVIIe–XVIIIe siècles.* La Crèche: Geste, 2007. Print.

Myers, Kathleen Ann. "Crossing Boundaries: Defining the Field of Female Religious Writing in Colonial Latin America." *Colonial Latin American Review* 9 (2000): 151–66. Print.

———. *Neither Saints nor Sinners: Writing the Lives of Women in Spanish America.* New York: Oxford UP, 2003. Print.

Nabarra, Alain. "Dunoyer, Anne Marguerite Petit (1663–1719)." *Dictionnaire des Journaux, 1600–1789.* Ed. Jean Sgard. 2 vols. Paris: Universitas, 1991. Print.

Nadelhaft, Ruth. "Domestic Violence in Literature: A Preliminary Study." *Mosaic* 17.2 (1984): 242–59. Print.

The New Oxford Annotated Bible. New rev. standard vers. Ed. Bruce M. Metzger and Roland E. Murphy. New York: Oxford UP, 1989. Print.

Nicole, Pierre. *Essais de morale.* Ed. Laurent Thirouin. Paris: PUF, 1999. Print.

Niderst, Alain. Introduction. Lafayette, *Romans* vii–xliv.

———. *Madeleine de Scudéry, Paul Pellisson et leur monde.* Paris: PUF, 1976. Print.

Nora, Pierre, ed. *Les Lieux de mémoire.* 1984. Paris: Gallimard, 1997. Print.

Norberg, Katheryn. "Incorporating Women/Gender into French History Courses, 1429–1789: Did Women of the Old Regime Have a Political History?" *French Historical Studies* 27.2 (2004): 243–66. Print.

Nye, Andrea. *The Princess and the Philosopher: Letters of Elisabeth of the Palatine to René Descartes.* Lanham: Rowman, 1999. Print.

Oberkirch, baronne d'. *Mémoires de la baronne d'Oberkirch sur la cour de Louis XVI.* 1853. Ed. Suzanne Burkard. Paris: Mercure de France, 1970. Print.

Offen, Karen. *European Feminisms, 1700–1950: A Political History.* Stanford: Stanford UP, 2000. Print.

O'Neill, Eileen. "Early Modern Women Philosophers and the History of Philosophy." *Hypatia* 20.3 (2005): 185–97. Print.

———. "Women Cartesians, 'Feminine Philosophy,' and Historical Exclusion." Bordo 232–57.

O'Reilly, Patrick, and Edouard Reitman. *Bibliographie de Tahiti et de la Polynésie française.* Paris: Musée de l'Homme, 1967. Print. Publications de la Société des Océanistes 14.

Orléans, Charlotte Elisabeth d'. *Lettres de la princesse Palatine, 1672–1772.* Paris: Mercure de France, 1981. Print.

Outram, Dorinda. *The Body and the French Revolution: Sex, Class, and Political Culture.* New Haven: Yale UP, 1989. Print.

Palmer, Melvin D. "Madame d'Aulnoy in England." *Comparative Literature* 27.3 (1975): 237–53. Print.

———. "Madame d'Aulnoy's Pseudo-Autobiographical Works on Spain." *Romanische Foschungen* 83 (1971): 220–29. Print.

Parker, Patricia. *Inescapable Romance: Studies in the Poetics of a Mode.* Princeton: Princeton UP, 1979. Print.

Pascal, Blaise. *Pensées.* Paris: Gallimard, 2004. Print.

———. *Pensées.* Ed. Philippe Sellier. Paris: Garnier, 1999. Print.

———. *Pensées. Les Provinciales, Pensées et opuscules divers.* Ed. Gérard Ferreyrolles and Philippe Sellier. Paris: Livre de Poche–Classiques Garnier, 2004. 755–1373. Print. La Pochothèque.

———. *Thoughts.* Trans. W. F. Trotter. Ed. T. S. Eliot. New York: Dutton, 1958. Print.

Pascal, Françoise. *L'Amoureux extravagant.* Gethner, *Femmes dramaturges* 1: 23–54.

———. *Le Commerce du Parnasse.* Ed. Deborah Steinberger. Exeter: U of Exeter P, 2001. Print.

———. *Endymion.* Gethner, *Femmes dramaturges* 2: 11–92.

———. *Letters from Parnassus.* Excerpts. Trans. Deborah Steinberger. *Writings by Pre-revolutionary French Women.* Ed. Anne R. Larsen and Colette H. Winn. New York: Garland, 2000. 289–304. Print.

Pascal, Jacqueline de Sainte-Euphémie. *Règlement pour les enfants de Port-Royal. Œuvres complètes d'Étienne et de Jacqueline Pascal.* Ed. Jean Mesnard. Vol 2. Paris: Brouwer, 1991. 1135–98. Print.

———. *A Rule for Children and Other Writings.* Ed. and trans. John J. Conley. Chicago: U of Chicago P, 2003. Print.

Pateman, Carol. *The Sexual Contract.* Stanford: Stanford UP, 1988. Print.

Pelous, Jean-Michel. *Amour précieux, amour galant, 1654–1675: Essai sur la représentation de l'amour dans la littérature et la société mondaines.* Paris: Klincksieck, 1980. Print.

Pepys, Samuel. *The Diary.* Ed. Richard De Gallienne. New York: Mod. Lib., 2001. Print.

Perkins, Wendy. "Le Libertinage de quelques poètes épicuriens à la fin du XVIIe siècle." *Laclos et le libertinage.* Paris: PUF, 1983. 21–46. Print.

———. "Mme Deshoulières: One of the 'Derniers Libertins'?" *Newsletter of the Society for Seventeenth-Century French Studies* 5 (1983): 125–33. Print.

Perrault, Charles. *Contes*. Paris: Bookking Intl., 1993. Print.

———. "Les Fées." Perrault, *Contes* 135–38.

———. *Parallèle des anciens et des modernes*. 1687. Ed. Hans Robert Jauss. Munich: Eidos, 1964. Print.

———. "Peau d'âne." *Contes*. Paris: Garnier, 1967. 51–75. Print.

———. *La Peinture*. Ed. Jean-Luc Gautier-Gentès. Genève: Droz, 1992. Print.

Perrault, Charles, François-Timoléon de Choisy, and Marie-Jeanne Lhéritier. *Histoire de la Marquise-Marquis de Banneville*. Ed. Joan DeJean. New York: MLA, 2004. Print.

Perry, Ruth. "Radical Doubt and the Liberation of Women." Bordo 169–89.

Peters, Jeffrey N. "Kingship and Paranoid Subjectivity in Marie-Catherine Desjardins's *Le Favori*." *French Forum* 25.3 (2000): 261–76. Print.

———. *Mapping Discord: Allegorical Cartogrpahy in Early Modern French Writing*. Newark: U of Delaware P, 2004. Print.

Phillips, Roderick. *Family Breakdown in Late Eighteenth-Century France: Divorce in Rouen, 1792–1803*. Oxford: Oxford UP, 1980. Print.

Picard, Roger. *Les Salons littéraires et la société française, 1670–1789*. New York: Brentano's, 1943. Print.

Pincas, Stéphane, and Maryvonne Rocher-Gilotte. *Versailles: The History of the Gardens and Their Sculpture*. Trans. Fiona Cowell. New York: Thames, 1996. Print.

Pingaud, Bernard. *Madame de La Fayette*. Paris: Seuil, 1997. Print.

Pizzey, Erin. *Scream Quietly or the Neighbours Will Hear*. 2nd ed. Harmondsworth: Penguin, 1979. Print.

Plantié, Christine. *L'Épistolaire, un genre féminin?* Paris: Champion, 1998. Print.

Plato. *The Collected Dialogues*. Ed. Edith Hamilton and Huntington Cairns. Trans. Lane Cooper. Princeton: Princeton UP, 1985. Print.

Plazenet, Laurence. *L'Ébahissement et la Délectation. Réception comparée et poétique du roman grec en France et en Angleterre aux XVIe et XVIIe siècles*. Paris: Champion, 1997. Print.

Poiron, Jean-Marc. "Elizabeth-Sophie Chéron et *La Coupe du Val-de-Grâce*." Démoris and Delpierre, *Homage* 9–26.

Pomarède, Vincent, and Marie-Claire Le Bourdellès. "*Le Déjeuner*." *Musée du Louvre*. Musée du Louvre, n.d. Web. 23 Aug. 2010.

Poncelin de la Roche-Tilhac, Jean-Charles. *Histoires des révolutions de Taïti*. Paris: Lamy, 1782. Print.

Pope, Alexander. "An Essay on Man, Epistle I." *The Major Works*. Ed. Pat Rogers. Oxford: Oxford UP, 2009. 270–80. Print.

Pósfay, Eva. "Mapping *La Princesse de Clèves*: A Spatial Approach." Beasley and Jensen 102–08.

Poulenc, François, and Georges Bernanos. *Dialogues des Carmélites: Opéra en trois actes et douze tableaux*. Paris: Ricordi, 1957. Print.

Poullain de la Barre, François. *De l'égalité des deux sexes*. Paris: Fayard, 1984. Print.

Poussin, Nicolas. *Autoportrait*. 1650. Oil on canvas. Musée du Louvre, Paris.

Les Précieuses ridicules. Dir. Georges Bensoussan. Writ. Molière. FR3, Néria Productions, Euripide Productions, and La Comédie Française, 1997. Television. Films for the Humanities, 2000.

Prévost, Antoine-François. *Histoire du chevalier des Grieux et de Manon Lescaut.* Ed. Pierre Malandain. Paris: Pocket, 1990. Print.

Puget de la Serre, Jean. *Le Secrétaire à la mode.* Amsterdam: L. Elzevier, 1663. Print.

Rabelais, François. *Pantagruel.* Ed. Marie-Madeleine Fragonard. Paris: Pocket, 1997. Print.

Racine, Jean. *Andromaque.* Paris: Larousse-Bordas, 1998. Print.

———. *Britannicus. Théâtre. Poésie.* Ed. Georges Forestier. Paris: Gallimard, 1999. 369–455. Print.

Rapley, Elizabeth. *A Social History of the Cloister: Daily Life in the Teaching Monasteries of the Old Regime.* Montreal: McGill-Queen's UP, 2001. Print.

Recueil des harangues prononcés par Messieurs de l'Académie française. Paris: Coignard, 1714. Print.

Reed, Sue Welsh. *French Prints from the Age of the Musketeers.* Boston: Museum of Fine Arts, 1998. Print.

Rétif de La Bretonne, Nicolas-Edme. *Ingénue Saxancour ou La Femme séparée.* Paris: Lattès, 1979. Print.

Revel, Emmanuelle, ed. *L'Autoportrait de Nicolas Poussin: Dossier pour enseignants.* Paris: Musée du Louvre, 1997. Print. Collection Arrêt sur Œuvre.

Rev. of *Lettres de Milady Juliette Catesby,* by Marie-Jeanne Riccoboni. *Année littéraire* 8 (1758): 289–301. Print.

Rev. of *Lettres de Milady Juliette Catesby,* by Marie-Jeanne Riccoboni. *Correspondance littéraire* 4 (1759): 98–99.

Rev. of *Lettres de Milady Juliette Catesby,* by Marie-Jeanne Riccoboni. *Journal encyclopédique* 3 (1759): 112–27. Print.

Rev. of *Lettres de Milady Juliette Catesby,* by Marie-Jeanne Riccoboni. *Mercure de France* June 1759: 73–87. Print.

Rev. of Le Mari sentimental, Lettres de Mistriss Henley, Justification de Mr Henley. *Année littéraire* 8 (1758): 169–78. Print. Rpt. in *Documentatieblad Werkgroep Achttiende Eeuw* 27–29 (1975): 210–14.

Rev. of Le Mari sentimental, Lettres de Mistriss Henley, Justification de Mr Henley. *Mercure de France* 22 Apr. 1786: 186–93. Print. Rpt. in *Documentatieblad Werkgroep Achttiende Eeuw* 27–29 (1975): 215–19.

Rev. of *Travels into Spain,* by Mme d'Aulnoy. *Amazon.* Amazon, n.d. Web. 27 July 2010.

Rey, Alain, et al., eds. *Dictionnaire historique de la langue française.* 3 vols. Paris: Dictionnaires Le Robert, 1992. Print.

Reynes, Geneviève. *Couvents de femmes: La Vie des religieuses contemplatives dans la France des XVIIe et XVIIIe siècles.* Paris: Fayard, 1987. Print.

Riccoboni, Marie-Jeanne de Heurles Laboras de Mezières. *Histoire du M. le marquis de Cressy.* Ed. Martine Reid. Paris: Gallimard, 2009. Print. Femmes des Lettres.

———. Letter to the editor. *Mercure de France* Mar. 1768: 53. Print.

———. *Lettres d'Adélaide de Dammartin, Comtesse de Sancerre, au comte de Nancé son ami.* 1767. *Œuvres de Madame Riccoboni.* 6 vols. Paris: Foucault, 1818. 4: 155–338. Print.

———. *Lettres de Milady Juliette Catesby à Milady Henriette Campley, son amie.* 1759. Ed. Sylvain Menant. Paris: Desjonquères, 1983. Print.

————. *Lettres de Mistriss Fanni Butlerd.* Genève: Droz, 1979. Print.

————. *Mme Riccoboni's Letters to David Hume, David Garrick and Sir Robert Liston: 1764–1783.* Ed. J. C. Nicholls. Oxford: Voltaire Foundation, 1976. Print.

————. *Suite de Marianne.* Marivaux, *Vie* 581–627.

Rich, Adrienne. *Of Woman Born: Motherhood as Experience and Institution.* New York: Norton, 1976. Print.

Richardson, Samuel. *Clarissa.* New York: AMS, 1990. Print.

————. *Pamela; or, Virtue Rewarded.* Oxford: Oxford UP, 2001. Print.

Richelet, Pierre. *Les Plus Belles Lettres des meilleurs auteurs français.* Lyon: Benoit Bailly, 1689. Print.

Ridicule. Dir. Patrice Leconte. Epithète Films, 1996. Film.

Rivera, Maria-Milagros. "Sexual Difference in History." European Feminisms: Theories and Practices of Sexual Difference. Chicago Humanities Inst. 16 May 1997. Address.

Riviere, Joan. "Weiblichkeit als Maske." *Internationale Zeitschrift für ärzliche Psychoanalyse* 15 (1929): 285–97. Print.

Robinson, Mary. "London's Summer Morning." *Selected Poems.* Ed. Judith Pascoe. Peterborough: Broadview, 2000. 352–53. Print.

Roche-Mazon, Jeanne. *Autour des contes de fées.* Paris: Didier, 1968. Print.

Rogers, Elizabeth Barlow. *Landscape Design: A Cultural and Architectural History.* New York: Abrams, 2001. Print.

Roland de La Platière, Marie-Jeanne Philipon. *Lettres.* Paris: Nationale, 1913–15. Print.

————. *Mémoires de Madame Roland.* Ed. Paul de Roux. Paris: Mercure de France, 1986. Print.

Rossetti, Christina. "Goblin Market." *Poems and Prose.* Ed. Jan Marsh. London: Everyman, 1994. 162–76. Print.

Rousseau, Jean-Jacques. *Discours sur les sciences et les arts.* Paris: Flammarion, 1990. Print.

————. *Discours sur l'origine et les fondements de l'inégalité parmi les hommes.* 1755. Rousseau, *Œuvres* 3: 111–237.

————. *Du contrat social.* Rousseau, *Œuvres* 3: 349–470.

————. *Émile et Sophie, ou les Solitaires.* Rousseau, *Œuvres* 4: 881–924.

————. *Émile, ou de l'éducation.* 1762. Rousseau, *Œuvres* 4: 241–868.

————. *Julie; or, The New Heloise: Letters of Two Lovers Who Live in a Small Town at the Foot of the Alps. The Collected Writings of Rousseau.* Vol. 6. Trans. Philip Stewart and Jean Vaché. Hanover: UP of New England, 1977. 1–612. Print.

————. *Julie, ou la Nouvelle Héloïse.* Paris: Gallimard, 1993. Print.

————. *La Nouvelle Héloïse.* Rousseau, *Œuvres* 2: 5–793.

————. *Œuvres complètes.* Ed. Bernard Gagnebin and Marcel Raymond. 5 vols. Paris: Gallimard, 1959–95. Print. Bibliothèque de la Pléiade.

Rousset, Jean. *La Littérature de l'âge baroque en France: Circé et le Paon.* Paris: Corti, 1954. Print.

Rubin, Gayle. "Thinking Sex: Notes for a Radical Theory of the Politics of Sexuality." *American Feminist Thought at Century's End: A Reader.* Ed. Linda S. Kauffman. Cambridge: Blackwell, 1993. 3–64. Print.

Russo, Elena. *La Cour et la ville dans la littérature classique aux Lumières*. Paris: PUF, 2002. Print.

———, ed. *Exploring the Conversible World: Text and Sociability from the Classical Age to the Enlightenment*. Spec. issue of *Yale French Studies* 92 (1997): 1–206. Print.

———. *Style of Enlightenment: Taste, Politics, and Authorship in Eighteenth-Century France*. Baltimore: Johns Hopkins UP, 2006. Print.

Sade, Donatien-Alphonse-François, marquis de. *La Marquise de Gange*. 1813. Ed. Hubert Juin. Paris: Belfond, 1965. Print.

Sainctonge, Louise-Geneviève Gillot' de. *Griselde*. Evain, Gethner, and Goldwyn 3: forthcoming.

Saint-Balmon, Alberte-Barbe de. *Les Jumeaux martyrs*. Ed. Carmeta Abbott and Hannah Fournier. Geneva: Droz, 1995. Print.

Sainte-Beuve, Charles-Augustin. "Une Ruelle poétique sous Louis XIV." *Œuvres*. Ed. Maxime Leroy. Vol. 2. Paris: Gallimard, 1956. 1304–27. Print.

Saint-Evremond, Charles de Marguetel de Saint-Denis, seigneur de. *Œuvres choisies*. Ed. M. Hippeau. Paris: Didot, 1852. 324–31. Print.

Saint-Simon, Louis de Rouvroy, duc de. *Mémoires*. Ed. Delphine de Garidel. Paris: Flammarion, 2001. Print.

Sales, François de. *Œuvres*. Ed. André Ravier and Roger Devos. Paris: Gallimard, 1969. Print.

Sawday, Jonathan. *The Body Emblazoned: Dissection and the Human Body in Renaissance Culture*. London: Routledge, 1995. Print.

Scarron, Paul. *Le Roman comique*. 1651–57. Ed. Jean Serroy. Paris: Gallimard, 1985. Print.

Schaeffer, Jean-Marie. "La Catégorie du romanesque." Declercq and Murat 291–302.

Schama, Simon. *Citizens: A Chronicle of the French Revolution*. New York: Knopf, 1989. Print.

Schiebinger, Londa. *The Mind Has No Sex: Women in the Origins of Modern Science*. Cambridge: Harvard UP, 1989. Print.

———. *Nature's Body*. Boston: Beacon, 1993. Print.

Schleiner, Winfried. "Early Modern Controversies about the One-Sex Model." *Renaissance Quarterly* 53.1 (2000): 180–91. Print.

Schröder, Volker. "Les Méditations de Mariane: La Matrice mystique des *Lettres portugaises*." *La Femme au XVIIe siècle: Actes du colloque de Vancouver, University of British Columbia, 5–7 octobre 2000*. Ed. Richard G. Hodgson. Tübingen: Narr, 2002. 283–99. Print.

Schwartz, Debora B. "Writing Her Own Life: Villedieu, Henriette-Sylvie de Molière and Feminine Empowerment." *Women in French Literature*. Ed. Michel Guggenheim. Saratoga: Anma, 1988. 77–89. Print.

Scott, Joan W. "Gender: A Useful Category of Historical Analysis." *American Historical Review* 91.5 (1986): 1053–75. Print.

———. "A Woman Who Has Only Paradoxes to Offer: Olympe de Gouges Claims Rights for Women." *Rebel Daughters: Women and the French Revolution*. Ed. Sara E. Melzer and Leslie W. Rabine. New York: Oxford UP, 1992. 102–20. Print.

Scudéry, Madeleine de. *Artamène; ou, Le Grand Cyrus*. Cambridge: Omnisys, 1990. Print.

————. *Célinte: Nouvelle Première.* Ed. Alain Niderst. Paris: Nizet, 1979. Print.

————. *Choix de Conversations de Mlle de Scudéry.* Ed. Phillip J. Wolfe. Ravenna: Longo, 1977. Print.

————. *Clélie, histoire romaine.* Abr. ed. Ed. Delphine Denis. Gallimard, 2006. Print.

————. *Clélie, histoire romaine.* Ed. Chantal Morlet-Chantalat. 5 vols. Paris: Champion, 2001–05. Print.

————. "Contre ceux qui parlent peu sérieusement de la religion." Scudéry, *Conversations sur divers sujets* 1: 173–99.

————. *Conversations nouvelles sur divers sujets.* 2 vols. Paris: Barbin, 1684. Print.

————. *Conversations sur divers sujets.* 2 vols. Paris: Barbin, 1680. Print.

————. "De la conversation." Scudéry, *"De l'air"* 67–75, 305–11.

————. "De l'air galant." Scudéry, *"De l'air"* 49–57.

————. *"De l'air galant" et autres conversations: Pour une étude de l'archive galante.* Ed. Delphine Denis. Paris: Champion, 1998. Print.

————. "De la magnificence et de la magnanimité." Scudéry, *Conversations nouvelles* 1: 1–118.

————. "De la manière d'écrire des letters." Scudéry, *"De l'air"* 139–58.

————. "De la politesse." Scudéry, *"De l'air"* 115–38.

————. "De la raillerie." Scudéry, *Conversations sur divers sujets* 2: 523–614.

————. "De l'ennui sans sujet." Scudéry, *Conversations nouvelles* 2: 457–502.

————. "De l'incertitude." Scudéry, *Morale* 1: 365–496.

————. "De parler trop, ou trop peu, et comment il faut parler." Scudéry, *Conversations sur divers sujets* 1: 200–50.

————. "Des passions que les hommes ont inventées." Scudéry, *Conversations sur divers sujets* 1: 271–309.

————. *Entretiens de morale.* 2 vols. Paris: Anisson, 1692. Print.

————. *Les Femmes illustres ou les harangues heroiques.* Paris, 1665. Print.

————. *La Morale du monde, ou Conversations [Conversations morales].* 2 vols. Paris: Guillain, 1686. Print.

————. *Nouvelles Conversations de morale.* 2 vols. Paris: Veuve de Mabre-Cramoisy, 1688. Print.

————. "On Conversation." Scudéry, *Selected Letters* 96–105.

————. "On Speaking Too Much or Too Little, and How to Speak Well." Scudéry, *Selected Letters* 105–17.

————. "On Wit." Scudéry, *Selected Letters* 117–39.

————. *Selected Letters, Orations, and Rhetorical Dialogues.* Ed. and trans. Jane Donawerth and Julie Strongson. Chicago: U of Chicago P, 2004. Print. The Other Voice in Early Modern Europe.

————. *The Story of Sapho.* Ed. and trans. Karen Newman. Chicago: U of Chicago P, 2003. Print. The Other Voice in Early Modern Europe.

Scudéry, Madeleine de, and Georges de Scudéry. *Artamène ou le Grand Cyrus.* Excerpts. Ed. Claude Bourqui and Alexandre Gefen. Paris: Flammarion, 2005. Print.

Sedgwick, Eve. *Between Men: English Literature and Male Homosocial Desire.* New York: Columbia UP, 1985. Print.

Seguin, Maria-Susana. Introduction. Aulnoy, *Relation* [2005] 7–26.

Seifert, Lewis C. *Manning the Margins*. Ann Arbor: U of Michigan P, 2009. Print.

Seifert, Lewis C., and Todd W. Reeser, eds. *French Masculinities*. Spec. issue of *L'Esprit Créateur* 43.2 (2003): 1–95. Print.

Serres, Michel. *The Parasite*. Trans. Lawrence R. Schehr. Baltimore: Johns Hopkins UP, 1982. Print.

Sévigné, Marie de Rabutin-Chantal, marquise de. *Correspondance*. Ed. Roger Duchêne. 3 vols. Paris: Gallimard, 1972–78. Print. Bibliothèque de la Pléiade.

———. *The Letters of Madame de Sévigné*. Ed. A. Edward Newton. 7 vols. Philadelphia: Horn, 1927. Print.

———. *Selected Letters*. Trans. Leonard Tancock. London: Penguin, 1982. Print.

Seward, Anna. "Sonnet: To France on Her Present Exertions." *Romantic Women Poets: An Anthology*. Ed. Duncan Wu. Oxford: Blackwell, 1997. 6–7. Print.

Shank, J. B. "Neither Natural Philosophy, nor Science, nor Literature: Gender and the Pursuit of Nature in Fontenelle's *Entretiens sur la pluralité des mondes habités*." *Men, Women, and the Birthing of Modern Science*. Ed. Judith P. Zinsser. Dekalb: Northern Illinois P, 2005. 86–110. Print.

Shapiro, Lisa. Volume editor's introduction. Elisabeth of Bohemia and Descartes 1–51.

Shaub, Jean-Frédéric. *La France espagnole. Les Racines hispaniques de l'absolutisme français*. Paris: Seuil, 2003. Print.

Shelley, Mary. *Frankenstein 1818 Text*. Ed. Marilyn Butler. Oxford: Oxford UP, 1993. Print.

Showalter, English. *The Evolution of the French Novel, 1641–1782*. Princeton: Princeton UP, 1972. Print.

Siraisi, Nancy. *Medieval and Early Renaissance Medicine: An Introduction to Knowledge and Practice*. Chicago: U of Chicago P, 1990. Print.

Sister Act. Dir. Emile Ardolino. Touchstone Pictures, 1992. Film.

"Si un homme doit se marier; si une femme doit se marier." *Extraordinaire* du *Mercure galant* Apr. 1679: 13–35. Microfilm. Bibliothèque Nationale de France, 1958.

Sol, Antoinette Marie. *Textual Promiscuities: Eighteenth-Century Critical Rewriting*. Lewisburg: Bucknell UP; London: Assoc. UPs, 2002. Print.

Spencer, Jane. *The Rise of the Woman Novelist: From Aphra Behn to Jane Austen*. Oxford: Blackwell, 1986. Print.

Staal-Delaunay, Marguerite-Jeanne Cordier, baronne de. *La Mode*. Gethner, *Femmes dramaturges* 2: 319–69.

Staël, Germaine de. *Corinne, ou l'Italie*. Ed. Simone Balayé. Paris: Gallimard, 1985. Print.

———. *De la littérature*. Paris: Flammarion, 1991. Print.

———. *De l'Allemagne*. Paris: Flammarion, 1968. Print.

———. "De l'esprit de conversation." Staël, *De l'Allemagne* 101–10.

———. Letter to Isabelle de Charrière. 23 Oct. 1793. Charrière, *Œuvres* 4: 234.

Stagl, Justin. *A History of Curiosity: The Theory of Travel, 1500–1800*. Chur: Harwood Acad., 1995. Print.

Stanton, Domna. "The Fiction of Préciosité and the Fear of Women." *Yale French Studies* 62 (1981): 107–34. Print.

———. "The Ideal of 'Repos' in Seventeenth-Century French Literature." *L'Esprit Créateur* 15.3 (1975): 79–104. Print.

Starobinski, Jean. "Sur Corneille." *L'Œil vivant: Corneille, Racine, Rousseau, Stendhal.* Paris: Gallimard, 1961. 29–67. Print.

Stedman, Allison. "Marie-Jeanne Lhéritier de Villandon." *Dictionnaire des femmes de l'ancien régime.* SIEFAR, 2006. Web. 24 Mar. 2010.

Steinberger, Deborah. Introduction. F. Pascal, *Commerce* v–xx.

Stella, Claudine, and Jacques Stella. *Games and Pastimes of Childhood.* New York: Dover, 1970. Print.

———. *Les Jeux et plaisirs de l'enfance, inventés par Jacques Stella et gravés par Claudine Bouzonnet Stella.* Paris: Galleries du Louvre, 1657. Print.

———. *Pastorales.* Paris: Galleries du Louvre, 1667. Print.

Stephens, Sonya, ed. *A History of Women's Writing in France.* Cambridge: Cambridge UP, 2000. Print.

Stevenson, Robert Louis. *The Strange Case of Dr. Jekyll and Mr. Hyde.* New York: Dover, 1991. Print.

Stirling, William, ed. *Mémoires de la cour d'Espagne sous le règne de Charles II, 1678–1682.* By Pierre de Villars. London: Trübner, 1861. Print.

Stolberg, Michael. "A Woman Down to Her Bones: The Anatomy of Sexual Difference in the Sixteenth and Early Seventeenth Centuries." *Isis* 94.2 (2003): 274–99. Print.

Stone, Harriet. *The Classical Model: Literature and Knowledge in Seventeenth-Century French Literature.* Ithaca: Cornell UP, 1986. Print.

———. *Tables of Knowledge: Descartes in Vermeer's Studio.* Ithaca: Cornell UP, 2006. Print.

Swift, Jonathan. *Gulliver's Travels. The Writings.* Ed. Robert A. Greenberg and William B. Piper. New York: Norton, 1973. 1–260. Print.

Tackett, Timothy. *When the King Took Flight.* Cambridge: Harvard UP, 2003. Print.

Tallemant des Réaux, Gédéon. *Historiettes.* Ed. Antoine Adam. 2 vols. Paris: Gallimard, 1960–61. Print.

Thacker, Christopher. *The History of Gardens.* Berkeley: U of California P, 1979. Print.

Thiesse, Anne-Marie, and Hélène Mathieu. "The Decline of the Classical Age and the Birth of the Classics." DeJean and Miller 74–96.

Thomas, Chantal. *The Wicked Queen: The Origins of the Myth of Marie-Antoinette.* New York: Zone, 2001. Print.

Timmermans, Linda. *L'Accès des femmes à la culture (1598–1715): Un Débat d'idées de Saint François de Sales à la Marquise de Lambert.* Paris: Champion, 1993. Print.

Todd, Janet. *The Sign of Angellica: Women, Writing, and Fiction, 1660–1800.* New York: Columbia UP, 1989. Print.

Tonolo, Sophie. "Aimer comme Amadis: Une Poétesse entre deux siècles." *Origines. Actes du 39e congrès annuel de la North American Society for Seventeenth-Century French Literature. University of Nebraska-Lincoln, 10–12 mai 2007.* Ed. Thomas M. Carr, Jr., and Russell Ganim. Tübingen: Narr, 2009. 273–86. Print.

Trouille, Mary Seidman. *Sexual Politics in the Enlightenment: Women Writers Read Rousseau.* Albany: State U of New York P, 1997. Print.

———. *Wife-Abuse in Eighteenth-Century France.* Oxford: Voltaire Foundation, 2009. Print.

Trousson, Raymond, ed. *Romans de femmes du XVIIIe siècle.* Paris: Laffont, 2000. Print.

Tucker, Holly. *Pregnant Fictions: Childbirth and the Fairy Tale in Early-Modern France.* Detroit: Wayne State UP, 2003. Print.

Turgot, Anne-Robert-Jacques. Letter to Mme de Graffigny. 1751. Graffigny, *Lettres* [2002] 277–88.

Urfé, Honoré d'. *L'Astrée.* Ed. Eglal Henein. Tufts U, n.d. Web. 14 Jan. 2011.

———. *L'Astrée.* Ed. Hugues Vaganay. 5 vols. Lyon: Masson, 1925. Print.

Valincour, Jean-Baptiste Trousset de. *Lettres à Madame la Marquise *** au sujet de La Princesse de Clèves.* 1678. Ed. Jacques Chupeau et al. Tours: U de Tours, 1972. Print.

Vega, Miguel Ángel. Introduction. Aulnoy, *Relación* 9–40.

Verdier, Gabrielle. "Comment l'auteur des *Fées à la mode* devint 'Mother Bunch': Métamorphoses de la Comtesse d'Aulnoy en Angleterre." *Marvels and Tales* 10.2 (1996): 285–309. Print.

———. "Memoirs, Publishing, Scandal: The Case of Mme D***[d'Aulnoy]." Winn and Kuizenga 397–414.

Vesalius. *De humani corporis fabrica. Wellcome Images: 2000 Years of Human Culture.* Wellcome Lib., n.d. Web. 28 Apr. 2010.

Viala, Alain. *La France galante.* Paris: PUF, 2008. Print.

———. *La Naissance de l'écrivain.* Paris: Minuit, 1985. Print.

———. "Racine et la 'Carte de Tendre.'" *La Licorne* 50 (1999): 369–87. Print.

Vigée Lebrun, Élisabeth. *Memoirs of Madame Vigée-Lebrun.* Trans. Lionel Strachey. New York: Doubleday, 1903. Print.

———. *Souvenirs.* 2 vols. Paris: Des Femmes, 1986. Print.

Villars, Pierre de. *Mémoires de la cour d'Espagne de 1679 à 1681.* Ed. Alfred Morel-Fatio. Paris: Plon, 1893. Print.

Villedieu, Mme de [Marie-Catherine Desjardins]. "Articles d'une intrigue de galanterie." *Madame de Villedieu (Hortense des Jardins), 1632–1692.* 2nd ed. Ed. Emile Magne. Paris: Mercure de France, 1907. 172–73. Print.

———. *Fables. Œuvres completes.* 1720. 3 vols. Geneva: Slatkine, 1971. Print.

———. *Le Favori.* Gethner, *Femmes dramaturges* 1: 55–126.

———. *Lettres et billets galants.* Paris: Société d'Étude du XVIIe Siècle, 1975. Print.

———. Love Notes and Letters *and* The Letter Case. Trans. and ed. Roxanne Decker Lalande. Madison: Fairleigh Dickinson UP, 2005. Print.

———. *Manlius.* Evain, Gethner, and Goldwyn 2: 323–94.

———. *Les Mémoires de la vie de Henriette-Sylvie de Molière.* Ed. René Démoris. Paris: Desjonquères, 2003. Print.

———. *The Memoirs of the Life of Henriette-Sylvie de Molière.* Trans. and ed. Donna Kuizenga. Chicago: U of Chicago P, 2004. Print.

———. *Nitétis.* Gethner, *Femmes dramaturges* 2: 93–156.

Vissière, Isabelle, ed. *Procès des femmes au temps des philosophes ou la violence masculine au XVIIIe siècle.* Paris: Des Femmes, 1985. Print.

Voltaire. Letter to Damilaville. 21 Jan. 1763. *The Complete Works of Voltaire*. Ed. Theodore Besterman et al. Vol. 109. Banbury: Voltaire Foundation, 1973. 429. Print.

———. "Les Oreilles du Comte Chesterfield et le chapelain Goudman." 1775. *Romans et contes*. Ed. Frédéric Deloffre and Jacques Van der Heuvel. Paris: Gallimard, 1979. 589–602. Print. Bibliothèque de la Pléiade.

Wartenberg, Thomas E. "Descartes's Mood: The Question of Feminism in the Correspondence with Elisabeth." Bordo 190–212.

Watt, Ian. *The Rise of the Novel*. Berkeley: U of California P, 1957. Print.

Weber, Alison, ed. *Approaches to Teaching Teresa of Ávila and the Spanish Mystics*. New York: MLA, 2009. Print.

Weiss, Charles. *Histoire des réfugiés protestants de France depuis la révocation de l'édit de Nantes jusqu'à nos jours*. 2 vols. Paris: Charpentier, 1853. Print.

White, Hayden. *Metahistory: The Historical Imagination in Nineteenth-Century Europe*. Baltimore: Johns Hopkins UP, 1973. Print.

Wiegman, Robyn. "Object Lessons: Men, Masculinity and the Sign of 'Women.'" *Signs* 26.2 (2001): 355–88. Print.

Wilkin, Rebecca M. *Women, Imagination and the Search for Truth in Early Modern France*. Aldershot: Ashgate, 2008. Print.

Winn, Colette H., and Donna Kuizenga, eds. *Women Writers in Pre-revolutionary France: Strategies of Emancipation*. New York: Garland, 1997. Print.

Wolfgang, Aurora. *Gender and Voice in the French Novel, 1730–1782*. Aldershot: Ashgate, 2004. Print.

———. Rev. of *The Other Enlightenment: How French Women Became Modern*, by Carla Hesse. *EBRO: Eighteenth-Century Book Reviews Online*. California State U, Long Beach, 2009. Web. 24 Mar. 2010.

Wollstonecraft, Mary. *A Vindication of the Rights of Woman*. London: Penguin, 1992. Print.

Woodrough, Elizabeth. "Aphra Behn and the French Astrea: Madame de Villedieu." *Europa* 1.4 (1995): 33–48. Print.

Wordsworth, William. *The Prelude. The Oxford Authors: William Wordsworth*. Ed. Stephen Gill. Oxford: Oxford UP, 1984. 375–590. Print.

Yardéni, Myriam. *Le Refuge huguenot: Assimilation et culture*. Paris: Champion, 2002. Print.

Zanger, Abby. "Making Sweat: Gender and the Sexuality of National Reproduction in the Marriage of Louis XIII." *Yale French Studies* 86 (1994): 187–205. Print.

———. "Marriage on the Margins of Monarchy: Politics and the Marriage Plot in the Motteville-Montpensier Correspondence." *Papers on French Seventeenth-Century Literature* 33.65 (2006): 339–54. Print.

———. *Scenes from the Marriage of Louis XIV: Nuptial Fictions and the Making of Absolutist Power*. Stanford: Stanford UP, 1997. Print.

———. "What the King Saw in the Belly of the Beast; or, How the Lion Got in the Queen: Allegories of Royal Procreation in the 1622 Royal Entry into Lyon." *The Body of the Queen: Gender and Rule in the Courtly World, 1500–2000*. Ed. Regina Schulte. Oxford: Berghahn, 2006. 103–24. Print.

Index

Aarne, Antti, 107
Abélard, 146
Adam, Antoine, 246, 248–49
Adams, Percy, 217
Adams, William Howard, 50
Addison, Joseph, 54
Aelders, Etta Palm d', 282
Alberti, Leon Battista, 267
Altman, Janet Gurkin, 77
Amerongen, Taets van, 162
Anderson, Elizabeth, 48
Angélique de Saint-Jean, 148, 151, 152
Angennes, Julie d', 247
Angoulême, duc d', 122
Anjou, Philippe d', 221n4
Anne of Austria, 5, 30, 31, 36, 37, 220n4, 263
Anne de Marquets, 145, 146
Apostolidès, Jean-Marie, 50
Aquinas, Thomas, 181
Archambault, Paul J., 38n1
Ardent, Fanny, 309
Arenal, Electa, 145
Aristotle, 4, 181, 182
Arnauld, Antoine, 182
Aronson, Nicole, 66
Astor, Dorian, 13n1
Atherton, Margaret, 295
Aubailly de La Berge, Mme, 134, 140, 141, 144n5
Aubignac, François Hédelin, abbé d', 231
Augustine, 179, 181
Aulnoy, François de La Motte, baron d', 216
Aulnoy, Marie-Catherine Le Jumel de Barneville, comtesse d', 6, 7, 11, 23, 62, 72, 79, 110, 212–21, 257, 311, 315
Austen, Jane, 23

Baillet, Adrien, 249
Ballaster, Ros, 253, 254, 256, 257
Balzac, Honoré de, 17
Barbier, Marie-Anne, 87, 89
Barbin, Claude, 78, 313
Baret, 155
Baridon, Michel, 50

Barrin, 155
Barthes, Roland, 120–21
Bartillat, 244
Bassy, Alain-Marie, 174
Bastoulh, Jean Raymond, 133
Batteux, Charles, 242
Bayle, Pierre, 110, 248
Bayreuth, Wilhelmina of, 157
Beasley, Faith E., 6, 7, 8, 9, 10, 22, 32, 56, 60, 62, 67, 68, 69, 71, 72, 73, 74, 103, 108, 206, 220n1, 318, 320, 328
Beauharnais, 155
Beaulieu, Jean-Philippe, 38n1
Beaumarchais, Pierre-Augustin Caron de, 147
Beauvoir, Simone de, 146
Beckstrand, Lisa, 4, 6, 9, 12, 73, 281, 285
Beebee, Thomas, 76
Béguin, Albert, 270
Behn, Aphra, 22, 79, 117, 257, 327–29
Bellart, Nicolas-François, 135, 137
Bennassar, Bartolomé, 218, 220n3
Bennassar, Lucile, 218, 220n3
Benoist, 155
Bensoussan, Georges, 312
Bérenguier, Nadine, 129
Bergmann, Emilie L., 145
Berling, Charles, 309
Bernard, 155
Bernard, Catherine, 7, 8, 87, 244
Bernier, François, 8, 71–72
Berrall, Julia S., 48
Bertaut, François, 218
Bertière, Simone, 125
Besenval, Pierre de, 122, 123, 125
Beugnot, Bernard, 24n5
Beyssade, Jean-Marie, 295, 301n2
Beyssade, Michelle, 295, 301n2
Biancolelli, Marie Thérèse, 158
Bignon, Jean-Paul, 41
Birkett, Mary Ellen, 11, 55, 55n1
Blake, William, 329–30
Blanc, Olivier, 289
Blanchard, Antoine, 128
Blanco, Pilar, 220n3
Blé, Mme, 132, 140, 143n2

Modern Language Association of America
Options for Teaching

Teaching Seventeenth- and Eighteenth-Century French Women Writers. Ed. Faith E. Beasley. 2011.

Teaching French Women Writers of the Renaissance and Reformation. Ed. Colette H. Winn. 2011.

Teaching Law and Literature. Ed. Austin Sarat, Cathrine O. Frank, and Matthew Anderson. 2011.

Teaching British Women Playwrights of the Restoration and Eighteenth Century. Ed. Bonnie Nelson and Catherine Burroughs. 2010.

Teaching Narrative Theory. Ed. David Herman, Brian McHale, and James Phelan. 2010.

Teaching Early Modern English Prose. Ed. Susannah Brietz Monta and Margaret W. Ferguson. 2010.

Teaching Italian American Literature, Film, and Popular Culture. Ed. Edvige Giunta and Kathleen Zamboni McCormick. 2010.

Teaching the Graphic Novel. Ed. Stephen E. Tabachnick. 2009.

Teaching Literature and Language Online. Ed. Ian Lancashire. 2009.

Teaching the African Novel. Ed. Gaurav Desai. 2009.

Teaching World Literature. Ed. David Damrosch. 2009.

Teaching North American Environmental Literature. Ed. Laird Christensen, Mark C. Long, and Fred Waage. 2008.

Teaching Life Writing Texts. Ed. Miriam Fuchs and Craig Howes. 2007.

Teaching Nineteenth-Century American Poetry. Ed. Paula Bernat Bennett, Karen L. Kilcup, and Philipp Schweighauser. 2007.

Teaching Representations of the Spanish Civil War. Ed. Noël Valis. 2006.

Teaching the Representation of the Holocaust. Ed. Marianne Hirsch and Irene Kacandes. 2004.

Teaching Tudor and Stuart Women Writers. Ed. Susanne Woods and Margaret P. Hannay. 2000.

Teaching Literature and Medicine. Ed. Anne Hunsaker Hawkins and Marilyn Chandler McEntyre. 1999.

Teaching the Literatures of Early America. Ed. Carla Mulford. 1999.

Teaching Shakespeare through Performance. Ed. Milla C. Riggio. 1999.

Teaching Oral Traditions. Ed. John Miles Foley. 1998.

Teaching Contemporary Theory to Undergraduates. Ed. Dianne F. Sadoff and William E. Cain. 1994.

Teaching Children's Literature: Issues, Pedagogy, Resources. Ed. Glenn Edward Sadler. 1992.

Teaching Literature and Other Arts. Ed. Jean-Pierre Barricelli, Joseph Gibaldi, and Estella Lauter. 1990.

New Methods in College Writing Programs: Theories in Practice. Ed. Paul Connolly and Teresa Vilardi. 1986.

School-College Collaborative Programs in English. Ed. Ron Fortune. 1986.

Teaching Environmental Literature: Materials, Methods, Resources. Ed. Frederick O. Waage. 1985.

Part-Time Academic Employment in the Humanities: A Sourcebook for Just Policy. Ed. Elizabeth M. Wallace. 1984.

Film Study in the Undergraduate Curriculum. Ed. Barry K. Grant. 1983.

The Teaching Apprentice Program in Language and Literature. Ed. Joseph Gibaldi and James V. Mirollo. 1981.

Options for Undergraduate Foreign Language Programs: Four-Year and Two-Year Colleges. Ed. Renate A. Schulz. 1979.

Options for the Teaching of English: Freshman Composition. Ed. Jasper P. Neel. 1978.

Options for the Teaching of English: The Undergraduate Curriculum. Ed. Elizabeth Wooten Cowan. 1975.